THE DIVINE CONSPIRACY

The kingdom of the heavens is similar to a bit of yeast which a woman took and hid in half a bushel of dough. After a while all the dough was pervaded by it.

JESUS OF NAZARETH

You must have often wondered why the enemy [God] does not make more use of his power to be sensibly present to human souls in any degree he chooses and at any moment. But you now see that the irresistible and the indisputable are the two weapons which the very nature of his scheme forbids him to use. Merely to override a human will (as his felt presence in any but the faintest and most mitigated degree would certainly do) would be for him useless. He cannot ravish. He can only woo. For his ignoble idea is to eat the cake and have it; the creatures are to be one with him, but yet themselves; merely to cancel them, or assimilate them, will not serve ... Sooner or later he withdraws, if not in fact, at least from their conscious experience, all supports and incentives. He leaves the creature to stand up on its own legs – to carry out from the will alone duties which have lost all relish ... He cannot 'tempt' to virtue as we do to vice. He wants them to learn to walk and must therefore take away his hand ... Our cause is never more in danger than when a human, no longer desiring, but still intending, to do our enemy's will, looks round upon a universe from which every trace of him seems to have vanished, and asks why he has been forsaken, and still obeys.

UNCLE SCREWTAPE
C. S. LEWIS, *THE SCREWTAPE LETTERS*

THE DIVINE CONSPIRACY

REDISCOVERING OUR HIDDEN LIFE IN GOD

DALLAS WILLARD

Fount
An Imprint of HarperCollins*Publishers*

Fount Paperbacks is an Imprint of HarperCollins*Religious*
Part of HarperCollins*Publishers*
77-85 Fulham Palace Road, London W6 8JB

First published in the United States in 1998 by HarperSanFrancisco

This edition first published in Great Britain in 1998
by Fount Paperbacks

9

A catalogue record for this book is available from the British Library

ISBN 000 628114 1

Printed and bound in Great Britain by
Clays Ltd, St Ives plc

R. R. Brown
Joe Henry Hankins
John R. Rice
Lee Roberson
J. I. Willard

'In those days there were giants in the land.'

CONTENTS

FOREWORD

The Divine Conspiracy is the book I have been searching for all my life. Like Michelangelo's Sistine ceiling, it is a masterpiece and a wonder. And like those famous frescoes, it presents God as real and present and ever reaching out to all humanity. I am struck by many things in *The Divine Conspiracy*. Let me mention a few.

First, I am struck by the comprehensive nature of this book. It gives me a *Weltanschauung*, a worldview. It provides me with the conceptual philosophy for understanding the meaning and purpose of human existence. It shows me how to make sense out of the whole of the biblical record. It helps me see that the teachings of Jesus are intelligent and vital and intently practical.

The breadth of the issues covered is astonishing: from the soul's redemption and justification to discipleship and our growth in grace to death and the state of our existence in heaven. The middle chapters rightly give concentrated attention to Jesus' teaching in the Sermon on the Mount, but Willard does even this in such a way that he actually teaches us the whole Bible – indeed, the whole of our life before God.

Then, too, his analysis of the contemporary scene is quite remarkable and comprehensive. Incisively, he uncovers the pretence of the various theories, facts and techniques of contemporary secular materialism, showing that 'they have not the least logical bearing upon the ultimate issues of existence and life'. Nor does the contemporary religious scene escape his incisive eye. In perhaps the most telling phrase of the book, he reveals the various 'theologies of sin management' that plague churches today, both conservative and liberal. This is a book that opens me to the big picture.

Second, I am struck by the accessibility of this book. I'm fully aware that the issues discussed here are of immense importance, yet it is all so understandable, so readable, so applicable. Perhaps I feared that a world-class philosopher would be unable to speak to my condition, but in this I was wrong. Again and again I found myself mirrored in Dr Willard's insights into human nature.

In addition, everything Willard deals with is so intently practical. Never allowing issues to stay theoretical, he constantly weaves them into the warp and woof of daily experience. His stories charm. His examples teach. Most of all, he deals with such huge human issues in such wise and sane ways.

This is never more true than in Chapter 9: 'A Curriculum for Christlikeness'. It contains a wealth of practical guidance into precisely how we come to love, honour and consistently obey 'God the Father almighty, maker of heaven and earth'.

Third, I am struck by the depth of this book. Willard is a master at capturing the central insight of Jesus' teachings. Perhaps this is because he takes Jesus seriously as an intelligent, fully competent Teacher. He writes, 'Jesus is not just nice, he is brilliant.'

Here I must comment on the depth of teaching on what we have come to call the Sermon on the Mount. Most writers turn these penetrating words of Jesus into a new set of soul-crushing laws. Others, feeling the teaching is impossible to obey, try to relegate it to another time, another place, another dispensation. Those who reject these two options usually think of it simply as a loose collection of nice sayings thrown together by unknown editors – interesting to read in a poetic sort of way, but having nothing essential to do with how we live today. What, I wondered, would Willard bring to the table?

A soul-satisfying banquet, that is what. No one I have read so effectively penetrates to the heart of Jesus' teaching. Willard's discussion of the 'Beatitudes', for instance, is simply stunning, upsetting many of our common notions of this famous passage. The entire book is well worth that discussion alone. But he gives us more, much more – a feast for the mind and the heart.

Which leads me to my fourth and final observation. I am struck by the warmth of this book. Rarely have I found an author with so penetrating an intellect combined with so generous a spirit. Clearly he has descended with the mind into the heart and from this place he touches us, both mind and heart.

Dallas Willard speaks words of grace and mercy to us all, and especially to those who have been crushed by the world in which we live: 'The flunk-outs and drop-outs and burned-outs. The broke and the broken. The drug heads and the divorced. The HIV positive and the herpes-ridden. The brain-damaged and the incurably ill. The barren and the pregnant too many times or at the wrong time. The over-employed, the under-employed, the unemployed. The unemployable. The swindled, the shoved-aside, the replaced. The lonely, the incompetent, the stupid.' In this, and so many other ways, I find this book speaks with compassion to where we all live and move and have our being.

I would place *The Divine Conspiracy* in rare company indeed: alongside the writings of Dietrich Bonhoeffer and John Wesley, John Calvin and Martin Luther, Teresa of Avila and Hildegard of Bingen, and perhaps even Thomas Aquinas and Augustine of Hippo. If the *parousia* tarries, this is a book for the next millennium.

RICHARD J. FOSTER

ACKNOWLEDGEMENTS

I am very grateful to many friends and readers who have encouraged and advised me through the years. At this point in life they are so many that I cannot begin to mention them individually. A few people, however, have really invested substantial efforts in thinking through some of the chapters of this book and advising me.

This is especially true of Bart Tarman, Ken Yee, John Ortberg, Trevor Hudson, Gary Rapkin, Scott Hilborn, Lynn Cory, Larry Burtoft, Greg Jesson, Richard Foster, Jim Smith, Randy Neal, Roger Freeman and Jane Lakes Willard.

I owe a special debt to Patricia Klein's fine sense of language and composition and to her persistence in helping me say as clearly as possible what I have to say. She deeply invested herself in the content of the book, and I am grateful. Virginia Rich and Terri Leonard made great improvements in the book by their editorial skills, and Mark Chimsky's encouraging words greatly strengthened me to finish the task. Bill Heatley and John S. Willard helped check the final proofs.

Jane, Richard, and Lynda Graybeal have, in addition, made it possible for me to write at all, especially by standing effectively against my too-great readiness to accept various kinds of commitments that make it impossible. But without Jane the writing would, for many reasons, never have been actually done. Her loving patience, insistence and assistance have been, as always, both incomparable and indispensable. This is her book.

All Saints, 1997

INTRODUCTION

My hope is to gain a fresh hearing for Jesus, especially among those who believe they already understand him. In his case, quite frankly, presumed familiarity has led to unfamiliarity, unfamiliarity has led to contempt and contempt has led to profound ignorance.

Very few people today find Jesus interesting as a person or of vital relevance to the course of their actual lives. He is not generally regarded as a real-life personality who deals with real-life issues but is thought to be concerned with some feathery realm other than the one we must *deal* with, and must deal with *now*. And, frankly, he is not taken to be a person of much ability.

He is automatically seen as a more or less magical figure – a pawn, or possibly a knight or a bishop, in some religious game – who fits only within the categories of dogma and of law. Dogma is what you have to believe, whether you believe it or not. And law is what you must do, whether it is good for you or not. What we have to believe or do *now*, by contrast, is real life, bursting with interesting, frightening and relevant things and people.

Now, in fact, Jesus and his words have never belonged to the categories of dogma or law, and to read them as if they did is simply to miss them. They are essentially subversive of established arrangements and ways of thinking. That is clear from the way they first entered the world, their initial effects and how they are preserved in the New Testament writings and live on in his people. He himself described his words as 'spirit and life' (John 6:63). They invade our 'real' world with a reality even more real than it is, which explains why human beings then and now have to protect themselves against them.

Dogma and law – wrongly, perhaps, but understandably – have come to have about them an air of arbitrariness. Because of how our minds have come down to us through history, dogma and law for most people today simply mean what God has *willed*. This view makes them important, and also dangerous, and that is appropriately acknowledged. But it breaks any connection with our sense of how things really are: with truth and reality. And our 'real life' is our truth and reality. It is where things actually happen, not a realm of supposed-to-bes that only threaten to make life harder, or possibly unbearable.

The life and words that Jesus brought into the world came in the form of information and reality. He and his early associates overwhelmed the ancient world because they brought into it a stream of life at its deepest, along with the best information possible on the most important matters. These were matters with which the human mind had already been seriously struggling for a millennium or more without much success. The early message was, accordingly, not experienced as something its hearers *had* to believe or do because otherwise something bad – something with no essential connection with real life – would happen to them. The people initially impacted by that message generally concluded that they would be fools to disregard it. That was the basis of their conversion.

Jesus himself was thought of as someone to admire and respect, someone you thought highly of and considered to be a person of great ability. Worship of him included this – not, as today, ruled it out. This attitude was naturally conveyed in such New Testament names and phrases as 'the Prince of life', 'the Lord of glory', 'abundant life', 'the inexhaustible riches of Christ' and so on. Today these phrases are emptied of most intellectual and practical content.

It is the failure to understand Jesus and his words as reality and vital information about life that explains why, today, we do not routinely teach those who profess allegiance to him how to do what he said was best. We lead them to profess allegiance to him, or we expect them to, and leave them there, devoting our remaining efforts to 'attracting' them to this or that.

True, you will find few scholars or leaders in Christian circles who deny that we are supposed to make disciples or apprentices to Jesus and teach them to do all things that Jesus said. There are a few here and there, but they are, at least, not widely influential. Jesus' instructions on this matter are, after all, starkly clear. We just don't do what he said. We don't seriously attempt it. And apparently we don't know how to do it. You have only to look honestly at our official activities to see this. It saddens me to say such things, and I do not mean to condemn anyone. But it is a matter of extreme importance, and unless it is openly acknowledged, nothing can be done about it.

So one is bound to look for an explanation of this state of affairs. How could the obligation be so clear and at the same time there be no attempt to meet it? The problem, we may be sure, lies very deep within the ideas that automatically govern our thinking about who we are, as Christians and as human beings, and about the relevance of Jesus to our cosmos and our lives.

In fact, it lies much deeper than anything we might appropriately feel guilty about. For it is not, truly, a matter of anything we do or don't do. It is a matter of how we *cannot but* think and act, given the context of our mental and spiritual formation. So any significant change can come only by breaking the stranglehold of the ideas and concepts that automatically shunt aside Jesus, 'the Prince of Life', when questions of concrete mastery of our life arise.

Whatever the ultimate explanation of it, the most telling thing about the contemporary Christian is that he or she simply has no compelling sense that understanding of and conformity with the clear teachings of Christ is of any vital importance to his or her life, and certainly not that it is in any way essential. We – including multitudes who have distanced themselves from any formal association with him – still manage to feel guilty with reference to those teachings, with a nervous laugh and a knowing look. But more often than not, I think, such obedience is regarded as just out of the question or impossible. This is largely because obedience is thought of solely in terms of law – which we shall have much to say about in what follows.

More than any other single thing, in any case, *the practical irrelevance of actual obedience to Christ* accounts for the weakened effect of Christianity in the world today, with its increasing tendency to emphasize political and social action as the primary way to serve God. It also accounts for the practical irrelevance of Christian faith to individual character development and overall personal sanity and well-being.

It is my hope with this book to provide an understanding of the gospel that will open the way for the people of Christ actually to do – do once again, for they have done it in the past – what their acknowledged Maestro said to do. Perhaps the day will come when the 'Great Commission' of Matthew 28:18–20 would be fully and routinely implemented as the objective, the 'mission statement', of the Christian churches, one-by-one and collectively.

Individual Christians still hear Jesus say, 'Whoever hears these words of mine and does them is like those intelligent people who build their houses upon rock,' standing firm against every pressure of life (Matt. 7:24–25). How life-giving it would be if their understanding of the gospel allowed them simply to reply, 'I will do them! I will find out how. I will devote my life to it! This is the best life strategy I ever heard of!' and then go off to their fellowship and its teachers, and into their daily life, to learn how to live in his kingdom as Jesus indicated was best.

My Assumptions About the Bible

It is tempting in such a project to enter the conflict – long-standing and currently at the boiling point – about the accessibility of the 'real' Jesus and his words to us now. Because I do not do so, I will simply state my assumptions about the Bible: On its human side, I assume that it was produced and preserved by competent human beings who were at least as intelligent and devout as we are today. I assume that they were quite capable of accurately interpreting their own experience and of objectively presenting what they heard and experienced in the language of their historical community, which we today can understand with due diligence.

On the divine side, I assume that God has been willing and competent to arrange for the Bible, including its record of Jesus, to emerge and be preserved in ways that will secure his purposes for it among human beings worldwide. Those who actually believe in God will be untroubled by this. I assume that he did not and would not leave his message to humankind in a form that can only be understood by a handful of late-twentieth-century professional scholars, who cannot even agree among themselves on the theories that they assume to determine what the message is.

The Bible is, after all, God's gift to the world through his Church, not to the scholars. It comes through the life of his people and nourishes that life. Its purpose is practical, not academic. An intelligent, careful, intensive but straightforward reading – that is, one not governed by obscure and faddish theories or by a mindless orthodoxy – is what it requires to direct us into life in God's kingdom. Any other approach to the Bible, I believe, conflicts with the picture of the God that, all agree, emerges from Jesus and his tradition. To what extent this belief of mine is or is not harmfully circular, I leave the philosophically minded reader to ponder.

I have freely translated and paraphrased scriptural passages to achieve emphases that seem to me important. When I quote versions other than the King James, that will be indicated.

Completing a Series

With this book I complete a trilogy on the spiritual life of those who have become convinced that Jesus is the One. In the first, *Hearing God* (previously *In Search of Guidance*), I attempted to make real and clear the intimate quality of life with him as 'a conversational relationship with God'.

But that relationship is not something that automatically happens, and we do not receive it by passive infusion. So the second book, *The Spirit of the Disciplines*, explains how disciples or students of Jesus can effectively interact with the grace and spirit of God to access fully the provisions and character intended for us in the gift of eternal life.

However, actual discipleship or apprenticeship to Jesus is, in our day, no longer thought of as in any way essential to faith in him. It is regarded as a costly option, a spiritual luxury, or possibly even an evasion. Why bother with discipleship, it is widely thought, or, for that matter, with a conversational relationship with God? Let us get on with what we have to *do*.

This third book, then, presents discipleship to Jesus as the very heart of the gospel. The really good news for humanity is that Jesus is now taking students in the master class of life. The eternal life that begins with confidence in Jesus is a life in his present kingdom, now on earth and available to all. So the message of and about him is specifically a gospel for our life now, not just for dying. It is about living now as his apprentice in kingdom living, not just as a consumer of his merits. Our future; however far we look, is a natural extension of the faith by which we live now and the life in which we now participate. Eternity is now in flight and we with it, like it or not.

In these three books there is very little that is new, though much that is forgotten. Indeed, if I thought it were new, I would certainly not advocate it or publish it. To see that it is old and only very recently forgotten, one need only compare it with the writings of P. T. Forsyth, C. S. Lewis, Frank Laubach, E. Stanley Jones, and George MacDonald, among many others of the quite recent past. Then, if one wishes, go on to the greater post-biblical sources such as Athanasius, Augustine, Anselm, Thomas, Luther and Calvin – and, finally, to the teachings about the world, the soul, and God that lie richly upon the pages of the Bible itself.

Chapter 1

ENTERING THE ETERNAL KIND OF LIFE NOW

> God's care for humanity was so great that he sent his unique Son among us, so that those who count on him might not lead a futile and failing existence, but have the undying life of God Himself.
>
> JOHN 3:16

> Jesus' good news, then, was that the Kingdom of God had come, and that he, Jesus, was its herald and expounder to men. More than that, in some special, mysterious way, he *was* the Kingdom.
>
> MALCOLM MUGGERIDGE,
> *JESUS: THE MAN WHO LIVES*

Life in the Dark

Recently a pilot was practising high-speed maneouvres in a jet fighter. She turned the controls for what she thought was a steep ascent – and flew straight into the ground. She was unaware that she was had been flying upside down.

This is a parable of human existence in our times – not exactly that everyone is crashing, though there is enough of that – but most of us as individuals and world society as a whole, live at high-speed and often with no clue to whether we are flying upside down or right-side up. Indeed, we are haunted by a strong suspicion that there may be no difference – or at least that it is unknown or irrelevant.

Rumours from the Intellectual Heights

That suspicion now has the force of unspoken dogma in the highest centres of Western learning. Of course, one has to assume in practice that there is a right-side up, just to get on with life. But it is equally assumed that right-side up is not a subject of *knowledge*.

Derek Bok was president of Harvard University for many years, and in his 'President's Report' for 1986–1987 he referred to some well-known moral failures in financial circles and the political life of America. He wondered out loud what universities might do to strengthen moral character in their graduates.

'Religious institutions,' he continued, 'no longer seem as able as they once were to impart basic values to the young. In these circumstances, universities, including Harvard, need to think hard about what they can do in the face of what many perceive as a widespread decline in ethical standards.'[1]

Bok points out that in other days 'the instructor's aim was ... to foster a belief in commonly accepted moral values' (p. 10). Now all is changed: 'Today's course in applied ethics does not seek to convey a set of moral truths but tries to encourage the student to think carefully about complex moral issues.' One senses that the governing assumption of his discussion is that these two objectives are mutually exclusive.

'The principal aim of the course,' Bok continues, 'is not to impart "right answers" but to make the students more perceptive in detecting ethical problems when they arise, better acquainted with the best moral thought that has accumulated through the ages and more equipped to reason about the ethical issues they will face' (p. 10).

Later he quotes Carol Gilligan to the effect that 'moral development in the college years thus centres on the shift from moral ideology to ethical responsibility' (p. 30). One should not miss the point that Bok puts 'right answers' in queer quotes, and that Gilligan holds what one has before college to be 'ideology' – that is, *irrational beliefs and attitudes*. They are faithfully expressing the accepted intellectual viewpoint on the common moral beliefs that guide ordinary human existence.

Finally, in coming to the conclusion of his report, President Bok remarks, 'Despite the importance of moral development to the individual student and the society, one cannot say that higher education has demonstrated a deep concern for the problem … Especially in large universities, the subject is not treated as a serious responsibility worthy of sustained discussion and determined action by the faculty and administration' (p. 31).

But the failure of will on the part of teachers that Bok courageously points out is inevitable. Had he crossed Harvard Yard to Emerson Hall and consulted some of the most influential American thinkers, he would have discovered that *there now is no recognized moral knowledge upon which projects of fostering moral development could be based.*

There is now not a single moral conclusion about behaviour or character traits that a teacher could base a student's grade on – not even those most dear to teachers, concerning fairness and diversity. If you lowered a student's grade just for saying on a test that discrimination is morally acceptable, for example, the student could contest that grade to the administration. And if that position on the moral acceptability of discrimination were the only point at issue, the student would win.

The teacher would be reminded that we are not here to impose our views on students, 'however misguided the student might be.' And if the administration of the university did not reach that decision, a court of law soon would.

Of course, if a student seriously wrote on a test that 7 times 5 equals 32, or that Columbus discovered America in 1520, we would be permitted to 'impose our views' in these cases. It would not matter by what route the student came to such conclusions because these cases concern matters that – quibbles aside – are regarded as known. That is what marks the difference.

Why Be Surprised?

But if indeed there is now no body of moral knowledge in our culture, then a number of things highly positioned people express surprise about are not surprising at all. Robert Coles, professor of psychiatry and medical humanities at Harvard and a well-known researcher and commentator on matters social and moral, published a piece in the *Chronicle of Higher Education* on 'The Disparity Between Intellect and Character.'[2] The piece is about 'the task of connecting intellect to character.' This task, he adds, 'is daunting.'

His essay was occasioned by an encounter with one of his students over the moral insensitivity – is it hard for him to say 'immoral behaviour'? – of other students, some of the best and brightest at Harvard. This student was a young woman of 'a Midwestern, working class background' where, as is well known, things like 'right answers' and 'ideology' remain strong. She cleaned student rooms to help pay her way through the university.

Again and again, she reported to Coles, people who were in classes with her treated her ungraciously because of her lower economic position, without simple courtesy and respect, and often were rude and sometimes crude to her. She was repeatedly propositioned for sex by one young student in particular as she went about her work. He was a man with whom she had had two 'moral reasoning' courses, in which he excelled and received the highest of grades.

This pattern of treatment led her to quit her job and leave school – and to something like an exit interview with Coles. After going over not only the behaviour of her fellow students, but also the long list of highly educated people who have perpetrated the atrocities for which the twentieth century is famous, she concluded by saying, 'I've been taking all these philosophy courses, and we talk about what's true, what's important, what's *good*. Well, how do you teach people to *be* good?' And, she added, 'What's the point of *knowing* good if you don't keep trying to *become* a good person?'

Professor Coles proceeds to comment on how ineffectual his efforts to respond to this young woman were. He seems genuinely conscience stricken that he *shrugged* in response to her disappointment. But he never confronts the fact that he certainly did not tell the students in his courses that they should not treat someone doing menial work with disdain, or that they should not proposition a classmate or anyone else who is cleaning their rooms.

There were no questions on his tests about these matters. He never deals with the fact that he could not use such questions because no one can now claim to know about such matters. The problem here is less one of connecting character to intellect than one of connecting intellectual to moral and spiritual realities. The trouble is precisely that character is connected with the intellect. The trouble is what is and is not in the intellect.

Indeed, in the current world of accepted knowledge one can't even *know* the truth of a moral theory or principle, much less a specific rule. You could never grade someone for holding Utilitarianism or Kantianism to be true or false. One can only know *about* such theories and principles and think about them in more or less clever ways. You can brightly discuss them. For that the young man got his A's. But that, of course, had no bearing on his character or behaviour because it is only literary or historical or perhaps logical expertise, not moral knowledge. And if you are already flying upside down and don't know it, your cleverness will do you little good.

The Incredible Power of 'Mere Ideas'

Now, both Bok and Coles are widely and justifiably recognized as people of fine character and intellect. They have a large measure of concern about the practical consequences of a culture that has accepted the view that what is good and right is not a subject of knowledge that can guide action and for which individuals can be held responsible. They have no way of dislodging this view, nor, I think, would they want to dislodge it. But they do not seem to realize the total futility of resisting its practical consequences without dislodging it from the popular as well as the academic mind.

John Maynard Keynes, who was perhaps an even more profound social observer than economist, remarks at the end of his best-known book that 'the ideas of economists and political philosophers, both when they are right and when they are wrong, are more powerful than is commonly understood. Indeed the world is ruled by little else. Practical men, who believe themselves to be quite exempt from any intellectual influences, are usually the slaves of some defunct economist. Madmen in authority, who hear voices in the air, are distilling their frenzy from some academic scribbler of a few years back.'[3]

One could wish this were true only of economics and politics. But it is true of life in general. It is true of religion and education, of art and media. For life as a whole, Keynes's words apply: 'I am sure that the power of vested interests is vastly exaggerated compared with the gradual encroachment of ideas.' Not immediately, as he acknowledges, but after a certain period of time. The ideas of people in current leadership positions are always those they took in during their youth. 'But, soon or late, it is ideas, not vested interests, which are dangerous for good or evil.'

The power of mere ideas is a matter about which intellectuals commonly deceive themselves and, intentionally or not, also mislead the public. They constantly take in hand the most powerful factors in human life, *ideas* and, most importantly, ideas about what is good and right. And how they handle and live them thoroughly pervades our world in its every aspect.

The complaint of the young Harvard woman to Professor Coles is actually a complaint about a system of ideas: a system of ideas about what is good and what is right. This system is one to which both President Bok and Professor Coles willingly subject themselves. It is conveyed to students – and readers, consumers of intellectual product – through the generations, and ever since the universities have become the authority centres of world culture it is wordlessly conveyed to world society. It conveys itself as simple reality and does so in such a way that it never has to justify itself. The truly powerful ideas are precisely the ones that never have to justify themselves.

The frequent attacks on 'Modernity' and 'Secularism' usually mistake where the problem lies. We are not primarily in a political battle, nor is there at bottom some kind of social conspiracy afoot. 'Secular humanism' is an idea movement, not the work of any individual, and before it, as a whole, individuals are little more than pawns.[4] The seeming triviality and irrelevance of the 'merely academic' is a major part of what misleads us about the power of mere ideas.

Merely Academic?

In 1889 the French novelist Paul Bourget wrote a novel, *The Disciple*. He described the 'egghead' existence of a noted philosopher and psychologist: seemingly lost in things 'merely academic', living up four flights of stairs, caught up in humdrum routines of meals and walks, coffee and lectures. Three times a week he had visits from scholars and students from four to six, and then dinner, short walk, a little more work and bed promptly at ten. It was the existence of an inoffensive, scholarly man who, in the words of his housekeeper, 'wouldn't hurt a fly.'

Then one day he was summoned to a criminal inquest concerning a brilliant young man who had been his student and had climbed those four flights of stairs to drink in illuminating and liberating discussions. In prison awaiting trial for murder, this young disciple had written an account of what he had done and of how those liberating doctrines enthusiastically discussed in the abstract had worked out in actual practice.[5] The results are only infrequently a matter of murder, but world as well as individual events ride upon the waters of an ideational sea. The killing fields of Cambodia come from philosophical discussions in Paris.[6]

The absurdity of our existence now falls upon the masses of humanity through several generations of intellectual and artistic elites. It surfaced in its modern form within a very small circle of intellectuals during the late eighteenth and early nineteenth centuries. It was temporarily restrained and was even in some measure utilized, by the various fine arts in the nineteenth and early twentieth centuries. Great literature, music and painting emerged, substantially in response to the spiritual crisis precipitated by massive shifts in ideas. But the fine arts capitulated to absurdity by the mid-twentieth century – having briefly exploited the 'cute' as a legitimate aesthetic category and then allowed a few quickly trite ways of being cute and clever to dominate the arts.

Cuteness, like cleverness, has certain aesthetic possibilities – as do sex and violence – but they are very limited. Picasso is the most familiar and brilliant illustration of how it can be well used and of how it goes to seed. But as we now know, masses of people can be cute, and clever as well, who have no ability or sense of art at all. As creators and consumers they fill the field of pop culture today, which is an economic enterprise and only by accident occasionally has something to do with art. Art objects are now commonly referred to as 'product' by those who handle them and only make news when they are sold for absurdly large sums or are stolen. Art is lost in pop 'art' as sport is lost in professional 'sport' – which is an oxymoron of the strongest kind. Absurdity reigns and confusion makes it look good.

Currently, through pop 'art' and the media the presumed absurdity of life that elites previously had to be very brilliant and work very hard to appreciate is mindlessly conveyed to hundreds of millions. It comes to us in Bart and Homer Simpson and endless sitcoms and soap operas involving doctors, lawyers and policemen, along with the bizarre selections and juxtapositions imposed by what is called news. You have only to 'stay tuned' and you can arrive at a perpetual state of confusion and, ultimately, despair with no effort at all.

Tolstoy's Journey

Leo Tolstoy's *A Confession* is possibly the most important document of the last two centuries for understanding our current plight. The 'dogmas of modern unbelief had captured his elite circle of Russian intellectuals, artists and members of the social upper crust, and the implications of it slowly destroyed the basis of his life. On those dogmas only two things are real: particles and progress. 'Why do I live?' he asked. And the answer he got was, 'In infinite space, in infinite time, infinitely small particles change their forms in infinite complexity, and when you have understood the laws of those mutations of form you will understand why you live on the earth.'[7]

'You are an accidentally united little lump of something,' the story continues. 'That little lump ferments. The little lump calls that fermenting its 'life'. The lump will disintegrate and there will be an end of the fermenting and of all the questions' (p. 31).

But the 'lump' dreams of progress: 'The faith of the majority of educated people of our day,' Tolstoy observes, 'was expressed by the word "progress". It then appeared to me that this word meant something. I did not as yet understand that, being tormented (like every vital man) by the question how it is best for me to live, in my answer, "Live in conformity with progress", I was like a man in a boat who when carried along by wind and waves should reply to what for him is the chief and only question, "Whither to steer", by saying, "We are being carried somewhere" ' (p. 12).

There has been no advance beyond this position since Tolstoy's day. If you look into the content of the most highly regarded video presentations or books on 'reality' or the cosmos, by people such as Carl Sagan or Stephen Hawking, you will see that it is all particles and progress. The very best presentation in recent years is a PBS television series called *A Glorious Accident*. The only difference from Tolstoy's time is, as already indicated, that the faith that passes as 'scientific' is available to all without effort.

And this does make a great difference. Tolstoy began to recover himself when he realized that 'I and a few hundred similar people are not the whole of mankind, and that I did not yet know the life of mankind' (p. 45). He could observe the mass of persons, the peasants, who in the most miserable of conditions found life deeply meaningful and even sweet. They had not heard about 'particles and progress'. But this is no longer possible. The peasants now watch TV and constantly consume media. There are no peasants now.

Smothered in Slogans

The mantle of intellectual meaninglessness shrouds every aspect of our common life. Events, things and 'information' flood over us, overwhelming us, disorienting us with threats and possibilities we for the most part have no idea what to do about.

Commercials, catch-words, political slogans and high-flying intellectual rumours clutter our mental and spiritual space. Our minds and bodies pick them up like a dark suit picks up lint. They decorate us. We willingly emblazon messages on our shirts, caps – even the seat of our trousers. Sometime back we had a campaign in America against roadside advertisement boards. But these were nothing compared to what we now post all over our bodies. We are immersed in birth-to-death and wall-to-wall 'noise' – silent and not so silent.

Must one not wonder about people willing to wear a commercial trademark on the outside of their shirts or caps or shoes to let others know who they are? And just think of a world in which little children sing, 'I wish I were a [certain kind of] wiener. That is what I really want to be. For if I were [that certain kind of] wiener. Everyone would be in love with me.'

Think of what it would mean to *be* a weenie, or for someone to love you as they 'love' a hot dog. Think of a world in which adults would pay millions of dollars to have children perform this song in 'commercials' and in which hundreds of millions, even billions, of adults find no problem in it. You are thinking of *our* world. If you are willing to be a weenie to be loved, what else would you be willing to do? Is it any wonder that depression and other mental and emotional dysfunctions are epidemic? Who is it, exactly, that is flying upside down now?

In the shambles of fragmented assurances from the past, our longing for goodness and rightness and acceptance – and orientation – makes us cling to bumper slogans, body graffiti and gift shop nostrums that in our profound upside-down-ness somehow seem deep but in fact make no sense: 'Stand up for your rights' sounds so good. How about 'All I ever needed to know I learned in kindergarten'? And 'Practise random kindnesses and senseless acts of beauty'? And so forth.

Such sayings contain a tiny element of truth. But if you try to actually plan your life using them you are immediately in deep, deep trouble. They will head you 180 degrees in the wrong direction. You might as well model your life on Bart Simpson or Seinfeld. But try instead 'Stand up for your responsibilities' or 'I don't know what I need to know and must now devote my full attention and strength to finding out' (Consider Prov. 3:7 or 4:7) or 'Practise routinely purposeful kindnesses and intelligent acts of beauty.'

Putting *these* into practice immediately begins to bring truth, goodness, strength and beauty into our lives. But you will never find them on a greeting card, plaque or bumper. They aren't thought to be smart. What is truly profound is thought to be stupid and trivial, or worse, boring, while what is actually stupid and trivial is thought to be profound. That is what it means to fly upside down.

All that is really profound in the cute wisdom is the awesome need of soul to which they incoherently respond. We sense the incoherence lying slightly beneath the surface, and we find the incoherence and lack of fit vaguely pleasing and true to life: What is the point of standing up for rights in a world where few stand up for their responsibilities? Your rights will do you little good unless others are responsible. And does one learn in kindergarten how to attract people and make a lot of money by writing books assuring people they already know all they need to know to live well? And how do you practise something that is random? Of course you can't. What is random may *hit* you, but whatever is purposely done is certainly not *random*. And no act of beauty is senseless, for the beautiful is never absurd. Nothing is more meaningful than beauty.

In fact, the popular sayings attract only because people are haunted by the idea from the intellectual heights that life is, in reality, absurd. Thus the only acceptable relief is to be cute or clever. In homes and on public buildings of the past, words of serious and unselfconscious exhortation, invocation and blessing were hung or carved in stone and wood. But that world has passed. Now the law is 'Be cute or die'. The only sincerity bearable is clever insincerity. That is what the clothing and greeting card graffiti really scream out. The particular 'message' doesn't matter.

And yet we have to act. The rocket of our life is off the pad. Action is forever. We are becoming who we will be – forever. Absurdity and cuteness are fine to chuckle over and perhaps to muse upon. But they are no place to live. They provide no shelter or direction for being human.

Word from a Different Reality

The Invitation

Yet, in the gloom a light glimmers and glows. We have received an invitation. We are invited to make a pilgrimage – into the heart and life of God. The invitation has long been on public record. You can hardly look anywhere across the human scene and not encounter it. It is literally 'blowing in the wind'. A door of welcome seems open to everyone without exception. No person or circumstance other than our own decision can keep us away. 'Whosoever will may come.'

The major problem with the invitation now is precisely over-familiarity. Familiarity breeds unfamiliarity – unsuspected unfamiliarity and then contempt. People think they have heard the invitation. They think they have accepted it – or rejected it. But they have not. The difficulty today is to hear it at all. Genius, it is said, is the ability to scrutinize the obvious. Written everywhere, we may think, how could the invitation be subtle or deep? It looks like the other graffiti and even shows up in the same places. But that is part of the divine conspiracy.

God's desire for us is that we should live in him. He sends among us the Way to himself. That shows what, in his heart of hearts, God is really like – indeed, what *reality* is really like. In its deepest nature and meaning our universe is a community of boundless and totally competent love.

God makes himself and his kingdom available, not in every way human beings have imagined, surely, but in a simple way – in a way that, paradoxically, is quite familiar to billions of people and that millions more have heard about. 'Paradoxically' because, though multitudes have heard about this Way, and even insist upon its rightness, humanity for the most part still lives in 'a far country'.

The Way we speak of is Jesus, the 'luminous Nazarene', as Albert Einstein once called him. Along with two thieves, he was executed by the authorities about two thousand years ago. Yet today, from countless paintings, statues and buildings, from literature and history, from personality and institution, from profanity, popular song and entertainment media, from confession and controversy, from legend and ritual – Jesus stands quietly at the centre of the contemporary world, as he himself predicted. He so graced the ugly instrument on which he died that the cross has become the most widely exhibited and recognized symbol on earth.

A World Historical Force

Jesus offers himself as God's doorway into the life that is truly life. Confidence in him leads us today, as in other times, to become his apprentices in eternal living. 'Those who come through me will be safe,' he said. 'They will go in and out and find all they need. I have come into their world that they may have life, and life to the limit.'

But intelligent, effectual entry into this life is currently obstructed by clouds of well-intentioned misinformation. The 'gospels' that predominate where he is most frequently invoked speak only of preparing to die or else of correcting social practices and conditions. These are both, obviously, matters of great importance. Who would deny it? But neither one touches the quick of individual existence or taps the depths of the reality of Christ. Our usual 'gospels' are, in their effects – dare we say it – nothing less than a standing invitation to omit God from the course of our daily existence.

Does Jesus only enable me to 'make the cut' when I die? Or to know what to protest, or how to vote or agitate and organize? It is good to know that when I die all will be well, but is there any good news for life? If I had to choose, I would rather have a car that runs than good insurance on one that doesn't. Can I not have both?

And what social or political arrangements – however important in their own right – can guide and empower me to be the person I know I ought to be? Can anyone now seriously believe that if people are only permitted or enabled to do what they want, they will then be happy or more disposed to do what is right?

Jaroslav Pelikan remarks that 'Jesus of Nazareth has been the dominant figure in the history of Western culture for almost twenty centuries. If it were possible, with some sort of super magnet, to pull up out of that history every scrap of metal bearing at least a trace of his name, how much would be left?'[8]

But just think how unlikely it would be that this great world-historical force, Jesus called 'Christ', could have left the depths of moment-to-moment human existence untouched while accomplishing what he has! More likely, we currently do not understand who he is and what he brings.

And what is it, really, that explains the enduring relevance of Jesus to human life? Why has he mattered so much? Why does he matter now? Why does he appear on the front covers of leading news magazines two millennia later? Why, even, is his name invoked in cursing more than that of any other person who has lived on earth? Why do more people self-identify as Christians – by some estimates 33.6 per cent of the world population – than any other world religion?[9] How is it that multitudes today credit him with their life and well-being?

I think we finally have to say that Jesus' enduring relevance is based on his historically proven ability to speak, to heal and empower the individual human condition. He matters because of what he brought and what he still brings to *ordinary* human beings, living their ordinary lives and coping daily with their surroundings. He promises wholeness for their lives. In sharing our weakness he gives us strength and imparts through his companionship a life that has the quality of eternity.

He comes where we are, and he brings us the life we hunger for. An early report reads, 'Life was in him, life that made sense of human existence' (John 1:4). To be the light of life, and to deliver God's life to women and men where they are and as they are, is the secret of the enduring relevance of Jesus. Suddenly they are flying right-side up, in a world that makes sense.

Entering the Ordinary

He slipped into our world through the backroads and outlying districts of one of the least important places on earth and has allowed his programme for human history to unfold ever so slowly through the centuries.

He lived for thirty years among socially insignificant members of a negligible nation – though one with a rich tradition of divine covenant and interaction. He grew up in the home of the carpenter for the little Middle-Eastern village of Nazareth. After his father, Joseph, died, he became 'the man of the house' and helped his mother raise the rest of the family. He was an ordinary workman: a 'blue-collar' worker.

He did all this to be with us, to be one of us, to 'arrange for the delivery' of his life to us. It must be no simple thing to make it possible for human beings to receive the eternal kind of life. But, as F. W. Faber opens one of his profound works, now 'Jesus belongs to us. He vouchsafes to put Himself at our disposal. He communicates to us everything of His which we are capable of receiving.'[10]

If he were to come today as he did then, he could carry out his mission through almost any decent and useful occupation. He could be an accountant, a computer engineer, a bank clerk, an editor, doctor, waiter, teacher, farmworker, lab technician or construction worker. He could run a housecleaning service or repair cars.

In other words, if he were to come today he could very well do what you do. He could very well live in your flat or house, hold down your job, have your education and life prospects, and live within your family, surroundings and time. None of this would be the least hindrance to the eternal kind of life that was his by nature and becomes available to us through him. Our human life, it turns out, is not destroyed by God's life but is fulfilled in it and in it alone.

Habitation of the Eternal

The obviously well kept secret of the 'ordinary' is that it is made to be a receptacle of the divine, a place where the life of God flows. But the divine is not pushy. As Huston Smith remarks, 'Just as science has found the power of the sun itself to be locked in the atom, so religion proclaims the glory of the eternal to be reflected in the simplest elements of time: a leaf, a door, an unturned stone.'[11] It is, of course, reflected as well in complicated entities, such as galaxies, music, mathematics and persons.

Now, considered apart from its Creator – which was never intended – the 'ordinary' truly is *so* ordinary and commonplace that it is of little interest or value. No atom by itself radiates solar power. In its own right everything is always just 'another one of those'. To be ordinary is to be only 'more of the same'. The *human* being screams against this from its every pore. To be just 'another one of those' is deadening agony for us. Indeed, it actually drives some people to their death. It was never God's intention for anyone.

This is why everyone, from the smallest child to the oldest adult, naturally wants in some way to be *extra*ordinary, *out*standing, making a unique contribution or, if all else fails, wants to be thought so – if only for a brief time. The fifteen minutes of fame that Andy Warhol said everyone would someday have, in the modern media-saturated world, may give desperate souls an assurance of uniqueness that could protect them from being 'nobody', at least in their own eyes.

The drive to significance that first appears as a vital need in the tiny child, and later as its clamourous desire for attention, is not egotism. Egotistical individuals see everything through themselves. They are always the dominant figures in their own field of vision.

Egotism is pathological self-obsession, a reaction to anxiety about whether one really does count. It is a form of acute *self*-consciousness and can be prevented and healed only by the experience of being adequately loved. It is, indeed, a desperate response to frustration of the need we all have to count for something and be held to be irreplaceable, without price.

Unlike egotism, the drive to significance is a simple extension of the creative impulse of God that gave us being. It is not filtered through self-consciousness any more than is our lunge to catch a package falling from someone's hand. It is outwardly directed to the good to be done. We were built to count, as water is made to run downhill. We are placed in a specific context to count in ways no one else does. That is our destiny.

Our hunger for significance is a signal of who we are and why we are here, and it also is the basis of humanity's enduring response to Jesus. For he always takes individual human beings as seriously as their shredded dignity demands, and he has the resources to carry through with his high estimate of them.

God's Kingdom Opened to All

Having established a beachhead of divine life in an ordinary human existence, Jesus finally stepped into the public arena to expose his life publicly and to make it available to the world. Mark's Gospel reports that 'Jesus then came into Galilee announcing the good news from God. "All the preliminaries have been taken care of," he said, "and the rule of God is now accessible to everyone. Review your plans for living and base your life on this remarkable new opportunity" ' (Mark 1:15).

In Matthew's account of Jesus' deeds and words, the formulation repeatedly used is the well-known 'Repent: for the kingdom of heaven is at hand' (3:2; 4:17; 10:7). This is a call for us to reconsider how we have been approaching our life, in light of the fact that we now, in the presence of Jesus, have the option of living within the surrounding movements of God's eternal purposes, of taking our life into his life.

What Jesus and his earliest friends meant by such words as these is made clear by the response they generated in hearers.

Around the age of thirty Jesus assumed the familiar role of rabbi, or teacher, within the traditions of Israel. His cousin, John the Baptizer, was the leading religious figure of the day. He was recognized by everyone at the time as a true prophet in the Old Testament pattern, the first in centuries. John's public endorsement of Jesus opened doors for him to begin his own work. But he began to minister, not in the bright lights of Jerusalem or even in his hometown of Nazareth, but in the farthest outposts of Jewish life in the Palestine of his day.

Capernaum and Bethsaida, at the north end of the Sea of Galilee, served as focal points of his earliest work. From there he ranged out into all of Galilee as well as into what is now southern Lebanon, the Golan Heights, Syria and Jordan. Wherever there were synagogues, his status as a rabbi opened doors for him to teach.

His speaking in synagogues in turn provided for the broadest possible penetration into the social fabric of his people, for the synagogues were central to their communities. His work began to have great effect far beyond the places he actually visited. Matthew gives us the picture:

> Jesus travelled all through Galilee teaching in the Jewish synagogues, everywhere preaching the Good News about the Kingdom of the Heavens.

> And he healed every kind of sickness and disease. The report of his miracles spread far beyond the borders of Galilee so that sick folk were soon coming to be healed from as far away as Syria. And whatever their illness or pain, or if they were possessed by demons, or were insane, or paralysed – he healed them all. Enormous crowds followed him wherever he went – people from Galilee and the Ten Cities, and Jerusalem and from all over Judea, and even from across the Jordan River (Matt. 4:23–25 LB).

Luke 8:1–3 seems to indicate that he systematically covered towns and villages in the area, announcing and exhibiting the rule, or 'kingdom', of God. His 'ministry team' included the Twelve Apostles, of course, but also a number of women he had healed. Along with others accompanying him, they supported the campaign out of their own pockets. His fame grew to the point where crowds were in the thousands. People trampled one another (Luke 12:1) and ripped roofs off houses (Mark 2:4) to gain access to him.

But they were only responding to *the striking availability of God to meet present human need through the actions of Jesus*. He simply was the good news about the kingdom. He still is.

Proprieties Aside

Some time later, towards the midpoint of his years in public ministry, Jesus reflected on a remarkable change that had occurred when his cousin, the Baptizer, passed the torch of God's word on to him.

John was, Jesus remarked, as great as any human being who ever lived. Yet, he still functioned from within the limited framework where God's action, rule or governance was primarily channelled through the official practices of Jewish rituals and institutions: through 'the law and the prophets', as that phrase was then used.

But since John, Jesus continued, we no longer 'stand on proprieties'. 'The Kingdom of the Heavens is subjected to violence and violent people take it by force' (Matt. 11:12). That is, the rule of

God, now present in the person of Jesus himself, submits to approaches that were previously not possible. Personal need and confidence in Jesus permits any person to blunder right into God's realm. And once in, they have an astonishing new status: 'Those least in the Kingdom of the Heavens are greater than John.'

The parallel passage in Luke 16:16 records Jesus as saying, 'The law and the prophets governed until John. But since then the kingdom of God is announced, and everybody is crowding into it.'

Concretely, how did that look? Here is just one of many illustrations that can be found in the Gospel stories.

A Harlot Crashes the Party

A very 'nice' man named Simon, a Pharisee, brought Jesus to dinner at his home in Capernaum (Luke 5). As they were reclining around the table, a woman known to be a harlot somehow came in, bringing with her an expensive flask of perfumed lotion. She certainly had overheard Jesus teaching and had seen his care for others. She was moved to believe that she too was loved by him and by the heavenly Father of whom he spoke. She was seized by a transforming conviction, an overwhelming faith.

Suddenly there she was, down on the floor by Jesus, tears of gratitude for him pouring down upon his feet. Drying them away with her hair, she then rained kisses upon his feet and massaged them with the lotion.

What a scene! That nice man, Simon, was taking it in, and – no doubt battling a surge of disapproval – he tried to put the best possible construction on it.

It just could not be that Jesus wasn't *nice*. Clearly he was a righteous man. So the only reason he would be letting this woman touch him, or even come near him, was that he didn't know she was a prostitute. And that, unfortunately, proved that Jesus didn't have 'it' after all. 'If this fellow really were a prophet,' Simon mused, 'he would know what this woman does, for she is filthy.' Perhaps Simon consoled himself with the thought that it is at least no sin not to be a prophet. It never occurred to him that Jesus would know exactly who the woman was and yet let her touch him.

But Jesus did know, and he also knew what Simon was thinking. So he told him a story of a man who lent money to two people: £50,000 to one and £5 to the other, let us say. When they could not repay, the man simply forgave the debts. 'Now Simon,' Jesus asked, 'which one will love the man most?' Simon replied that it would be the one who had owed most.

That granted, Jesus positioned Simon and the streetwalker side by side to compare their hearts:

> 'Look at this woman,' he said. 'When I entered your home, you didn't bother to offer me water to wash the dust from my feet, but she has washed them with her tears and wiped them with her hair. You refused me the customary kiss of greeting, but she has kissed my feet again and again from the time I first came in. You neglected the usual courtesy of olive oil to anoint my head, but she has covered my feet with rare perfume. Therefore her sins – and they are many – are forgiven, for she loved me much; but one who is forgiven little, shows little love.' (Luke 7:44–47 LB)

'Loved me much!' Simply that, and not the customary proprieties, was now the key of entry into the rule of God.

Jesus went on to say to the woman, 'Your sins are forgiven. Your faith has saved you. Go with peace in your heart.' Here is God's rule in action.

We must not overlook the connection between faith and love. The woman *saw* Jesus and recognized who he was and who dwelt in him. That vision was her faith. She knew he was forgiving and accepting her before he ever said, 'Your sins are forgiven.' She knew because she had seen a goodness in him that could only be God, and it broke her heart with gratitude and love.

Speaking in the language of today, we would say she went 'nuts' about Jesus. Her behaviour obviously was the behaviour of a 'nutty' person. (We really do have to use colloquial language to capture responses to Jesus. More formal, literary or theological language cannot do it.) When we see Jesus as he is, we must turn away or else shamelessly adore him. That must be kept in mind for any authentic understanding of the power of Christian faith. This woman, unlike nice Simon, was not about to turn away.

The Presence of God in Action

Such a response, along with many others familiar from the Gospels, illustrates how Jesus' hearers understood the invitation to base their own lives on the rule of God 'at hand'. Of course they had no general understanding of what was involved, but they knew Jesus meant that he was acting with God and God with him, that God's rule was effectively present through him.

The familiar stories, traditions and rituals of Israel enabled them to know the practical significance of this. They were stories and traditions of individual human beings whose lives were interlaced with God's action. Abraham, David, Elijah were well known to all. And the routinely practised rituals of Israel were often occasions when God acted. Everyone knew that whoever trustingly put themselves in his hands, as this poor scandalous woman did, were in fact in the hands of God. And God's deeds bore out his words.

When he announced that the 'governance' or rule of God had become available to human beings, he was primarily referring to what he could do for people, God acting with him. But he was also offering to communicate this same 'rule of God' to others who would receive and learn it from him. *He was himself the evidence for the truth of his announcement about the availability of God's kingdom, or governance, to ordinary human existence.*

This explains why, as everyone saw, he did not teach 'in the manner of the scribes' but instead 'as having authority in his own right' (Matt. 7:29). Scribes, expert scholars, teach by citing others. But Jesus was, in effect, saying, 'Just watch me and see that what I say is true. See for yourself that the rule of God has come among ordinary human beings.'

'Already during Jesus' earthly activity,' Hans Küng has pointed out, 'the *decision for or against the rule of God* hung together with the *decision for or against himself*' (italics mine). The presence of Jesus upon earth, both before and after his death and resurrection, means that God's rule is here now. 'In this sense,' Küng continues, 'the *immediate expectation* ... [of the kingdom] ... *has been fulfilled*' (italics mine).[12]

God's Rule Extended Onward Through Us

From the very beginning of his work, those who relied on him had, at his touch, entered the rule, or governance, of God and were receiving its gracious sufficiency. Jesus was not just acting for God but also *with* God – a little like the way, in a crude metaphor, I act with my power steering, or it with me, when I turn the wheel of my car.

And this 'governance' is projected through those who receive him. When we receive God's gift of life by relying on Christ, we find that God comes to act with us as we rely on him in our actions. That explains why Jesus said that the least in the kingdom of the heavens are greater than John the Baptist – not, of course, greater in themselves, but as a greater power works along with them. The 'greater' is not inherent, a matter of our own substance, but *relational*.

So, C. S. Lewis writes, our faith is not a matter of our hearing what Christ said long ago and 'trying to carry out'. Rather, 'The real Son of God is at your side. He is beginning to turn you into the same kind of thing as Himself. He is beginning, so to speak, to 'inject' His kind of life and thought, His *Zoe* [life], into you; beginning to turn the tin soldier into a live man. The part of you that does not like it is the part that is still tin.'[13]

Jesus' words and presence gave many of his hearers faith to see that when he acted God also acted, that the governance or 'rule' of God came into play and thus was *at hand*. They were aware of the invisible presence of God acting within the visible reality and action of Jesus, the carpenter rabbi.

Some years of reflection and further experience with Jesus and the kingdom enabled his people to describe him in lofty language as 'the icon of the unseeable God' (Col. 1:15). Today we might say *photo* or *snapshot* instead of *icon*. He was the 'exact picture' or 'precise representation of God's substance' (Heb. 1:3). But that time was not yet. It was to still uncomprehending ears that Jesus said, 'Those who have seen me have seen the Father.'

Made to Rule

What a 'Kingdom' Is

To gain deeper understanding of our eternal kind of life in God's present kingdom, we must be sure to understand what a *kingdom* is. Every last one of us has a 'kingdom' – or a 'queendom' or a 'government' – a realm that is uniquely our own, where our choice determines what happens. Here is a truth that reaches into the deepest part of what it is to be a person.

Some may think it should not be so. John Calvin remarked rather balefully, 'Everyone flatters himself and carries a kingdom in his breast.'[14] He understood this to mean that 'there is nobody who does not imagine that he is really better than the others.' Perhaps this is so for human beings as they are. All too easily, at least, we presume to rule others – in opinion and word, if not in deed.

But it is nevertheless true that we are made to 'have dominion' within an appropriate domain of reality. This is the core of the likeness or image of God in us and is the basis of the destiny for which we were formed. We are, all of us, never-ceasing spiritual beings with a unique eternal calling to count for good in God's great universe.

Our 'kingdom' is simply *the range of our effective will*. Whatever we genuinely have the say over is in our kingdom. And our having the say over something is precisely what places it within our kingdom. In creating human beings God made them to rule, to reign, to have dominion in a limited sphere. Only so can they be persons.

Any being that has say over nothing at all is no person. We only have to imagine what that would be like to see that this is so. Such 'persons' would not even be able to command their own body or their own thoughts. They would be reduced to completely passive observers who count for nothing, who make no difference.

The sense of having some degree of control over things is now recognized as a vital factor in both mental and physical health and can make the difference between life and death in those who are seriously ill.[15] Anyone who has raised a child, or has even supervised the work of others, knows how important it is to *let them do it* – whatever 'it' may be – and to do so as soon as that is practically feasible.

Obviously, having a place of rule goes to the very heart of who we are, of our integrity, strength and competence.

By contrast, attacks on our personhood always take the form of diminishing what we can do or have say over, sometimes up to the point of forcing us to submit to what we abhor. In the familiar human order, slaves are at the other end of the spectrum from kings. Their bodies and lives are at the disposal of another. Prisoners are, in most cases, several degrees above slaves. And, as the twentieth century has taught us, thought control is worst of all. It is the most heinous form of soul destruction, in which even our own thoughts are not really ours. It reaches most deeply into our substance.

God's 'Creation Covenant' with Human Beings

Keeping in mind these truths about personality, we will not be surprised at the Bible's simple, consistent picture of human beings in relation to God. The human job description (the 'creation covenant', we might call it) found in Chapter 1 of Genesis indicates that God assigned to us collectively the *rule* over all living things on earth. We are responsible before God for life on the earth (vv. 28–30).

However unlikely it may seem from our current viewpoint, God equipped us for this task by framing our nature to function in a conscious, personal relationship of interactive responsibility *with* him. We are meant to exercise our 'rule' only in union with God, as he acts with us. He intended to be our constant companion or co-worker in the creative enterprise of life on earth. That is what his love for us means in practical terms.

Now, what we can do by our unassisted strength is very small. What we can do acting *with* mechanical, electrical or atomic power is much greater. Often what can be accomplished is so great that it is hard to believe or imagine without some experience of it. But what we can do with these means is still very small compared to what we could do acting in union with God himself, who created and ultimately controls all other forces.

Lamentably, we fell away from our intended divine context and from the task for which we are by nature fitted. We mistrusted and distanced ourselves from God and then, very naturally, from one another. In our arrogance and fear we flounder through our existence on our own. The earth itself is 'subjected to futility' because of this (Rom. 8:20). However we may picture the original event, 'the fall', one cannot deny that such mistrust pervasively characterizes human life today and that things do not go well on earth. History and the eleven o'clock news leave no doubt.

But at the same time our fundamental make-up is unchanged. The deepest longings of our heart confirm our original calling. Our very being still assigns us to 'rule' in our life circumstances, whatever they may be. If animals are in trouble anywhere, for example, people generally feel they should do something about it – or at least that someone should. And we still experience ourselves as creative will, as someone who accomplishes things, constantly desiring to generate value, or what is good, from ourselves and from our environment. We are perhaps all *too* ready, given our distorted vision and will, to take charge of the earth.

Apart from harmony under God, our nature-imposed objectives go awry. The social and individual chaos of human desires sees to it. Much of our time and energy is spent trying to dominate others or escape domination by them, from 'office politics' to tribal warfare to international relations on a global scale.

In the biblical account of our fall from God, we were assigned to earn our bread by the sweat of our face. The sweat comes from our own energies, which is all we have left after losing our roots in God's own life. But we relentlessly try to earn our bread by the sweat of someone else's face, even when it might be easier to use our own. Perhaps John Calvin was not totally wrong about us.

Redemption of Our Rule

God nevertheless pursues us redemptively and invites us individually, every one of us, to be faithful to him in the little we truly 'have say over'. There, at every moment, we live in the interface between our lives and God's kingdom among us. If we are faithful to him here, we learn his co-operative faithfulness to us in turn. We discover the effectiveness of his rule with us precisely in the details of day-to-day existence.

Frank Laubach wrote of how, in his personal experiment of moment-by-moment submission to the will of God, the fine texture of his work and life experience was transformed. In January of 1930 he began to cultivate the habit of turning his mind to Christ for one second out of every minute.[16]

After only four weeks he reported, 'I feel simply carried along each hour, doing my part in a plan which is far beyond myself. This sense of co-operation with God in little things is what so astonishes me, for I never have felt it this way before. I need something, and turn round to find it waiting for me. I must work, to be sure, but there is God working along with me.'[17]

From a lonely missionary post in the Philippines, God raised Frank Laubach to the status of Christian world statesman and spokesman for Christ. He founded the World Literacy Crusade, still in operation today, and without any political appointment he was influential on United States foreign policy in the post-World War II years. But he was forever and foremost Christ's man, and always knew that his brilliant ideas and incredible energy and effectiveness derived from his practise of constant conscious interface with God.

Our Rule Extended – into Eternity

When we submit what and where we are to God, our rule or dominion then increases. In Jesus' words from the parable of the talents (Matt. 25), our Master says, 'Well done! You were faithful with a few things, and I will put you in charge of many things. Share what your Lord enjoys'; that is, share the larger direction or governance of things for good (cf. Luke 16:1–12). For God is unlimited creative will and constantly invites us, even now, into an ever larger share in what he is doing. Like Jesus, we can enter into the work we see our Father doing (John 5:17–19).

In accord with his original intent, the heavenly Father has in fact prepared an individualized kingdom for every person, from the outset of creation. That may seem impossible to us. But we do have a very weak imagination towards God, and we are confused by our own desires and fears, as well as by gross misinformation. It is a small thing for him.

As we learn through increasing trust to govern our tiny affairs with him, the kingdom he had all along planned for us will be turned over to us, at the appropriate time. 'Come you who are under my Father's blessing and take over the government assigned to you from the beginning' (Matt. 25:34).

Accordingly, in the last chapter of the Bible we see God's purposes in creation come round full circle in eternity: 'The Lord will be their light, and they shall reign for ever and ever' (Rev. 22:5).

God's Kingdom

Now God's own 'kingdom', or 'rule', is the range of his effective will, where what he wants done is done. The person of God himself and the action of his will are the organizing principles of his kingdom, but everything that obeys those principles, whether by nature or by choice, is *within* his kingdom.[18]

The Old Testament book of Psalms comes to a joyous, breathtaking celebration of God's kingdom in Psalms 145–150. The picture there presented must be kept in mind whenever we try to understand his kingdom. Then we will not doubt that that kingdom has existed from the moment of creation and will never end (Ps. 145:13; Dan. 7:14). It cannot be 'shaken' (Heb. 12:27f.) and is totally good. It has never been in trouble and never will be. It is not something that human beings produce or, ultimately, can hinder. We do have an invitation to be a part of it, but if we refuse we only hurt ourselves.

Accordingly, the kingdom of God is not essentially a social or political reality at all. Indeed, the social and political realm, along with the individual heart, is the only place in all of creation where the kingdom of God, or his effective will, is currently permitted to be absent. That realm is the 'on earth' of the Lord's Prayer that is opposed to the 'in heaven' where God's will is, simply, done. It is the realm of what is cut out 'by hands', opposed to the kingdom 'cut out without hands' of Daniel, Chapter 2.

Thus, contrary to a popular idea, the kingdom of God is not *primarily* something that is 'in the hearts of men'. That kingdom *may* be there, and it may govern human beings through their faith and allegiance to Christ. At the present time it governs them only through their hearts, if at all. But his kingdom is not something confined to their hearts or to the 'inner' world of human consciousness. It is not some matter of inner attitude or faith that might be totally disconnected from the public, behavioural, visible world. It always pervades and governs the whole of the physical universe – parts of planet earth occupied by humans and other personal beings, the satanic, slightly excepted for a while.

Also, God did not start to bring his kingdom, the 'kingdom of the heavens' as Jesus often called it, into existence through Jesus' presence on earth. All too frequently it is suggested that he did. But Jesus' own gospel of the kingdom was not that the kingdom was about to come, or had recently come, *into existence*. If we attend to what he actually said, it becomes clear that his gospel concerned only the new accessibility of the kingdom to humanity through himself.

And, in any case, if Jesus had come announcing the existence of the kingdom, it would have been no more newsworthy to his hearers than an announcement that Moses had given laws. The 'gospel' of the Old Testament, if you wish, was simply 'Our God reigns!' (Isa. 52:7; Pss. 96, 97, 99). Everyone knew that. It was the cry of deliverance as Israel emerged from Egypt through the Red Sea (Exod. 15:18). It was understood by all that 'God caused His glorious arm to go at the right hand of Moses' (Isa. 63:12). That 'arm' was, simply, God's rule in action.

So when Jesus directs us to pray, 'Thy kingdom come', he does not mean we should pray for it to come into existence. Rather, we pray for it to take over at all points in the personal, social and political order where it is now excluded: 'On earth as it is in heaven.' With this prayer we are invoking it, as in faith we are acting it, into the real world of our daily existence.

Within his overarching dominion God has created us and has given each of us, like him, a range of will – beginning from our minds and bodies and extending outward, ultimately to a point not wholly predetermined but open to the measure of our faith. His intent is for us to learn to mesh our kingdom with the kingdoms of others. Love of neighbour, rightly understood, will make this happen. But we can only love adequately by taking as our primary aim the integration of our rule with God's. That is why love of neighbour is the second, not the first, commandment and why we are told to seek first the kingdom, or rule, of God.

Only as we find that kingdom and settle into it can we human beings *all* reign or rule together with God. We will then enjoy individualized 'reigns' with neither isolation nor conflict. This is the ideal of human existence for which secular idealism vainly strives. Small wonder that, as Paul says, 'Creation eagerly awaits the revealing of God's children' (Rom. 8:19).

The Kingdom Is Now 'at Hand'

These matters are now widely misunderstood. The invitation to come out of the darkness and live right-side up in the light makes no sense to many. Thus we need to restate and further explain some of the essential points we have already made about the eternal kind of life now available to us within the ever-present governance of God.

Jesus came among us to show and teach the life for which we were made. He came very gently, opened access to the governance of God with him, and set afoot a conspiracy of freedom in truth among human beings. Having overcome death he remains among us. By relying on his word and presence we are enabled to reintegrate the little realm that makes up our life into the infinite rule of God. And that is the eternal kind of life. Caught up in his active rule, our deeds become an element in God's eternal history. They are what God and we do together, making us part of his life and him a part of ours.

'Ultimate reality' – to speak grandly – permits itself to be addressed and dealt with through the Son of man, Jesus. Indeed, by taking the title Son of man, he staked his claim to be all that the human being was originally supposed to be – and surely much more. Colloquially we might describe him as humanity's 'fair-haired boy', the one who expresses its deepest nature and on whom its hopes rest. Older theologians soberly referred to him as 'the representative man' or the 'federal head' of humanity.

We have noted how he entered human history through the life of an ordinary family. But then, as God's flash point in re-igniting eternal life amongst us, he inducts us into the eternal kind of life that flows through himself. He does this first by bringing that life to bear upon our *needs*, and then by diffusing it throughout our *deeds* – deeds done with expectation that he and his Father will act with and in our actions.

Because of so much misunderstanding on this particular point, we must re-emphasize that in speaking of the kingdom of the heavens being 'at hand', Jesus was not speaking of something that was about to happen but had not yet happened and might not.[19]

In the course of human events there are always plenty of things that are on the horizon of possibility but do not come about or that come about later. And there certainly is a dimension of still future realization of God's rule. But the term *eggiken* – usually translated as 'is at hand' or 'has drawn nigh' in such passages as Matt. 3:2; 4:17; 10:7; Mark 1:15; and Luke 10:9–11 – is a verb form indicating a past and completed action. It is best translated simply 'has come'.[20]

The reality of God's rule, and all of the instrumentalities it involves, is present in action and available with and through the person of Jesus. That is Jesus' gospel. The obvious present reality of the kingdom is what provoked the responses we have just discussed. New Testament passages make plain that this kingdom is not something to be 'accepted' now and enjoyed later, but something to be entered now (Matt. 5:20; 18:3; John 3:3–5). It is something that already has flesh-and-blood citizens (John 18:36; Phil. 3:20) who have been transformed into it (Col. 1:13) and are fellow workers in it (Col. 4:11).

The apostle Paul on one occasion describes it simply as 'righteousness and peace and joy' of a type that only occurs 'through the energizing of the Holy Spirit' (Rom. 14:17). That it is not *of*, or not derived from, this world or 'here' does not mean that it is not real or that it is not *in* this world (John 18:36). It is, as Jesus said, constantly in the midst of human life (Luke 17:21; cf. Deut. 7:21). Indeed, it means that it is more real and more present than any human arrangement could ever possibly be.

In the Midst of Many Kingdoms

We Become Bearers of God's Rule 'at Hand'

Those who have been touched by forgiveness and new life and have thus entered into God's rule become, like Jesus, *bearers of that rule*. We must re-emphasize this point also.

Once in replying to some of his critics Jesus made this statement: 'If I by the finger of God expel demons from people, then it is the Kingdom of God that has come upon you' (Luke 11:20). It came in his person and acted in his actions. This was not an entirely new phenomenon in biblical events. When the Egyptian magicians in Pharaoh's court saw what happened at the word of Moses, they acknowledged, 'This is the finger of God' (Exod. 8:19). And the Ten Commandments were said to have been inscribed in stone by the finger of God (Exod. 31:18).

But the divine co-action was to be true for Jesus' trainees, or apprentices, also. After a time of instruction he sent them out to do what he did. As they went they were to heal the sick and announce that 'the Kingdom of God has come upon you' (Luke 10:9). Even those who refused their ministry were to be informed that 'the Kingdom' had come to them (v. 11).

C. H. Dodd strikingly expresses how God's kingdom was present with Christ and his apostles:

> In what sense, then, did Jesus declare that the Kingdom of God was present? Our answer must at least begin with His own answer to John: 'The blind see, the lame walk, the lepers are cleansed, the deaf hear, the dead are raised, the poor have the Gospel preached to them.' In the ministry of Jesus Himself the divine power is released in effective conflict with evil.[21]

But Other Kingdoms Remain

One thing that may mislead us about the meaning of 'at hand' in Jesus' basic message is the fact that *other* 'kingdoms' are still present on earth along with the kingdom of the heavens. They too are 'at hand'. That is the human condition. Persons other than God, such as you or I, are still allowed on earth to have a 'say' that is contrary to his will. A kingdom of darkness is here, certainly, and the kingdoms of many individuals who are still 'trying to run their own show'.

All of this God still permits. And the lack of human unity in intelligent love under God not only leaves us at the mercy of man-made disasters, such as wars, famine and oppression, but also prevents our dealing successfully with many so-called natural evils, such as disease, scarcity and weather-related disasters. So, along with the 'already here' there obviously remains a 'not yet' aspect with regard to God's present rule on earth.

The present situation of kingdoms in conflict is one eloquently portrayed in the Twenty-third Psalm: 'In the valley of the shadow of death I will fear no evil.' Yes, but the 'evil' is very much here to be feared. And: 'Thou preparest a table before me in the presence of mine enemies.' The 'enemies' are certainly here, but we are safe in God's hands even though other 'kingdoms' loom over us and threaten us.

Sometimes the places where God's effective or actual rule is not yet carried out, and his will is not yet done, lie *within* the lives and little kingdoms of those who truly have been invaded by the eternal kind of life itself – those who really do belong to Christ because his life is already present and growing within them.

The 'interior castle' of the human soul, as Teresa of Avila called it, has many rooms, and they are slowly occupied by God, allowing us time and room to grow. That is a crucial aspect of the conspiracy. But even this does not detract from the reality of the 'kingdom among us'. Nor does it destroy the choice that all have to accept it and bring their life increasingly into it.

Right beside and among the kingdoms that are not God's stands his kingdom, always 'at hand'. It is that of Jesus and his heavenly Father. It can be ours as well. The door is open, and life in that kingdom is real. Even now 'the whole earth is full of His glory' (Isa. 6:3). True, few see it. The earth is *not yet* 'filled with the *knowledge* of the glory of the Lord, as the waters cover the sea.' But that too one day 'shall be' (Heb. 2:14).

Electricity Is 'at Hand'

As a child I lived in an area of southern Missouri where electricity was available only in the form of lightning. We had more of that than we could use. But in my senior year of high school the REA (Rural Electrification Administration) extended its lines into the area where we lived, and electrical power became available to households and farms.

When those lines came by our farm, a very different way of living presented itself. Our relationships to fundamental aspects of life – daylight and dark, hot and cold, clean and dirty, work and leisure, preparing food and preserving it – could then be vastly changed for the better. But we still had to believe in the electricity and its arrangements, understand them, and take the practical steps involved in *relying* on it.

You may think the comparison rather crude, and in some ways it is. But it will help us to understand Jesus' basic message about the kingdom of the heavens if we pause to reflect on those farmers who, in effect, heard the message: 'Repent, for electricity is at hand.' Repent, or turn from their kerosene lamps and lanterns, their ice-boxes and cellars, their scrub-boards and rug beaters, their woman-powered sewing machines and their radios with dry-cell batteries.

The power that could make their lives far better was right there near them where, by making relatively simple arrangements, they could utilize it. Strangely, a few did not accept it. They did not 'enter the kingdom of electricity'. Some just didn't want to change. Others could not afford it, or so they thought.

Another image may help us understand this 'available' aspect of the kingdom, which is so easily overlooked. Think of visiting in a home where you have not been before. It is a fairly large house, and you sit for a while with your host in a living room or on the veranda. Dinner is announced, and he ushers you down a hall, saying at a certain point, 'Turn, for the dining room is at hand,' or more likely, 'Here's the dining room.' Similarly Jesus directs us to his kingdom.

In these images something absolutely crucial to Jesus' message is emphasized. There is no suggestion that electricity or the dining room hasn't happened yet but is about to happen or about to be there – possibly if someone welcomes it or *lets* it come. Rather, they have now become available. And, similarly, the kingdom of God is also right beside us. It is indeed The Kingdom Among Us. You can reach it from your heart with your mouth – through even a shaky and stumbling confidence and confession that Jesus is the death-conquering Master of all (Rom. 10:9).

To be sure, that kingdom has been here as long as we humans have been here, and longer. But it has been available to us through simple confidence in Jesus, the Anointed, only from the time he became a public figure. It is a kingdom that, in the person of Jesus, welcomes us just as we are, just where we are, and makes it possible for us to translate our 'ordinary' life into an eternal one. It is so available that everyone who from the centre of his or her being calls upon Jesus as Master of the Universe and Prince of Life will be heard and will be delivered into the eternal kind of life.

Two Who Called

A close friend of our family, Gary Smith, was under zero religious influence of any kind until he was about thirty years of age. Trained and employed as a meteorologist, he was living in a suburban setting with his family. He and his wife, Diane, started sending their children to Sunday school, thinking that that was 'the suburban thing to do'. After some time Gary became concerned about what the children were being taught. And who was this 'Jesus' after all?

He was awakened one night by what he could only describe as a 'yearning' to go into the living room with pencil and paper. When he walked into that room, he found himself 'surrounded with love', and he 'knew' the presence of Jesus Christ. As he later said, it was 'too tangible' to be the Holy Spirit, yet it was not visible.

Soon he found himself writing over and over on the paper, 'I don't care! I don't care!' His concerns about who this 'Jesus' was did not matter anymore in view of the presence he had encountered. He became a Presbyterian pastor, widely known and loved in the Los Angeles area.

Jesus is now throughout the world, and he currently hears those who cry out for him even more effectively than he did in 'the days of his flesh'. He even reaches those who have very little knowledge about him.

David (Paul) Cho now heads Yoido Full Gospel Church in Seoul, Korea, generally regarded as the largest church in the world today. But as a young man he was a Buddhist, dying of tuberculosis in hopeless poverty. He had heard that 'the God of the Christians' helped people, healed people, so where he was he simply *asked* 'their' God to help him.

And their God did. He healed this young Korean man, and taught him, and gave him an abundance of the kingdom life that was and is in Jesus, the Son of man. And now that same life flows through David Cho to thousands of others.

Do Jesus and his Father hear Buddhists when they call upon them? They hear *anyone* who calls upon them. 'The Lord is near to the brokenhearted, and saves those who are crushed in spirit' (Ps. 34:18). There is no distinction between 'Jew and Greek', between those who have 'it' – however humans may define 'it' – and those who do not, 'for the same one is Lord of all, abounding in riches to all who call upon him' (Rom. 10:12).

You cannot call upon Jesus Christ or upon God and not be heard. You live in their house, their *ecos* (Heb. 3:4). We usually call it simply 'the universe'. But they fully occupy it. It is their place, their 'kingdom', where through their kindness and sacrificial love we can make our present life an eternal life. Only as we understand this, is the way open for a true ecology of human existence, for only then are we dealing with what the human habitation truly is.

And the God who hears is also one who speaks. He has spoken and is sill speaking. Humanity remains his project, not its own, and his initiatives are always at work among us. He certainly 'gives us space', as we say, and this is essential. But he continues to speak in ways that serious inquirers can hear if they will. We need not, as earlier described, stagger onward in darkness concerning what is truly good and really right. We need not fly upside down. There is a right-side up, and we can find it. But we don't *have* to. We are free. For now.

Chapter 2

GOSPELS OF SIN MANAGEMENT

> He then helped them understand the scriptures, which foretold that the Anointed One would be killed, and would rise from the dead, and that repentance and forgiveness of sins would be offered in his name to every ethnic group on earth, beginning from Jerusalem. 'You are the ones to do it,' he said … 'But stay in town until you have been clothed with power from the heights.'
>
> LUKE 24:45–49

> We have so persistently dissembled the power of the Gospel … that it is pardonable if those who judge of it by us should doubt whether it is anything more efficacious and inspiring than the pathetic guesses which adorn the writings of philosophy.
>
> CANON B. F. WESTCOTT,
> THE GOSPEL OF THE RESURRECTION

The Invitation Diminished

How does the grand invitation to life sound today?

The bumper sticker gently imposes its little message: Christians Aren't Perfect, Just Forgiven. A popular song of some years ago said that the words of the prophets are written on the subway walls. Where there are no subways, bumpers will do.

Just forgiven? And is that really all there is to being a Christian? The gift of eternal life comes down to that? Quite a retreat from living an eternal kind of life now!

Christians certainly aren't perfect. There will always be need for improvement. But there is a lot of room between being perfect and being 'just forgiven' as that is nowadays understood. You could be *much* more than forgiven and still not be perfect. Perhaps you could even be a person in whom Jesus' eternal kind of life predominates and still have room for growth.

Now this bit of bumper-sticker theology has migrated to Christian trinkets. There is a little bookmark adorned with flowers, bows, green sprigs and fourteen tiny pink hearts, with a tassel at the top. In the centre is a wide-eyed teddy bear that looks as if it might have inadvertently just done something naughty. The message below is – as you will now expect – 'Christians aren't perfect, just forgiven.'

Well, it certainly needs to be said that Christians are forgiven. And it needs to be said that forgiveness does not depend on being perfect. But is that really what the slogan communicates?

Unfortunately, it is not. What the slogan really conveys is that forgiveness alone is what Christianity is all about, what is genuinely essential to it.

It says that you can have a faith in Christ that brings forgiveness, while in every other respect your life is no different from that of others who have no faith in Christ at all. This view so pleasingly presented on bumpers and trinkets has deep historical roots. It is by now worked out in many sober tomes of theology, lived out by multitudes of those who sincerely self-identify as Christians.

Bar-Code Faith

Think of the bar codes now used on goods in most stores. The scanner responds only to the bar code. It makes no difference what is in the bottle or package that bears it, or whether the sticker is on the 'right' one or not. The calculator responds through its electronic eye to the bar code and totally disregards everything else. If the ice cream sticker is on the dog food, the dog food is ice cream, so far as the scanner knows or cares.

On a recent radio programme a prominent minister spent fifteen minutes enforcing the point that 'justification', the forgiveness of sins, involves *no change at all* in the heart or personality of the one forgiven. It is, he insisted, something entirely external to you, located wholly in God himself.

His intent was to emphasize the familiar Protestant point that salvation is by God's grace only and is totally independent of what we may do. But what he in fact *said* was that being a Christian has nothing to do with the kind of person you are. The implications of this teaching are stunning.

The theology of Christian trinkets says there is something about the Christian that works like the bar code. Some ritual, some belief, or some association with a group affects God the way the bar code affects the scanner. Perhaps there has occurred a moment of mental assent to a creed, or an association entered into with a church. God 'scans' it, and forgiveness floods forth. An appropriate amount of righteousness is shifted from Christ's account to our account in the bank of heaven, and all our debts are paid. We are, accordingly, 'saved'. Our guilt is erased. How could we not be Christians?

For some Christian groups the 'account' has to be appropriately serviced to keep the debts paid up, because we really are not perfect. For others – some strongly Calvinist groups – every debt past, present and future is paid for at the initial scan. But the essential thing in either case is the forgiveness of sins. And the pay-off for having faith and being 'scanned' comes at death and after. Life now being lived has no necessary connection with being a Christian as long as the 'bar code' does its job.

We do hear a lot of discussion concerning what *good* Christians do and do not do. But of course it is not necessary to be a *good* Christian in order to be forgiven. That's the main point of the bar code, and it is correct.

Would God Really Do It That Way?

Many are distressed about this disjunction between faith and life, but they remain firmly pinned to it by their ideas about salvation. Many others are angry with such a view of being Christian because to them it seems irresponsible. They contemptuously refer to it as 'cheap grace' or 'fire insurance'. Some people actually reject Christianity because of it, while others insist that faith in Christ is a matter of righteous living in the social arena, standing up against social evils on behalf of love and justice.

But, to be quite frank, grace is cheap from the point of view of those who need it. That is why attacks on 'cheap grace' never make much difference. To try to rule out unheroic Christianity by making grace expensive will only add to confusion about matters of vast importance. And if a fire is likely, it would not be a mark of wisdom to forgo insurance that really is available.

No one need worry about our getting the best of God in some bargain with him, or that we might somehow succeed in using him for our purposes. ('All this and heaven too', as is sometimes humorously said.) Anyone who thinks this is a problem has seriously underestimated the intelligence and agility of our Father in the heavens. He will not be tricked or cheated. Any arrangement God has established will be right for him and right for us. We can count on it.

The real question, I think, is whether God *would* establish a bar code type of arrangement at all. It is we who are in danger: in danger of missing the fullness of life offered to us. Can we seriously believe that God would establish a plan for us that essentially bypasses the awesome needs of present human life and leaves human character untouched?

Would he leave us even temporarily marooned with no help in our kind of world, with our kinds of problems: psychological, emotional, social and global? Can we believe that the essence of Christian faith and salvation covers nothing but death and after? Can we believe that being saved really has nothing whatever to do with the kinds of persons we are?

And for those of us who think the Bible is a reliable or even significant guide to God's view of human life, can we validly interpret its portrayal of faith in Christ as one concerned only with the management of sin, whether in the form of our personal debt or in the form of societal evils?

Some Puzzling Facts

According to Gallup surveys, 94 per cent of Americans believe in God and 74 per cent claim to have made a commitment to Jesus Christ.[1] About 34 per cent confess to a 'new birth' experience. These figures are shocking when thoughtfully compared to statistics on the same group for unethical behaviour, crime, mental distress and disorder, family failures, addictions, financial misdealings and the like.

Of course there are always shining exceptions. But could such a combination of profession and failure really be the 'life and life abundantly' that Jesus said he came to give? Or have we somehow developed an understanding of 'commitment to Jesus Christ' that does not break through to his living presence in our lives? Without question, it is the latter that has occurred, and with heart-rending consequences.

One of the leading Christian magazines in this country recently editorialized about a rumour to the effect that a leader at a certain evangelical institution had resigned because of 'moral failure.'[2] The rumour was confirmed, but the magazine decided not to report on this case.

In explaining their decision, the editors comment that these cases are so numerous that the magazine has 'been forced to set criteria to decide which ones are newsworthy.' They did not run a story in the present instance because 'the individual was not a top-level leader'.

The point of the editorial had been to discuss the speed and power of the 'grapevine' in such cases. But these cases – grapevine and all – provoke deeper reflections on what must be the faith and interior life of our leaders and of those many Christians who make up the 'grapevine'. Are we to suppose that everyone, from Mother Teresa to Hitler, is really the same on the inside, but that some of us are just vigilant or 'lucky' enough to avoid doing what we all really want to do? Are we to suppose that God gives us nothing that really influences character and spirituality? Are we to suppose that in fact Jesus has no substantial impact on our 'real lives'?

Helmut Thielicke points out that we often wonder if the celebrities who advertise foods and beverages actually consume what they are selling.[3] He goes on to say that this is the very question most pressing for those of us who speak for Christ. Surely something has gone wrong when moral failures are so massive and widespread among *us*. Perhaps we are not eating what we are selling. More likely, I think, what we are 'selling' is irrelevant to our real existence and without power over daily life.

God Really Doesn't Change Our Behaviour?

A well-known leader who has spent most of his life in Christian service, much of it at a national level, recently turned fifty. Looking back, he comments in his monthly magazine column that 'in these last four decades my faith has truly taken a beating.' He tells how from his conversion at the age of ten he was taught that 'if I was a Christian, then *people would see a marked difference in my life!!!* And … that the closer I was to God – the more spiritual I was – the greater and *more visible* that difference would be' (italics mine).

Now at fifty he has seen so many of his mentors 'who stumbled and fell, never again to recover their faith; so many "truths" about the Gospel that turned out to be false; so many casualties, so many losses, so many assumptions that turned out to be just that – assumptions, not truth.' Finally, he says, 'I don't believe that anymore.'

He still believes that Jesus changes you, but his definition of 'change' has changed. 'Whatever the change is, it is not so much outward as it is inward. This difference that God makes is often visible *only* to God … and no one else … I haven't abandoned my faith, I have abandoned a way of *looking* at my faith … Life is different. But what is different is different from what I thought.'[4]

The suggestion is that the change that makes a person Christian, whatever that is, may be totally undetectable from the human point of view. Only God's 'scanner' can detect it. Apparently that is 'Christian reality' now.

At least many of our best-known leaders seem to think so.[5]

Shifting the Focus

But now let us try out a subversive thought. Suppose our failures occur, not in spite of what we are doing, but precisely because of it.

Suppose, to illustrate, that those who guide our school systems seriously considered the possibility that the low attainments of schoolchildren are not in spite of what is done with them in school, but largely because of what they are taught and how they are taught. Or suppose that the American national legislature began to think that its failure to come to grips with the national debt or violence in the streets is not in spite of what the legislature does, but because of it.

It may be hard to take such a suggestion seriously, but to do so might well provide a basis for genuine solutions to problems that now seem unsolvable.

A leading American pastor laments, 'Why is today's church so weak? Why are we able to claim many conversions and enrol many church members but have less and less impact on our culture? Why are Christians indistinguishable from the world?'[6]

Should we not at least consider the possibility that this poor result is not in spite of what we teach and how we teach, but precisely because of it? Might that not lead to our discerning why the power of Jesus and his gospel has been cut off from ordinary human existence, leaving it adrift from the flow of his eternal kind of life?

We will come back to this question later, at the end of this chapter and in Chapters 8 and 9.

Gospels of Sin Management

The current situation, in which faith professed has little impact on the whole of life, is not unique to our times, nor is it a recent development. But it is currently at an acute stage. History has brought us to the point where the Christian message is thought to be *essentially* concerned only with how to deal with sin: with wrongdoing or wrong-being and its effects. Life, our actual existence, is not included in what is now presented as the heart of the Christian message, or it is included only marginally. That is where we find ourselves today.

Once we understand the disconnection between the current message and ordinary life, the failures just noted at least make a certain sense. They should be expected. When we examine the broad spectrum of Christian proclamation and practice, we see that the only thing made essential on the right wing of theology is forgiveness of the individual's sins. On the left it is removal of social or structural evils. The current gospel then becomes a 'gospel of sin management'. Transformation of life and character is no part of the redemptive message. Moment-to-moment human reality in its depths is not the arena of faith and eternal living.

To the right, being a Christian is a matter of having your sins forgiven. (Remember that bumper sticker?) To the left, you are Christian if you have a significant commitment to the elimination of social evils. A Christian is either one who is ready to die and face the judgement of God or one who has an identifiable commitment to love and justice in society. That's it.

The history that has brought this about – being filtered through the Modernist/Fundamentalist controversy that consumed American religion for many decades and still works powerfully in its depths – also has led each wing to insist that what the other takes for essential *should not* be regarded as essential.

What right and left have in common is that neither group lays down a coherent framework of knowledge and practical direction adequate to personal transformation towards the abundance and obedience emphasized in the New Testament, with a corresponding redemption of ordinary life. What is taught as the essential message about Jesus has no natural connection to entering a life of discipleship to him.

Of course the Christian gospel and being a Christian have not always been thought of in this way. Anyone familiar with the bright lights of Christian history will know this to be so. And there are at present rare, bright exceptions to the rule. The influential Anglican Bishop Stephen Neill, for example, says simply: 'To be a Christian means to be like Jesus Christ.' And, 'Being a Christian depends on a certain inner relatedness to the living Christ. Through this relatedness all other relationships of a man – to God, to himself, to other people – are transformed.'[7]

But the inevitable question will then be: Who is a Christian by such a standard of authentic Christlikeness? It surely resonates well with biblical teachings and with the high moments of Christian history. And the depressing statistics of human failure referred to a few paragraphs back would be radically reduced.

No doubt! But what then are we to say about the multitudes, right and left along the theological spectrum, who today self-identify as Christians while having hardly a whiff of Christlikeness about them and no idea that it might even be possible – who perhaps even have a settled conviction that genuine Christlikeness is impossible? What is the gospel they have heard?

The Gospel on the Right

The Atonement as the Whole Story

If you ask anyone from that 74 per cent of Americans who say they have made a commitment to Jesus Christ what the Christian gospel is, you will probably be told that Jesus died to pay for our sins, and that if we will only believe he did this, we will go to heaven when we die.

In this way what is only one theory of the 'atonement' is made out to be the whole of the essential message of Jesus. To continue with theological language for the moment, *justification* has taken the place of *regeneration*, or new life.[8] Being let off the divine hook replaces possession of a divine life 'from above'. For all of the talk about the 'new birth' among conservative Christians, there is an almost total lack of understanding of what that new birth is in practical terms and of how it relates to forgiveness and imputed or transmitted righteousness.

Moreover, what it is to *believe* that Jesus died for us is currently explained in various ways, with differing degrees and forms of creedal content or association with a local church or denomination. Indeed, as we shall see presently, this issue – what the faith that saves is – is a flash point of current controversy. But for some time now the belief required to be saved has increasingly been regarded as a totally private act, 'just between you and the Lord.' Only the 'scanner' would know.

And so the only sure outcome of belief is that we are 'just forgiven'. We are justified, which is often explained by saying that, before God, it is 'just-as-if-I'd' never sinned at all. We may not have done or become anything positive to speak of. But when we come to heaven's gate, they will not be able to find a reason to keep us out. The mere record of a magical moment of mental assent will open the door.

Practically, there has always been a great problem with knowing for sure that you have performed the right private or mental act, because its only essential effect is a change in the books of heaven, and these cannot be seen now. Thus there occurs the familiar and often bitter struggle in the Protestant tradition to know whether or not you are 'among the elect' and will certainly 'get in'.

On the understanding of the theological right there is no behaviour that absolutely indicates belief and none that is absolutely ruled out by it. Grace and forgiveness (salvation) by grace, 'plus nothing and minus nothing', is thought to require that. To insist that something more than mere faith must be present would be to add 'works' on to pure grace. And that, we know from our Protestant cultural heritage, cannot be done.

'Lordship Salvation'

Widespread acceptance of this interpretation of salvation within the evangelical and conservative churches of North America is what has produced the situation sketched earlier, in which those who profess Christian commitment consistently show little or no behavioural and psychological difference from those who do not. This in turn has led to what is called the 'Lordship salvation' debate among leading evangelicals and their followers.

The issues involved in that debate may seem a little difficult to follow, but a brief examination of them will do much to aid us in understanding how things now stand with the invitation to life as commonly heard.

One of the most influential writers in the conservative camp today is John MacArthur. He has defended the view that you *cannot* have a 'saving' faith in Jesus Christ without also intending to obey his teachings. You must accept him as *Lord*, hence the name *Lordship salvation*.[9] Obviously, for MacArthur, you can and must say much more about a Christian than that he or she is forgiven. He has painstakingly defended his view by biblical exposition and historical and theological analysis.

In replying to MacArthur, Charles Ryrie states that 'the Gospel that saves is believing that Christ died for our sins and rose from the dead.'[10] 'The good news,' he continues, 'is that Christ has done something about sin [paid for it] and that He lives today to offer His forgiveness to me.'

In supporting his position, Ryrie provides a clarification of what he calls 'the issue in reference to the Gospel':

> Some of the confusion regarding the meaning of the Gospel today may arise from failing to clarify the issue involved. The issue is, How can my sins be forgiven? What is it that bars me from heaven? What is it that prevents my having eternal life? The answer is sin. Therefore, I need some way to resolve that problem. And God declares that the death of His son provides forgiveness of my sin … Through faith I receive Him and His forgiveness. Then the sin problem is solved, and I can be fully assured of going to heaven.[11]

Ryrie does not try to support his claim that removal of sin-guilt (not of sin itself, as his words might suggest), to secure entrance into heaven after death, is *the* problem or issue. He quite correctly assumes that all parties to the current debate will agree with him about this. But in the face of Christian history and of the biblical record, that claim does need support – support it can never find. The Christian tradition certainly deals with guilt and the afterlife, but by no means does it take them to be *the only* issues involved in salvation.

This fact is hidden from Ryrie and others on his side by their own systematic way of reading New Testament references to faith or belief in Christ and to 'the gospel' so that they fit their account of what is at issue.

For example, he states that all of Matthew's references to the gospel of the kingdom have to do with the coming of the Messiah to rule the earth in the Millennium. The Millennium is a projected one-thousand-year period when the actual government on earth will be under the personal direction of a returned Jesus. The 'kingdom' that the good news is about is said by Ryrie and many others to be the very same thing as this future millennial reign – a future political reality, not the present action of God's will in creation and in Christ.

Could this possibly be correct? Certainly if we substitute the phrase *millennial reign* for *the kingdom* in such passages as Matt. 6:33 and 8:12, we get language that makes little or no sense: 'Seek ye first the millennial reign of God' and 'the children of the millennial reign shall be cast out.' We need an explanation of why *kingdom* must mean something different in such passages while allegedly meaning 'millennial reign' in 'gospel' contexts such as Matt. 4:17 and 9:35.

If, by contrast, we understand the kingdom of God to be simply what God is actually doing, as previously explained, then the 'kingdom' passages in the Gospels all make sense, and yet leave plenty of room to deal with future dimensions of the kingdom, including a millennial reign of a political nature.

Ryrie is so sure that the saving gospel is about Jesus' death that, in Matthew's story of Mary Magdalene's anointing of Jesus for burial, he simply inserts the words *about his death* after the word *gospel* in Matt. 26:13. This makes the passage say, in Ryrie's words, 'that wherever the good news *about His death* was preached, Mary Magdalene's good deed of anointing Him in anticipation of that death would be known' (italics mine).[12] But the scripture text itself simply says, 'Wherever this gospel is preached' and does not indicate that it is 'about his death' at all. The gospel certainly includes the death of Jesus for humankind, but much more besides.

Salvation Cut Off from Life

Construing texts in this manner makes it possible for Ryrie, and many others, to make a distinction between what you believe for salvation and other things you can correctly believe about Christ. In itself a perfectly correct and helpful distinction, it still must be used with care.

'To believe in Christ for salvation,' he says, 'means to have confidence that He can remove the guilt of sin and give eternal life [read *heaven*]. It means to believe that He can solve the problem of sin [read *guilt*] which is what keeps a person out of heaven.'[13]

There are a multitude of things that, according to Ryrie, you can correctly believe about Christ but are not required to believe for salvation, among them:

> You can believe that what He taught while on earth was good, noble and true, and it was ... You can believe He is able to run your life, and He surely is able to do that, and He wants to. But these are not issues of salvation. That issue is whether or not you believe that His death paid for all your sin and that by believing in Him you can have forgiveness and eternal life. (p. 74)

'When one believes, he commits to God,' Ryrie explains. 'Commits what? His eternal destiny. That's the issue, not the years of his life on the earth' (p. 123). The non-salvation 'issues belong to Christian living' or 'relate to the Christian life, not to the issue of salvation.' 'I do not need to settle issues that belong to Christian living in order to be saved' (p. 40).

But Is That *the* Issue?

The difference between adherents of Lordship salvation and its critics has to do with what makes up saving faith. But we should also consider where the two sides agree. They agree that being lost or saved is solely a matter of demerit and merit, on what it is for faith to be *saving* faith, and on what being 'saved' amounts to. These points form the heart of the gospel on the theological right.

Also, the phrase *eternal destiny* is used much by all parties. They all agree that the matter at issue is what Ryrie says it is: forgiveness of sins because of transferred merit, with the resultant admission to heaven after death. You are saved if you have got this, and saving faith is the personal quality or attitude that is required to 'get' it. The point of difference is over what that faith is that saves. What exactly must one believe if the belief is to save us?

MacArthur agrees with his critics that the issue at stake in salvation is forgiveness and eternal destiny. If he did not, there would be no significant disagreement at all; the two sides would just be talking about different things. MacArthur would be saying that in order to have A (salvation) you must have B (commitment to Lordship), and his critics would be replying, 'No, in order to have C (another 'salvation'), you do *not* have to have B.'

Associated with this agreement that the issue in salvation is only 'heaven or hell' is a further agreement that being saved is a forensic or legal condition rather than a vital reality or character. No one is in this 'saved' condition until *declared* to be so by God. We do not enter it by something that happens to us, or in virtue of a reality that moves into place in our life, even if that reality is God himself. The debate then is about what must be true of us *before* God will declare us to be in the saved condition.

Finally, the two sides agree that getting into heaven after death is the sole *target* of divine and human efforts for salvation. It is what such efforts are aimed at, rather than a by-product or natural outcome of something else that is the target.

But we get a totally different picture of salvation, faith and forgiveness if we regard having life from the kingdom of the heavens now – the eternal kind of life – as the target. The words and acts of Jesus naturally suggest that this is indeed salvation, with discipleship, forgiveness and heaven to come as natural parts. And in this he only continues the teachings of the Old Testament. The entire biblical tradition from beginning to end is one of the intimate involvement of God in human life – or else alienation from it. That is the biblical alternative for life now. 'The crooked man is an abomination to the Lord,' as the proverb sums it up, 'but He is intimate with the upright' (Prov. 3:32 NAS).

Recalling Abraham's Faith and Righteousness

Abraham believed God and it was reckoned to him as righteousness, we are told (Gen. 15:6). *What* did Abraham believe that led God to declare or 'reckon' him righteous? Was it that God had arranged payment for his sins? Not at all. The story makes it very clear that Abraham believed God was going to give him a male baby, an heir, and through that baby a multitude of descendants who would possess the land promised to him. He trusted God, of course, but it was for things involved in his current existence.

He believed that *God would interact with him now* – just as those who later gathered around Jesus did. He even dared to ask God how he could know that the promise of a male heir would be fulfilled. In response, God directed him to prepare animals for sacrifice. Abraham did so and then waited for God to act (Gen. 15:8–11). He waited until God materialized fire 'out of thin air'. God acted from surrounding space, the atmosphere – that is, from the 'first heaven' of the Bible. *This* was the answer to Abraham's question. Much later 'God visited Sarah' and Isaac was conceived (Gen. 21:1).

In the face of such faith, God declared Abraham to be righteous. Does that mean he declared he would go to heaven when he died? Not precisely that, but certainly that Abraham's sins and failures would not cut him off from God in the present moment and in their ongoing relationship in life together. But *would* he go to heaven when he died? Of course! What else would God do with such a person? They were friends, a fact made much of in scripture (2 Chron. 20:7; Isa. 41:8; James 2:23), as we are to be friends of Jesus by immersing ourselves in his work (John 15:15). No friend of God will be in hell. Jesus even assured us that 'whoever, as one of his apprentices, gives a "little one" just a cup of cold water to drink shall not lose his reward' (Matt. 10:42).

Certainly forgiveness and reconciliation are essential to any relationship where there has been offence, and also between us and God. We cannot pass into a new life from above without forgiveness. Certainly it is Christ who made possible such a transition, including forgiveness, through his life and his death. We must be reconciled to God and he to us if we are going to have a life together. But such a reconciliation involves far more than the forgiveness of our sins or a clearing of the ledger. And the faith and salvation of which Jesus speaks obviously is a much more positive reality than mere reconciliation. The stories of Abraham and other biblical characters beautifully illustrate this.

The issue, so far as the gospel in the Gospels is concerned, is whether we are alive to God or dead to him. Do we walk in an interactive relationship with him that constitutes a new kind of life, life 'from above'? As the apostle John says in his first letter, 'God has given undying life to us, and that life is in his Son. Those who have the Son have life' (1 John 5:11–12).

What must be emphasized in all of this is the difference between trusting Christ, the real person Jesus, with all that that naturally involves, versus trusting some arrangement for sin-remission set up through him – trusting only his role as guilt remover. To trust the real person Jesus is to have confidence in him in every dimension of our real life, to believe that he is right about and adequate to everything.

Ryrie comments, with reference to the use of 'gospel' in the Gospels of Mark and Luke, 'Our Lord is the central theme of the good news.'[14] And this is certainly right. But he and many others see no distinction between saying that and saying, 'The Gospel is the good news about the death and resurrection of Christ' – or that it claims an *arrangement* for forgiveness of sin has been made that leaves Christ, the now living person, simply irrelevant to our present existence.

The sensed irrelevance of what God is doing to what makes up our lives is the foundational flaw in the existence of multitudes of professing Christians today. They have been led to believe that God, for some unfathomable reason, just thinks it appropriate to transfer credit from Christ's merit account to ours, and to wipe out our sin debt, upon inspecting our mind and finding that we believe a particular theory of the atonement to be true – even if we trust everything but God in all other matters that concern us.

It is left unexplained how it is that one can rely on Christ for the next life without doing so for this one, trust him for one's eternal destiny without trusting him for 'the things that relate to Christian life.' Is this really possible? Surely it is not! Not within one life.

When all is said and done, 'the gospel' for Ryrie, MacArthur, and others on the theological right is that Christ made 'the arrangement' that can get us into heaven. In the Gospels, by contrast, 'the gospel' is the good news of the presence and availability of life in the kingdom, now and forever, through reliance on Jesus the Anointed. This was Abraham's faith, too. As Jesus said, 'Abraham saw my time and was delighted' (John 8:56).

Accordingly, the only description of eternal life found in the words we have from Jesus is 'This is eternal life, that they [his disciples] may know you, the only real God, and Jesus the anointed, whom you have sent' (John 17:3). This may sound to us like 'mere head knowledge'. But the biblical 'know' always refers to an intimate, personal, interactive relationship. Thus the prophet speaks for God in saying to Israel, 'You are the only ones I have known from among all of the families of the earth' (Amos 3:2). And Mary, in response to the angel's statement that she would bear a child, asks, 'How can that be, since I know no man?' (Luke 1:35). Obviously God knows *about* other families on the earth, as Mary knows about men. The eternal life of which Jesus speaks is not knowledge about God but an intimately interactive relationship with him.

The Gospel on the Left

The Gospel as Entirely Social

At the opposite end of the theological spectrum stand a large number of ministers, priests and congregations who take an entirely different view of what the issue is in the gospel and of the gospel itself.

It would be a mistake, however, to refer to them as 'liberal' without considerable qualification. They are, indeed, the legitimate offspring of the liberal Christian church of the nineteenth century and the first half of the twentieth. But anyone really familiar with ministers and theologians from the *older* liberalism (up to the nineteen sixties) may find many of them closer to MacArthur and Ryrie, in the substance of their teachings as well as in their morality and practical spirituality, than to the currently dominant figures and teachings of the Christian left.

By the late 1950s and early 1960s, the older liberal theology, with its 'social gospel', had pretty well proven itself unable to accomplish the transformation of human existence that it had envisaged and promised. Bludgeoned to its knees by world events, its intellectual capital exhausted and incapable of providing concepts that could clarify exactly what was happening in Western life and society at the time, it awakened to find itself, as a social and institutional reality, on the side of the oppressor when the civil rights movement began to dawn.

Quickly, liberal leadership moved to an activist posture. In 1963 the National Council of Churches (NCC) in America adopted a policy of direct participation in the struggle of black Americans for social and economic equality. Shortly afterwards came involvement in protests over the war in Vietnam and also in movements of liberation in other countries. Later came issues of gender, sexual preference, ecology, speciesism and generalized 'correctness'.

Religion Becomes Social Ethics

By 1963 the NCC leadership had for some time been preoccupied with the question of the church's nature and mission, hence with the basic nature of the Christian gospel. James Findlay has shown how this laid the foundation for the move into activism, recovering an element of the social gospel radicalism of the 1920s and 1930s.[15]

For many individuals who engaged in civil rights actions, Findlay points out, it was a life-transforming moment. He quotes one of the northern white clergy who had participated in the famous Mississippi summer project of 1964: 'It was the most intense moment of my life. There was no other moment in my life when I had such a certainty that this was where I ought to be, that this is where the church ought to be, and that ... my presence was the presence of the church.' Twenty years later, Findlay reports, this individual still relives the exhilarating and transformative impact of his modest role in the civil rights struggle of the 1960s.[16]

James Traub, in an essay published in 1994, speaks of 'those like me, who grew up listening to Martin Luther King, Jr., and who found in the redemptive language of the civil rights movement a virtual substitute for religious belief.'[17]

However, for many in the liberal church, clergy and layperson alike, that language was not just a substitute for religious belief. It *became* their faith. Or perhaps we should say that their religious belief became commitment to civil rights in some broadened sense – including, more recently, a right not even to have offensive symbolism or language used in your presence.

To be committed to the oppressed, to liberation, or just to 'community' became for many the whole of what is essential to Christian commitment. The gospel, or 'good news', on this view, was that God himself stood behind liberation, equality and community; that Jesus died to promote them, or at least for lack of them; and that he 'lives on' in all efforts and tendencies favouring them. For the theological left, simply this became the message of Christ.

The older liberal theology, which indeed was still primarily *a theology* or a view of God, died and was resurrected in the form of a social ethic that one could share with people who had no reliance on a present God or a living Christ at all. Total inclusivism of all beliefs and practices except oppressive ones, such as the exclusivism of traditional Christianity itself, was the natural next step.

God and Jesus Immanent in Human Love

No minister or theologian was more influential in popularizing this view than John A. T. Robinson. According to him,

> the Christian God is not remote. He is involved; he is implicated. If Jesus Christ means anything, he means that God belongs to this world ... We all need, more than anything else, to love and be loved ... We need to be accepted as persons, as whole persons, for our own sake. And this is what true love does. It accepts people, without any strings, simply for what they are. It gives them worth. It 'makes their lives.'[18]

The death of Jesus, still to be regarded as the central event for historic Christianity, comes in here:

> That is what we see Jesus doing in the Gospels, making and remaking men's lives, bringing meaning back to them. In him we see love at work, in a way

> that the world has never seen before or since. And that's why the New Testament sees God at work in him – for God is love. In the cross that love comes out to the uttermost. 'There's love for you!' says Calvary. And in the Resurrection we see that not even death was able to destroy its power to transform and heal. Love still came out on top.'[19]

This is the gospel of the current Christian left: Love comes out on top. And, of course, for that we should all devoutly hope.

Correspondingly, as Robinson says, 'The Christian is the man who believes in *that* love [Jesus' kind] as the last word for his life' (p. 52). And the *real* Jesus, as is now commonly said, is 'one who identified with and loves oppressed people and those who are different,' calling us to do the same. These words now express the redemptive vision of the Christian left, just as 'trusted Christ for forgiveness' or 'prayed to receive Jesus' does for the right.

The Political and Social Meaning of Love

But, just as there was a serious question as to what constitutes saving faith, so there is a problem with the precise nature of redemptive love. In this world there are many things called love. Which love is it that is God? And who is the God that is love?

Here the descent of the current Christian left from the older liberal theology stands out. Robinson and those who adopt his version of the gospel rarely miss a chance to dismiss the 'old man in the sky' view of God. Bishop James Pike used to say, 'I don't believe in a God that tinkers,' thus dismissing actual answers to prayer requests from human beings.[20] He granted that prayer may make some mysterious, unscientific adjustment in life, but it will not evoke 'answers' in any straightforward sense of the term – certainly not one that changes what would happen in the 'natural' order anyway. So prayer proves to be little more than a ritual hand-waving at the cosmos that may, at most, bring personal comfort or help us improve our attitudes.

But what do these theologians really accomplish with their revised view of God – other than aligning themselves with a view of natural reality and life that they can take to be more scientific? Is it not simply the destruction of any workable sense in which God and Jesus are *persons*, now alive and accessible, standing in an interactive relationship with those who rely on them?

Such a relationship, as we have seen, was called 'eternal life' by Jesus himself. But in the hands of the theological left, church creed and ritual become mere comforting symbols of 'another' realm, remote and inaccessible at best, and possibly one of mere imagination or sentiment.

Unfortunately this 'other realm' is not capable of giving any straightforward sense to the Twenty-third Psalm or the Lord's Prayer, for example, or to Christ's promise that he is with us always. The new theology takes the view William James once described as a 'universalistic' or 'refined' supernaturalism. It 'confines itself to sentiments about life as a whole,' he noted, while 'the essence of practical religion … evaporates.'[21]

Robbed of its reference to a transcendent spiritual being or substance that nonetheless personally engages with humanity while holding them responsible to its specific directives on how to live, this 'love' ('God') has no recourse but to become whatever the current ideology says it is. Currently that means not treating people as different, while liberating them and enabling them to do what they want.

But this 'gospel' turns out in practice to be little more than another version of the world-famous American dream. Other words associated with it are 'egalitarianism', 'happiness' and 'freedom'. As a professor of education at Bradley University recently stated, the American dream is that 'people can do or be what they want if they just go ahead and do it.'[22] Desire becomes sacred, and whatever thwarts desire is evil or sin. We have from the Christian left, after all, just another gospel of sin management, but one whose substance is provided by Western social and political ideals of human existence in a secular world.

The Gospel Gap

Could we then have a bumper sticker that reads, 'Christians aren't perfect, just committed to Liberation'?

Quite possibly. The current gospels, left and right, exhibit the very same type of conceptual disconnection from, and practical irrelevance to, the personal integrity of believers – and certainly so, if we put that integrity in terms of biblically specific 'Christlikeness'. And both lack any essential bearing upon the individual's life as a whole, especially upon occupations or work time and upon the fine texture of our personal relationships in the home and neighbourhood. This is true even though everyone agrees that it ought not to be so.

To reiterate, that irrelevance to life stems from the very content of those 'gospels': from what they state, what they are about. They concern sin guilt or structural evils (social sins) and what to do about them. That is all. That real life goes on without them is a *natural* consequence of this.

In *The Search for God at Harvard*, Ari Goldman tells of one of his classmates in the Divinity School who was 'out' at school and, indeed, was head of the Gay and Lesbian Caucus. After graduation she received an appointment as an associate pastor. The local congregation of the United Church of Christ that appointed her also ordained her.

She found the moment of laying on of hands from the congregants very moving. But the congregation did not know she was a lesbian. 'I never raised the issue with them,' she said. 'If I did, I would never have gotten the job. Sure, there is a degree to which I am leading a dual life, but that doesn't seem like a problem right now.'[23]

How very familiar such evasion and irresponsibility is. How crassly common. Everyone knows what it is, but 'business is business'. Similar cases exist at all points on the theological spectrum. Sins turn out to be astonishingly non-partisan and unoriginal. (Wouldn't we almost be relieved to find one that is truly original?) Where for this woman is faith in Christ? Is it irrelevant? Or simply powerless? Would not God be with her if she told the truth? But, once again, overall abundance of life and obedience to moral standards that we all know to be valid have no inherent connection to the gospels of sin management. As we have pointed out, being 'right' or 'left' make no difference on this basic point.

Towards Integration of Life and Faith

The Case of the Missing Teacher

So as things now stand we have, on the one hand, some kind of 'faith in Christ' and, on the other, the life of abundance and obedience he is and offers. But we have no effective bridge from the faith to the life. Some do work it out. But when that happens it is looked upon as a fluke or an accident, not *a normal and natural part of the regular good news itself*. Prayer also may seem to 'work' for some. But who knows how or why? And anyway, effectiveness in prayer is not required – either to go to heaven when you die or to be committed to the cause of liberation.

We settle back into *de facto* alienation of our religion from Jesus as a friend and teacher, and from our moment-to-moment existence as a holy calling or appointment with God. Some will substitute ritual behaviour for divine vitality and personal integrity; others may be content with an isolated string of 'experiences' rather than transformation of character.

Right at the heart of this alienation lies the absence of Jesus the teacher from our lives. Strangely, we seem prepared to learn how to live from almost anyone but him. We are ready to believe that the 'latest studies' have more to teach us about love and sex than he does, and that Louis Rukeyser knows more about finances. 'Dear Abby' can teach us more about how to get along with our family members and co-workers, and Carl Sagan is a better authority on the cosmos. We lose any sense of the difference between information and wisdom, and act accordingly.

Where we spontaneously look for 'information' on how to live shows how we truly feel and who we really have confidence in. And nothing more forcibly demonstrates the extent to which we automatically assume the irrelevance of Jesus as teacher for our 'real' lives.

Historically, conservative Christians became suspicious of any talk of Jesus as 'teacher' because liberals, or 'Modernists', used it as a way of saying that he was not the divine Son and supernatural saviour but 'just a good man'. In addition, their understanding of salvation by grace alone cut off from the 'essentials' in Christian faith his teachings about life and God's kingdom. As we have seen, being a Christian then comes to have nothing to do with the kind of person one is.

The Modernists, by contrast, professed to regard him as a great teacher. But then they presented him as fundamentally mistaken about major elements of his own message, such as when his kingdom would come, and they explained away all his sayings and deeds that required supernatural interaction – his teaching and practice of prayer, for example. Thus they made it impossible in practice to take him seriously as a teacher.

Thomas Oden points out that 'it becomes difficult if not impossible to build a plausible Christology out of a naïve, mistaken, hapless or ignorant Jesus.'[24] And we should add, 'Or on a historically inaccessible Jesus,' as he is almost universally taken to be by the theological left.

We should not be surprised, then, that while those to the left claimed to regard Jesus' ethical teachings highly, the ethic they ascribed to him turns out upon examination to be derived from the reflections of philosophers such as Locke, Rousseau, Kant and Marx – or even, in more recent years, thinkers such as Martin Heidegger, Jean-Paul Sartre or Michel Foucault. The Modernists, no more than the conservatives, were about to accept as actually binding upon themselves the plain teachings of the Gospels as we have them.

This remarkable reticence extends even to the Ten Commandments and to all the specific moral directives of the Judeo-Christian heritage. Amid much talk, there is little resolute conformity to them. Some current critics of the U.S. Supreme Court like to point out that it does not allow the Ten Commandments, though written upon the walls of its own chambers, to be displayed in schools.

But where do we find churches, right or left, that put them on their walls? The Ten Commandments really aren't very popular anywhere. This is so in spite of the fact that even a fairly general practise of them would lead to a solution of almost every problem of meaning and order now facing Western societies. They are God's best information on how to lead a basically decent human existence.

The disappearance of Jesus as teacher explains why today in Christian churches – of whatever leaning – little effort is made to teach people to do what he did and taught. Once again, it is a natural consequence of our basic message. Who among us has personal knowledge of a seminar or course of study and practice being offered in a 'Christian Education Programme' on how to 'love your enemies, bless those that curse you, do good to those that hate you and pray for those who spit on you and make your life miserable'? (Matt. 5:44). Much less, then, one on how to conduct our business or profession on behalf of Jesus Christ (Col. 3:17–23). The most common response by Christians in the 'real' world to Christ's teachings is, precisely, 'Business is Business'. And we all know what that means.

Sincere teaching on such matters simply does not appear on the Christian's intellectual horizon as something that might be done. We do not seriously consider Jesus as our teacher on how to live, hence we *cannot* think of ourselves, in our moment-to-moment existence, as his students or disciples. So we turn to popular speakers and writers, some Christians and some not – whoever happens to be writing books and running talk shows and seminars on matters that concern us.

The Centrality of the Pulpit

We return now to a point made earlier in this chapter, when we spoke of 'Shifting the Focus'. And for the moment we speak specifically to those of us who teach and lead, bearing the pastoral role in churches and in society.

The situation we have just described – the disconnection of life from faith, the absence from our churches of Jesus the teacher – is not caused by the wicked world, by social oppression, or by the stubborn meanness of the people who come to our church services and carry on the work of our congregations. It is largely caused and sustained by the basic message that we constantly hear from Christian pulpits. We are flooded with what I have called 'gospels of sin management', in one form or another, while Jesus' invitation to eternal life now – right in the midst of work, business and profession – remains for the most part ignored and unspoken.

'Must not all who speak for Christ constantly ask themselves these crucial questions:

> Does the gospel I preach and teach have a natural tendency to cause people who hear it to become full-time students of Jesus?
>
> Would those who believe it become his apprentices as a natural 'next step'?
>
> What can we reasonably expect would result from people actually believing the substance of my message?

The condition so eloquently deplored by numerous leaders already quoted in this chapter is nothing but *the natural consequence of the basic message of the church as it is heard today*. It would be foolish to expect anything else other than precisely what we have got.

A saying among management experts today is, 'Your system is perfectly designed to yield the result you are getting.' This is a profound though painful truth that must be respected by all who have an interest in Christian spiritual formation, whether for themselves as individuals or for groups or institutions.

We who profess Christianity will believe what is constantly presented to us as gospel. If gospels of sin management are preached, they are what Christians will believe. And those in the wider world who reject those gospels will believe that what they have rejected is the gospel of Jesus Christ himself – when, in fact, they haven't yet heard it.

And so we have the result noted: the resources of God's kingdom remain detached from human life. There is no gospel for human life and Christian discipleship, just one for death or one for social action. The souls of human beings are left to shrivel and die on the plains of life because they are not introduced into the environment for which they were made, the living kingdom of eternal life.

To counteract this we must develop a straightforward presentation, in word and life, of the reality of life now under God's rule, through reliance upon the word and person of Jesus. In this way we can naturally become his students or apprentices. We can learn from him how to live our lives as he would live them if he were we. We can enter his eternal kind of life now.

The Kingdom Must Make Sense

But this cannot come about unless what Jesus himself believed, practised and taught *makes sense* to us. And his message must come to us free of the deadening legalisms, political sloganeering and dogmatic traditionalisms long proven by history to be soul-crushing dead ends. Obviously it does not so come to us now, and this is a fact widely recognized.

At the 1974 Lausanne Conference on World Evangelization, Michael Green asked rhetorically, 'How much have you heard here about the Kingdom of God?' His answer was, 'Not much. It is not our language. But it was Jesus' prime concern.'[25]

Dr I. Howard Marshall of the University of Aberdeen has commented, 'During the past sixteen years I can recollect only two occasions on which I have heard sermons specifically devoted to the theme of the Kingdom of God … I find this silence rather surprising because it is universally agreed by New Testament scholars that the central theme of the teaching of Jesus was the Kingdom of God.'[26]

Peter Wagner, perhaps the best-known leader in the worldwide 'church growth' movement, also refers to the unanimous opinion of modern scholarship that the kingdom of God was the message of Jesus. Then he adds,

> I cannot help wondering out loud why I haven't heard more about it in the thirty years I have been a Christian. I certainly read about it enough in the Bible … But I honestly cannot remember any pastor whose ministry I have been under actually preaching a sermon on the Kingdom of God. As I rummage through my own sermon barrel, I now realize that I myself have never preached a sermon on it. Where has the Kingdom been?[27]

Does what we have discussed in this chapter not make it clear that serious difficulties currently bar people of good intent from an effectual understanding of Jesus' gospel for life and discipleship in his kingdom? We must now try to identify and remove these difficulties. If we cannot remove them, no gospel we bring can have a natural tendency to lead onward into a life of discipleship to Jesus and to personal fulfilment in the kingdom of the heavens.

Chapter 3

WHAT JESUS KNEW: OUR GOD-BATHED WORLD

While man is at home with animals and the stars, he is also the cosmic neighbour of the Absolute.

GUSTAVE MARTELET, *THE RISEN CHRIST AND THE EUCHARISTIC WORLD*

In the world of Faith the heavens above the city are friendly and near: they are the upper chamber of every house.

MAX PICARD, *THE FLIGHT FROM GOD*

Re-Visioning God and His World

Jesus' good news about the kingdom can be an effective guide for our lives only if we share his view of the world in which we live. To his eyes this is a God-bathed and God-permeated world. It is a world filled with a glorious reality, where every component is within the range of God's direct knowledge and control – though he obviously permits some of it, for good reasons, to be for a while otherwise than as he wishes. It is a world that is inconceivably beautiful and good because of God and because God is always in it. It is a world in which God is continually at play and over which he constantly rejoices. Until our thoughts of God have found every visible thing and event glorious with his presence, the word of Jesus has not yet fully seized us.

The novelist Vladimir Nabokov writes of a moment of awakening in one of his characters who, watching an old woman of the streets drink a cup of coffee given to her,

> became aware of the world's tenderness, the profound beneficence of all that surrounded me, the blissful bond between me and all of creation; and I realized that joy ... breathed around me everywhere, in the speeding street sounds, in the hem of a comically lifted skirt, in the metallic yet tender drone of the wind, in the autumn clouds bloated with rain. I realized that the world does not represent a struggle at all, or a predaceous sequence of chance events, but shimmering bliss, beneficent trepidation, a gift bestowed on us and unappreciated.[1]

God's Joyous Being

Central to the understanding and proclamation of the Christian gospel today, as in Jesus' day, is a re-visioning of what God's own life is like and how the physical cosmos fits into it. It is a great and important task to come to terms with what we really think when we think of God. Most hindrances to the faith of Christ actually lie, I believe, in this part of our minds and souls. If he cannot help us with understanding God's life, he cannot help us at all to that salvation/life that is by faith. But of course he can and he does.

We should, first, think that God leads a very interesting life, and that he is full of joy. Undoubtedly he is the most joyous being in the universe. The abundance of his love and generosity is inseparable from his infinite joy. All of the good and beautiful things from which we occasionally drink tiny droplets of soul-exhilarating joy, God continuously experiences in all their breadth and depth and richness.

While I was teaching in South Africa some time ago, a young man named Matthew Dickason took me out to see the beaches near his home in Port Elizabeth. I was totally unprepared for the experience. I had seen beaches, or so I thought. But when we came over the rise where the sea and land opened up to us, I stood in stunned silence and then slowly walked towards the waves. Words cannot capture the view that confronted me. I saw space and light and texture and colour and power … that seemed hardly of this earth.

Gradually there crept into my mind the realization that God sees this all the time. He sees it, experiences it, knows it from every possible point of view, this and billions of other scenes like and unlike it, in this and billions of other worlds. Great tidal waves of joy must constantly wash through his being.

It is perhaps strange to say, but suddenly I was extremely happy for God and thought I had some sense of what an infinitely joyous consciousness he is and of what it might have meant for him to look at his creation and find it 'very good'.

We pay a lot for a tank with a few tropical fish in it and never tire of looking at their brilliant iridescence and marvellous forms and movements. But God has *seas full of them*, which he constantly enjoys. (I can hardly take in these beautiful little creatures one at a time.)

We are enraptured by a well-done movie sequence or by a few bars from an opera or lines from a poem. We treasure our great experiences for a lifetime, and we may have very few of them. But he is simply one great inexhaustible and eternal experience of all that is good and true and beautiful and right. This is what we must think of when we hear theologians and philosophers speak of him as a perfect being. *This is his life.*

A short while ago the Hubble Space Telescope gave us pictures of the Eagle Nebula, showing clouds of gas and microscopic dust reaching six trillion miles from top to bottom. Hundreds of stars were emerging here and there in it, hotter and larger than our sun. As I looked at these pictures, and through them at the past and ongoing development of the cosmos, I could not help but think of Jesus' words before he left his little band of students: 'In my father's house there are many places to live. I go to get some ready for you.'

Human beings can lose themselves in card games or electric trains and think they are fortunate. But to God there is available, in the language of one reporter, 'Towering clouds of gases trillions of miles high, backlit by nuclear fires in newly forming stars, galaxies cartwheeling into collision and sending explosive shock waves boiling through millions of light-years of time and space.'[2] These things are all before him, along with numberless unfolding rosebuds, souls and songs – and immeasurably more of which we know nothing.

The poet William Cowper appropriately exclaimed of God:

> Deep in unfathomable mines
> Of never ending skill,
> He treasures up his bright designs,
> And works his sovereign will.[3]

Now, Jesus himself was and is a joyous, creative person. He does not allow us to continue thinking of our Father who fills and overflows space as a morose and miserable monarch, a frustrated and petty parent, or a policeman on the prowl.

One cannot think of God in such ways while confronting Jesus' declaration 'He that has seen me has seen the Father.' One of the most outstanding features of Jesus' personality was precisely an abundance of joy. This he left as an inheritance to his students, 'that their joy might be full' (John 15:11). And they did not say, 'Pass the aspirin', for he was well known to those around him as a happy man. It is deeply illuminating of kingdom living to understand that his steady happiness was not ruled out by his experience of sorrow and even grief.

So we must understand that God does not 'love' us without liking us – through gritted teeth – as 'Christian' love is sometimes thought to do. Rather, out of the eternal freshness of his perpetually self-renewed being, the heavenly Father cherishes the earth and each human being upon it. The fondness, the endearment, the unstintingly affectionate regard of God towards all his creatures is the natural outflow of what he is to the core – which we vainly try to capture with our tired but indispensable old word *love*.

Finding Language to Express This Great God

It is, frankly, hard today to think adequately of God – or perhaps to think of him at all. Our intellectual history works against it, and we certainly do not get much training for it. Frankly, our daily experience, under pressure from many quarters, constantly keeps us from thoughtful living and 'dumbs us down', in many ways – especially theologically. But the resulting lack of adequate ideas and terminology does great harm to our faith. It insulates our real life from what we say we believe. We cannot, even by a miracle, believe a blank or a blur, much less *act* on it. There is no 'what' for our minds and lives to lay hold of in such a case – or it is the wrong 'what'.

To trust in *God*, we need a rich and accurate way of thinking and speaking about him to guide and support our life vision and our will. Such is present in the biblical language, of course, and it continued to be carefully crafted in the works of Christian writers well into the twentieth century.

Still today the Old Testament book of Psalms gives great power for faith and life. This is simply because it preserves a conceptually rich language about God and our relationships to him. If you bury yourself in Psalms, you emerge knowing God and understanding life.

And that is by no means a matter, as some suggest, of the 'poetic effect' of the great language. No mere emotional lift is involved. What makes the language great and provides the emotional lift is chiefly its picture of God and of life. We learn from the psalms how to think and act in reference to God. We drink in God and God's world from them. They provide a vocabulary for living Godward, one inspired by God himself. They show us who God is, and that expands and lifts and directs our minds and hearts.

But because of ideas arising out of the eighteenth century – focused primarily through 'British Empiricism' and the Kantian/Rationalist reaction to it in Germany – the richly informative language needed to nourish thoughtful faith in God is no longer functional in our cultural setting.

The ideas of Modernity now dominate the academic centres of the world, even where they are not consciously identified or understood, and even where they are explicitly rejected. This is also true of many of the Christian seminaries where ministers and teachers are educated, and where it is commonly thought to be a deep question whether or not we can succeed in thinking about God at all or can speak intelligibly of him.

We are all products of this modern thought system, and you yourself can test its power by observing your response to a representative statement about God from a century or so ago.

In the grand and carefully phrased old words of Adam Clarke, God is

> the eternal, independent and self-existent Being; the Being whose purposes and actions spring from himself, without foreign motive or influence; he who is absolute in dominion; the most pure, the most simple, the most spiritual of all essences; infinitely perfect; and eternally self-sufficient, needing nothing that he has made; illimitable in his immensity, inconceivable in his mode of existence and indescribable in his essence; known fully only by himself, because an infinite mind can only be fully comprehended by itself. In a word, a Being who, from his infinite wisdom, cannot err or be deceived, and from his infinite goodness, can do nothing but what is eternally just, and right and kind.[4]

It would be surprising if you found this easy reading. However, it is a lot like Shakespeare – not just old, but incredibly rich. Possibly you even began to think the words are just meaningless. Nevertheless, with some earnest thought we can all appreciate what a vast difference it would make in anyone's life to actually believe in such a God as these words portray. Think of someone whose every action, whose slightest thought or inclination, automatically assumes the reality of the God Adam Clarke describes.

When you do this you will have captured nothing less than the thought of Jesus himself, along with the faith and life he came to bring. And with such realities in mind, it then becomes illuminating to say that God is love. This proves to be very different from forcing a bedraggled human version of 'love' into a mental blank where God is supposed to be, and then identifying God as *that*.

The Heavens as the Human Environment

Some Advice on Living

With this magnificent God positioned among us, Jesus brings the assurance that our universe is *a perfectly safe place for us to be*. The very heart of his message, as well as of his personality and actions, is found in such well-known words as these from Matthew 6:

> My advice would be not to worry about what is going to happen to you: about what you will have to eat or drink, or about what clothes you will wear. Your life doesn't consist of eating, and there is much more to your body than clothing. Take a lesson from the birds of heaven. They don't sow or reap or hoard away in granaries, and your Father – the One in the heavens around you – sees to it that they have food. Aren't you more important than birds?
>
> Who can change their physical features by worrying about them? And as for worrying about clothes, well, look at the little flowers out in the fields. They just pop right up. They don't slave away getting or making clothes. But King Solomon in his best outfit was not as glorious as one of these. Now if God so adorns the wild grasses – which are here for a day, and the next day are burned for fuel – won't he do even better by you? You mini-faiths!
>
> So don't worry about things, saying, 'What are we going to eat?' or 'Will we have anything to drink?' or 'What will we wear?' (People who don't know God at all do that!) For your Father – the One in the heavens around you – knows you need these things. Instead, make it your top priority to be part of what God is doing and to have the kind of goodness he has. Everything else you need will be provided.

> Tomorrow? Don't worry about it. You can do your worrying about tomorrow tomorrow. And anyway, enough will happen today to keep you in things to worry over until bedtime.

The Heavens Are Also Here

This bold and slyly humorous assurance about all the basic elements of our existence – food and drink, clothing and other needs of life – can only be supported on a clear-eyed vision that a totally good and competent God is right here with us to look after us. And his presence is precisely what the word *heaven* or, more accurately, *the heavens* in plural, conveys in the biblical record as well as through much of Christian history.[5]

The Old Testament experience of God is one of the direct presence of God's person, knowledge and power to those who trust and serve him. Nothing – no human being or institution, no time, no space, no spiritual being, no event – stands between God and those who trust him.

The 'heavens' are always there with you no matter what, and the 'first heaven', in biblical terms, is precisely the atmosphere or air that surrounds your body. We saw what this meant for Abraham's experience in an earlier chapter, and we will go more deeply into it in what follows. But it is precisely from the space immediately around us that God watches and God acts.

When Paul on Mars Hill told his Greek inquisitors that in God we 'live and move and exist', he was expressing in the most literal way possible the fact learned from the experience of God's covenant people, the Jews. He was not speaking metaphorically or abstractly.

The same is true when Jesus chided Nicodemus, who took himself to be a 'teacher in Israel', for not understanding the birth 'from above' – the receiving of a superhuman kind of life from the God who is literally with us in surrounding space. To be born 'from above', in New Testament language, means to be interactively joined with a dynamic, unseen system of divine reality in the midst of which all of humanity moves about – whether it knows it or not. And that, of course, is 'The Kingdom Among Us'.[6]

Perhaps we all are far too much like Nicodemus. In a church service we may heartily sing the grand old hymn, 'O Worship the King ... Whose robe is the light, whose canopy space':

> Thy bountiful care, what tongue can recite?
> It breathes in the air; it shines in the light;
> It streams from the hills; it descends to the plain;
> And gently distills in the dew and the rain.[7]

But do we actually believe this? I mean, are we ready automatically to *act as if* we stand here and now and always in the presence of the great being described by Adam Clarke, who fills and overflows all space, including the atmosphere around our body? Some serious attention to specific experiences of God's covenant people through the ages may help us to have such a faith for ourselves.

Heaven Invading Human Space

Abraham, of course, leads the way. Hagar, his outcast concubine, turned away from her desperate child because she could not stand to watch him die of thirst in the desert. But 'God heard the voice of the lad; and the angel of God called to Hagar out of heaven, and said to her, Hagar, what is wrong? Don't be afraid. For God has heard the voice of the boy there ... And God opened her eyes, and she saw a well of water' (Gen. 21:17–19).

Some years later Abraham was about to sacrifice Isaac, 'And the angel of the Lord called unto him out of heaven and said ... Don't touch the boy' (Gen. 22:11–15). In such passages 'heaven' is never thought of as far away – in the clouds perhaps, or by the moon. It is always right here, 'at hand'.

Jacob on the run, asleep in a ditch on his pillow of stone, saw the earth and heaven connected by a passageway, with angels coming and going, and the Lord himself standing *beside him*. He awoke in awe, saying, 'God lives here! ... I've stumbled into his home! This is the awesome entrance to Heaven' (Gen. 28:12–19 LB).

God spoke to Moses *from heaven* in the presence of the people of Israel while giving the Ten Commandments (Exod. 20), and thundered *from heaven* upon the enemies of Israel during battle (1 Sam. 7:10). On numerous occasions fire materialized out of the air (Gen. 15:17; Exod. 13:21; 1 Kings 18:38; 2 Kings 1:10; 1 Chron. 21:26, etc.). The manifestation in atmospheric fire became almost a routine event in Israel's history, so much so that God came to be known as a consuming fire (Deut. 4:24; Heb. 12:29) – a fire that is also love.

These are just a few of the constant interactions of 'heaven' with God's people in the Old Testament. They show us that heaven is here and God is here, because God and his spiritual agents act here and are constantly available here.

Hence the general conclusion reached by the faithful community: 'The eyes of the Lord run back and forth across the whole earth, to show himself strong on behalf of them whose heart is perfect towards him' (2 Chron. 16:9). And again: 'The eyes of the Lord are upon the righteous, and his ears are open unto their cry. The face of the Lord is against them that do evil, to wipe the memory of them off the earth. The righteous cry, and the Lord hears and delivers them out of all their troubles' (Ps. 34:15–17). These and many other statements from God's chosen people make clear their understanding that God is actually here.

The New Testament Experience

Exactly the same types of events continue in New Testament times. Of course, incarnation in the person of Jesus is the most complete case of 'God with us' or 'Immanuel'. The apostle John, who as a youth was the closest of companions with Jesus, marvels in his old age that he and others had with their physical senses – their ears, eyes and hands – known the very source of life, which was from the beginning of everything (1 John 1:1).

Thus the sight of Jesus interacting with the enveloping kingdom day after day; his transfiguration and his resurrection presence; his ascension; the coming of the spirit with a sound 'from heaven' – that is, out of the atmosphere – where he recently had gone, which then filled the room where his disciples were waiting, resting visibly on them as flames of fire; that steady stream of interactions of God's new people on earth with angelic beings, the substance of 'Jacob's ladder' mentioned above – all of these gave the early church the strongest possible impression of the reality and immediate presence of the kingdom of Christ.

It is necessary to emphasize that the events in question were real events and that they provide the basis for a biblical and practical understanding of how God is really in our world. But we may have seen too many 'special effects' from television and Hollywood, where appearances with no corresponding reality are produced. Many of our day no longer have the ability to read the Bible or historic Christian events realistically, as if they really happened as described.

We know all about 'simulations', we think. Moreover, we have heard of psychological 'projection', and our heads are full of pseudo-scientific views that reject a spiritual world and insist that space is empty and matter the only reality. So we are prepared to treat all of this long historical record as a matter of 'visions' that are 'only imagination', or as outright delusions, not as perceptions of reality. And we slump back into those materialistic mythologies of our culture that are automatically imparted to us by 'normal' life as what 'everyone knows'.

Embarrassing Translations?

The inability to accept the fact that our familiar atmosphere is a 'heaven' in which God dwells and from which he deals with us leads to some curious translations of biblical texts. In Acts 11:5–9, within a span of five verses, exactly the same phrase, *tou ouranou*, is translated in three different ways by the New American Standard Version, and by most others. It is translated 'the sky' in verse 5, 'the air' in verse 6, and 'heaven' in verse 9.

This, you may recall, is where Peter in a trance sees a sheet with all kinds of animals on it being let down through *the atmosphere* (*tou ouranou*). Among them are birds of *the atmosphere*. And he hears a voice from *the atmosphere* telling him to rise and eat.

Now our English *sky* means something quite different from *air*, and *heaven* means something quite different from either. The translation becomes entangled in these meanings. The sky is more a limit than a place, and as a place it is farther away than the air. Hence, we say, 'The sky's the limit', not 'The air's the limit'. Heaven, of course, is strictly out of sight for us, beyond the moon for sure and quite likely 'beyond' the physical cosmos.

A consistent translation of *tou ouranou* drawing upon the biblical context could use 'air' or 'atmosphere' in each occurrence, as I have just done, and thus give the precise content of Peter's experience. God spoke to Peter from the surrounding 'thin air', where birds fly and from which the sheet came. This conveys quite a different impression from the standard translations, which usually only speak of 'heaven' in this passage.

Similarly, God spoke to Moses from the midst of the fire on Sinai and from above the 'Mercy Seat' in the tabernacle (Num. 7:89). In each case it was from our 'air'. But the ideology that dominates our education and thought today makes it hard to accept this straightforward fact.

The damage done to our practical faith in Christ and in his government-at-hand by confusing heaven with a place in distant or outer space, or even beyond space, is incalculable. Of course God is there too. But instead of heaven and God also being always present with us, as Jesus shows them to be, we invariably take them to be located far away and, most likely, at a much later time – not here and not now. And we should then be surprised to feel ourselves alone?

The Experience Continues Today

Experiences of God in space around us are by no means restricted to the biblical record. They leave many people sceptical or uncomfortable, but they continue to occur up to the present day. Groups I speak to almost always have people in them who have experienced some manifestation of God from and in the space where they are.

I find that if you can establish a mood of confidence among them there will be some and often several in almost any group with such a story to tell. These stories do not always involve visual experiences alone, but often hearing and touch as well. And I do not have in mind the cases in which, as we often say, the presence of God is 'felt'.

A well-known Christian teacher, Sundar Singh, was born and raised a Sikh in Rampur, India, around the turn of the twentieth century. As a boy he was placed in a Presbyterian mission school, where he developed a 'love/hate' relationship with the Christian gospel. For some time he had been in a condition of inner turmoil. Then one morning he arose very early to pray, as was Sikh custom. In his distress He cried out, 'Oh God, if there be a God, show me the right way, and I will become a Sadhu [holy man]; otherwise I will kill myself.'

At about a quarter to five in the morning, his room was filled with light. He looked outside, thinking there must be a fire, but he saw none. Continuing to pray, he suddenly saw before him a glorious face filled with love. At first he thought it was Buddha or Krishna or some other deity. But a voice in Hindustani said, 'How long will you persecute me? Remember, I died for you; I gave my life for you.'

Seeing the scars on his body, Sundar Singh recognized Jesus and saw that he was alive, not someone who died centuries ago. He fell at his feet and accepted him as master and worshipped him. Afterwards he became a world-famous example of God's life present among human beings.[8]

This kind of experience, involving here a notable person of public record, is characteristic of many biblical and extrabiblical personalities alike. God, Christ, angels or other unusual phenomena are experienced in surrounding space, in the atmosphere – the 'first heaven' of the biblical world. Recall, for example, the story of Gary Smith at the end of Chapter 1. It is but one of multitudes.[9]

Of course, such experiences do not glorify those who have them. They do not create an elite class of believers. Balaam's donkey remained a donkey after he had seen the angel and miraculously discussed the matter with his master. Moreover, Jesus' words to Thomas always remain true: 'Blessed are those who believe without seeing.'

Indeed they are blessed! And not because that shows some especially meritorious exertion or commitment on their part. Rather, it is because the most important things in our human lives are nearly always things that are invisible. That is even true without special reference to God. People who cannot believe without seeing are desperately limited in all their relationships. Yet God does show himself from time to time in the space of those who seek him, and over time he leaves among his people visible reminders of his constant though invisible presence.

So, in summary, the reason the Judeo-Christian witness regards surrounding space as full of God is that that is where it has from time to time experienced him. That is where he has manifested himself. Jehovah naturally became known among the Israelites as 'the God of the Heavens' through the progression of their historical experience.[10]

Matthew, the quintessentially Judaic Gospel, as a matter of course utilizes the phrase *the kingdom of the heavens* to describe God's rule, or 'kingdom'. It captures that rich heritage of the Jewish experience of the nearness of God that is so largely lost to the contemporary mind. This heritage is a primary revelation of the nature of God. Thus it forms the mark of identification of the one we address in the central prayer of Christendom: 'Our Father, the One in the heavens …'(Matt. 6:9).

'Kingdom of the Heavens' and 'Kingdom of God'

Accordingly, a difference in terminology that at first seems insignificant in fact reaches deeply into the heart of Jesus' message about this world we live in. The phrase *kingdom of the heavens* occurs thirty-two times in Matthew's Gospel and never again in the New Testament. By contrast, the phrase *kingdom of God* occurs only five times in that Gospel but is the usual term used in the remainder of the New Testament. What is the significance of this variation in terminology?

Generally speaking, scholars have treated the variation as of no significance at all. This is unfortunate, for reasons that should now be clear. C. H. Dodd is characteristic with his statement: 'The two expressions, "The Kingdom of God" and "The Kingdom of Heaven", the latter of which is peculiar to the First Gospel, are synonymous, the term 'heaven' being common in Jewish usage as a reverential periphrasis for the divine name.'[11]

Now it is certainly true that the word *heaven* is often used in the Bible to refer to God's realm – though I think never, strictly speaking, to God himself. But this does not mean that the terms are synonymous. The two phrases in question refer to the same reality in some contexts, but they always refer to it in different ways and communicate importantly different things about it.

The very fact that heaven could be used loosely to refer to God at all is deeply instructive of how God relates to us, once you realize what 'the heavens' are. It tells us exactly where God is in relation to the human world. On the other hand, omission of these meanings by speaking only of the kingdom of God creates a vacuum that makes it easy to misunderstand Jesus and his teachings. The problem is made much worse by how we are taught to think of space today.

Space Inhabited by God

Spirit and Space

At no place, I think, does our contemporary mind-set more strongly conflict with the life and good news of Jesus than over the understanding of space. If we are to make sense of Jesus' teaching and practice of the kingdom of the heavens, we must understand what spirit and the spiritual are and how they are in space.

Confusing God with his historical manifestations in space may have caused some to think that God is a Wizard-of-Oz or Sistine-Chapel kind of being sitting at a location very remote from us. The universe is then presented as, chiefly, a vast empty space with a humanoid God and a few angels rattling around in it, while several billion human beings crawl through the tiny cosmic interval of human history on an oversized clod of dirt circling an insignificant star.

Of such a 'god' we can only say, 'Good riddance!' It seems that when many people try to pray they do have such an image of God in their minds. They therefore find praying psychologically impossible or extremely difficult. No wonder.

But the response to this mistake has led many to say that God is not in space at all, not that 'old man in the sky', but instead is 'in' the human heart. And that sounds nice, but it really does not help. In fact, it just makes matters worse. 'In my heart' easily becomes 'in my imagination'. And, in any case, the question of God's relation to space and the physical world remains unresolved. If he is not in space at all, he is not in human life, which is lived in space. Those vast oceans of 'empty space' just sit there glowering at the human 'heart' realm where God has, supposedly, taken refuge from science and the real world.

This ill-advised attempt to make God near by confining him to human hearts robs the idea of his direct involvement in human life of any sense. Ironically it has much the same effect as putting God in outer space or beyond. It gives us a pretty metaphor but leaves us vainly grasping for the reality. We simply cannot solve the problem of spirit's relation to space by taking spirit out of space, either beyond space or 'in' the heart.[12] We must gain a deeper understanding of what 'spirit' is.

The Human Spirit

The spirit and the space most familiar to each one of us are contained in our own personality. The necessary path of understanding lies in reflecting on our own make-up.

I am a spiritual being who currently has a physical body. I occupy my body and its environs by my consciousness of it and by my capacity to will and to act with and through it. I *occupy* my body and its proximate space, but I am not localizable in it or around it. You cannot find me or any of my thoughts, feelings, or character traits in any part of my body. Even I cannot. If you wish to find *me*, the last thing you should do is open my body to take a look – or even examine it closely with a microscope or other physical instruments.

For many years in Moscow there was a scientific institute where the brains of great Communists – leaders, scientists and artists – were preserved and slices taken to be analyzed under the microscope. Technicians hoped to find the secret of great Communist personalities right there in their great Communist brains. Of course, they found nothing of personal greatness there. They were looking in the wrong place and in the wrong way. To be sure, the brain is a relatively more important and interesting piece of flesh, but nothing of intellect, creativity or character is to be found in it.

That very *unity of experiences* that constitutes a human self cannot be located at any point in or around this body through which we live, not even in the brain. Yet I am present as agent or causal influence with and about my body and its features and movements. In turn, what my body undergoes and provides influences my life as a personal being. And through my body, principally through my face and gestures, or 'body language', but also verbally, I can make myself present to others.[13]

The human face, and especially the eyes, are not just additional physical objects in space. We say that the eyes are the windows of the soul, and there is much truth to it. They and the face and hands are areas in space where the spiritual reality of the person becomes present to others. There the inmost being of the individual pours forth, though of course the person is no more literally identical with his or her face or eyes than with lungs or toenails or brain.

Interestingly, 'growing up' is largely a matter of learning to hide our spirit behind our face, eyes and language so that we can evade and manage others to achieve what we want and avoid what we fear. By contrast, the child's face is a constant epiphany because it doesn't yet know how to do this. It cannot manage its face. This is also true of adults in moments of great feeling – which is one reason why feeling is both greatly treasured and greatly feared.

Those who have attained considerable spiritual stature are frequently noted for their 'childlikeness.' What this really means is that they do not use their face and body to hide their spiritual reality. In their body they are genuinely present to those around them. That is a great spiritual attainment or gift.

Now, roughly speaking, *God relates to space as we do to our body*. He occupies and overflows it but cannot be localized in it. Every point in it is accessible to his consciousness and will, and his manifest presence can be focused in any location as he sees fit. In the incarnation he focused his reality in a special way in the body of Jesus. This was so that we might be 'enlightened by the knowledge of the glory of God in the face of Jesus Christ' (2 Cor. 4:6).

The traditional Christian understanding is that every physical object and every natural law is a manifestation of God's willing. This does not have to be taken in the sense that he is every second consciously choosing, for example, that this electron should be circling that neutron or that this pillar should be supporting that house. No doubt he could do that if he wished. But it is true in the same sense that the arrangement of the furniture in your apartment is a manifestation of your will. It is as you have provided for and want it to be, though you are not always thinking of that arrangement and 'willing' it. It is also a continuing revelation of you to all who know you well.

God Wants to Be Seen

Similarly, God is, without special theophanies, seen everywhere by those who long have lived for him. No doubt God wants us to see him. That is a part of his nature as outpouring love. Love always wants to be known. Thus he seeks for those who could safely and rightly worship him. God wants to be present to our minds with all the force of objects given clearly to ordinary perception.

In a beautiful passage Julian of Norwich tells of how once her 'understanding was let down into the bottom of the sea,' where she saw 'green hills and valleys.' The meaning she derived was this:

> If a man or woman were there under the wide waters, if he could see God, as God is continually with man, he would be safe in soul and body, and come to no harm. And furthermore, he would have more consolation and strength than all this world can tell. For it is God's will that we believe that we see him continually, though it seems to us that the sight be only partial; and through this belief he makes us always to gain more grace, for God wishes to be seen, and he wishes to be sought, and he wishes to be expected, and he wishes to be trusted.[14]

Seeing is no simple thing, of course. Often a great deal of knowledge, experience, imagination, patience and receptivity are required. Some people, it seems, are never able to see bacteria or cell structure through the microscope. But seeing is all the more difficult in spiritual things, where the objects, unlike bacteria or cells, *must be willing to be seen*.

Persons rarely become present where they are not heartily wanted. Certainly that is true for you and me. We prefer to be wanted, warmly wanted, before we reveal our souls – or even come to a party. The ability to see and the practice of seeing God and God's world comes through a process of seeking and growing in intimacy with him.

But as we can expect to make progress in the seeing of any subject matter, so also it is with God. Towards the end of his life Brother Lawrence remarked, 'I must, in a little time, go to God. What comforts me in this life is that I now see Him by faith; and I see Him in such a manner as might make me say sometimes, *I believe no more, but I see.*'[15] The heavens progressively open to us as our character and understanding are increasingly attuned to the realities of God's rule from the heavens.

The Myth of Empty Space

So we should assume that space is anything but empty. This is central to the understanding of Jesus because it is central to the understanding of the rule of God from the heavens, which is his kingdom among us. Travelling through space and not finding God does not mean that space is empty any more than travelling through my body and not finding me means that I am not here.

In *Out of the Silent Planet*, C. S. Lewis gives an imaginative description of how one of his main characters, Ransom, experiences a 'progressive lightening and exultation of heart' as the airship carrying him moves away from the earth:

> A nightmare, long engendered in the modern mind by the mythology that follows in the wake of science was falling off him. He had read of 'Space': at the back of his thinking for years had lurked the dismal fancy of the black, cold vacuity, the utter deadness, which was supposed to separate the worlds. He had not known how much it affected him till now – now that the very name 'Space' seemed a blasphemous libel for this empyrean ocean of radiance in which they swam … He had thought it barren: he saw now

> that it was the womb of worlds, whose blazing and innumerable offspring looked down nightly even upon the earth with so many eyes – and here, with how many more![16]

Some may object that this is only literature. Yes, but it is nonetheless helpful in loosening the baseless images that, without scientific validation of any sort, flood in from the culture of pseudoscience to paralyse faith. Sometimes important things can be presented in literature or art that cannot be effectively conveyed in any other way.

Certainly mere space travel is not the way to discover the divine richness that fills all creation. That discovery comes through personal seeking and spiritual reorientation, as well as God's responsive act of making himself present to those ready to receive. Only then we cry with the Seraphim, 'Holy! Holy! Holy!' as we find 'the whole earth full of his glory'.

In a striking comparison, Ole Hallesby points out that the air our body requires envelops us on every hand. To receive it we need only breathe. Likewise, 'The "air" which our souls need also envelops all of us at all times and on all sides. God is round about us in Christ on every hand, with his many-sided and all-sufficient grace. All we need to do is to open our hearts.'[17]

All Things Visible and Invisible

What, Then, Is *Spiritual* Reality?

Perhaps this helps us get a start on rethinking the problem of how God is present around us in space and of what 'the kingdom of the heavens' is. But we must press on towards a still deeper understanding of the spirit and the spiritual.

And for this we look once again to personality as we find it in ourselves. For it is in persons, or 'selves' – and their experiences of feeling, thought and will – that we primarily come to know precisely what the spiritual is. 'Spiritual' is not just something we *ought* to be. It is something we are and cannot escape, regardless of how we may think or feel about it. It is our nature and our destiny.

NON-PHYSICAL. When we say that it is the personal that is the spiritual, we mean, negatively, that the spiritual is something not perceptible by any one of the five senses. In yourself, in others, or in God himself, it does not have physical properties such as shape, size and weight, or colour, flavour, odour and texture. Thus, when in 2 Cor. 4:18 Paul speaks of drawing life from the non-visible by focusing our minds and expectations on it, as opposed to the visible – 'we are looking not at things which are seen, but at those which are not seen' – he is, of course, referring to the realm of persons and to God above all.

Your *thought* of or your *wish* for a candy bar or for success in your profession is a trivial example of something you are sharply aware of and can describe in some detail. But you do not touch or smell it, nor would stronger light or glasses enable you to 'see' it better. It simply does not have the characteristics revealed to the physical senses. And that is no objection to it, for if it had such properties it could not be a thought or a wish. This observation is associated with the fact already considered: that such a thought or wish is not localizable in space.

THE ULTIMATE POWER. In finding the spiritual not to be physical we do not mean to deny that it has power or energy. It most certainly does. And this is a major point for the positive characterization of the spiritual. Spirit is a form of energy, for it does work, and whatever does work has power. In the biblical view it is, of course, the ultimate form of power on which all other forms rest.[18]

To consider the simplest of cases, once again, if you are now seated in a room probably everything you see around you owes its existence, or at least its presence there, to the feelings, ideas and willings of one or more persons. Again, when you look up and see an aeroplane flying overhead, you are looking at something that owes its existence to the spiritual reality, the mind and will, of the human being. Aeroplanes do not grow on trees.

THOUGHT. But any positive characterization of the spiritual must also mention that, besides having power, persons, or selves, and their experiences are consciously directed upon various subject matters that concern them. That is, persons *think*, and their thoughts pick out or select specific objects past, present or future. This is the activity of mind. It is the cognitive aspect of the spiritual being a person is. No physical thing has it.

VALUING. Then, as we also know, persons will be favourably disposed towards some things of which they think and set against others (this is feeling, emotion or valuation). That makes us capable of *choosing* and acting with reference to them. This is our *will*.

Each of these dimensions or aspects of the personal or spiritual is something we find in ourselves, even though not by sight, hearing, smell or other physical senses. And we find them flowing there so richly that it is impossible for us to describe our own existence in anything like its actual fullness of detail.

The Centrality of Will or Heart

It is the 'will' aspect of personal/spiritual reality that is its innermost core. In biblical language the will is usually referred to as 'heart'. This it is that organizes all the dimensions of personal reality to form a life or a person. The will, or heart, is the executive centre of the self. Thus the centre point of the spiritual in humans as well as in God is self-determination, also called freedom and creativity.

Little children quickly learn to make things and to give them to those they love. If their souls are not crushed by life, as so many unfortunately are, they will continue to do this throughout their lives and at death will wish to leave to others things they have produced or secured by their own efforts.

Creative people in leadership (human affairs), in the arts and in the realm of intellect are the most highly admired among us. Sometimes the creativity is a matter of steadfast faithfulness to ideals or relationships. We always place a tremendous premium on what comes from the centre of our being, the heart. It, more than anything else, is what we are.

Commenting on how our strength, intelligence, wealth or good luck 'makes us feel ourselves a match for life,' William James adds, 'but deeper than all such things, and able to suffice unto itself without them, is the sense of the amount of effort which we can put forth.' This 'effort seems to belong to an altogether different realm, as if it were the substantive thing which we *are*, and those were but externals which we *carry*.' Our 'consents or non-consents,' as James calls them, 'seem our deepest organs of communication with the nature of things! What wonder if the effort demanded by them be the measure of our worth as men ... the one strictly underived and original contribution which we make to the world!'[19]

And as for God, the highest biblical revelation of God's metaphysical nature is Exod. 3:14. There, in response to Moses' question about his nature or who he is, God replies, 'I am that I am' – a Being that exists totally from its own resources. The Father has life 'in himself', we are later told by Jesus, and has given the same kind of life to the Son (John 5:26). Nothing other than God has this character of *totally* self-sufficient being or self-determination.

But every human being nevertheless has a will, or will power. It is our inclination and capacity to act on our own and to produce what we find to be good – to be freely creative. Because we have will we are not *things*. We have in us the capacity to be self-determined to some significant degree. Without will we would have no life that is recognizably human.

We briefly discussed this in an earlier chapter. There, you may recall, we were describing the 'kingdom' that belongs to every human being by nature. And we saw how grace, through confidence in Jesus, permits our kingdom to grow into a union with the kingdom of God.

The heart, or will, simply is spirit in human beings. It is the human spirit, and the only thing in us that God will accept as the basis of our relationship to him. It is the spiritual plane of our natural existence, the place of truth before God, from where alone our whole lives can become eternal.

The *Substantiality* of the Spiritual

We pull all these thoughts together by saying that spirit is *unbodily personal power*. It is primarily a *substance*, and it is above all God, who is both spirit and substance.

To understand spirit as 'substance' is of the utmost importance in our current world, which is so largely devoted to the ultimacy of matter. It means that spirit is something that exists in its own right – to some degree in the human case, and absolutely so with God. Thoughts, feelings, willings and their developments are so many dimensions of this spiritual substance, which exercises a power that is outside the physical. Space is occupied by it, and it may manifest itself there as it chooses. This is how Jesus sees our world. It is part of his gospel.

Because we are spiritual beings, as just explained, it is for our good, individually and collectively, to live our lives in interactive dependence upon God and under his kingdom rule. Every kind of life, from the cabbage to the water buffalo, lives from a certain world that is suited to it. It is called to that world by what it is. There alone is where its well-being lies. Cut off from its special world it languishes and eventually dies.

This is how the call to spirituality comes to us. We ought to be spiritual in every aspect of our lives because *our* world is the spiritual one. It is what we are suited to. Thus Paul, from his profound grasp of human existence, counsels us, 'To fill your mind with the visible, the "flesh", is death, but to fill your mind with the spirit is life and peace' (Rom. 8:6).

As we increasingly integrate our life into the spiritual world of God, our life increasingly takes on the substance of the eternal. We are destined for a time when our life will be entirely sustained from spiritual realities and no longer dependent in any way upon the physical. Our dying, or 'mortal' condition, will have been exchanged for an undying one and death absorbed in victory.[20]

The Human Quandary

Of course that destiny flatly contradicts the usual human outlook, or what 'everyone knows' to be the case. I take this to be a considerable point in its favour. Our 'lives of quiet desperation', in the familiar words of Thoreau, are imposed by hopelessness. We find our world to be one where we hardly count at all, where what we do makes little difference, and where what we really love is unattainable, or certainly is not secure. We become frantic or despairing.

In his book *The Doors of Perception*, Aldous Huxley remarks, 'Most men and women lead lives at the worst so painful, at the best so monotonous, poor and limited that the urge to escape, the longing to transcend themselves if only for a few moments, is and has always been one of the principal appetites of the soul.'[21] They are relentlessly driven to seek, in H. G. Wells's phrase, 'Doors in the Wall' that entombs them in life.

Huxley was sure that 'the urge to escape from selfhood and the environment is in almost everyone almost all the time' (p. 63). Therefore the need for frequent 'chemical vacations from intolerable selfhood and repulsive surroundings' would never change. The human need could only be met, in his view, by discovery of a new drug that would relieve our suffering species without doing more harm than good in the long run (pp. 64–65).

In *A Confession*, Leo Tolstoy relates how the drive towards goodness that moved him as a boy was erased by his experiences in society. Later in life, after overwhelming success as a writer, he nevertheless sank into psychological paralysis brought on by his vision of the futility of everything. The awareness that the passage of time alone would bring everything he loved and valued to nothing left him completely hopeless. For years he lived in this condition, until he finally came to faith in a world of God where all that is good is preserved.

A Solution in the 'Mind of the Spirit'

That is precisely the world of the spiritual that Jesus opened to humanity long ago and still opens to those who seek it. Observing the faith of simple peasants and the deeply meaningful (though painful) lives that flowed from it, Tolstoy was led onward to Jesus and his message of the kingdom of God. That message then showed him the way to the spiritual world and the 'mind of the spirit', which, as Paul also said, is 'life and peace'.

The mind or the minding of the spirit is life and peace precisely because it locates us in a world adequate to our nature as ceaselessly creative beings under God. The 'mind of the flesh', on the other hand, is a living death. To it the heavens are closed. It sees only 'That inverted Bowl they call the Sky, Whereunder crawling cooped we live and die.'[22] It restricts us to the visible, physical world where what our hearts demand can never be. There, as Tolstoy saw with disgust, we find we constantly must violate our conscience in order to 'survive'.

Jesus, by contrast, brings us into a world without fear. In his world, astonishingly, there is nothing evil we must do in order to thrive. He lived, and invites us to live, in an undying world where it is safe to do and be good. He was understood by his first friends to have 'abolished death and brought life and immortality to light through the gospel' (2 Tim. 1:10). Thus our posture of confident reliance upon him in all we do allows us to make our life undying, of eternal worth, integrated into the eternal vistas and movements of the Spirit.

Human existence understood in the context of this full world of God – 'all things visible and invisible', to use the biblical language – can be as good as we naturally hope for it to be and think it ought to be, though perhaps not in the precise terms that would first come to our minds. In far better terms, really, because God is constantly poised to do 'exceedingly abundantly above all that we ask or imagine, in terms of the energy that is working in us' (Eph. 3:20).

Death Dismissed

Carelessness About Death

Once we have grasped our situation in God's full world, the startling disregard Jesus and the New Testament writers had for 'physical death' suddenly makes sense. Paul bluntly states, as we have just seen, that Jesus abolished death – simply did away with it. Nothing like what is usually understood as death will happen to those who have entered his life.

To one group of his day, who believed that 'physical death' was the cessation of the individual's existence, Jesus said, 'God is not the God of the dead but of the living' (Luke 20:38). His meaning was that those who love and are loved by God are not allowed to cease to exist, because they are God's treasures. He delights in them and intends to hold on to them. He has even prepared for them an individualized eternal work in his vast universe.

At this present time the eternally creative Christ is preparing places for his human sisters and brothers to join him. Some are already there – no doubt busy with him in his great works. We can hardly think that they are mere watchers. On the day he died, he covenanted with another man being killed along with him to meet that very day in a place he called Paradise. This term carries the suggestion of a lovely gardenlike area.

Too many are tempted to dismiss what Jesus says as just 'pretty words'. But those who think it is unrealistic or impossible are more short on imagination than long on logic. They should have a close look at the universe God has *already* brought into being before they decide he could not arrange for the future life of which the Bible speaks.

Anyone who realizes that reality is God's, and has seen a little bit of what God has *already* done, will understand that such a 'Paradise' would be no problem at all. And there God will preserve every one of his treasured friends in the wholeness of their personal existence precisely because he treasures them in that form. Could he enjoy their fellowship, could they serve him, if they were 'dead'?

We have already used the words of Vladimir Nabokov once in this chapter to express the reality of God's world and its closeness to us. In a letter to his mother to console her on the death of his father, he wrote,

> Three years have gone – and every trifle relating to father is still as alive as ever inside me. I am so certain, my love, that we will see him again, in an unexpected but completely natural heaven, in a realm where all is radiance and delight. He will come towards us in our shared bright eternity, slightly raising his shoulders as he used to do, and we will kiss the birthmark on his hand without surprise. You must live in expectation of that tender hour, my love and never give in to the temptation of despair. Everything will return.[23]

Now, of course, if one simply doesn't believe in the God we have been talking about, then one must make of Jesus whatever one can. This, unfortunately, is all too common. Perhaps people should be required to say, when they begin to interpret Jesus, whether they believe in his God or not. Then we would have a pretty good idea of what to expect.

Never Taste Death

In any case, Jesus made a special point of saying that those who rely on him and have received the kind of life that flows in him and in God will never experience death. Such persons, he said, will never *see* death, never *taste* death (John 8:51–52). On another occasion he says simply that 'everyone living and believing in me shall never die' (11:26).

So as we think of our life and make plans for it, we should not be anticipating going through some terrible event called 'death', to be avoided at all costs even though it can't be avoided. That is the usual attitude for human beings, no doubt. But, immersed in Christ in action, we may be sure that our life – yes, that familiar one we are each so well acquainted with – will never stop. We should be anticipating what we will be doing three hundred or a thousand or ten thousand years from now in this marvellous universe.

The hymn *Amazing Grace* was found in a recent *USA Today* poll to be America's favourite hymn. It is sung at Boston Pops concerts and played at military and police funerals. It is now a solid part of American if not Western culture, and it accurately presents the future of redeemed humanity:

> When we've been there ten thousand years,
> Bright shining as the sun,
> We've no less days to sing God's praise,
> Than when we first begun.

Could this be the actual truth about our case? Jesus' word to us would most certainly be, 'Believe it!' We are never-ceasing spiritual beings with an eternal destiny in the full world of God.

When Mickey Mantle was dying of diseases brought on by a life of heavy drinking, he said that he would have taken better care of himself had he only known how long he was going to live. He gives us a profound lesson. How should we 'take care of ourselves' when we are never to cease? Jesus shows his apprentices how to live in the light of the fact that they will never stop living. This is what his students are learning from him.

Moving out of Our 'Tent', or Temporary House

Of course something is going to happen. We will leave our present body at a certain point, and our going and what we leave behind will not seem pleasant to those who care for us. But we are at that point, as Paul also says, simply 'absent from the body and present with the Lord' (2 Cor. 5:8).

Early Christians spoke of their condition at physical death as being 'asleep'. We are then, as we say even now of a sleeping person, 'dead to this world'. To those who remain behind there is an obvious, if superficial, similarity between the body of one who sleeps and that of one who has stepped into the full world.

But there was no intention in this language to say we will be unconscious. Consciousness continues while we are asleep, and likewise when we 'sleep in Jesus' (1 Thess. 4:14; Acts 7:60). The difference is simply a matter of what we are conscious of. In fact, at 'physical' death we *become* conscious and enjoy a richness of experience we have never known before.

The American evangelist Dwight Moody remarked towards the end of his life, 'One day soon you will hear that I am dead. Do not believe it. I will then be alive as never before.' When the two guards came to take Dietrich Bonhoeffer to the gallows, he briefly took a friend aside to say, 'This is the end, but for me it is the beginning of life.'[24]

How then are we to think about the transition? Failure to have a way of thinking about it is one of the things that continues to make it dreadful even to those who have every confidence in Jesus. The unimaginable is naturally frightening to us. But there are two pictures that I believe to be accurate as well as helpful.

They can help us know what to expect as we leave 'our tent,' our body (2 Cor. 5:1–6).

One was made famous by Peter Marshall some years ago. It is the picture of a child playing in the evening among her toys. Gradually she grows weary and lays her head down for a moment of rest, lazily continuing to play. The next thing she experiences or 'tastes' is the morning light of a new day flooding the bed and the room where her mother or father took her. Interestingly, we never remember falling asleep. We do not 'see' it, 'taste' it.

Another picture is of one who walks to a doorway between rooms. While still interacting with those in the room she is leaving, she begins to see and converse with people in the room beyond, who may be totally concealed from those left behind. Before the widespread use of heavy sedation, it was quite common for those keeping watch to observe something like this. The one making the transition often begins to speak to those who have gone before. They come to meet us while we are still in touch with those left behind. The curtains part for us briefly before we go through.

Speaking of the magnificence of this passage into the full world of 'the heavens reopened', John Henry Newman remarks, 'Those wonderful things of the new world are even now as they shall be then. They are immortal and eternal; and the souls who shall then be made conscious of them will see them in their calmness and their majesty where they have ever been ... The life then begun, we know, will last forever; yet surely if memory be to us then what it is now, that will be a day much to be observed unto the Lord through all the ages of eternity.'[25] It will be our birthday into God's full world.

The Dual Context of Life in God's World

According to the wisdom of Jesus, then, every event takes on a different reality and meaning, depending on whether it is seen only in the context of the visible or also in the context of God's full world, where we all as a matter of fact live. Everything he taught presupposes this, and to be his students we must understand and accept it. It is in this sense 'axiomatic'.

In a familiar Gospel story Jesus is sitting near the offering box in the temple. He watches while rich men cast in their sizeable gifts. Then comes a poor widow who casts in all she owns, two of the tiniest coins in use at the time. He then comments to his students that the widow has put more in the offering than all the others did.

Viewed in the context of the physical or merely human, these can only be more 'pretty words'. That, in fact, is true of nearly everything Jesus said, for he lived and taught in full view of the heavens opened. This causes multitudes to dismiss his teachings as 'unrealistic'. They do not see his world.

Obviously, in some sense, the widow did not cast in more. But viewed in the context of what God does with her action and what he does, or rather does not do, with the actions of the others, it is a strictly literal truth that she cast in more. It was of greater value. More of value was done with the widow's pennies than with the 'large' gifts of the others. The context of The Kingdom Among Us transforms the respective actions. 'Little is much,' we say, 'when God is in it.' And so it is. Really.

Which Side Really Is Up?

The First Shall Be Last and the Last First

This story calls to our attention The Great Inversion that lies at the heart of the good news (or gospel) of Jesus and his people. The scene at the offering box in the temple is an illustration. What turns up so graphically in that case is actually a general structure that permeates the message of the Bible as a whole and the reality portrayed therein.

This structure indicates that humanity is routinely flying upside down, and at the same time it provides a message of hope for everyone who counts on God's order, no matter his or her circumstance. There is none in the humanly 'down' position so low that they cannot be lifted up by entering God's order, and none in the humanly 'up' position so high that they can disregard God's point of view on their lives.

We see this inversion at play in the patriarchs, Abraham, Isaac and Jacob: drifters who yet managed great wealth and owned by promise the land in which they wandered. Everything rested on the fact that God was obviously, tangibly *with them*. They were positively frightening to their neighbours (Gen. 26:27–29).

Again, the children of Israel were the most deprived segment of Egyptian society. Yet they 'triumphed over the horse and the rider in the midst of the sea.' The barren, the widow, the orphan, the eunuch, the alien, all models of human hopelessness, are fruitful and secure in God's care. They are repeatedly invoked in Old Testament writings as testimony to the great inversion between our way and God's way (e.g., Isa. 56:3–8).

This inversion becomes so well known as the biblical revelation of God progresses that it is treated as a formal literary device in teaching God's perspective and how he works. Ezekiel contemplates the complete destruction of the royal house and government of Israel as it stood in his time. Babylon would destroy it utterly. Over against this collapse of a physical and social reality, he depicts God's way: taking a tiny sprig from a cedar, planting it on the high mountains of Israel, totally independent of human care.

That sprig represented the humanly 'kingdomless' remnant of the Jewish people. 'It will bring forth boughs and bear fruit, and become a stately cedar,' the prophet says for God. 'The birds of every kind will nest under it; they will nest in the shade of its branches. And all the trees of the field will know that I am the Lord; I bring down the high tree, exalt the low tree, dry up the green tree, and make the dry tree flourish. I am the Lord; I have spoken and I will perform it' (Ezek. 17:22–24 NAS).

Jesus renewed this image in his parable of the kingdom of the heavens as a tiny seed that grows into a large plant where birds can make their home (Matt. 13:31–32). In that parable he refers precisely to the growth of his people in the earth without reference to human government. His government from the heavens is quite sufficient for them.

To see everything from the perspective of 'the heavens opened' is to see all things as they are before God. The Kingdom Among Us is simply God himself and the spiritual realm of beings over which his will perfectly presides – 'as it is in the heavens'.

That kingdom is to be sharply contrasted with the kingdom of man: the realm of human life, that tiny part of visible reality where the human will for a time has some degree of sway, even contrary to God's will. 'The heavens are the heavens of the Lord,' the psalmist said, 'but the earth He has given to the sons of men' (115:16 NAS). And as things now stand we must sigh, 'Alas for the earth!'

To become a disciple of Jesus is to accept now that inversion of human distinctions that will sooner or later be forced upon everyone by the irresistible reality of his kingdom. How must we think of him to see the inversion from our present viewpoint? We must, simply, accept that he is the best and smartest man who ever lived in this world, that he is even now 'the prince of the kings of the earth' (Rev. 1:5). Then we heartily join his cosmic conspiracy to overcome evil with good.

The Resistance Built into Our Daily Life

Human life certainly resists the great inversion. To it, the very idea of any such inversion is an insult and an illusion. Our civilization is at present in the advanced stages of what Max Picard described as 'the flight from God'. The idea of an all-encompassing, all-penetrating world of God, interactive at every point with our lives, where we can always be totally at home and safe regardless of what happens in the visible dimension of the universe, is routinely treated as ridiculous.

It is not hard to see the concrete and oppressive form that the flight from God takes today. There is, for example, no field of expertise in human affairs where interaction with God is a part of the subject matter or practice that must be mastered in order to be judged competent. This is true of chemistry and public administration, but it is also true of education, nursing, police work and often, astonishingly, Christian ministry itself. It is true of marriage and parenting. Just observe how people are taught and certified or judged competent in any of these fields, and you will be staring the flight from God straight in the face.

All of us live in such a world, for we live by our competencies. Our souls are, accordingly, soaked with secularity. In any context in which people are supposed to be smart and informed, even the most thoughtful and devout Christian will find it hard to make a convincing presentation of the relevance of God and his spiritual world to 'real life.'

The 'real' world has little room for a God of sparrows and children. To it, Jesus can only seem 'otherworldly' – a good-hearted person out of touch with reality. Yes, it must be admitted that he is influential, but only because he affirms what weak-minded and fainthearted individuals fantasize in the face of a brutal world. He is like a cheerleader who continues to shout, 'We are going to win,' though the score is 98 to 3 against us in the last minute of the game.

When this cheerleading approach to the 'real world' triumphs among those who profess Christ, they may then have faith in faith but will have little faith in God. For God and his world are just not 'real' to them. They may believe in believing but not be able to rely on God – like many in our current culture who love love but in practice are unable to love real people. They may believe in prayer, think it quite a good thing, but be unable to pray believing and so will rarely, if ever, pray at all.

I personally have become convinced that many people who believe in Jesus do not actually believe in God. By saying this I do not mean to condemn anyone but to cast light on why the lives of professed believers go as they do, and often quite contrary even to what they sincerely intend.

Jesus, Master of Intellect

The Growing Wave of Unfaith

The 'cultural reality' that so cuts the nerve of effective discipleship today has been coming upon us over a lengthy period. For centuries it was fostered within a narrow circle of intellectuals. Bishop Joseph Butler, at the end of the seventeenth century, referred to these 'advanced thinkers' sarcastically by remarking that 'Christianity seems at length to have been found out to be fictitious.'[26]

The nineteenth century saw a bitter intellectual struggle in the centres of learning of the Western world, in which the long-accepted outlook of Jesus, as I am presenting it here, lost its standing as an intellectual option. Not that Christian faith is merely an intellectual matter, but it came in this period to be identified with ideas and attitudes simply irrelevant to reality.[27]

By the mid-twentieth century, the dominant attitude within those academic circles that stand guard over our belief system was well expressed in words from Evelyn Waugh's *Brideshead Revisited*. Charles Ryder, the protagonist in that novel, comments on the religion of the other central character:

> Sebastian's faith was an enigma to me at that time, but not one which I felt particularly concerned to solve ... The view implicit in my education was that the basic narrative of Christianity had long been exposed as a myth, and that opinion was now divided as to whether its ethical teaching was of present value, a division in which the main weight went against it; religion was a hobby which some people professed and others not; at the best it was slightly ornamental, at the worst it was the province of 'complexes' and 'inhibitions' – catchwords of the decade – and of the intolerance, hypocrisy and sheer stupidity attributed to it for centuries. No one had ever suggested to me that these quaint observances expressed a coherent philosophic system and intransigent historical claims; nor, had they done so, would I have been much interested.[28]

These words perfectly express the crushing weight of the secular outlook that permeates or pressures every thought we have today. Sometimes it even forces those who self-identify as Christian teachers to set aside Jesus' plain statements about the reality and total relevance of the kingdom of God and replace them with philosophical speculations whose only recommendation is their consistency with a 'modern' mind-set.

The powerful though vague and unsubstantiated presumption is that *something has been found out* that renders a spiritual understanding of reality in the manner of Jesus simply foolish to those who are 'in the know'. But when it comes time to say exactly what it is that has been found out, nothing of substance is forthcoming.

Thus Rudolf Bultmann, long regarded as one of the great leaders of twentieth-century thought, had this to say: 'It is impossible to use electric light and the wireless and to avail ourselves of modern medical and surgical discoveries, and at the same time believe in the New Testament world of spirits and miracles.'[29]

To anyone who has worked through the relevant arguments, this statement is simply laughable. It only shows that great people are capable of great silliness. Yet this kind of 'thinking' dominates much of our intellectual and professional life at present, and in particular has governed by far the greater part of the field of biblical studies for more than a century.

The Smartest Man in the World

But the baseless presumption in question must be seen for the empty prejudice it is if we are to enrol with serious intent in Jesus' school of life. Though this is not the place to discuss it, you can be very sure that nothing fundamental has changed in our *knowledge* of ultimate reality and the human self since the time of Jesus.[30]

Many will be astonished at such a remark, but it at least provides us with a thought – that nothing fundamental has changed from biblical times – that every responsible person needs to consider at least once in his or her lifetime, and the earlier the better. And as for those who find it incredible – I constantly meet such people in my line of work – you only need ask them exactly *what* has changed, and where it is documented, and they are quickly stumped. Descending to particulars always helps to clear the mind.

The multitudes of theories, facts and techniques that have emerged in recent centuries have not the least logical bearing upon the ultimate issues of existence and life. In this respect they only serve to distract and confuse a people already harassed witless by their slogans, scientific advances, 'labour-saving' devices and a blizzard of promises about when and how 'happiness' is going to be achieved. Vague references to 'particles and progress' do not provide a coherent picture of life.

In any case, we can say with even greater certainty that, if we go with the currents of modernity, we shall never make sense of Jesus' gospel for life and discipleship. Quite simply, his work and teaching, as well as the main path of historical Christianity that sprang from him, is essentially based upon the substantial reality of the spirit and of the spiritual world. They cannot be separated from it. At this point in our history we have had enough experience at attempting that separation for any candid and informed person to know it cannot be done.

Our commitment to Jesus can stand on no other foundation than a recognition that he is the one who knows the truth about our lives and our universe. It is not possible to trust Jesus, or anyone else, in matters where we do not believe him to be competent. We cannot pray for his help and rely on his collaboration in dealing with real-life matters we suspect might defeat his knowledge or abilities.

And can we seriously imagine that Jesus could be *Lord* if he were not smart? If he were divine, would he be dumb? Or uninformed? Once you stop to think about it, how could he be what we take him to be in all other respects and not be the best-informed and most intelligent person of all, the smartest person who ever lived?

That is exactly how his earliest apprentices in kingdom living thought of him. He was not regarded as, perhaps, a magician, who only knew 'the right words' to get results without understanding or who could effectively manipulate appearances. Rather, he was accepted as the ultimate scientist, craftsman and artist.

The biblical and continuing vision of Jesus was of one who made all of created reality and kept it working, literally 'holding it together' (Col. 1:17). And today we think people are smart who make light bulbs and computer chips and rockets out of 'stuff' already provided! He made 'the stuff'!

Small wonder, then, that the first Christians thought he held within himself 'all of the treasures of wisdom and knowledge' (Col. 2:3). This confidence in his intellectual greatness is the basis of the radicalism of Christ-following in relation to the human order. It sees Jesus now living beyond death as 'the faithful witness, the first-born of the dead, the ruler of the kings of the earth, ... the first and the last, the living One,' the one who can say 'I was dead, and behold, I am alive forever more, the master of death and the world of the dead' (Rev. 1:5, 18).

Master of Molecules

At the literally mundane level, Jesus knew how to transform the molecular structure of water to make it wine. That knowledge also allowed him to take a few pieces of bread and some little fish and feed thousands of people. He could create matter from the energy he knew how to access from 'the heavens', right where he was.

It cannot be surprising that the feeding of the thousands led the crowds to try to force him to be their king. Surely one who could play on the energy/matter equation like that could do anything. Turn gravel into gold and pay off the national debt! Do you think he could get elected president or prime minister today?

He knew how to transform the tissues of the human body from sickness to health and from death to life. He knew how to suspend gravity, interrupt weather patterns and eliminate unfruitful trees without saw or axe. He only needed a word. Surely he must be amused at what Nobel prizes are awarded for today.

In the ethical domain he brought an understanding of life that has influenced world thought more than any other. We shall see what this means in chapters to follow. And one of the greatest testimonies to his intelligence is surely that he knew how to enter physical death, actually to die, and then live on beyond death. He seized death by the throat and defeated it. Forget cryonics!

Death was not something others imposed on him. He explained to his followers in the moment of crisis that he could at any time call for 72,000 angels to do whatever he wanted. A mid-sized angel or two would surely have been enough to take care of those who thought they were capturing and killing him. He plainly said, 'Nobody takes my life! I give it up by choice. I am in position to lay it down, and I am in position to resume it. My father and I have worked all this out' (John 10:18).

All these things show Jesus' cognitive and practical mastery of every phase of reality: physical, moral and spiritual. He is Master only because he is Maestro. 'Jesus is Lord' can mean little in practice for anyone who has to hesitate before saying, 'Jesus is smart.'

He is not just nice, he is brilliant. He is the smartest man who ever lived. He is now supervising the entire course of world history (Rev. 1:5) while simultaneously preparing the rest of the universe for our future role in it (John 14:2). He always has the best information on everything and certainly also on the things that matter most in human life. Let us now hear his teachings on who has the good life, on who is the truly blessed.

Chapter 4

WHO IS REALLY WELL OFF? – THE BEATITUDES

> Blessed are the sat upon, spat upon, ratted on.
>
> PAUL SIMON

> Blessed are the spiritually deprived, for they too find the kingdom of the heavens.
>
> MATT. 5:3

> But many who are first will be last, and many who are last will be first.
>
> MATT. 19:30 NIV

The Puzzle of the Beatitudes

What we have come to call the Sermon on the Mount is a concise statement of Jesus' teachings on how to actually live in the reality of God's present kingdom available to us from the very space surrounding our bodies. It concludes with a statement that all who hear and do what he there says will have a life that can stand up to everything – that is, a life for eternity because it is already in the eternal (Matt. 7:24–25).

As outstanding thinkers before and after him have done, Jesus deals with the two major questions humanity always faces.

First there is the question of which life is the good life. What is genuinely in my interest, and how may I enter true well-being. Of course we already know that life in the life of God will be the good life, and Jesus' continual reassertion of the direct availability of the kingdom always kept that basic truth before his students and his hearers.

But exactly who is and who is not assured of such a life was a subject of much confusion in his day, as it is today. What came to be called the Beatitudes were given by him to help clarify this matter. They and the vital epilogue that accompanies them occupy Matt. 5:3–20.

The second question Jesus deals with in the sermon concerns who is truly a good person. Who has the kind of goodness found in God himself, constituting the family likeness between God and his children? This is dealt with in the remainder of the sermon, from 5:20 to 7:27. We shall return to Jesus' answer to this question in the chapter immediately to follow.

It is for a very good reason that Jesus' teachings here in response to these two great questions have proven to be the most influential such teachings ever to emerge on the face of this weary planet. That is by no means to say that all else produced in human history is worthless. Far from it. But his teachings on what is good for human beings are, taken as a whole, unique and uniquely deep and powerful.

To come to a full understanding of their force and depth nothing would be more useful than the most candid and thorough comparison of them with all of the promising alternatives.[1] But that requires a different kind of book from this one, and we simply cannot undertake such a comparison here. We shall concentrate directly on what Jesus himself taught. And the first question is, Who is it, according to Jesus, that has the good life?

Pretty Poison?

The Beatitudes of Jesus drive home his answer to this question. They are among the literary and religious treasures of the human race. Along with the Ten Commandments, the Twenty-third Psalm, the Lord's Prayer, and a very few other passages from the Bible, they are acknowledged by almost everyone to be among the highest expressions of religious insight and moral inspiration. We can savour them, affirm them, meditate upon them, and engrave them on plaques to hang on our walls. But a major question remains: How are we to live in response to them?

This is not an idle question. Misunderstanding of the 'blesseds' given by Jesus in Matthew 5 and Luke 6 have caused much pain and confusion down through the ages and continue to do so today. Strangely enough, his blesseds have not uniformly been a blessing. For many they have proved to be nothing less than pretty poison.

Once after I had spoken on the Beatitudes, a lady approached me expressing great relief at what she had just heard. She told me her son had dropped his Christian identification and left the church because of the Beatitudes. He was a strong, intelligent man who had made the military his profession. As often happens, he had been told that the Beatitudes – with its list of the poor and the sad, the weak and the mild – were a picture of the ideal Christian. He explained to his mother very simply: 'That is not me. I can never be like that.'

Certainly this man was not perfect as he stood and could have made several changes for the better. But is that what we're supposed to do with the Beatitudes – 'Be like that'? Frankly, most people think so. But they could hardly be more mistaken. More common than such outright rejection of Christianity so understood is a constant burden of guilt conscientiously borne for not being, or not wanting to be, on this list of the supposedly God-preferred. This kind of guilt also feeds a morbid streak that unfortunately persists in historical Christianity and has greatly weakened its force for good in history and in individual lives. On the other hand, pride often visibly swells in those who think of themselves as conforming to the 'blesseds'.

Teaching from the Context

It will help us know what to do – and what not to do – with the Beatitudes if we can discover what Jesus himself was doing with them. That should be the key to understanding them, for after all they are his Beatitudes, not ours to make of them what we will. And since great teachers and leaders always have a coherent message that they develop in an orderly way, we should assume that his teaching in the Beatitudes is a clarification or development of his primary theme in this talk and in his life: *the availability of the kingdom of the heavens.*[2] How, then, do they develop that theme?

In Chapter 4 of Matthew we see Jesus proclaiming his basic message (v. 17) and demonstrating it by acting with God's rule from the heavens, meeting the desperate needs of the people around him. As a result, 'Sick folk were soon coming to be healed from as far away as Syria. And whatever their illness or pain, or if they were possessed by demons, or were insane, or paralysed – he healed them all. Enormous crowds followed him wherever he went' (4:23–25 LB).

Having ministered to the needs of the people crowding around him, he desired to teach them and moved to a higher position in the landscape – 'up on the hill' (Matt. 5:1 BV) – where they could see and hear him well. But he does not, as is so often suggested, withdraw from the crowd to give an esoteric discourse of sublime irrelevance to the crying need of those pressing upon him. Rather, in the midst of this mass of raw humanity, and with them hanging on every word – note that it is they who respond at the end of the discourse – Jesus teaches his students or apprentices, along with all who hear, about the meaning of the availability of the heavens.

I believe he used the method of 'show and tell' to make clear the extent to which the kingdom is 'on hand' to us. There were directly before him those who *had just received* from the heavens through him. The context makes this clear. He could point out in the crowd now this individual, who was 'blessed' because The Kingdom Among Us had just reached out and touched them with Jesus' heart and voice and hands. Perhaps this is why in the Gospels we only find him giving Beatitudes from the midst of a crowd of people he had touched.

And so he said, 'Blessed are the spiritual zeros – the spiritually bankrupt, deprived and deficient, the spiritual beggars, those without a wisp of 'religion' – when the kingdom of the heavens comes upon them.'

Or, 'Blessed are the poor in spirit, for theirs is the kingdom of the heavens.' This, of course, is the more traditional and *literally* correct translation of Matt. 5:3. The poor in spirit are blessed as a result of the kingdom of God being available to them in their spiritual poverty. But today the words 'poor in spirit' no longer convey the sense of spiritual destitution that they were originally meant to bear. Amazingly, they have come to refer to a praiseworthy condition. So, as a corrective, I have paraphrased the verse as above. No doubt Jesus had many exhibits from this category in the crowd around him. Most, if not all, of the Twelve Apostles were of this type, as are many now reading these words.

'Spiritual Zeros' Also Enjoy Heaven's Care

Standing around Jesus as he speaks are people with no spiritual qualifications or abilities at all. You would never call on them when 'spiritual work' is to be done. There is nothing about them to suggest that the breath of God might move through their lives. They have no charisma, no religious glitter or clout.

They 'don't know their Bible.' They 'know not the law,' as a later critic of Jesus' work said. They are 'mere laypeople' who at best can fill a pew or perhaps an offering plate. No one calls on them to lead a service or even to lead in prayer, and they might faint if anyone did.

They are the first to tell you they 'really can't make heads nor tails of religion.' They walk by us in the hundreds or thousands every day. They would be the last to say they have any claim whatsoever on God. The pages of the Gospels are cluttered with such people. And yet: 'He touched me.' The rule of the heavens comes down upon their lives through their contact with Jesus. And then they too are blessed – healed of body, mind or spirit – in the hand of God.

A minister tells of trying to lead home Bible studies among the poor of northern Mexico. In such studies participation is, of course, always encouraged. He related that, at the beginning, he would read a passage from scripture and ask, 'What do you think?' No response. Just silence. Over and over this happened. Finally he realized that no one ever asks the poor what they *think*. That also is a part of what it means to be poor 'in spirit'. No one imagines you could have any thoughts worth sharing. Real poverty in the human order is almost automatically taken as a sign of failure in every respect.

It is deeply revealing of how we think about God to see the way translators struggle to make this condition of 'spiritual poverty' something good in its own right and thus deserving of blessing. Those who do not give the literal meaning indicated most commonly put something like being 'humble-minded' in its place.[3]

The first edition of the New English Bible, for example, said, 'How blest are those who know that they are poor.' That is a clear mistranslation, however, that the second edition has fortunately recognized by returning to 'Blessed are the poor in spirit.'

The generally excellent Berkeley version reads, 'Blessed are they who know their spiritual poverty, for theirs is the kingdom of heaven.' Once again an obvious mistranslation when compared with the Greek. It is a mistranslation driven by the necessity to make sense of something one just does not understand. If the Greek language wishes to say something about knowing or realizing one has no spiritual goods, it certainly has adequate resources to do so. But it says nothing of all that.

This struggle with the translation reflects our intense need to find in the condition referred to something good, something God supposedly desires or even requires, that then can serve as a 'reasonable' basis for the blessedness he bestows. But that precisely misses the point that the very formulation of the Beatitudes should bring to our attention.

Jesus did not say, 'Blessed are the poor in spirit *because* they are poor in spirit.' He did not think, 'What a fine thing it is to be destitute of every spiritual attainment or quality. It makes people worthy of the kingdom.' And we steal away the much more profound meaning of his teaching about the availability of the kingdom by replacing the state of spiritual impoverishment – in no way good in itself – with some supposedly praiseworthy state of mind or attitude that 'qualifies' us for the kingdom.[4]

In so doing we merely substitute another banal legalism for the ecstatic pronouncement of the gospel. Those poor in spirit are called 'blessed' by Jesus, not because they are in a meritorious condition, but because, *precisely in spite of and in the midst of their ever so deplorable condition*, the rule of the heavens has moved redemptively upon and through them by the grace of Christ.

Alfred Edersheim is therefore exactly right in saying that

> in the Sermon on the Mount ... the promises attaching, for example, to the so-called 'Beatitudes' must not be regarded as the *reward* of the spiritual states with which they are respectively connected, nor yet as their result. It is not *because* a man is poor in spirit that his is the Kingdom of Heaven, in the sense that the one state will grow into the other, or be its result; still less is the one the reward of the other. The connecting link is in each case Christ Himself: because He ..., 'has opened the Kingdom of Heaven to all believers.'[5]

Staying in Charge

Those spiritually impoverished ones present before Jesus in the crowd are blessed only because the gracious touch of the heavens has freely fallen upon them. But the mistranslations noted remain attractive because they suit our human sense of propriety, which cries out against God's blessing on people just because of their need and just because he chooses – or perhaps just because someone asked him to.

This same sense of propriety may even allow us to totally bypass contact with Jesus in his own Beatitudes. Indeed, most interpretations of his words manage to forget that he is even on the scene.

If all we need to be blessed in the kingdom of the heavens is to be humble-minded through recognizing our spiritual poverty, then let's just do that and we've got bliss cornered. We escape the humiliation of spiritual incompetence because, strange to say, we have managed to turn it into spiritual attainment just by acknowledging it. And we escape the embarrassment of receiving pure mercy, for our humble recognition makes blessedness somehow appropriate.

We have egg on our face perhaps, but at least we know it – and then can wear it defiantly, even proudly, like a badge of virtue. We have salvaged an impressive bit of righteousness for ourselves. And anyway, aren't all good people humble-minded? So all good people have the kingdom of the heavens! What necessary place does Jesus have in this – other than having the good sense to see it and say it?

And of course this also means that we can very neatly tell people how to engineer their way into the kingdom. Perhaps many will find that they are already there! 'Just be humble-minded,' it is said. (Who doesn't think that he or she is humble-minded? Perhaps there are some.) Such a solution will have great appeal to intellectual and scholarly types, who, in my experience, especially take pride in being humble about their minds.

But such a way of reading the Beatitudes also gives various other kinds of people automatic access to the kingdom of the heavens in terms nicely suited to them – especially if they have a distant God and not a present King. If they are not in a position to be humble-minded, they perhaps can manage to mourn, or be meek, or become persecuted, and then one of the other Beatitudes will, on the interpretation in question, take over to secure their blessedness.

Here we have full-blown, if not salvation by works, then possibly salvation by attitude. Or even by situation and chance, in case you happen to be persecuted, for example – meritorious attitude or circumstance guarantees acceptance with God! Can we really imagine that Jesus had anything like this in mind?

And What of Those Not on 'the List'?

We round out this popular approach to the Beatitudes with its final, fatal step. Not only are the conditions cited – poverty of spirit, mourning, meekness and so on – meritorious ones that somehow make it 'only right' for God to match them with beatitude, and not only can you be sure of being in the kingdom if you appropriately flee or fall into these conditions, but if you are *not* in these conditions, you certainly cannot be blessed. If you're not on the list, you're not in the kingdom. You may not even make it into 'heaven' when you die. I have heard this stated by many Christian teachers.

If Jesus' aim here is to tell us how to qualify for kingdom life, must we not believe he gave us a complete list? If that were his aim, would he have failed to mention other possible ways of attaining the kingdom? That the list is complete and exclusive of other ways into the kingdom may seem proved by the 'woes' or 'miseries' pronounced alongside the 'blesseds' in Saint Luke's version:

> How sad for you who have wealth!
> That's all the comfort you'll have.
> How sad for you who are now well-fed!
> It won't help in the hunger to come.
> How sad for you who are laughing it up now!
> Grief and tears are on their way.
> How sad when everybody says you're wonderful!
> Their fathers said the same about lying prophets.

Are not the wealthy those who fail to be poor, the laughers those who do not mourn, the popular those who are not persecuted?

What could be more plain? If the usual interpretation of Jesus' Beatitudes as directions on how to attain blessedness is correct, you would *have to be* poor, have to mourn, be persecuted and so forth, to be among the blessed. We would therefore expect anyone who seriously accepted this interpretation to seek to become poor, sad, persecuted and so on, but very few people actually do this. Can it be enough just to feel guilty for not doing it?

Not for Today?

So one can easily see why many have decided that the Sermon on the Mount, which opens with the Beatitudes, cannot be meant for today – 'this dispensation' or the present age – but should come into force in the Millennium, or possibly only in the afterlife. Ours is the age of *grace*, they say. Haven't we suffered long to establish this? Because being in the kingdom of God is, on the usual interpretation of the Beatitudes, obviously not a matter of grace but of attaining to special conditions, the present age cannot be the age of the kingdom. That is the thinking of many.[6]

Such an interpretation readily accounts for the fact that among Evangelicals, up until about twenty years ago, one could not teach kingdom principles for present living without being regarded as preaching a mere 'social' gospel. Such a gospel sought to realize the kingdom of God by emphasizing legal and social reforms in line with Christian imperatives. And it was indeed, for all its good intent, a form of 'works salvation' – one that now lives on in the fully secularized 'social ethics' movement. Of course the only salvation in question for it was one from deprivation and suffering in this life.

But to suppose that Jesus' teaching about the kingdom of the heavens is not for today is exactly like holding that the Twenty-third Psalm is not for today. It is true that Jesus' call to the kingdom NOW, just like that psalm, is of such a radical nature, is so utterly subversive of 'life as usual', that anyone who takes it seriously will be under constant temptation to disconnect it from 'normal' human existence. Thus it is that 'The Lord is my Shepherd' is written on many more tombstones than lives.

On the other hand, the clear intent of the New Testament as a whole is that Jesus' teachings are meant to be applied now. For if they are not, neither is the remainder of what the New Testament says about life. You cannot consistently say that the great passages such as Romans 8, 1 Corinthians 13, Colossians 3 and Galatians 5, for example, are for now – as everyone admits – while relegating the Sermon on the Mount and other Gospel passages to the next dispensation or life. This cannot be, simply because they actually say the same things.

They say, for example, 'put on as God's select people, holy and beloved, the inner qualities of mercy, kindness, humbleness of mind, meekness, patience' (Col. 3:12). Or again, 'Love suffers long and is kind. Love does not envy. Love does not exalt itself, is not vain, does not do stupid things, is not acquisitive, is not easily irritated, does not dwell on what is bad. Love is not happy because of evil but rejoices in what is true. Love holds up under anything, has confidence in everything, hopes no matter what and puts up with everything imaginable' (1 Cor. 13:4–7).

The opposition at this point so frequently hypothesized between the teachings of Paul 'for the church age' and those of Jesus for 'another time' simply will not stand scrutiny. If your mind and life really does conform to what is said in Paul's letters, you will find little that is new when you turn to the Sermon on the Mount.

Instead of denying the relevance of Jesus' teachings to the present, we must simply acknowledge that he has been wrongly interpreted. The Beatitudes, in particular, are not the teachings on *how* to be blessed. They are not instructions to do anything. They do not indicate conditions that are especially pleasing to God or good for human beings.

No one is actually being told that they are better off for being poor, for mourning, for being persecuted, and so on, or that the conditions listed are recommended ways to well-being before God or man. Nor are the Beatitudes indications of who will be on top 'after the revolution'. *They are explanations and illustrations, drawn from the immediate setting, of the present availability of the kingdom through personal relationship to Jesus.* They single out cases that provide proof that, in him, the rule of God from the heavens truly is available in life circumstances that are beyond all human hope.

Clues to how we have gone wrong in approaching them lie in what we have already said, but now we must look more closely at *how* Jesus taught, at the strategy of his approach to teaching and learning. Doing this will enable us to return to the Beatitudes with the joy and insight they brought to his first hearers.

The Beatitudes simply cannot be 'good news' if they are understood as a set of 'how-tos' for achieving blessedness. They would then only amount to a new legalism. They would not serve to throw open the kingdom – anything but. They would impose a new brand of Phariseeism, a new way of closing the door – as well as some very gratifying new possibilities for the human engineering of righteousness.

Dealing with the Soul in Depth

Jesus' Manner of Teaching

As already suggested by our reference to 'show and tell', Jesus teaches contextually and concretely, from the immediate surroundings, if possible, or at least from events of ordinary life. This is seen in his well-known use of the parable – which, from its origin in the Greek word *paraballein*, literally means to throw one thing down alongside another. Parables are not just pretty stories that are easy to remember; rather, they help us understand something difficult by comparing it to, placing it beside, something with which we are very familiar, and always something concrete, specific.

Jesus' 'concrete' method of teaching goes far beyond use of parables, however. You see it also in the way in which he capitalizes upon events that happen around him as he goes about his work. On one occasion as he teaches, for example, a man calls out from the crowd, asking him to make his brother divide their inheritance and give him his part so he can start living. Jesus responds with a story about a person who has all the wealth he desires – and yet has nothing (Luke 12).

Another time, his mother and brothers send word through the crowds swarming him that they want to speak to him. He takes the occasion to call attention to the new family under the heavens, pointing out that those who do the will of his Father in the heavens are all brothers and sisters and mothers to him in the kingdom family (Matt. 12).

Still another time, the Passover meal is eaten with his closest disciples. Around the simple elements of bread and wine Jesus conveys the deepest meanings of his death for our new life 'from above': '*This* is my body'; '*This* is my blood' (Matt. 26)

Nothing is more concretely powerful than body and blood.

Teaching to Correct Prevailing Assumptions and Practices

But his use of concreteness in teaching takes yet another form, one absolutely necessary for our understanding of the Beatitudes. This use is found where he corrects a *general* assumption or practice thought to govern the situation at hand. He does this by pointing out that the case before him provides an exception and shows the general assumption or practice to be an unreliable guide to life under God.

Mark, Chapter 10, gives us the familiar story of the 'rich young ruler', which turns out to have interesting implications for the first beatitude in Luke: 'Blessed are the poor'. The common assumption of the time, as in many times since, was that the prosperity of the rich indicated God's special favour. How else could they be rich, since it is, supposedly, God himself who controls the wealth of the earth? But this young man loved his wealth more than he loved God. When faced with the option of continuing to run his business or to serve God, he chose his riches – though with great reluctance.

Jesus then commented to his students on how hard it was for the rich to put themselves under the rule of God, to enter the kingdom. Because of the common assumption that wealth *meant* God's favour, they were stunned. In response to their amazement he went on to explain, 'How hard it is for those who trust wealth to enter the kingdom! A camel can pass through the eye of a needle easier than a rich man can enter the kingdom of God.' But this 'explanation' totally lost them. They were 'astonished out of measure' and muttered to one another, 'Who then *can* be saved?' (v. 26).

It is crucial to note here what Jesus did *not* say. He did not say that the rich cannot enter the kingdom. In fact he said they could – with God's help, which is the only way anyone can do it. Nor did he say that the poor have, on the whole, any advantage over the rich so far as 'being saved' is concerned. By using the case at hand, he simply upset the prevailing general assumption about God and riches. For how *could* God favour a person, however rich, who loves him less than wealth?

So being rich does not mean that one is in God's favour – which further suggests that being poor does not automatically mean one is out of God's favour. The case of the rich young ruler corrects the prevailing assumption, shocking the hearers but making it possible to think more appropriately of God's relation to us.

Don't Have Your Relatives for Dinner?

A striking illustration of this type of teaching is found in Luke 14. Here Jesus is at 'Sunday dinner' in the house of a religious leader. Noting that the host had invited only his kinfolk and well-to-do neighbours, he remarks, 'When you have people in for a meal, don't invite your relatives, friends and wealthy neighbours, who will only pay you back by having you over. Instead, when you have a feast invite the poor, the maimed, the lame and the blind, who cannot pay you back, and you will be paid back when the just are raised from the dead' (vv. 12–14).

Now this may immediately become your favourite verse in the Bible, depending on your relatives! You are plainly told not to have them over for dinner. But do we really need to say that Jesus is not forbidding you to have family members over for dinner – even though he explicitly says we are not to? Some of us might be glad if he did, but that isn't what he is saying.

We are not, then, disobeying him if we have our mother or aunt and uncle or even some financially comfortable neighbour over for dinner. Everything depends on what is in our heart. He simply uses the particular occasion to correct the prevailing practice of neglecting those in real need while we feast with the full who will reciprocate by doing something for us.

He is, on the other hand, most certainly telling us to provide for more than our little circle of mutual appreciation, and thus to place ourselves in the larger context of heaven's rule where we have a different kind of mind and heart regardless of who we do or do not have over for dinner.

The Case of the Good Samaritan

Sometimes several 'techniques of concreteness' come together in one of Jesus' teachings. Thus the *parable*, the *occasion* and the *case* contradicting the prevailing general assumption all come together in the illustration of 'the good Samaritan' (Luke 10).

The occasion here is one in which an expert in the law is testing Jesus' doctrinal correctness and gets caught in his own trap. Having agreed with Jesus that to 'inherit eternal life' you must love your neighbour as you love yourself, he finds that requirement more stringent than he likes.

The 'expert' then, in the manner of experts, tries to wriggle off the hook by raising a quibble-question: 'Who is my neighbour?' That is just the sort of thing 'experts' pride themselves on – a general question that will leave us exactly where we began in practice. He was trying to justify himself because he surely knew that he had not loved his neighbours as he loved himself. But now Jesus has him in the palm of his hand. He will give him and everyone standing by a number of lessons that they will not have to write down or 'capture on tape' to remember.

Of course the words good Samaritan do not occur in the story. For those listening to Jesus, that phrase would have been what we call an 'oxymoron': a combination of words that makes no sense. For the Jews generally, at that time, we could say that 'the only good Samaritan was a dead Samaritan.'

Jesus masterfully develops the story in such a way that the Samaritan slips in towards the end, before the door of the mind can be shut. The Samaritan concretely embodies the answer to the quibble-question about who neighbours are, and he simultaneously blasts aside general assumptions about who 'of course' inherits eternal life.

The story has a man travelling from Jerusalem to Jericho, when bandits grab him, beat him half to death, strip him of everything and leave him in the road. So here is a naked, bleeding man lying in a coma, or at least unable to move, and down the road comes a priest. The priest (a minister?) sees the messy situation and gives it as wide a berth as possible, moving on down the road. Then a Levite (a deacon or trustee?) – perhaps having observed the priest – does exactly the same thing. This fellow wasn't *their* neighbour! They had no responsibility for him. They didn't even know him. And probably they were hurrying to Jerusalem to 'do something religious'. Who could expect them to risk becoming ritually unclean just to help someone?

Such is often the life and thoughts of those who are not destitute of spiritual things – not 'poor in spirit' – but instead are loaded with them.

Now along comes the despised half-breed, the Samaritan. Of the truly spiritual, as any Jew would know, he hasn't a glimmer. *Couldn't* have. But the key to this man – as, indeed, to the priest and the Levite – is his heart. The mere sight of the victim immediately 'filled him with pity.' Of course that made him rush to the poor fellow and give him such immediate first aid as he could.

But he did not stop there and wish him well. Instead he put him on his own donkey, walked him along to a 'motel' and watched over him that day and night. The next day he got the manager to promise to take care of the victim until he recovered. He then left some money with him and assured him that he would cover any further expenses on his return trip.

Now Jesus is really rubbing it in. And yet the story is very true to life. This is one of those cases where, in what might very well be a mere parable, Jesus also could easily be telling a story of something that had actually happened. It is the sort of thing that all of his hearers knew does happen. It is the sort of thing that still happens today.

When Jesus then drives the point home with his question, 'Which of the three was a neighbour to the victim of the crime?' there is only one way any decent person could answer. To quibble further would be to reveal a hopelessly godless heart. So the theological expert manages to reply, 'The neighbour is the one who had mercy on him.' He cannot bring himself to say, 'The Samaritan.'

How to Make a Neighbour

But we must say it, and we must understand what it means. It means that the general assumptions of Jesus' hearers about who has eternal life have to be revised in the light of the condition of people's hearts. The story does not teach that we can have eternal life just by loving our neighbour. We cannot get away with that nice legalism either. The issue of our posture towards God still has to be taken into account. But in God's order nothing can substitute for loving people. And we define who our neighbour is by our love. We make a neighbour of someone by caring for him or her.

So we don't first define a class of people who will be our neighbours and then select only them as the objects of our love – leaving the rest to lie where they fall. Jesus deftly rejects the question 'Who is my neighbour?' and substitutes the only question really relevant here: 'To whom will I be a neighbour?' And he knows that we can only answer this question case by case as we go through our days. In the morning we cannot yet know who our neighbour will be that day. The condition of our hearts will determine who along our path turns out to be our neighbour, and our faith in God will largely determine whom we have strength enough to make our neighbour.

If Jesus were here today, the story would be told differently. The words *good Samaritan* now identify a person of an especially good sort in our society. We even have 'good Samaritan' laws to protect them when they do 'their good deeds'.

To make his point now, Jesus might have to put the 'good Samaritan' in the place of the priest or Levite as he originally told the story. Or if he were in Israel now, he would probably tell a story about the 'good Palestinian'. The Palestinians, on the other hand, would hear about the 'good Israeli'.

In the United States, of course, he would tell us about the 'good Iraqi', 'good Communist', 'good Muslim' and so on. In some quarters it would have to be the good feminist or good homosexual. In yet others the good Christian or good church member would have the appropriate shock value. Indeed, given some current secular attitudes, to speak of the good priest or good deacon might be very effective. All of these break up pet generalizations concerning who most surely is or is not leading the eternal kind of life.

In the story of the good Samaritan, Jesus not only teaches us to help people in need; more deeply, he teaches us that we cannot identify who 'has it', who is 'in' with God, who is 'blessed', by looking at exteriors of any sort. That is a matter of the heart. There alone the kingdom of the heavens and human kingdoms great and small are knit together. Draw any cultural or social line you wish, and God will find his way beyond it. 'Human beings look at the outer appearance, but Jehovah looks on the heart' (1 Sam. 16:7). And 'what humanity highly regards can be sickening to God' (Luke 16:15).

Why Jesus Teaches in This Manner

This 'concrete' or contextual method of teaching is obviously very different from how we attempt to teach and learn today, and the difference makes it difficult for us to grasp what precisely it is that Jesus is teaching. What he is saying cannot be understood unless we appreciate how he teaches, and we cannot appreciate how he teaches unless we take into account something of the world within which his teaching occurred.

We must recognize, first of all, that the aim of the popular teacher in Jesus' time was not to impart information, but to make a significant change in the lives of the hearers. Of course that may require an information transfer, but it is a peculiarly modern notion that the aim of teaching is to bring people to know things that may have no effect at all on their lives.

In our day learners usually think of themselves as containers of some sort, with a purely passive space to be filled by the information the teacher possesses and wishes to transfer – the 'from jug to mug model'. The teacher is to fill in empty parts of the receptacle with 'truth' that may or may not later make some difference to the life of the one who has it. The teacher must get the information *into* them. We then 'test' the patients to see if they 'got it' by checking whether they can *reproduce* it in language rather than watching how they live.

Thus if we today were invited to hear the Sermon on the Mount – or, more likely now, the 'Seminar at the Sheraton' – we would show up with notebooks, pens and tape recorders. We would be astonished to find the disciples 'just listening' to Jesus and would look around to see if someone was taping it to make sure that everyone could 'get it all' if they wanted to.

Working our way through the crowd to the right-hand man, Peter, we might ask where the conference notebooks and other material were and be further astonished when he only says, 'Just listen!' Perhaps we push the 'record' button as we sit down, thankful that we at least will have captured all the spiritual information – if the batteries aren't dead or the tape doesn't stick.

The situation of teacher/learner was really so different in Jesus' day that we can hardly picture it to ourselves. Writing was not all that uncommon, but it was not really an option for someone trying to 'get' what a teacher was saying. And then it is simply a fact that no value was placed on mere 'information' as we know it today.

Of course information relevant to a real need has always been prized. But to want merely to 'know stuff' such as we usually get today out of a high school and college education would have been thought laughable – if it could have been thought at all. 'Trivial Pursuit' certainly never would have caught on as a game back then. (And a thoughtful person today might well wonder about a society in which it could catch on as the educational system is near a state of collapse. But that is another story!)

The teacher in Jesus' time – and especially the religious teacher – taught in such a way that he would impact the life flow of the hearer, leaving a lasting impression without benefit of notes, recorders or even memorization. Whatever did not make a difference in that way just made no difference. Period. And, of course, this is true to the laws of the mind and self.

I recall with perfect clarity where I was and what I was doing when I heard that John Kennedy had been shot. My brother Duane and I were playing basketball with other students in the old gymnasium at the University of Wisconsin in Madison. We had just finished a game and were walking off the court. I remember exactly which corner of the gym and which way I was facing the instant I heard. I never wrote it down, and I never memorized it. Millions of people today can make a similar report on their own experience of this event.

We automatically remember what makes a real difference in our life. The secret of the great teacher is to speak words, to foster experiences, that impact the active flow of the hearer's life. That is what Jesus did by the way he taught. He tied his teachings to concrete events that make up the hearers' lives. He aimed his sayings at their hearts and habits as these were revealed in their daily lives.

He still takes us today in the fullness of our flight, moving right along, assuming our assumptions, and he gently but firmly lets the air out of our balloon. And as he does so, we don't have to try to 'get it' and remember it. It has stuck in our life, whether we want it or agree with it or not. We will eventually have to come to terms with it somehow. The parables, the incidents, the cases where our guiding generalization about 'how things are' just won't fit, sit in our minds and go off like the 'tiny time capsules' of popular medications. The master teacher has done his work – or rather, keeps on doing his work.

Jesus not only taught in this manner; he also taught his students in the kingdom to teach in the same way – using, of course, a parable. 'So every bible scholar who is trained in the kingdom of the heavens is like someone over a household that shows from his treasures things new and things old' (Matt. 13:52 REV). By showing to others the presence of the kingdom in the concrete details of our shared existence, we impact the lives and hearts of our hearers, not just their heads. And they won't have to write it down to hold on to it.

What Jesus Really Had in Mind with His Beatitudes

A Look at Luke's Version of the Beatitudes

Armed, now, with this understanding of the manner in which Jesus teaches, let us return to the Beatitudes – and this time to Luke's version, which seems more relentless and harder to 'pretty up' than Matthew's, and where 'blesseds' also are accompanied by the very uncompromising 'woes' referred to earlier.

The setting here is somewhat different from that recorded in Matthew. It seems to me we are not dealing with a different record of the same sermon, though many of the same topics are treated.[7] Here Jesus has just spent all night out in the hills in prayer, preparing to appoint twelve of his students to be his special emissaries, or 'apostles,' to world history.

Early in the morning he calls the disciples to him and names the twelve 'winners'. Then they go together down to a plain where 'great numbers of people' from all quarters had gathered 'to listen to him, and to be cured of their diseases … and everyone in the crowd was trying to touch him, because power went out from him and cured them all' (6:17–19 REV).

In this familiar context he turns to his students and lists four groups of people who are blessed as God's provisions from the heavens come upon them.

The poor.
The hungry.
The grief-stricken.
Those hated and hurt because of associating with Jesus.

These are, once again, precisely people from the crowd surrounding him. Truly it would be difficult to make these kinds of people look good. I have yet to find anyone attempting to translate the first beatitude of Luke as 'Blessed are those who think they are poor.' Yet of course, as church history shows, there have been many who have taught that poverty, misery and martyrdom are meritorious conditions that somehow make you holy and justify blessedness from God.

Just as plainly, however, there have been multitudes who have been poor, hungry and grief-stricken, and who have remained as ungodly as sin itself – appropriate compassion for them notwithstanding. There have also been many who because of reproach for Jesus' sake have rejected him and have filled their lives with bitterness against God and man. They are anything but blessed.

These are things that we all know to be true. 'Though I bestow all my goods to feed the poor,' Paul points out, 'and though I give my body to be burned, and fail to love as God does, it is of no gain to me.' So whatever the point of the Beatitudes, it cannot be that they state conditions that guarantee God's approval, salvation or blessing.

Similarly, unless we suffer from a remarkably restricted range of acquaintances, we all know that there are people who please God and have his blessing *without* being poor, hungry, grief-stricken or persecuted. They trust Jesus with all their heart, and they love and serve their neighbours and others in his name. Their hearts are full of peace and joy in believing, and they 'do justice, love mercy and walk humbly with their God.' Only those blinded by their prior commitments can continue to insist that it is necessary to be on this list of 'blesseds' in order to live under the blessing of God.

The Beatitudes as Kingdom Proclamation

What then does Jesus say to us with his Beatitudes? How are we to live in response to them? That is the question we asked at the outset of this chapter, and it is now time to answer it.

We have already indicated the key to understanding the Beatitudes. They serve to clarify Jesus' fundamental message: the free availability of God's rule and righteousness to all of humanity through reliance upon Jesus himself, the person now loose in the world among us. They do this simply by taking those who, from the human point of view, are regarded as most hopeless, most beyond all possibility of God's blessing or even interest, and exhibiting them as enjoying God's touch and abundant provision from the heavens.

This fact of God's care and provision proves to all that no human condition excludes blessedness, that God may come to any person with his care and deliverance. God does sometimes help those who cannot, or perhaps just do not, help themselves. (So much for another well-known generalization!) The religious system of his day left the multitudes out, but Jesus welcomed them all into his kingdom. Anyone could come as well as any other. They still can. That is the gospel of the Beatitudes.

Just look at the list of the 'written off', of the 'sat upon, spat upon, ratted on'. It is interesting that Simon and Garfunkel got Jesus' point in their old song, even though many of us 'scribes' miss it. We have already considered the spiritually bankrupt or deprived.

Now we pass on to those who mourn. Luke refers to them as 'the weeping ones' (6:21): men or women whose mates have just deserted them, leaving them paralysed by rejection, for example; a parent in gut-wrenching grief and depression over the death of a little daughter; people in the sunset of their employable years who have lost their careers or businesses or life savings because of an 'economic downturn' or the takeover of the company in which they had invested themselves. So many things to break the heart! But as they see the kingdom in Jesus, enter it and learn to live in it, they find comfort and their tears turn to laughter. Yes, they are even better off than they were before their particular disaster.

Then there are the meek. ('Blessed are the meek: for they shall inherit the earth.') These are the shy ones, the intimidated, the mild, the unassertive. They step off the sidewalk to let others pass as if it were only right, and if something goes wrong around them, they automatically feel it must have something to do with them. When others step forward and speak up, they shrink back, their vocal chords perhaps moving but producing no sound. They do not assert their legitimate claims unless driven into a corner and then usually with ineffectual rage. But as the kingdom of the heavens enfolds them, the whole earth is their Father's – and theirs as they need it. The Lord is their shepherd, they shall not want.

Next are those who burn with desire for things to be made right. ('Blessed are they which do hunger and thirst after righteousness: for they shall be filled.') It may be that the wrong is in themselves. Perhaps they have failed so badly that night and day they cringe before their own sin and inwardly scream to be made pure. Or it may be that they have been severely wronged, suffered some terrible injustice, and they are consumed with longing to see the injury set right – like parents who learn that the murderer of their child has been quickly released from prison and is laughing at them. Yet the kingdom of the heavens has a chemistry that can transform even the past and make the terrible, irretrievable losses that human beings experience seem insignificant in the greatness of God. He restores our soul and fills us with the goodness of rightness.

The merciful are here also. ('Blessed are the merciful: for they shall obtain mercy.') The worldly wise will, of course, say, 'Woe to the merciful, for they shall be taken advantage of.' And outside heaven's rule there is nothing more true. My mother and father went bankrupt and lost their clothing business in the early 1930s, just before I was born. Those were depression years, and they simply could not make people pay for what they needed. Clothing was given 'on credit' when it was clear there would be no payment.

A familiar story, no doubt. The merciful are always despised by those who know how to 'take care of business'. Yet outside the human order, under the great profusion of heaven's goodness, they themselves find mercy to meet their needs, far beyond any 'claim' they might have on God.

And then there are the pure in heart, the ones for whom nothing is good enough, not even themselves. ('Blessed are the pure in heart: for they shall see God.') These are the perfectionists. They are a pain to everyone, themselves most of all. In religion they will certainly find errors in *your* doctrine, your practice and probably your heart and your attitude. They may be even harder on themselves.

They endlessly pick over their own motivations. They wanted Jesus to wash his hands even though they were not dirty and called him a glutton and a wine-biber.

Their food is never cooked right; their clothes and hair are always unsatisfactory; they can tell you what is wrong with everything. How miserable they are! And yet the kingdom is even open to them, and there at last they will find something that satisfies their pure heart. *They will see God*. And when they do they will find what they have been looking for, someone who is truly good enough.

The peacemakers are here too. ('Blessed are the peacemakers: for they shall be called the children of God.') They make the list because outside the kingdom they are, as is often said, 'called everything *but* a child of God.' That is because they are always in the middle. Ask the policeman called in to smooth out a domestic dispute. There is no situation more dangerous. Neither side trusts you. Because they know that you are looking at both sides, you can't possibly be on their side.

But under God's rule there is recognition that in bringing good to people who are in the wrong (as both sides usually are) you show the divine family resemblance, 'because God himself is kind to the ungrateful and the wicked' (Luke 6:35 REB). The peacemaker deals precisely with the ungrateful and the wicked, as anyone who has tried it well knows.

And then we have those who are attacked because of their stand for what is right. ('Blessed are they which are persecuted for righteousness' sake: for theirs is the kingdom of heaven.') These often not only suffer momentary harassment, but see their lives ruined or are killed simply for refusing to be compliant with what is wrong.

Laws are sometimes passed to protect 'whistle-blowers' in certain cases, but what the law can protect you from falls far short of the damage that is often done. Most of what is wrong in human affairs simply can't be dealt with by law. It is a terrible position to be in. Yet these, too, can be possessed by the kingdom of the heavens, and when they are, that is enough to allow them to enjoy a blessed life. They experience an unshakable security in which they cannot be harmed.

Finally we see those insulted, persecuted and lied about because they have 'gone off their rocker and taken up with that Jesus.' That is certainly how his disciples were viewed at the time. 'They actually think this carpenter from Hicksville is the one sent to save the world!' It is almost impossible for anyone who has not received this sort of treatment to understand how degrading it is.

From the human point of view, this may be the position most removed from God's blessing, because you are, in the eyes of surrounding society, precisely offending against God. Thus, when they kill you they think they are doing God a favour (John 16:2). Yet, Jesus says, jump for joy when this happens, from the knowledge that even now you have a great and imperishable reward in God's world, in the heavens. Your reputation stands high before God the Father and his eternal family, whose companionship and love and resources are now and forever your inheritance.

Sometimes I am told that the reading of the Beatitudes given here works well for all except the ones about hungering and thirsting for righteousness and being pure of heart. But if the old 'engineering' or legalistic interpretation is wrong, it is wrong for these as well. It is unlikely to the extreme that Jesus would have been doing one thing with the remainder of his Beatitudes and then switch back for these two alone. Moreover, I believe the reading I have given of these two is inherently credible once you consider the various permissible translations of terms like *dikaiosunen* (v. 6) and *hoi katharoi te kardia* (v. 8).

Beatitude under the Personal Ministry of Jesus

Thus by proclaiming blessed those who in the human order are thought hopeless, and by pronouncing woes over those human beings regarded as well off, Jesus opens the kingdom of the heavens to everyone.

Two other well-known scenes from Jesus' life emphasize the connection of the Beatitudes to the life and ministry of Jesus.

The first is from his visit back to his hometown of Nazareth riding the wave of popularity that greeted his entrance into public life. His growing fame went before him, and at the Sabbath gathering he indicated his desire to read and comment on scripture, as was commonly done.

He read from the prophet Isaiah: 'The Spirit of the Lord is upon me. For he has anointed me to proclaim good news to the poor. He has sent me to announce that captives are released, that the blind have their sight, that the oppressed are empowered, and that this is a time when the Lord's favours are open to people' (Luke 4:18–19). He then let his townspeople know that he was the very one through whom these blessings would come to them.

Their response was violent. They tried to kill him because they understood clearly that he was claiming to be God's anointed leader, whereas they knew him to be only 'Joseph's son', the carpenter, who had worked for wages from many of those present.

But notice who is among those listed by Jesus using the words of the prophet: the poor, the captives, the blind and the oppressed. Clearly this is the same type of list found in the Beatitudes of both Matthew and Luke. It is a list of people humanly regarded as lost causes, but who yet, at the hand of Jesus, come to know the blessing of the kingdom of the heavens.

The second scene comes later in his ministry. John the Baptizer has been in prison for some time now but has been following Jesus' work from his cell. John had all along been very limited in his understanding of Jesus. It was not his job to understand him. But he became increasingly concerned when Jesus did not do what any red-blooded Messiah would surely do: take the government in hand and set the world right. So he finally sends his own disciples to ask directly whether he, Jesus, is the one supposed to come, the one with the anointing, or whether they should expect someone else.

Jesus directed John's students simply to report back to him what they had heard and seen around Jesus: 'The blind see, the lame walk, lepers are made clean, the deaf hear, the dead are revived and the poor hear some real good news.' Then he added, in beatitude language, 'And blessed are those who are not disappointed with me' (Matt. 11:4–6).

The word here translated 'blessed,' *makarios*, is the same as that used in Matthew 5 and Luke 6. It refers to the highest type of well-being possible for human beings, but it is also the term the Greeks used for the kind of blissful existence characteristic of the gods. More important, however, note here the list of 'hopeless cases' that are blessed through the sufficiency of God to meet them in their appalling need. The personal ministry of Jesus from his present kingdom brings them beatitude.

Indeed, such transformation of status for the lowly, the humanly hopeless, as they experience the hand of God reaching into their situation, is possibly the most pervasive theme of the biblical writings. Certainly it is a major component of the great inversion discussed in our previous chapter.

Some of the more significant passages stressing the transformation of status under God are the 'Song of Moses and Miriam' in Exodus 15, the prayer of Hannah in 1 Samuel 2, the story of David and Goliath in 1 Samuel 17, Jehoshaphat's prayer and battle in 2 Chronicles 20 and the 'magnificat' of the virgin Mary in Luke 1. Psalms 34, 37, 107 and others celebrate this theme of God's hand lifting up those cast down and casting down those lifted up in the human scheme. The reigning of God over life is the good news of the whole Bible: 'How beautiful upon the mountains are the feet of him who brings good tidings, who publishes peace, who brings good tidings of well-being, who publishes salvation, who says to Zion, "Your God reigns!"' (Isa. 52:7).

It is precisely this God-based inversion that Jesus expresses in his oft-repeated sayings about the reversal of the 'firsts' and 'lasts.' No doubt the initial response of most of us when we hear about God's care for us is that he is going to secure the various projects that we have our hearts set upon. In the setting of the 'rich young ruler' story discussed earlier, Peter pointed out to Jesus that he and the other disciples had, unlike that wealthy young man, left everything to follow him. 'What will we get for this?' he wanted to know.

Jesus replied that they would be rewarded in this life many times over for all their sacrifices and given eternal life in the world to come. 'But,' he added, 'many who are first shall be last, and the last shall be first' (Mark 10:31). He knew that much of what Peter and the others thought to be important was not really so, and that what they thought to be of no importance was often of great significance before God. Their thinking would have to be rearranged before they could understand their 'reward' for leaving all to follow him. So he adds his 'reversal' formula to help them keep thinking.

In general, many of those thought blessed or 'first' in human terms are miserable or 'last' in God's terms, and many of those regarded as cursed or 'last' in human terms may well be blessed or 'first' in God's terms, as they rely on the kingdom of Jesus. Many, but not necessarily *all*. The Beatitudes are lists of human 'lasts' who at the individualized touch of the heavens become divine 'firsts'. The gospel of the kingdom is that no one is beyond beatitude, because the rule of God from the heavens is available to all. Everyone can reach it, and it can reach everyone. We respond appropriately to the Beatitudes of Jesus by living as if this were so, as it concerns others and as it concerns ourselves.

Making This Message Personal to Us Today

And on Your List of the Blessed?

You are really walking in the good news of the kingdom if you can go with confidence to any of the hopeless people around you and effortlessly convey assurance that they can now enter a blessed life with God.

Who would be on your list of 'hopeless blessables' as found in today's world? Certainly all of those on Jesus' lists, for though they are merely illustrative, they also are timeless. But can we, following his lead as a teacher, concretize the gospel even more for those around us? Who would you regard as the most unfortunate people around you?

A Silly Side of Salvation?

There is, first of all, a silly side to this question – which turns suddenly sombre. If you look at advertising and current events in the print and other media – for example, as you encounter them in supermarket checkouts, newsagents and bookshops or on television and radio – you might think that the most unfortunate people in the world today are the fat, the misshapen, the bald, the ugly, the old and those not relentlessly engaged in romance, sex and fashionably equipped physical activities.

The sad truth is that many people around us, and especially people in their teens and young adulthood, drift into a life in which being thin and correctly shaped, having 'glorious' hair, appearing youthful and so forth, are the only terms of blessedness or woe for their existence. It is all they know. They have heard nothing else. Many people today really are in this position.

If you judge from what they devote time and effort to, you have the stark realization that to be fat, have thinning hair or a bad complexion, be wrinkled or flabby, is experienced by them as unconditional personal condemnation. They find themselves beyond the limits of human acceptability. This is a fact about them, regardless of how silly it may seem. To say, 'How silly of you!' is not exactly to bring Jesus' good news of the kingdom to them.

Instead, Jesus took time in his teaching to point out the natural beauty of every human being. He calls attention to how the most glamorous person you know ('Solomon in all his splendour') is not as ravishingly beautiful as a simple field flower. Just place a daffodil side-by-side with anyone at the president's inaugural ball or at the motion-picture Academy Awards, and you will see. But the abundant life of the kingdom flowing through us makes us of greater natural beauty than the plants. 'God who makes the grass so beautiful – here today and tomorrow burned for fuel – will clothe you 'mini-faiths' even more beautifully' (Matt. 6:30).

This is the gospel for a silly world, all the more needed because the silly is made a matter of life and death for many. Sin, for that matter, is silly. If the kingdom did not reach us in our silliness who would be saved? Lostness does not have to wear a stuffed shirt to find redemption.

So we must see from our heart that:

> Blessed are the physically repulsive,
> Blessed are those who smell bad,
> The twisted, misshapen, deformed,

The too big, too little, too loud,
The bald, the fat and the old –
For they are all riotously celebrated in the party of Jesus.

And the More Serious Side

Then there are the 'seriously' crushed ones: The flunk-outs and drop-outs and burned-outs. The broke and broken. The drug heads and the divorced. The HIV-positive and herpes-ridden. The brain-damaged, the incurably ill. The barren and the pregnant too-many-times or at the wrong time. The overemployed, the underemployed, the unemployed. The unemployable. The swindled, the shoved aside, the replaced. The parents with children living on the street, the children with parents not dying in the 'rest' home. The lonely, the incompetent, the stupid. The emotionally starved or emotionally dead. And on and on and on. Is it true that 'Earth has no sorrow that heaven cannot heal?'[8] It is true! That is precisely the gospel of heaven's availability that comes to us through the Beatitudes. And you don't have to wait until you're dead. Jesus offers to all such people as these the present blessedness of the present kingdom – regardless of circumstances. The condition of life sought for by human beings through the ages is attained in the quietly transforming friendship of Jesus.

And the Immoral

Even the moral disasters will be received by God as they come to rely on Jesus, count on him, and make him their companion in his kingdom. Murderers and child-molesters. The brutal and the bigoted. Drug lords and pornographers. War criminals and sadists. Terrorists. The perverted and the filthy and the filthy rich. The David Berkowitzs ('Son of Sam'), Jeffrey Dahmers and Colonel Noriegas.

Can't we feel some sympathy for Jesus' contemporaries, who huffed at him, 'This man is cordial to sinners, and even eats with them!' Sometimes I feel I don't really want the kingdom to be open to such people. But it is. That is the heart of God. And, as Jonah learned from his experience preaching to those wretched Ninevites, we can't shrink him down to our size.

In Paul's first letter to the church at Corinth, he gives an awesome list of those who, continuing in their evil, cannot 'inherit the kingdom': 'fornicators, idolaters, adulterers, male prostitutes, active homosexuals, thieves, the greedy, drunkards, slanderers and swindlers' (6:10). Then he adds, 'And such were some of you, but you were cleansed, made holy and justified in the name of the Lord Jesus Christ and by the Spirit of our God.'

If I, as a recovering sinner myself, accept Jesus' good news, I can go to the mass murderer and say, 'You can be blessed in the kingdom of the heavens. There is forgiveness that knows no limits.' To the pederast and the perpetrator of incest. To the worshipper of Satan. To those who rob the aged and weak. To the cheat and the liar, the bloodsucker and the vengeful: Blessed! Blessed! Blessed! As they flee into the arms of The Kingdom Among Us.

These are God's grubby people. In their midst a Corrie Ten Boom takes the hand of the Nazi who killed her family members. The scene is strictly not of this earth. Any spiritually healthy congregation of believers in Jesus will more or less look like these 'brands plucked from the burning'. If the group is totally nice, that is a sure sign something has gone wrong. For here are the foolish, weak, lowly and despised of this world, whom God has chosen to cancel out the humanly great (1 Cor. 1:26–31; 6). Among them there indeed are a few of the humanly wise, the influential and the socially elite. They belong here too. God is not disturbed by them. But the Beatitudes is not even a list of spiritual giants. Often you will discern a peculiar nobility and glory on and among these 'blessed' ones. But it is not from them. It is the effulgence of the kingdom among them.

These Are to Be the Salt of the Earth, Light of the World

Speaking to these common people, 'the multitudes', who through him had found blessing in the kingdom, Jesus tells them it is they, not the 'best and brightest' on the human scale, who are to make life on earth manageable as they live from the kingdom (Matt. 5:13–16). God gives them 'light' – truth, love and power – that they might be the light for their surroundings. He makes them 'salt', to cleanse, preserve and flavour the times through which they live.

These 'little' people, without any of the character or qualifications humans insist are necessary, are the only ones who can actually make the world work. It is how things are among them that determines the character of every age and place. And God gives them a certain radiance, as one lights a lamp to shed its brilliance over everyone in the house. Just so, Jesus says to those he has touched, 'Let your light glow around people in such a way that, seeing your good works, they will exalt your Father in the heavens' (Matt. 5:16).

The complete obliteration of social and cultural distinctions as a *basis* for life under God was clearly understood by Paul as essential to the presence of Jesus in his people. It means nothing less than *a new type of humanity*, 'Abraham's seed'. Those who, in Paul's language, have 'put on Christ' make nothing of the distinctions between Jew and Greek, between slave and free, between male and female. If they 'are Christ's', they inherit life in the kingdom, just as Abraham did through his faith (Gal. 3).

In a parallel statement to the disciples in Colossae, Paul says that in the new humanity, whose knowledge of reality conforms to the viewpoint of the Creator, no distinction is drawn between Greek and Jew, between those who are circumcised and those who are not, barbarian, Scythian, slave or free, because the Christ in each one is the only thing that matters (Col. 3:10–11).

Inclusion of the Scythian here is instructive and should be understood to refer to the very lowest possibility of humanity. The Scythian was the barbarian's barbarian, thought of as an utterly brutal savage – largely because he was. Yet, 'Blessed are the Scythians.' They are as blessable in the kingdom as the most proper Jew or Greek.

Paul's policy with regard to the redemptive community simply followed the gospel of the Beatitudes. He refused to base anything on excellence of speech, understanding and culture *as attainments of human beings*. Rather, in building the work of God he would disregard everything in the new humankind but what came from Jesus in his crucifixion and beyond: 'I resolved to regard nothing in your midst except Jesus Christ and him crucified' (1 Cor. 2:2). Or, as he says in 2 Corinthians 5:16–17, 'From now on we disregard all common human distinctions between people, and even though we have known Christ in human terms, we no longer do so. So if anyone is "in Christ" they are a new type of creation, where the old categories drop away and the individual emerges in a new order.'

Surely it is this radically revolutionary outlook that explains why Jesus, in completing his statement on the 'blesseds' and God's government in Matthew 5, finds it necessary to caution, 'Don't think I have come to abolish the Law and the Prophets' – that is, to abolish the entire established order as far as his hearers were concerned.

Obviously he had to say this because that is precisely what his hearers were thinking! They could think nothing else! They had not heard just another powerless list of legalisms, however pretty, and they knew it. They had heard an upside down world being set right-side up.

The Law and the Prophets had been twisted around to authorize an oppressive, though religious, social order that put glittering humans – the rich, the educated, the 'well-born', the popular, the powerful and so on – in possession of God. Jesus' proclamation clearly dumped them out of their privileged position and raised ordinary people with no human qualifications into the divine fellowship by faith in Jesus.

That is a powerful message, enough to thoroughly confuse a simple people who lived with their noses to the grindstone and knew no order other than the one imposed upon them by religious experts zealously defending their own privileges. So Jesus cautions them to respect the law – to fulfil it, not abolish it – as he then moves on, in Matt. 5:20 and following, to where he will explain what the law really means for human life under God. Exactly how they are to respect the law and move beyond the righteousness of the scribes and the Pharisees we shall see in the next chapter.

Chapter 5

THE RIGHTNESS OF THE KINGDOM HEART: BEYOND THE GOODNESS OF SCRIBES AND PHARISEES

No good tree produces bad fruit, nor any bad tree good fruit … The good person, from the good treasured up in his heart, produces what is good.

LUKE 6:43–45

The command 'Be ye perfect' is not idealistic gas. Nor is it a command to do the impossible. He is going to make us into creatures that can obey that command.

C. S. LEWIS, MERE CHRISTIANITY

Master of Moral Understanding

When Jesus deals with moral evil and goodness, he does not begin by theorizing. He plunges immediately (Matt. 5:21–44) into the guts of human existence: raging anger, contempt, hatred, obsessive lust, divorce, verbal manipulation, revenge, slapping, suing, cursing, coercing and begging. It is the stuff of soap operas and the daily news – and real life.

He takes this concrete approach because his aim is to enable people to be good, not just talk about it. He actually knows how to enable people to be good, and he brings his knowledge to bear upon life as it really is, not some intellectualized and sanctified version thereof.

He knows that people deeply hunger to be good but cannot find their way. No one wishes to do evil for its own sake, we just find it unfortunately 'necessary.' We want to be good but are ready to do evil, and we come prepared with lengthy justifications.

Accordingly, John Milton correctly put the words 'Evil be thou my good' in the mouth of Satan. Satan might be able to take what is evil as his direct and ultimate goal just to oppose God. Those words truly are demonic, not human. By contrast, a little girl in Sunday school expressed the human ambiguity well. When asked what a lie is, she replied, 'A lie is an abomination to God and a very present help in time of trouble.'

Having illustrated concretely, in situations of grimy realism (Matt. 5:20–44), what it is like to be a really good person – one who has found the kingdom and is living in its ways – Jesus then proceeds, in the immediately following verses, to give his overall picture of moral fulfilment and beauty in the kingdom of the heavens. It is one of heartfelt love towards all, including those who would be happy if we dropped dead. This love does not consist of acts and projects but is a pervasive condition of vision, joy and love in which we habitually reside. It is a love of the same quality as God's love (Matt. 5:45–48). We are to be 'perfect' or whole as our Father, the one in the heavens, is perfect and whole.

Thus in the span of a few words Jesus moves from bitingly specific reality into the comprehensiveness of theory – a moral theory of great force, fully developed by Christians of later centuries such as Aurelius Augustine, Thomas Aquinas, John Wesley and Dietrich Bonhoeffer. But he never loses sight of the real-life context in which the theory must translate into action, for his purpose is not to give a theory – he can leave that to others – but to start a historical movement.

Historically Profound Moral Understanding

What Jesus had to say about human good and evil was of sufficient depth, power and justification to dominate European culture and its offshoots for two millennia. Nobody even has an idea of what 'Europe' and the 'Western world' would mean apart from Jesus and his words. The historian of morals W. E. H. Lecky describes the teachings of Jesus as 'an agency which all men must now admit to have been, for good or for evil, the most powerful moral lever that has ever been applied to the affairs of man.'[1]

A contemporary historian, Michael Grant, comments,

> The most potent figure, not only in the history of religion, but in world history as a whole, is Jesus Christ: the maker of one of the few revolutions which have lasted. Millions of men and women for century after century have found his life and teaching overwhelmingly significant and moving. And there is ample reason … in this later twentieth century why this should still be so.[2]

Friedrich Nietzsche is usually thought of as a bitter opponent of Jesus. But he clearly saw his indispensable role in the civilization into which Nietzsche himself had been born. He also understood that the modern world had moved off its foundations in the Christian traditions of moral goodness, and that cataclysmic changes were to come because of this. They have come and they are coming.

For over two hundred years now in the Western world, those 'advanced thinkers' referred to by Bishop Butler in our previous chapter have tried to make secularized human nature and intellect, free of any dependence upon Jesus and his teachings, serve as the basis for moral understanding and practice.

Leading figures who still thought of themselves as profoundly Christian, such as Immanuel Kant and G. F. W. Hegel, played a major role in this effort. They developed a version of Christianity that, ironically, did not even require Jesus to have existed. They seriously took this to be an advantage for their works.

What Jesus taught was said by them to be contained in human rationality as such. Today it is more likely to be said that it is contained in 'the human quest for meaning or wholeness.' Moral understanding can, allegedly, be established by careful human thought and experience apart from any historical tradition. But the centuries-long attempt to devise a morality from within merely human resources has now proved itself a failure.

The Talk on the Hill

Before turning directly to Jesus' powerful picture of the kingdom heart in Matthew 5, however, a few misunderstandings must be cleared away.

First, what is now called his Sermon on the Mount (Matt. 5–7) should indeed be read as a sermon, as one unified discourse. To be sure, it is not what might be called a sermon today. Neither was it given in the seclusion of a genuine mountain. It is not 'preachy', of course, and is far too dense in content to function as a sermon in contexts where 'sermons' now occur. It is 'a talk', we would probably say, and one given for the benefit of a large crowd of common folk, who heard it and enjoyed it on gently rolling pastures by the Sea of Galilee.

Now, to say that this passage in the Gospel of Matthew was a sermon or a talk means that it is organized around one purpose and develops along a single line of thought. This is crucial for a correct understanding of what he is saying here. It was a great day in my own life when I came across some words by the old Princeton homileticist A. W. Blackwood, who stated the necessity of reading the Sermon on the Mount *as* a sermon. He had discerned its masterful unity.

At the time, I didn't even think it was *permissible* so to read it. I had been given to understand that the 'sermon' was actually a collection of stray 'sayings' that unknown 'editors" had thrown together as one might throw marbles into a sack. Hence one could only take up the 'sayings' one by one, like marbles or jewels, and ponder what they might mean taken in isolation.

As a result the 'sermon' remained a baffling text to me, as it seems to remain for most scholars to this day. Clarence Bauman opens his study of nineteen radically different and opposed interpretations of it with the statement that it is 'an enigma to the modern conscience.'[3] He goes on to say, 'The Sermon on the Mount is the most important and most controversial biblical text' (p. 3).

The implications of this statement are simply staggering, as Bauman himself recognizes. The most important text is an enigma? That this could be so is deeply revelatory of the condition of the church in the modern world. We are scattered, wandering, and have no clear and comprehensive message for life because our most important text is an enigma. It does not function as the clear guide to life that its author intended.

When taken as independent sayings, the various statements the 'sermon' contains will certainly be regarded as 'laws' dictating what we are to do and not to do. They will then be seen to prescribe impossibilities and, in some cases, to be simply ridiculous. For example, the comment on cutting off your hands or punching out your eyes (Matt. 5:29–30) is most often presented as a *serious* recommendation from Jesus, though not one to be taken literally. (As we shall see later, he was in fact teaching precisely the futility of any such actions. They would make no difference, because true rightness remains a matter of one's heart.)

Why, then, is it important that we understand Matthew 5–7 as one talk or sermon? It is important because, unless we understand it as one discourse, purposively organized by its highly competent speaker, its parts – the particular statements made – will be left at the mercy of whatever whims may strike readers as they contemplate each pearl of wisdom. Their meaning cannot then be governed by the unity of the discourse as a whole. And this is, for the most part, exactly what happens today.

The most constant 'whim' historically, has been the disastrous idea just mentioned: that Jesus is here giving *laws*. For if that is all he is doing, they will certainly be laws that are impossible to keep. The keeping of law turns out to be an inherently self-refuting aim; rather, the inner self must be changed. Trying merely to keep the law is not wholly unlike trying to make an apple tree bear peaches by tying peaches to its branches.

Yes, impossible, one standard reaction now has it. That's what they are – but therefore all the more suited to thoroughly crush human hopes than were the laws of Moses, forcing us to turn to grace for forgiveness. Jesus is presented as more relentless and meaner than Moses. And we have all been subjected to so much well-intentioned meanness that we are prepared to believe it. The holier, the harder, we think. We could hardly be more wrong!

The aim of the sermon – forcefully indicated by its concluding verses – is to help people come to hopeful and realistic terms with their lives here on earth by clarifying, in concrete terms, the nature of the kingdom into which they are now invited by Jesus' call: 'Repent, for life in the kingdom of the heavens is now one of your options.' The separate parts of the discourse are to be interpreted in the light of this single purpose. They are not to be read as one disconnected statement after another. One must discern the overall plan of life within which the separate parts of the discourse make sense.

So, far from being additional *laws* to crush us or show us we can't make it on our own (of course we can't!), the separate parts are distinct perspectives on the sweet life of love and power, of truth and grace, that those who count on Jesus can even now lead in his kingdom. 'The law came by Moses, but grace and truth came through Jesus the Anointed' (John 1:17). His teachings illustrate how those alive in the kingdom can live, through the days and hours of their ordinary existence, on their way to the full world of God.

The Brilliance of Jesus: One Final Look

To prepare us to appreciate the richness and rigor of the Discourse on the Hill, we must return for one final emphasis upon a theme struck at the end of Chapter 3. There we noted a misunderstanding of Jesus that treats him as nice but not very intelligent. That misunderstanding is the death knell of discipleship, for it locates him outside the company of those who have knowledge and therefore deprives us of the practical power of his teachings.

If you play a game of word association today, in almost any setting, you will collect some familiar names around words such as *smart*, *knowledgeable*, *intelligent* and so forth. Einstein, Bill Gates (of Microsoft) and the obligatory rocket scientists, will stand out. But one person who pretty certainly will not come up in this connection is Jesus.

Here is a profoundly significant fact: In our culture, among Christians and non-Christians alike, Jesus Christ is automatically disassociated from brilliance or intellectual capacity. Not one in a thousand will spontaneously think of him in conjunction with words such as *well-informed*, *brilliant* or *smart*.

Far too often he is regarded as hardly conscious. He is looked on as a mere icon, a wraithlike semblance of a man, fit for the role of sacrificial lamb or alienated social critic, perhaps, but little more.

A well-known 'scholarly' picture has him wandering the hills of Palestine, deeply confused about who he was and even about crucial points in his basic topic, the kingdom of the heavens. From time to time he perhaps utters disconnected though profound and vaguely radical irrelevancies, now obscurely preserved in our Gospels.

Would you be able to trust your life to such a person? If this is how he seems to you, are you going to be inclined to become his student? Of course not. We all know that action must be based on knowledge, and we grant the right to lead and teach only to those we believe to know what is real and what is best.

The world has succeeded in opposing intelligence to goodness. A Russian saying speaks of those who are 'stupid to the point of sanctity.' In other words, you have to be really dumb in order to qualify for saintliness. Centuries ago, even, when Dante assigned the title 'master of those who know', he mistakenly gave it to Aristotle, not Jesus, for Jesus is *holy*.

Tertullian, a famous Christian leader of the second and third centuries, asked rhetorically, 'What has Jerusalem to do with Athens, the Church with the Academy, the Christian with the heretic?'[4] The correct answer, he supposed, was, 'Nothing whatsoever.' Devotion to God is independent of human knowledge. Of course, the modern secular outlook rigorously opposes sanctity to intelligence. And today any attempt to combine spirituality or moral purity with great intelligence causes widespread pangs of 'cognitive dissonance'. Mother Teresa, no more than Jesus, is thought of as smart – nice, of course, but not really *smart*. 'Smart' means good at managing how life 'really' is.

For all the vast influence he has exercised on human history, we have to say that Jesus is usually seen as a frankly pathetic individual who lived and still lives on the margins of 'real life'. What lies at the heart of the astonishing disregard of Jesus found in the moment-to-moment existence of multitudes of professing Christians is a simple lack of respect for him. He is not seriously considered or presented as a person of great ability. What, then, can devotion or worship mean, if simple respect is not included in it? Not much.

The picture the ordinary person today has of Jesus' surroundings in his earthly lifetime seems largely determined by what his homeland, Palestine, looked like to famous nineteenth-century tourists such as Mark Twain. Their impressions of Jesus' social setting remains today in the minds of most people. We imagine a desolate land of ruins, perhaps with a few peasants and ignorant villagers, Jesus among them. But there is no truth in this. In fact, his own society should be thought of as the equivalent in its world to Israel's place in the world today.

In Jesus' day Jerusalem was a glorious city, routinely flooded by hundreds of thousands of visitors, including multitudes of brilliant people from all over the 'known' world. It was a cosmopolitan environment, interacting with the entire Roman world and more. What was known and discussed anywhere was known and discussed there. It was in such surroundings that, already as a lad of twelve, he held spellbound for several days some of the best minds in the land. Thankfully, recent archaeological and historical work has done much to give us a correct picture of the rich culture in which Jesus worked and lived, and of which he was a part.[5]

Outlining the 'Sermon'

The brilliance and profundity of Jesus stand out in the overall structure and outline of The Discourse on the Hill, as he forcefully conveys an understanding of human life that actually works. The talk as a whole is given, of course, under the assumption of the availability of the kingdom he proclaimed. Within that framework, the first part of the talk (on the 'blesseds' and the light and salt of the earth) revises prevailing assumptions about human well-being by presenting unlikely kinds of people who in fact found and still find blessedness in the kingdom. We dealt with this part of the sermon in the previous chapter.

The radical shift of perspective with regard to 'the good life' and who has it led Jesus' hearers to begin suspecting that 'the law' was irrelevant to their life in God's world. On the one hand, they were sure that their own lives fell short of the law, and those 'in charge' never let them forget it. But, on the other hand, Jesus had said that blessedness was still theirs in the kingdom. It sounded to them as if Jesus had set the law aside.

However, 'the law' they had in mind and that they rubbed up against every day was not the law of God. It was a contemporary version of religious respectability, very harsh and oppressive in application, that Jesus referred to as 'the goodness of scribes and Pharisees' (5:20). Law as God intended it remains forever essential to the kingdom, and Jesus made it clear to his hearers that his aim is to bring those who follow him into fulfilment of the true law. The fulfilment he had in mind was not for the purpose of making them humanly *acceptable*. That is quite another matter. But fulfilment of God's law is important because the law is good. It is right for human life. And the presence of the kingdom brings us all that is right for human life.

In Matt. 5:20–48, then, we find out precisely what fulfilment of the law would look like in daily life. In this crucial passage, where the rightness of the kingdom heart is most fully displayed, there is a sequence of contrasts between the older teaching about what the good person would do – for example, not murder – and Jesus' picture of the kingdom heart. That heart would live with full tenderness towards everyone it deals with. This passage in Matthew 5 moves from the deepest roots of human evil, burning anger and obsessive desire, to the pinnacle of human fulfilment in *agape*, or divine love. In this way the entire edifice of human corruption is undermined by eliminating its foundations in human personality.

The remainder of the Discourse on the Hill, chapters 6 and 7, then provides a sequence of warnings about practices and attitudes that will deflect us from living from the kingdom. First there is a warning about trying to secure ourselves by depending on realities other than the kingdom: on our religious/moral reputation before human beings (6:1–18) and on material goods or wealth (6:19–34). This is 'the mind of the flesh', which in Romans 8 the apostle Paul called, simply, 'death'. We will deal with these matters in Chapter 6.

Then there is a warning about trying to control others by 'judging', blaming, condemning them. The apostle Paul later contrasted the 'ministry of condemnation' with the 'ministry of the Spirit' or 'ministry of righteousness' (2 Cor. 3:6–10). Jesus was fully aware of the 'ministry' of condemnation and its futility. By contrast, he shows us how we can really help our loved ones and others in 'The Community of Prayerful Love' (the title for Chapter 7).

Finally, Jesus gives us urgent warnings about failing to actually *do* what he calls us to do in his teachings and mentions the specific things that are most likely to trip us up in this regard. Dietrich Bonhoeffer forcefully states, 'The only proper response to this word which Jesus brings with him from eternity is simply to do it.'[6] Remarkably, almost one sixth of the entire Discourse (fifteen of ninety-two verses) is devoted to emphasizing the importance of actually doing what it says. Doing and not just hearing and talking about it is how we know the reality of the kingdom and integrate our life into it. This final section therefore concludes with the well-known images of the wise man who builds his house upon the rock (he is the one *doing* the words of Jesus), as compared to the other man, who does not.

The simple but powerful structure of the Discourse on the Hill can therefore be represented as follows:

1. Background assumption: life in the kingdom through reliance upon Jesus (Matt. 4:17–25; Chapters 1 to 3 of this book are devoted to this topic).
2. It is ordinary people who are the light and salt of the world as they live the blessed life in the kingdom (5:1–20, and Chapter 4 of this book).
3. The kingdom heart of goodness concretely portrayed as the kind of love that is in God (5:21–48, and the present chapter of this book).
4. Warning: against false securities – reputation and wealth (Matt. 6, and Chapter 6 of this book).
5. Warning: against 'condemnation engineering' as a plan for helping people. A call to the community of prayerful love (Matt. 7:1–12, and Chapter 7 of this book).

6. Warnings: about how we may fail actually to do what the Discourse requires, and the effects thereof (7:13–27).

The Sequential Order in the Discourse Must Be Respected

To understand correctly *what* Jesus is teaching us to do in his Discourse, we must keep the *order* of the treatment in mind and recognize its importance. That is what we would naturally expect when we realize that we are hearing from someone who has absolute mastery of the subject matter with which he is dealing and is absolute master of how to present it. The later parts of the Discourse presuppose the earlier parts and simply cannot be understood unless their dependence upon the earlier parts is clearly seen.

For example, receiving the teaching about anger and contempt (5:21–26) depends upon our having received the teaching about our well-being and blessedness. Conversely, having received the teaching about well-being, the teaching about anger and contempt will be recognized as good and right.

Again, if I have been freed from anger, contempt and obsessive desire and am pervaded by the love that is the family resemblance of those alive in the kingdom of the Father, I am freed from the need to secure myself by reputation or wealth. Conversely, if I am not immersed in the reality of this kingdom of love, it will not seem good or right to me to forgo reputation, pride, vanity and wealth, and I will inescapably be driven to pursue them.

If we do not keep the *sequential order* of kingdom life in mind, as Jesus certainly did, it will seem that each new topic in his Discourse is being taken up on its own, with no connection to what has already been dealt with. The Discourse will therefore make little or no sense as a guide to what to do. This is the predicament of those who, for example, from the viewpoint of the current state of their own chaotic souls, look with bewilderment at, say, the 'command' to offer the other cheek for a slapping or to do good to those who hate them. They quite naturally see this as impossible or as something that would make their life wretched. For they are thinking of their life as the one they now have, untouched by the more fundamental parts of Jesus' teaching, given earlier.

The various scenes and situations that Jesus discusses in his Discourse on the Hill are actually *stages* in a progression towards a life of *agape* love. They progressively presuppose that we know where our well-being really lies, that we have laid aside anger and obsessive desire, that we do not try to mislead people to get our way, and so on. Then loving and helping those who hurt us and hate us, for example, will come as a natural progression. Doing so will seem quite right, and we will be able to do so.

A similar point is to be made regarding not performing to be seen, not relying on wealth, not using condemnation to straighten people out, and so on. Taken strictly in the order Jesus presents them they provide the foundation for a practical strategy for becoming the beings God created us to be. We must constantly review and remember them until they form a part of our conscious minds.

The Law and the Soul

The 'Beyond' of Actual Obedience

It is precisely Jesus' grasp of the structure in the human soul that also leads him to deal primarily with the *sources* of wrongdoing and not to focus on actions themselves. He thus avoids the futility, which we have already pointed out, of making law ultimate. Wrong action, he well knew, is not the problem in human existence, though it is constantly taken to be so. It is only a symptom, which from time to time produces vast evils in its own right.

Going to the source of action is a major part of what he has in mind by saying that one must 'go beyond the goodness of scribes and Pharisees.' One must surpass humanly contrived religious respectability 'if one is to mesh their life with the flow of the kingdom of the heavens' (5:20).

True enough, he also meant that we are actually to *do* what the law, as God intended it, says to do. And that too was quite 'beyond' the goodness of the scribes and Pharisees.[7] They talked a lot of law, but they did not keep it. Thus Jesus told his hearers to do what the religious authorities say, 'for they sit in Moses' seat. But beware of doing what they do. They say and do not' (Matt. 23:3).

Now confidence in the Christ is, correctly understood, inseparable from the fulfilling of the law. People came to him on one occasion and asked, 'What shall we do to work the works of God?' (John 6:28). His reply was, 'You do the work of God when you place your confidence in the one he sent.' We would now say, and say correctly, 'Trust Jesus Christ.' But we have already seen in previous chapters how the idea of having faith in Jesus has come to be totally isolated from being his apprentice and learning how to do what he said.

The tragic result of this separation is seen all around us today. What we are looking at in the contemporary Western world is precisely what he himself foretold. We *have* heard him. For almost two millennia we have heard him, as already noted. But we have chosen to not do what he said. He warned that this would make us 'like a silly man who built his house on a sand foundation. The rain poured down, and the rivers and winds beat upon that house, and it collapsed into a total disaster' (Matt. 7:26–27). We today stand in the midst of precisely the disaster he foretold, 'flying upside down' but satisfied to be stoutly preaching against 'works' righteousness.

If people in our Christian fellowships today were to announce that they had decided to keep God's law, we would probably be sceptical and alarmed. We probably would take them aside for counselling and possibly alert other responsible people in the group to keep an eye on them. We would be sure nothing good would come of it. We know that one is not *saved* by keeping the law and can think of no other reason why one should try to do it.

This leaves us caught in a strange inversion of the work of the Judaizing teachers who dogged the footsteps of Paul in New Testament days. As they wanted to add obedience to ritual law to faith in Christ, we want to subtract moral law from faith in Christ. How to combine faith with obedience is surely the essential task of the church as it enters the twenty-first century.

The Centrality of God's True Law to Human Life

The law that God had truly given to Israel was, until the coming of Messiah, the most precious possession of human beings on earth. *That* law consisted of fundamental teachings such as the Ten

Commandments, the 'Hear, O Israel …' of Deuteronomy. 6:4–5, the great passage on neighbour love in Leviticus 19:9–18, and the elaborations and applications of them by the Jewish prophets up to John the Baptizer.

'What great nation is there,' Moses exclaims, 'that has statutes and judgments as righteous as this whole law that I am setting before you today?' (Deut. 4:8). The ancient writers knew well the desperate human problem of knowing how to live, and they recognized the law revealed by Jehovah, Israel's covenant-making God, to be the only real solution to this problem.

God's true law also possessed an inherent beauty in its own right, as an expression of the beautiful mind of God. It is profound truth and therefore precious in its own right. In Psalm 119 and elsewhere, we see how the devotee of the law, Jehovah's precious gift, was ravished by its goodness and power, finding it to be the perfect guide into the blessed life in God. It was a constant delight to the mind and the heart.

We must understand that Jesus, the faithful Son, does not deviate at all from this understanding of the law that is truly God's law. He could easily have written Psalm 119 himself. When asked by an earnest though misguided young man what he should do to receive eternal life, Jesus replies, 'Keep the law' (Mark 10:19). There was no double entendre whatsoever here, as so many 'saving interpretations' would have it. The same response is given to a professional expert in the law who asked the same question in the process of giving Jesus a test for orthodoxy and ability (Luke 10:28).

In both cases, as it turned out, the inquirer wanted to get by with the cut-down and distorted version of the law that dominated their social setting. But this 'righteousness of the scribes and Pharisees', as Jesus called it, was *not* the law of God, as we have indicated. And Jesus, in his firm but gentle way, would not co-operate with their delusions.

When he confronted them with the law that was truly God's, they each in their own way flunked the test they professed to have passed. But this does not in the least detract from the fact that God's law is an unspeakably good and precious thing, and that to live within it is to live the life that is eternal. To be sure, law is not the source of rightness, but it is forever the *course* of rightness.

Accordingly, in his Discourse on the Hill Jesus responds to his hearers' emerging idea that the law is to be abolished (Matt. 5:17) by making the strongest possible statement to the contrary. So long as creation stands, not the least element of the law – not 'one jot or one tittle' of what God intended with it – will be retracted (5:18). This must be, simply because the law is good. It is right. That, and not some sense of his offended dignity, is why God stands behind it.

A time will come in human history when human beings will follow the Ten Commandments and so on as regularly as they now fall to the ground when they step off a roof. They will then be more astonished that someone would lie or steal or covet than they now are when someone will not. The law of God will then be written in their hearts, as the prophets foretold (Jer. 31:33; Heb. 10:16). This is an essential part of the future triumph of Christ and the deliverance of humankind in history and beyond.

From the viewpoint of the kingdom of the heavens or from God's perspective, Jesus points out, those who do the commandments and teach them are the greatest among human beings, whereas those who break the least of the genuine commandments of God and teach others to do so are the worst of human beings (Matt. 5:19).

The law of God marks the movements of God's kingdom, of his own actions and of how that kingdom works. When we keep the law, we step into his ways and drink in his power. Jesus shows us those ways even more fully and leads us into them. 'If you love me,' he said, 'do what I have said. And I will ask the Father and he will give you an additional strengthener, who will never leave you' (John 14:15–16).

The Deeper 'Beyond' from Which Actions Come

But the question is, How can one keep the law? Jesus well knew the answer to this question, and that is why he told those who wanted to know how to work the works of God to put their confidence in the one God had sent (John 6:29). He knew that we cannot keep the law by trying to keep the law. To succeed in keeping the law one must aim at something other and something more. One must aim to become the *kind of person* from whom the deeds of the law naturally flow. The apple tree naturally and easily produces apples because of its inner nature. This is the most crucial thing to remember if we would understand Jesus' picture of the kingdom heart given in the Sermon on the Mount.

And here also lies the fundamental mistake of the scribe and the Pharisee. They focus on the *actions* that the law requires and make elaborate specifications of exactly what those actions are and of the manner in which they are to be done. They also generate immense social pressure to force conformity of action to the law as they interpret it. They are intensely self-conscious about doing the right thing and about being thought to have done the right thing.

But the inner dimensions of their personality, their heart and character, are left to remain contrary to what God has required. That heart will, of course, ultimately triumph over their conscious intentions and arrangements, and they will in fact do what they know to be wrong. Their words, especially, will reveal the contents of their heart (Matt. 12:34). And their need to appear righteous 'before men' (Luke 15:15) then forces them into hypocrisy. Hypocrisy becomes the spirit, or 'yeast', that pervades and colours their entire existence (Luke 12:1).

One can hardly exaggerate the extent to which this deadly 'yeast' infects human relationships all around us. One could wish only religious people were subject to it.

A Lesson from the Dishwasher and the Farmer

In his efforts to help us understand the connection between the inner dimensions of personality and the outward revelations of it in action, and thus build a strategy for becoming the persons God knows we ought to be, Jesus brings lessons from the common knowledge of life, as was his manner (Matt. 13:52).

First from the dishwasher: 'You fine folk,' he says to the religiously proper, 'are in real trouble! Ever so carefully you wipe clean the outside of the cup or dish. But that leaves the inside full of criminality and self-indulgence. When, by contrast, you first scrub the inside of a cup, the outside becomes clean in the process' (Matt. 23:25–26).

It is easy to clean the outside of a cup without washing the inside, but it is hard to wash the inside thoroughly and leave the outside dirty. Washing the inside has as its natural accompaniment the cleansing of the outside. Only a spot here or there may be left.

Another lesson comes from the farmer. It is one that Jesus refers to repeatedly, and others in the New Testament take it up as well. A good tree, he notes, produces good fruit, and a bad tree bad fruit (Luke 6:43–45). His little brother James extends the point by observing that the fig tree does not bear olives, nor a grapevine figs (James 3:12).

Actions do not emerge from nothing. They faithfully reveal what is in the heart, and we can know what is in the heart that they depend upon. Indeed, everyone does know. That is a part of what it is to be a mentally competent human being. The heart is not a mystery at the level of ordinary human interactions. We discern one another quite well.

When we hear the daily litany of evil deeds that comes to us through the media, for example, we all know well enough, if we can stand to think of it, what kind of inner life and character produces those deeds – even though in a certain sense we still may say we 'just can't understand how anyone could do such things.' The same is true of behaviour in the home or at work.

It is the inner life of the soul that we must aim to transform, and then behaviour will naturally and easily follow. But not the reverse. A special term is used in the New Testament to mark the character of the inner life when it is as it should be. This is the term *dikaiosune*.

Dikaiosune

Jesus' account of *dikaiosune*, or of being a really good person, is given in Matt. 5:20–48. We need to stop for a comment on this special term that plays such a large part in the thought world of classical and Hellenistic Greek culture, as well as in the language of the Bible and in the early form of Christianity that emerged to conquer the Greco-Roman world of the second and third centuries.

The human need to know how to live is perennial. It has never been more desperate than it is today, of course – in Los Angeles and New York, in London, Paris and Berlin. But this need is *always* desperate. That is an unalterable part of the human condition. It is especially urgent in times and places where there is social instability. Such instability does not allow us to maintain the illusion that being a good Jones or Catholic or American or Armenian or Jew solves the problem. We have to have something deeper.

The search for something deeper had become a serious intellectual and spiritual project in the Mediterranean world by the fifth century B.C. or even earlier. That search was, in fact, worldwide in scope,[8] but nowhere did it achieve a higher result than in the great prophets of Israel, such as Amos, Micah and Isaiah.

Its first thorough and systematic treatment within the powers of human reason is found in Plato's *Republic*, which would be more accurately translated *The City*. This book is really a study of the human soul and of the condition in which the soul must be in order for human beings to live well and manage to do what is right. The condition required is called, precisely, *dikaiosune* in the *Republic*. This is exactly the term that Jesus centres on in his Discourse on the Hill, as we have it in the Greek language. It is usually translated 'justice' in Plato's texts. But this is, once again, an unfortunate translation, for *dikaiosune* is only indirectly related to what we today understand by justice.

The best translation of *dikaiosune* would be a paraphrase: something like 'what that is about a person that makes him or her really right or good.' For short, we might say 'true inner goodness'. Plato (following Socrates) tries to give a precise and full account of what this true inner goodness is.

In establishing the central term of ethical understanding, Aristotle replaced his teacher Plato's word, *dikaiosune*, with *arete*, usually translated 'virtue'. Historically, Aristotle won the terminological battle, and virtue has, more than any other term, stood through the ages for the heart of human rightness. It represents a combination of skill, wisdom, power and steadfastness for good that makes it very attractive.

The Old Testament book of Proverbs is actually more focused on *arete* than upon *dikaiosune*, and *arete* also occurs in the New Testament writings: for example, in Phil. 4:8 and 2 Pet. 1:3–5. Still, in the Hebrew and New Testament traditions, *dikaiosune* remains preferred. Perhaps this is because it retains a note of emphasis upon relationship of the soul to God, whereas *arete* predominantly stresses human ability and fulfilment by itself. Of course no contemporary ethical expert would be caught dead discussing 'righteousness', though virtue has recently experienced something of a revival in the field.

A couple of centuries after Plato – certainly beginning sometime prior to 285 B.C. – the Old Testament began to be translated into Greek, yielding the text we call the Septuagint. The term *dikaiosune* was used to translate the Hebrew terms *tsedawkaw* and *tsehdek*, usually rendered in English as 'righteousness'. Thus, a great central text of the Old Testament, Gen. 15:6, tells us, 'And Abram believed God, and it was counted to him for *dikaiosune*.' And we see in Isaiah: 'All our *dikaiosune* is like filthy rags' (64:6). And again in Amos: 'But let judgement roll down as water and *dikaiosune* as an impassable flood' (5:24).

As a result, the two greatest traditions of moral reflection in the ancient world are brought together in the term *dikaiosune*. It re-emerges in the teachings of Jesus, three centuries after the creation of the Greek Old Testament, and becomes the central term in the understanding of Christian salvation represented in the New Testament. Indeed, for Paul, the redemptive act of Jesus becomes the key to understanding the very *dikaiosune* of God himself (Rom. 1–8). It is the person of Jesus and his death for us that makes clear what it is about God that makes him 'really good'.

Six Contrasts of the Old and the New Moral Reality

In Matthew, Chapter 5, Jesus works us through six situations in which the goodness that lives from the heart and through The

Kingdom Among Us is contrasted with the old *dikaiosune* focused merely on 'doing the right thing'.

Situation	Old *Dikaiosune*	Kingdom *Dikaiosune*
1. Irritation with ones associates. (vv. 21–26)	No murder.	Intense desire to be of help. No anger or contempt.
2. Sexual attraction. (vv. 27–30)	No intercourse.	No cultivation of lust.
3. Unhappiness with marriage partner. (vv. 31–32)	If you divorce, give 'pink slip'.	No divorce, as then practised.
4. Wanting someone to believe something. (vv. 33–37)	Keep vows or oaths made to convince.	Only say how things are or are not. No verbal manipulation.
5. Being personally injured. (vv. 38–42)	Inflict exactly the same injury on the offender.	Don't harm, but help, the one who has damaged you.
6. Having an enemy. (vv. 43–48)	Hate your enemy.	Love and bless your your enemy, as the heavenly Father does.

And now with the preliminaries about the structure and progress of the Discourse on the Hillside before us, we can begin to immerse ourselves in the substance of Jesus' teachings on the rightness of the kingdom heart. The remainder of this chapter will be devoted to examining each of these situations in depth. Having worked through these contrasts in well-known and frequent life situations, one should be able to see very clearly the kind of inner character or heart that belongs to those whose life truly flows from the kingdom of God.

In the Cauldron of Anger and Contempt

The Primacy of Anger in the Order of Evil

The first illustration of kingdom *dikaiosune* is drawn from cases in which we are displeased with our 'brother' and may allow ourselves to treat him with anger or contempt.

When we trace wrongdoing back to its roots in the human heart, we find that in the overwhelming number of cases it involves some form of anger. Close beside anger you will find its twin brother, contempt. Jesus' understanding of them and their role in life becomes the basis of his strategy for establishing kingdom goodness. It is the elimination of anger and contempt that he presents as the first and fundamental step towards the rightness of the kingdom heart.

Pointing to the moral inadequacy of the commandment not to kill as a guide to relationships with others who anger us, Jesus goes deeper, and yet deeper, into the texture of human personality: 'But what I say is that anyone who becomes intensely angry [*orgizomenos*] with those around them shall stand condemned before the law' (5:22). He uses exactly the same phrase, 'shall stand condemned before the law', to apply to anger as the old teaching applied to murder.

What Anger Is

And when we look carefully at anger we can see why such a strong statement is justified. In its simplest form, anger is a spontaneous response that has a vital function in life. As such, it is not wrong. It is a *feeling* that seizes us in our body and immediately impels us towards interfering with, and possibly even harming, those who have thwarted our will and interfered with our life.

Indeed, anger is in its own right – quite apart from 'acting it out' and further consequences – an injury to others. When I discover your anger at me, I am *already* wounded. Your anger alone will very likely be enough to stop me or make me change my course, and it will also raise the stress level of everyone around us. It may also evoke my anger in return. Usually it does, precisely because your anger places a restraint on me. It crosses my will. Thus anger feeds on anger. The primary function of anger in life is to alert me to an obstruction to my will, and immediately raise alarm and resistance, before I even have time to think about it.

And if that were all there was to anger, all would be well. Anger in this sense is no sin, even though it is still better avoided where possible. (Headaches are no sin, but do we really need them?) Anger would then perform its vital function, as physical pain does, and pass with the occasion. But the anger that is a reality among us is much more than this and quickly turns into something that is inherently evil.

To understand why, we need to take a still closer look at what anger is. It is primarily a function of the human will, and this in several respects. It spontaneously arises in us, as just noted, when our will is obstructed. That is what occasions it. But as a response towards those who have interfered with us, it includes a will to harm them, or the beginnings thereof. Some degree of malice is contained in every degree of anger.[9] That is why it always hurts us when someone is angry at us.

Consequently, we would not choose to have others angry at us unless some ulterior end were to be gained by it. We know that people who are angry at us will our harm, and by just their look (or refusal to look) or the raising of their voice (or not speaking at all) they *intend* to make a painful impression on us. They certainly succeed.

Anger and the Wounded Ego

But it is a third possible involvement of the will in anger that makes it so deadly as to deserve the censure Jesus places upon it. We can and usually do choose or will *to be* angry. Anger first arises spontaneously. But we can actively receive it and decide to indulge it, and we usually do. We may even become an angry person, and any incident can evoke from us a torrent of rage that is kept in constant readiness.

This is actually the case with those who are caught up in the current epidemic of 'road rage'. The explosion of anger *never* simply comes from the incident. Most people carry a supply of anger around with them. Perhaps it comes along with that 'quiet desperation' that, according to Henry David Thoreau, characterizes the life of most people. Increasingly, now, the desperation is not so quiet.

But why, one might ask, would people embrace anger and indulge it? Why would they, as they do so often, bloat their bodies with anger or wear it like a badge of honour while it radiates real and potential harm, not only to its proper object, the one who thwarted their will in the first place, but to others standing by – often with deadly effects on their own life and health and happiness? It is well established today that many people are killed by their own anger.[10] Untold many others die of second-hand anger, like second-hand smoke. In Los Angeles and other cities, hardly a week goes by without the death of a child from bullets fired at others in anger.

The answer to this question of why people embrace anger and cultivate it is one we must not miss if we are to understand the ways of the human heart. Anger indulged, instead of simply waved off, always has in it an element of self-righteousness and vanity. Find a person who has embraced anger, and you find a person with a wounded ego.

The importance of the self and the real or imaginary wound done to it is blown out of all proportion by those who indulge anger. Then anger can become anything from a low-burning resentment to a holy crusade to inflict harm on the one who has thwarted me or my wishes or bruised my sense of propriety. It may explode on anything and anyone within reach. I may become addicted to the adrenaline rush and never feel really alive except when my anger is pumping.

Only this element of self-righteousness can support me as I retain my anger long after the occasion of it or allow its intensity to heat to the point of totally senseless rage. To rage on I must regard myself as mistreated or as engaged in the rectification of an unbearable wrong, which I all too easily do.

Anger embraced is, accordingly, inherently disintegrative of human personality and life. It does not have to be specifically 'acted out' to poison the world. Because of what it is, and the way it seizes upon the body and its environment just by being there, it cannot be hidden. All our mental and emotional resources are marshalled to nurture and tend the anger, and our body throbs with it. Energy is dedicated to keeping the anger alive: we constantly remind ourselves of how wrongly we have been treated. And when it is allowed to govern our actions, of course, its evil is quickly multiplied in heart-rending consequences and in the replication of anger and rage in the hearts and bodies of everyone it touches.

Anger As Now Practised and Encouraged

In the United States there are around 25,000 murders each year. There are 1,000 murders in the workplace, and a million people are injured in the workplace by violent attacks from co-workers.[11] Most of the workplace murders occur after long periods of open rage and threats, and many involve multiple murders of innocent bystanders. It is a simple fact that none of the 25,000 murders, or only a negligible number of them, would have occurred but for an anger that the killers chose to embrace and indulge.

Anger and contempt are the twin scourges of the earth. Mingled with greed and sexual lust (to be discussed later), these bitter emotions form the poisonous brew in which human existence stands suspended. Few people ever get free of them in this life, and for most of us even old age does not bring relief.

Once you see those emotions for what they are, the constant stream of human disasters that history and life bring before us can also be seen for what *they* are: the natural outcome of human choice, of people choosing to be angry and contemptuous. It is a miracle there are not more and greater disasters. We have to remember this when we read what Jesus and other biblical writers say about anger. To cut the root of anger is to wither the tree of human evil. That is why Paul says simply, 'Lay aside anger' (Col. 3:8).

Yet influential people tell us today that we *must* be angry, that it is necessary to be angry to oppose social evil. The idea goes deep into our thinking. I was once counselling a Christian couple about family matters and suggested that they should not discipline their child in anger. They replied in amazement, 'You mean we should just punish him in cold blood?' They had no idea of how their sense of righteousness had become intertwined with anger.

A leading social commentator now teaches that despair and rage are an essential element in the struggle for justice.[12] He and others who teach this are sowing the wind, and they will reap the whirlwind, the tornado. Indeed, we are reaping it now in a nation increasingly sick with rage and resentment of citizen towards citizen. And often the rage and resentment is upheld as justified in the name of God.

But there is nothing that can be done with anger that cannot be done better without it. The sense of self-righteousness that comes with our anger simply provokes more anger and self-righteousness on the other side. Of course, when nothing is done about things that are wrong, anger naturally builds and finally will break into action, whether in a family or a nation. That is inevitable and even necessary *outside* The Kingdom Among Us.

But the answer is to right the wrong in persistent love, not to harbour anger, and thus to right it without adding further real or imaginary wrongs. To retain anger and to cultivate it is, by contrast, 'to give the devil a chance' (Eph. 4:26–27). He will take the chance, and there will be hell to pay. The delicious morsel of self-righteousness that anger cultivated always contains comes at a high price in the self-righteous reaction of those we cherish anger towards. And the cycle is endless as long as anger has sway.

Contempt Is Worse Than Anger

But contempt is a greater evil than anger and so is deserving of greater condemnation. Unlike innocent anger, at least, it is a kind of studied degradation of another, and it also is more pervasive in life than anger. It is never justifiable or good. Therefore Jesus tells us, 'Whoever says "Raca" to his brother shall stand condemned before the Sanhedrin, the highest court of the land' (v. 22).

The Aramaic term *raca* was current in Jesus' day to express contempt for someone and to mark out him or her as contemptible. It may have originated from the sound one makes to collect spittle from the throat in order to spit. In anger I want to hurt you. In contempt, I don't care whether you are hurt or not. Or at least so I say. You are not worth consideration one way or the other. We can be angry at someone without denying their worth. But contempt makes it easier for us to hurt them or see them further degraded.

Today, of course, we would not say, 'Raca'. But we might call someone a twit or a twerp, maybe a dork or a nerd. These are the gentler words in our vocabulary of contempt; when it really gets going, it becomes filthy. Our verbal arsenal is loaded with contemptuous terms, some with sexual, racial or cultural bearing, others just personally degrading. They should never be uttered.

The intent and the effect of contempt is always to exclude someone, push them away, leave them out and isolated. This explains why filth is so constantly invoked in expressing contempt and why contempt is so cruel, so serious. It breaks the social bond more severely than anger. Yet it may also be done with such refinement.

How often we see it, in the school playground, at a party, even in the home or church! Someone is being put down or oh so precisely omitted, left out. It is a constant in most of human life. In the course of normal life one is rarely in a situation where contempt is not at least hovering in the wings. And everyone lives in terror of it. It is never quite beyond the margins of our consciousness.

But those who are 'excluded' are thereby made fair game for worse treatment. Conversely, respect automatically builds a wall against mistreatment. In family battles the progression is nearly always from anger to contempt (always expressed in vile language) to physical brutality. Once contempt is established, however, it justifies the initial anger and increases its force.

Recently cultural observers have noted the overwhelming rise in the use of filthy language, especially among young people. Curiously, few have been able to find any grounds for condemning it other than personal taste. How strange! Can it be that they actually find contempt acceptable, or are unable to recognize it? Filthy language and name calling is *always* an expression of contempt. The current swarm of filthy language floats upon the sea of contempt in which our society is now adrift.

Some attention has recently been paid to twelve-year-old or fourteen-year-old children who kill people for no apparent reason. Commentators have remarked on the lack of feeling in these young killers. But when you observe them accurately, you will see that they are indeed actuated by a feeling. Watch their faces. It is contempt. They are richly contemptuous of others – and at the same time terrified and enraged at being 'dissed', which is their language for contempt.

Jesus' comment here (Matt. 5:22) is that anyone who says, 'Raca', to an associate is rightly to be singled out by the highest authorities in the land – 'the council' or Sanhedrin – for appropriate and obviously serious penalties. Contemptuous actions and attitudes are a knife in the heart that permanently harms and mutilates people's souls.

That they are so common does not ease their destructiveness. In most professional circles and 'high' society, where one might hope for the highest moral sensitivity, contempt is a fine art. Practising it is even a part of being 'in good standing'. Not to know whom and how to despise is one of the surest of signs that you are not quite with it and are yourself mildly contemptible.

In his marvellous little talk 'The Inner Ring', C. S. Lewis comments that 'in all men's lives at certain periods, and in many men's lives at all periods between infancy and extreme old age, one of the most dominant elements is the desire to be inside the local Ring and the terror of being left outside.'[13]

To *belong* is a vital need based in the spiritual nature of the human being. Contempt spits on this pathetically deep need. And, like anger, contempt does not have to be acted out in special ways to be evil. It is inherently poisonous. Just by being what it is, it is withering to the human soul. But when expressed in the contemptuous phrase – in its thousands of forms – or in the equally powerful gesture or look, it stabs the soul to its core and deflates its powers of life. It can hurt so badly and destroy so deeply that murder would almost be a mercy. Its power is also seen in the intensity of the resentment and rage it always evokes.

'You Fool!'

But Jesus notes one stage further in the progression of internal evil that may be there without murder occurring: 'And whoever says 'You fool!' shall merit condemnation to the fires of gehenna' (v. 22).

'You fool!' said with that characteristic combination of freezing contempt and withering anger that Jesus had in mind, is a deeper harm than either anger or contempt alone. *Twerp* or *twit* usually is not said in anger but even with a certain amusement. *Fool*, on the other hand, in the biblical sense, is an expression of malice as well as contempt.

Actually, that word will no longer do to capture the sense of Jesus' teaching here and, in fact, is now closer to *twerp* than it is to what he had in mind. Thus one who would follow Jesus' 'law' by not calling people fools today gets off easy. We have plenty of other terminology that would allow us to go ahead and do exactly what he was in fact condemning, without using the word *fool*.

The dominant sense of *fool* in our culture is that of a benign folly, as in 'Feast of Fools', an ancient idea that became the title of a popular book some years back. Excuse the crudity, but the nearest equivalent of the biblical *fool* in today's language would be something more like *stupid bastard* or *f— jerk*, as said to someone who either has just messed up something important we were doing to meet a deadline or has just cut us up in traffic. One would hardly speak of a 'Feast of Stupid Bastards' in the same celebratory sense.

The fool, in biblical language, is a combination of stupid perversity and rebellion against God and all that sensible people stand for. He is willfully perverted, rebellious, knowingly wicked to his own harm. The Old Testament book of Proverbs carefully delineates his soul. 'The fool,' we are told, 'is arrogant and careless' (Prov. 14:16). 'A fool doesn't care about understanding, but only in displaying his own heart' (18:2). 'Like a dog that re-eats its own vomit, a fool repeats his folly over and over' (26:11). And so on and so on.

To brand someone 'fool' in this biblical sense was a violation of the soul so devastating, of such great harm, that, as Jesus saw, it would justify consigning the offender to the smouldering rubbish-dump of human existence, *gehenna*. It combines all that is evil in anger as well as in contempt. It is not possible for people with such attitudes towards others to live in the movements of God's kingdom, for they are totally out of harmony with it.

These Three Prohibitions Are Not Laws

Today one is apt to feel that Jesus is taking all this too seriously. But what is it, exactly, that is being done in the delineation of this threefold progression of prohibitions from anger to contempt to verbal desecration? The answer is that Jesus is giving us a revelation of the preciousness of human beings. He means to reveal the value of persons. Obviously merely not killing others cannot begin to do justice to that.

By no means, however, is he simply giving here three more things not to do, three more points on a 'list' of things to be avoided. Certainly, we are not to do them, but *that* is not the point. If that were all, the enterprising human mind would soon find its way around them. Don't we already know that not getting angry is the way some people have of winning? And don't we hear people say, 'I don't get mad. I just get even'? One doesn't have to be mad to be mean.

So here as elsewhere in his lovely Discourse on the Hillside, we need to put the idea of laws entirely out of our minds. Jesus is working, as already indicated, at the much deeper level of the *source* of actions, good and bad. He is taking us deeper into the kind of beings we are, the kind of love God has for us, and the kind of love that, as we share it, brings us into harmony with his life. No one can be 'right' in the kingdom sense who is not transformed at this level. And then, of course, the issue of *not* being wrongly angry, *not* expressing contempt, *not* calling people 'stupid bastards,' and so on is automatically taken care of.

When I go to New York City, I do not have to think about *not* going to London or Atlanta. People do not meet me at the airport or station and exclaim over what a great thing I did in *not* going somewhere else. I took the steps to go the New York City, and that took care of everything.

Likewise, when I treasure those around me and see them as God's creatures designed for his eternal purposes, I do not make an additional point of not hating them or calling them twerps or fools. *Not* doing those things is simply a part of the package. 'He that loves has fulfilled the law,' Paul said (Rom. 13:8). Really.

On the other hand, not going to London or Atlanta is a poor plan for going to New York. And *not* being wrongly angry and so on is a poor plan for treating people with love. It will not work. And, of course, Jesus never intended it to be such a plan. For all their necessity, goodness, and beauty, laws that deal only with actions, such as the Ten Commandments, simply cannot reach the human heart, the *source* of actions. 'If a law had been given capable of bringing people to life,' Paul said, 'then righteousness would have come from that law' (Gal. 3:21). But law, for all its magnificence, cannot do that. Graceful relationship sustained with the masterful Christ certainly can.

We learn this in our discipleship to Christ.

Positive Illustrations of the Kingdom Heart

But the revelation of kingdom goodness relative to our interactions with others is not yet complete. Showing that anger and contempt are such serious matters only lays a foundation for the final move in this first contrast that Jesus makes between the kingdom heart and the older teaching about 'rightness'. Now he states a remarkable 'therefore' that leads us out of mere negations or prohibitions into an astonishing positive regard for our neighbour, whom we are to love as God loves.

Referring to what has just been made clear, Jesus says 'therefore' (v. 23). *Because* the reality of the human soul and God's regard for it in his kingdom are so great, what kind of positive caring makes us at home in the kingdom life? Two illustrations are given of what, once again, law could never capture:

First, you are with the Temple officials before the altar, about to present your sacrifice to God (Matt. 5:23–24). It is one of the holiest moments in the ritual life of the faithful. The practice was that nothing should interrupt this ritual except some more important ceremonial matter that required immediate attention.

Suddenly, right in the midst of it all, you remember a brother who is mad at you. Realizing how important it is for his soul to find release, and pained by the break between yourself and him, you stop the ritual. You walk out of it to find him and make up. *That* illustrates the positive goodness of the kingdom heart.

To get the full impact of this illustration we have to imagine ourselves being married or baptized or ordained to some special role, such as pastor. In the midst of the proceedings, we walk out to seek reconciliation with someone who is not even there. That pictures the kingdom love that is kingdom rightness.

Jesus' selection of this scene to illustrate the quality of the kingdom heart continues the long-established prophetic emphasis in

Israel, which always weighted the moral over the ritual. 'Behold, I would have mercy and not sacrifice' (Hos. 6:6). Eduard Schweizer comments, 'When a cultic act is stopped for the sake of one's brother, as Jesus requires, cultic ideology has been fundamentally overcome.'[14]

Now just think of what the quality of life and character must be in a person who would routinely interrupt sacred rituals to pursue reconciliation with a fellow human being. What kind of thought life, what feeling tones and moods, what habits of body and mind, what kinds of deliberations and choices would you find in such a person? When you answer these questions, you will have a vision of the true 'rightness beyond' that is at home in God's kingdom of power and love.

Of course the *legalistic* tendency in the human self will immediately go to work. It seems never to rest. It will ask, What if my brother refuses to be reconciled? Am I never to go to church again? ('First be reconciled to your brother and then come and offer your gift.') Do I always have to do this, no matter what else is at issue in the situation? The answer is, Obviously not! Jesus is not here giving a law that you must never carry through with your religious practice if an associate has something against you. He is not stating a law like 'Thou shalt not kill'. The aim of his *illustration* – and it is an illustration – is to bring us to terms with what is in our hearts and, simultaneously, to show us the rightness of the kingdom heart.

We do not control outcomes and are not responsible for them, but only for our contribution to them. Does our heart long for reconciliation? Have we done what we can? Honestly? Do we refuse to substitute ritual behaviours for genuine acts of love? Do we mourn for the harm that our brother's anger is doing to his own soul, to us and to others around us? If so, we are beyond 'the righteousness of scribes and Pharisees' and immersed in God's ways. We can certainly find an appropriate way to act from such a heart without being given a list of things to do.

The second illustration of an action typical of the kingdom heart is drawn from the case in which we have an *adversary* before the legal system. Today it would probably mean someone is suing us.

Here Jesus tells us to be well disposed or kindly minded (*eunoon*) towards our adversary in the preliminary interactions that might lead up to a trial. Try, with genuine love for the adversary, to resolve the matter before it comes to trial. We might cordially meet with him or her, for example, and just ask with sincerity what we could do to help. That is the sort of thing the kingdom heart will do.

By truly loving our adversary, we stand within the reality of God's kingdom and resources, and it is very likely we will draw our adversary into it also. Things are really different there, and a resolution manifesting the divine presence becomes possible. See what will happen. Venture on the kingdom. That is how we 'seek' it.

If we do not approach our 'adversary' in this way, we limit ourselves and our adversary to the human system and its laws, and we will endure the bitter fruit of it. We probably will not escape it until it has totally drained us. How realistic Jesus' description is of a process we constantly see about us today! Currently some of our courts are imprisoning children because they refuse to visit their father who has left the family. Such a system, one can only say, may be unavoidable now, but it is too crude for human existence by anyone's thoughtful standards.

It is crucial to realize that Jesus does not here say that we should simply give in to the demands of an adversary. To be of a kindly or favourable mind towards an adversary or anyone else does not mean to do what they demand. It means to be genuinely committed to what is good for them, to seek their well-being. This may even require that we *not* give in to them. But there are many ways of holding the line, some of God, some not.

Likewise, he does not forbid us to go to court. Yet how many people, looking for a law, have falsely supposed he does. But that is simply not there in his words. Nevertheless, a man of my acquaintance was in business with someone who took ruinous advantage of him. This man gave in to his partner's illegitimate demands and actions and did not go to law over the matter. He presumed that Jesus had laid down a law to that effect. As it turned out, he was expecting God to see to it that he suffered no loss. But he suffered a great loss. And now he is very angry at God, and not at God alone.

Jesus here gives us a second illustration, then, of how the kingdom heart will respond. He does not tell us what to do, but how to do it. Indeed, go to court or not – as makes sense in the circumstances. But do whatever you do without hostility, bitterness and the merciless drive to *win*. Be prepared to sacrifice your interest for that of another if that seems wise. And keep a joyous confidence in God regardless of what happens.

Standing in the kingdom, we make responsible decisions in love, with assurance that how things turn out for us does not really matter that much because, in any case, we *are* in the kingdom of the heavens. In that kingdom nothing that can happen to us is 'the end of the world.'

Through these two illustrations we finally see the kingdom goodness placed side by side with the mere goodness of not killing, which then looks quite empty by contrast. If we made laws of these illustrations and followed them, would that make us right towards our brother or sister? Not at all. We could do these things and yet find many other ways to hate and hurt our neighbour. We would miss the whole point.

The Destructiveness of Fantasized Desire

The Poison of Sexual Desire Indulged and Fantasized Desire

In his Discourse on the Hillside Jesus treats hostility at greater length than any of the other matters he takes up. This is certainly because it is most fundamental. If you pull contempt and unrestrained anger out of human life, you have thereby rid it of by far the greater part of wrong acts that actually get carried out.

But in this first concretely displayed contrast between the old and the new *dikaiosune* Jesus also gives us space to pick up on *how* he is treating his subject matter. Now it will be possible to deal somewhat more briefly with the five remaining contrasts brought up in his exposition of kingdom rightness.

The second contrast he deals with concerns sex. Of course he is right on target for today. Sex and violence are the two things that are repeatedly cited as the areas of our greatest problems, in life as in the media. Violence is the sure overflow of anger and contempt in the heart. Anger and contempt constantly intermingle, both with each other and with the torrents of fantasized gratifications that also inhabit the human heart: such as those for fame, drugs and alcohol, power and money. Hungers for these dominate a social framework in which a seemingly unlimited range of desires are constantly pushing their claims for 'liberation' into unlimited satisfaction.

In dealing with sex, as with verbal and physical violence, Jesus takes for the point of contrast one of the Ten Commandments as used in the current setting: 'You shall not commit adultery.' Strictly speaking, this prohibits a married person's having sexual intercourse with someone other than his or her spouse. As with murder, it is an absolute prohibition, and there is no question of its being right under any circumstances to murder or to commit adultery.

Yet, as we have seen with murder, the mere fact that you do not commit adultery with a certain man or woman does not mean that your relation to that person in the domain of sexuality is as it should be or that you yourself are what you ought to be with reference to your sexuality.

Jesus was confronted with multitudes of men who thought of themselves as good, as right, in their sexual life because they did not do the specific thing forbidden by the commandment. They were like those who thought they were right in relation to their fellow men because they had not killed them.

But Jesus was aware, as we may easily notice today, that the very same people who thought of themselves as sexually pure and right would follow a woman with their eyes, lavishing their lookings upon her, tracing out by sight the lineaments of her body with a look of absorbed lusting upon their face and posture. They obviously take great pleasure in this activity, fantasizing what touching, caressing and entering this body would be like.

Everyone knows about this kind of activity, and there are few who have not at some time engaged in it to some degree. No doubt the same was true even in Jesus' day. But it goes on among all types of men, including ministers and university professors, and, in this day of equal opportunity, among women as well and between members of the same sex. Jesus' teaching here is that a person who cultivates lusting in this manner is not the kind of person who is at home in the goodness of God's kingdom.

Job's Eyes

In the book of Job, dated by some as the oldest book in the Bible, there is a very analytic statement of the course of sexual involvement (Job 31). As is well known, Job is protesting his integrity on all fronts. He is aware of the issue Jesus is addressing and has a well-thought-out policy concerning it. 'I made a covenant with my eyes,' he says. He had, as it were, an understanding with them that they would not engage in lusting. 'How,' he asks, 'could I ogle a young woman,' a 'virgin'? The salacious gaze would be seen by God. And it would certainly lead into deceitful actions (v. 5). But God knows that none of this is a part of his life (v. 6).

Job is so emphatic about his purity in this area that he goes into great detail concerning the all-too-familiar course of wrong sexual involvement and its consequences. Obviously he knew exactly what goes on. 'If my feet have carried me to the wrong places,' he says, 'or if my heart has walked after my eyes, or my hand is defiled because it has touched what it ought not to touch, then let my children belong to others. And if my heart has been captured by the wife of another, and I have sought for an opportunity with her, then may my wife be possessed by other men' (Job 31:5–8).

To be right sexually before God is to be precisely as Job was. It is to be the kind of person who has a detailed and established practice of not engaging his or her bodily parts and perceptions, thoughts and desires in activities of sexual trifling, dalliance and titillation. It is to be the kind of person whose feet, eyes, hands, heart and all the rest simply walk within the good policy that he or she has adopted because of the knowledge that it is good and right.

Adultery 'in the Heart'

So in this area Jesus is not exactly making points unheard of among human beings. All except those committed to a course of self-justification will understand clearly what he is talking about and will recognize that it is not good. He says simply that those who 'look upon a woman *for the purpose of lusting* for her – using her visual presence as a means of savouring the fantasized act – has thereby committed adultery with her in his heart' (Matt. 5:28).

In other words, all the elements of a genuine act of adultery other than the overt movements of the body are present in such a case. The heart elements are there. Usually the only thing lacking for overt action is the occasion. When the heart is ready, the action will occur as occasion offers. Just as the thief is the person who would steal if circumstances were right, so the adulterer is the one who would have wrongful sex if the circumstances were right. Usually that means if he or she could be sure it would not be found out. This is what Jesus calls 'adultery in the heart.' In it, the person is not caring for, but using, the other. The condition is wrong even though sexual relations do not occur.

When one is inhabited by fantasizing visual lusting, it, like anger and contempt, makes its presence known. It is detectable in one's 'body language' and expressions. As a result it has pervasive effects on everyone in the situation, even though it is not 'acted out'. Indeed, being what it is, a condition of the embodied social self, it is *always* acted out to some degree and simply cannot be kept a private reality. 'The look' is a public act with public effects that restructure the entire framework of personal relations where it occurs.[15]

The person subjected to the fantasy, as well as others alongside, is deeply affected by such lusting. And it nearly always produces some degree of inappropriate action, including all of the behaviour now classified as sexual harassment. Indeed, it is in itself a form of harassment unless it is invited. The person subjected to it and everyone else nearby must 'deal with it', often by constant planning and managing. Sexual harassment as we know it would simply disappear under Jesus' ethic of sexuality.

Also eliminated would be the unfair treatment of those who do not attract the lusting look. They do not have the 'sexual edge' that facilitates others, often quite subtly, on the path of life: favourable attention, a more 'forgiving' application of standards of performance, advancement in position and financial reward. And of course they cannot usually say anything at all about this because it would be a humiliating admission of their 'unattractiveness'. In silence they suffer.

But Actual Adultery Is Worse

Accordingly, no one can be in harmony with The Kingdom Among Us who indulges and cultivates this type of absorbing desire. That they do not actually commit adultery is, however, important. Actual adultery involves all the wrong of 'adultery in the heart' and much more besides. Jesus never suggests that actual adultery is acceptable if it is only done 'in the right way', or that if you are already engaged in heart adultery you might just as well go all the way. He knew how terribly disruptive it was of life. The classical moralist Aristotle, who lived four centuries before Jesus, also held that adultery was simply wrong. There is no such thing, he says, as 'committing adultery with the right woman, at the right time and in the right way, for it is ... simply wrong.'[16] And until the mid-twentieth century it was generally assumed that this was the correct view.

Today, of course, this view has almost totally changed. It would be hard to find any current writer in ethics who would regard adultery as simply wrong. Actually, almost anything in the way of sexual relations is now regarded as correct as long as both parties consent to it. You will now hear it explained that adultery is not even committed as long as no child is conceived. For the 'real' prohibition all along, some say, was not against sexual relations, but against fathering a child on someone else's wife or by someone else's husband and thus 'adulterating' the man's family lineage.

More commonly, now, it is thought that sex is right with anyone you love in the sense of a 'romantic' involvement. And on the other hand sex without romantic feelings is thought to be wrong even if the sexual partners are married. Often the 'romantic love' in question turns out upon examination to be nothing more than precisely that fantasized lusting that Jesus called 'adultery in the heart'. One is not in love but in lust, which glorifies itself as something deeper in order to have its way.

It is almost inconceivable today that the rightness or wrongness of sexual intercourse would have nothing whatsoever to do with what now passes for romantic love. Yet that is the biblical view generally: the rightness of sex is tied instead to a solemn and public covenant for life between two individuals, and sexual arousal and delight is a response to the gift of a uniquely personal intimacy with the whole person that each partner has conferred in enduring faithfulness upon the other.

Intimacy is the mutual mingling of souls who are taking each other into themselves to ever increasing depths. The truly erotic is the mingling of souls. Because we are free beings, intimacy cannot be passive or forced. And because we are extremely finite, it must be exclusive. This is the metaphysical and spiritual reality that underlies the bitter violation of self experienced by the betrayed mate. It also makes clear the scarred and shallow condition of those who betray.

The profound misunderstandings of the erotic that prevail today actually represent the inability of humanity in its current Western edition to give itself to others and receive them in abiding faithfulness.[17] Personal relationship has been emptied out to the point where intimacy is impossible. Quite naturally, then, we say, 'Why not?' when contemplating adultery. If there is nothing there to be broken, why worry about breaking it?

One of the most telling things about contemporary human beings is that they cannot find a reason for not committing adultery. Yet intimacy is a spiritual hunger of the human soul, and we cannot escape it. This has always been true and remains true today. We now keep hammering the sex button in the hope that a little intimacy might finally dribble out. In vain. For intimacy comes only within the framework of an individualized faithfulness within the kingdom of God. Such faithfulness is violated by 'adultery in the heart' as well as by adultery in the body.

Anger and Contempt in Sex

Of course such covenant-framed intimacy as just referred to is an expression of the same heart of love that Jesus refers to in his earlier discussion of anger, contempt and associated feelings. And the orderly progression of his Discourse comes immediately into play here. The sexual delight that goes naturally with the unique covenantial intimacy of marriage is totally destroyed by anger and contempt. How many marriage unions are fatally undermined because of contempt that one mate has for the other? Sometimes it is for the body, sometimes for the mind, talents or family, or for something he or she has done. The contempt always elicits anger, which elicits anger in turn and so on. It's a familiar story. These wounds seldom heal, but instead fester and grow. Further 'sex' under such contempt-filled conditions usually will only deepen them.

Anger and contempt between mates makes sexual delight between them impossible, and when such an important need is unmet, people are, almost invariably, drawn into the realm of fantasy. Dissatisfied mates project fantasy images that the real people in their lives are forced, in one way or another, to fit into – or fall short of. This leads to increased frustration, producing more anger and contempt.

Hostile feelings may even become essential to sexual stimulation. Then straightforward sexual stimulation and gratification become impossible. 'Kinkiness' and degradation (humiliation, bondage, etc.) become necessary for sexual arousal to occur. Finally, the anger and contempt cycle comes back into play again, this time turned against those who do not approve of abnormal sexual needs and behaviour, or even against oneself.

The overt sexiness of many magazines on a newsagent's shelves, advertising, romance novels and nearly all movie and television productions is always an exercise in fantasy sexuality, and it feeds into the path of frustration, anger and contempt just described. In charting one's course in life, it is important never to forget that many things that cannot be called wrong or evil are nevertheless not good for us.

Of course when we arrive at outright pornography we can see, if we have eyes and brains left, that it always involves some element of contempt or even disgust. Those presented in it are *obviously* being used, hence are even regarded by the viewer as 'deserving' disgust or even pain. There is no question of an appropriate human relation to them.

The idea of 'girl next door' pornography, pushed so hard by publications in recent years, is simply an absurdity. Pornography lives in the hostile and degraded imagination along with 'adultery in the heart'. Jesus' teaching here reaches the depths of the human soul and body and makes us aware of dimensions of real or possible darkness within us that, like Job, we must simply stay away from.

But Merely to Think or Desire Is Not Wrong

On the other hand, we must be careful to recognize that sexual desire is not wrong as a natural, uncultivated response, any more than anger is, or pain. It has a vital function in life, and as long as it performs *that* function it is a good and proper thing.

Moreover, when we only *think* of sex with someone we see, or simply find him or her attractive, that is not wrong, and certainly is not what Jesus calls 'adultery in the heart'. Merely to be *tempted* sexually requires that we think of sex with someone we are not married to, and that we desire the other person – usually, of course, someone we see. But temptation also is not wrong, though it should not be willfully entered. Jesus himself came under it, experienced it and understood it.

Therefore those translations of Matt. 5:28 that say, 'Everyone who looks at a woman *and* desires her,' or 'everyone who looks at a woman with desire,' are terribly mistaken. They do much harm, especially to young people. For they totally change the meaning of the text and present 'adultery in the heart' as something one cannot avoid, as something that just happens to people with no collusion of their will.

That on this reading to be tempted would be to sin *should* have been enough, by itself, to show that such translations are mistaken. No translation of scripture can be correct that contradicts basic principles of biblical teaching as a whole.

The terminology of 5:28 is quite clear if we will but attend to it, and many translations do get it right. The Greek preposition *pros* and the dative case are used here. The wording refers to looking at a woman with *the purpose* of desiring her. That is, we desire to desire. We indulge and cultivate desiring because we enjoy fantasizing about sex with the one seen. Desiring sex is the purpose for which we are looking.

Another New Testament passage very graphically speaks of those who have 'eyes full of adultery' (2 Pet. 2:14). These are people who, when they see a sexually attractive person, do not see the person but see themselves sexually engaging him or her. They see adultery occurring in their imagination. Such a condition is one we can and should avoid. It is a choice.

For many people, unfortunately, it has become a chosen habit. But it still is not something that merely *happens* to them. These are not unwilling victims without any choice in the matter. It isn't like the law of gravity. The desire is desired, embraced, indulged, elaborated, fantasized. It is the purposeful entertaining and stimulation of desire that Jesus marks as the manifestation of a sexually improper condition of the soul. No one has to do this or be this, unless perhaps he or she has already advanced to a stage of compulsive disorder or possession. In that case, of course, the person needs help that goes beyond instruction and advice.

Not Enough Just to Avoid Adultery in the Heart

But can we then make Jesus' teaching about adultery in the heart a *law* that states what rightness is in the sexual domain? Would we certainly have a right heart in this domain if we did not commit adultery *and* did not visually indulge absorbing lust?

Not at all. This would be, once again, to take his illustration of sexual wrongness and turn it into a law of righteousness. And that will make us miss the point of his teaching altogether, which is the condition of the inmost self, or 'heart'.

The case of obsessive lusting illustrates a wrongness of the inner self that may still be there even if no outward act of adultery is committed. Yes, but sexual wrongness can still be present when one does not look on persons to fantasize sex with them. To avoid just this is no guarantee of being sexually sound. And to make a law that says, 'Don't look to lust,' and assume that obeying it is to be righteous is a mistake. It all depends on how it is done and what else is going on in the heart.

For example, there have been men, even groups of men, who made it their goal not to look lustfully at a woman. (They thus made the typically pharisaical mistake of trying to control the act instead of changing the source.) And they have achieved that goal. They did not look at a woman for years, not even their mother or sister. They would not allow themselves to be in the company of a woman or see one under any circumstances. They would not allow themselves to be where a woman was visible.[18]

Well, one might say, that would certainly solve the problem of conforming to Jesus' new *law* on sexual rightness. If you don't see a woman at all, you cannot look at her to cultivate desire of her. Or suppose I train myself to hate women in order not to desire them? This also has been done. Am I therefore right sexually? Is this the way of The Kingdom Among Us?

One hardly has to ask the question to know how misguided it is. Could one possibly say that this would constitute a loving relationship to women, including those in one's family circle? Obviously not. Historically such a 'solution' has been associated with regarding the woman as the problem, or even as inherently evil. Though there no doubt are times when, man or woman, we can only run from temptation, or simply avoid the possibility, that must be regarded as a temporary expedient. It cannot serve as a permanent solution. It cannot change who we are. One cannot live by it.

Reductio ad Absurdum of Rightness in Terms of Acts

Indeed, the attempt to solve the problem of right sexual behaviour by a law or laws that govern specific behaviours is what Jesus is addressing in Matt. 5:29–30: 'If your right eye makes you sin, gouge it out and fling it from you. Better that one of your bodily parts rot than that your whole body rot in *gehenna*' (v. 29). And likewise for your right hand (v. 30).

Jesus is saying that if you think that laws can eliminate being wrong you would, to be consistent, cut off your hand or gouge out your eye so that you could not possibly do the acts the law forbids.

Now, truly, if you blind yourself you cannot look at a woman to lust after her, because you cannot look on her at all. And if you sufficiently dismember yourself, you will not be able to do any wrong *action*. This is the logic by which Jesus reduces the righteousness of the scribes and Pharisees to the absurd.

In their view, the law could be satisfied, and thus goodness attained, if you avoided sinning. You are right if you have done nothing wrong. You could avoid sinning if you simply eliminated the bodily parts that make sinful actions possible. Then you would roll into heaven a mutilated stump.

Of course being acceptable to God is so important that, if cutting bodily parts off could achieve it, one would be wise to cut them off. Jesus seems to have made this very point on some occasions (Matt. 18:8–9; Mark 9:43). But so far from suggesting that any advantage before God could actually be gained in this way, Jesus' teaching in this passage is exactly the opposite. The mutilated stump could still have a wicked heart. The deeper question always concerns who you are, not what you did do or can do. What *would* you do if you could?[19] Eliminating bodily parts will not change that.

If you dismember your body to the point where you could never murder or even look hatefully at another, never commit adultery or even look to lust, your heart could still be full of anger, contempt and obsessive desire for what is wrong, no matter how thoroughly stifled or suppressed it may be. 'From within, out of the heart of men, the thoughts of evil proceed: fornications, thefts, murders, adulteries, acts of greed and iniquity, as well as deceit, lewdness, the envious glare, blasphemy, arrogance and foolishness – all of these evils come from inside and pollute the person' (Mark 7:21–23).

The goodness of the kingdom heart, by contrast, is the positive love of God and of those around us that fills it and crowds out the many forms of evil. From that goodness come deeds of respect and purity that characterize a sexuality as it was meant by God to be.

Beyond the Divorce Papers

Now we come to arrangements that did not quite have the status of law in the fullest sense, but nonetheless are understandings that in important ways defined the 'old' rightness being displaced by the presence of the kingdom. And the first of these arrangements concerns divorce.

One of the most important things in the male mind of Jesus' day, and perhaps every day, was to be able to get rid of a woman who did not please him. And on this point the man really had great discretion, whereas from the woman's point of view divorce was simply brutal and, practically speaking, could not be chosen. When Jesus gave his teaching that divorce as then practised was unacceptable, the men who were his closest students responded by saying, 'If that is how things are, it's better not to marry at all!' (Matt. 19:10).

A man was generally thought to be righteous or good in the matter of divorce if, when he sent his wife away, he gave her a written statement that declared her to be divorced. She at least had, then, a certificate to prove her status as unmarried. This allowed her to defend herself against a charge of adultery if found with a man, for such a charge could result in her death. It also made it possible for her to seek marriage to another, or, if all else failed, to make her living as a prostitute.

Certainly there was long-standing disagreement among the interpreters of the law as to whether the man was free to divorce his wife 'for every reason whatsoever' (Matt. 19:3), or only for adultery. The Pharisees dragged Jesus into this controversy, and he clearly took the highly restrictive position of the school of Shammai, which allowed divorce only on 'moral' grounds. The school of Hillel, by contrast, permitted it 'for every reason'. For example, if the wife burned the food or merely oversalted it. Rabbi Akibah even allowed divorce if the husband merely saw a woman whose appearance pleased him better and he wanted her as wife instead of a wife he had.[20]

In practice, however, a woman knew very well that she *could* be divorced for any reason her husband chose. The law as practised was entirely favourable to the husband's slightest whim, even though the Mosaic codes, chiefly found in Deuteronomy 22–24, are obviously much more restrictive and require some sort of sexual impropriety in the woman. They also specify conditions under which a man entirely loses the right to divorce a woman.

When Jesus himself comes to deal with the rightness of persons in divorce, he does not forbid divorce absolutely, but he makes it very clear that divorce was never God's intent for men and women in a marriage. The intent in marriage is a union of two people that is even deeper than the union of parents and children or any other human relationship. They are to become 'one flesh', one natural unit, building one life, which therefore could never lose or substitute for one member and remain a whole life (Matt. 19:5; Gen. 2:24).

The Principle of Hardness of Heart

Yet he does not say that divorce is never permissible. To begin with, he accepts the Mosaic exception of 'uncleanness', which may have covered a number of things but chiefly referred to adultery (Matt. 5:32; 19:8–9). His interpretation of the grounds of the Mosaic exception is not, however, simply that adultery and the like are intrinsically so horrible that a marriage relationship cannot survive them. That, of course, is really not true. Many marriages have survived them. Misunderstanding this point, some people even today think that where there is adultery divorce is *required* by the biblical teachings. But it is not.

Rather, it is the hardness of the human heart that Jesus cites as grounds for permitting divorce in case of adultery. In other words, the ultimate grounds for divorce is human meanness. If it weren't for that, even adultery would not legitimate divorce. No doubt what was foremost in his mind was the fact that the woman could quite well wind up dead, or brutally abused, if the man could not 'dump' her. It is still so today, of course. Such is 'our hardness of heart'. Better, then, that a divorce occur than life be made unbearable. Jesus does nothing to retract this principle.

But though not absolutely ruling out divorce, he makes very incisive comments about what divorce does to people. First of all, he insists, as already noted, that divorce was never God's intention for men and women in a marriage. Divorce disrupts a natural unit in a way that harms its members for life, no matter how much *worse* it would have been for them to stay together. Marriage means that 'they are no longer two, but one flesh' (Mark 10:8). This is an arrangement in nature that God has established, and no human act can change that order.

Perhaps one of the hardest things for the contemporary mind to accept is that life runs in natural cycles that cannot be disrupted without indelible damage to the individuals involved. For example, a child that does not receive proper nutrition in its early years will suffer negative effects for the rest of its life. The deficiency cannot be made up later. And failure of a newborn baby to bond with its mother in its early weeks is thought by many researchers to do irreparable psychological damage.[21]

These are representative of a wide range of natural cycles to be found in human life. We now know that even the physical structure of the brain will never develop in certain crucial directions unless it does so within a particular period of the individual's life. In the order of nature some things can simply never be regained if they are lost.

Divorce also powerfully disrupts one of the major natural cycles of human existence. And the individuals involved can never be the same – whether or not a divorce was, everything considered, justifiable. That is why no one regards a divorce as something to be chosen for its own sake, a 'great experience', perhaps. But of course a brutal marriage is not a good thing either, and we must resist any attempt to classify divorce as a special, irredeemable form of wickedness. It is not. It is sometimes the right thing to do, everything considered.

Second – and this is the main point of the teaching in Matt. 5:31–32 – just the fact that a man (or woman) has given the woman (or man) a 'pink slip' and 'done everything legally' does not mean that he or she has done right or has been a good person with regard to the relationship. This is what Jesus is denying with his teaching here, for that is precisely what the old *dikaiosune*, as operative among the men of his time, affirmed.

Forced into 'Adultery'

Third, he very clearly gives his reasons for rejecting the old view of rightness in divorce by saying that anyone who sends away his wife on grounds other than 'uncleanness' *forces* her into adultery, and whoever takes as wife a woman who has been sent away from another engages in adultery (Matt. 5:32; 19:9).[22] This is not to forbid divorce, but it is to make clear what its effects are. What, exactly, do these statements mean?

In the Jewish society of Jesus' day, as for most times and places in human history, the consequences of divorce were devastating for the woman. Except for some highly unlikely circumstances, her life was, simply, ruined. No harm was done to the man, by contrast, except from time to time a small financial loss and perhaps bitter relationships with the ex-wife's family members.

For the woman, however, there were only three realistic possibilities in Jesus' day. She might find a place in the home of a generous relative, but usually on grudging terms and as little more than a servant. She might find a man who would marry her, but always as 'damaged goods' and sustained in a degraded relationship. Or she might, finally, make a place in the community as a prostitute. Society simply would not then, as ours does today, support a divorced woman to any degree or allow her to support herself in a decent fashion.

These circumstances explain why Jesus says that to divorce a woman causes her to commit adultery and to marry a divorced woman is to commit adultery (Matt. 5:32; 19:9). To *not* marry again was a terrible prospect for the woman. It meant, in nearly every case, to grow old with no children as well as with no social position, a perpetual failure as a human being. But to marry was to live in a degraded sexual relationship the rest of her life, and precious few husbands would allow her to forget it. As in the phrase 'adultery in the heart', Jesus speaks of being forced into 'adultery' to point out the degraded sexual condition that was, then if not now, sure to be the result of divorce.

Is It Then Better Not to Marry?

As noted already, when his apprentices heard what Jesus said about divorce, they immediately concluded that it was better not to marry at all than to be unable to get rid of a woman easily (Matt. 19:10). But Jesus, like Paul later (1 Cor. 7:9), points out that not marrying can also force one into an impossible situation. It is, accordingly, an option only for those especially qualified for it (vv. 11–12). More important, of course, he knew that the resources of the kingdom of the heavens were sufficient to resolve difficulties between husband and wife and to make their union rich and good before God and man – provided, of course, that both are prepared to seek and find these resources.

And we must remember, of course, what we have been saying all along about the order in the Sermon on the Mount. It is not an accident that Jesus deals with divorce *after* having dealt with anger, contempt and obsessive desire. Just ask yourself how many divorces would occur, and in how many cases the question of divorce would never even have arisen, if anger, contempt and obsessive fantasized desire were eliminated. The answer is, of course, hardly any at all.

In particular, the brutal treatment that women received in divorce in Jesus' day – and now men too in our day – would simply not happen. Hard hearts may make divorce necessary to avoid greater harm, and hence make it permissible. But kingdom hearts are not hard, and they together can find ways to bear with each other, to speak truth in love, to change – often through times of great pain and distress – until the tender intimacy of mutual, covenant-framed love finds a way for the two lives to remain one, beautifully and increasingly.

Is, then, divorce ever justifiable for Jesus? I think it clearly is. His principle of the hardness of hearts allows it, though its application would require great care. Perhaps divorce must be viewed somewhat as the practice of triage in medical care. Decisions must be made as to who cannot, under the circumstances, be helped. They are then left to die so that those who can be helped should live. A similar point applies to some marriages. But just as with the case of going to trial, discussed earlier, *it is never right to divorce as divorce was then done and as it is now usually done.* And it makes no difference today whether you are a man or a woman.

Divorce, if it were rightly done, would be done as an act of love. It would be dictated by love and done for the honest good of the people involved. Such divorce, though rare, remains nonetheless possible and may be necessary. If it were truly done on this basis, it would be rightly done, in spite of the heartbreak and loss it is sure to involve.

This position certainly represents a change on my part. I recall with embarrassment sitting around a seminar table at the University of Wisconsin in the early sixties. The professor had not yet arrived for our seminar in formal logic, and one of the class members was talking about his divorce proceedings. Without being asked for my opinion, I ventured to say, 'Divorce is always wrong.'

Looking back on it, the strangest thing of all was that no one objected to what I said or even to my saying it. Everyone seemed accepting of it. Of course that was because my words represented a cultural assumption of those days. But in fact I was vastly ignorant of the things men and women do to one another.

Later I came across the situation of a devout woman whose husband had married her as a cover for his homosexuality. He consummated the marriage so it couldn't be annulled, and after that he had nothing to do with her. They had no personal relationship at all. He would bring his male friends home and, in her presence, have sex in the living room or wherever else they pleased any time they pleased. Her religious guides continued to tell her that she must stay in 'the marriage', while she died a further death every day, year after year.

I was simply an ignorant young man full of self-righteous ideas. This and later episodes of discovery educated me in the hardness of the human heart. But Jesus, of course, always knew.

Transparent Words and Unquenchable Love

A Yes That Is Just a Yes

The fourth point upon which Jesus contrasts the older rightness with the rightness of the kingdom concerns the practice of giving oaths or *swearing by* something of importance, especially God himself, in order to lend weight to a statement one is making. In a society like our own, where the sacred is not real – not *really* real – oaths may only have the effect of a legal formality that makes possible the crime of perjury, of lying 'under oath'. But in a world where people actually believe, 'the oath confirms what is said and puts an end to any dispute' (Heb. 6:16).

Thus even today you hear people say, 'I swear by all that's holy,' for example. We say, 'By God.' We 'swear on a stack of Bibles.' And so forth. We invoke God to damn. We cry out, 'Jeeeeezuss Kuuriiist!'

Why is it we do this? Obviously, habit. But where did the habit come from? Something pretty deep, no doubt.

In this matter of invoking God or other things associated with him, the old rightness held that you could cite high and holy things as much as you pleased, as long as not obviously 'in vain' or foolishly, of course (Exod. 20:7). The one thing you had to be careful about was fulfilling anything you said you would do 'before God'. 'You shall fulfil your oaths to the Lord' (Matt. 5:33).

But Jesus goes right to the heart of why people swear oaths. He knew that they do it to impress others with their sincerity and reliability and thus gain acceptance of what they are saying and what they want. It is a method for getting their way.

They are declaring some promise or purpose or some point of information or knowledge dear to them. They want their hearers to accept what they say and do what they want. So they say, 'By God!' or, 'God knows!' to lend weight to their words and presence. It is simply a device of manipulation, designed to override the judgement and will of the ones they are focusing upon, to push them aside, rather than respecting them and leaving their decision and action strictly up to them.

The problem with 'swearing' or the making of oaths – which was really a huge part of life in Jesus' world – is not just that it involves taking the name of God in vain, or using it lightly and without love and respect for him. It does that often, no doubt, but not always. The evil of it that he addresses is that it is an inherently wrong approach to other human beings.

Thus Jesus says simply, 'Swear not at all. Not by heaven, for it is God's to reside in, his 'throne', nor by the earth, for that too is God's, his 'footstool', nor by Jerusalem, the holy city, for it is his city. Don't even make an oath upon your head, for it too is not under your power. You cannot make one hair on it white or black' (5:34–36).

Little brother James echoes this point, as he does so many others in the Sermon on the Mount: 'But above all, brothers, don't swear, neither by heaven, nor by the earth, nor any other oath. Let the yes be yes and the no be no, that you not fall under condemnation' (5:12).

The essence of swearing or making oaths is to try to use something that, though impressive, is irrelevant to the issues at hand to get others to believe you and let you have your way. This is wrong. It is unlike God. And just making sure you perform on any promises made to God in the course of it (the old rightness) does not make it right. Of course you should keep promises you make to God in any circumstances. But the wrongness of swearing lies deeper. We are making use of people, trying to bypass their understanding and judgement to trigger their will and possess them for our purposes. Whatever consent they give to us will be uninformed because we have short-circuited their understanding of what is going on.

Swearing is, then, a version of what is often called a 'song and dance'. It is very common in people who are 'selling' something, either figuratively, as in political life, or really. In Southern California there is a well-known car salesman who uses running chatter on TV about him and his 'dog, Spot.' 'Spot' may be anything, such as an ostrich or a hippopotamus, that this man is riding or strolling along with in front of his acres of more or less used cars.

Why does he do this? To create an atmosphere for prospective buyers that will incline them to buy from him. (Perhaps they will trust him more if he seems jolly or doesn't look too smart.) It certainly is not for the purpose of respecting or serving his customers. There are many ways he could do that if he chose, but he would rather do things that would help him sell cars.

Many people make a good living doing nothing but uttering in attractive or coercive ways 'yeses' that are not really yeses at all, and 'noes' that are not noes. In social or political contexts, we now call them 'spin doctors'.

The inherent wrongness of such projects makes Jesus simply say, 'Don't do it.' Swearing, or the 'song and dance' in general, does not respect those at whom it is directed. As God's free creatures, people are to be left to make their decisions without coercion or manipulation. Hence, 'let your affirmation be just an affirmation,' a yes, and your denial be just a denial, a no. Anything more than this 'comes from evil' – the evil intent to get one's way by verbal manipulation of the thoughts and choices of others.

Kingdom rightness respects the soul need of human beings to make their judgements and decisions solely from what they have concluded is best. It is a vital, a biological need. We do not thrive, nor does our character develop well, when this need is not respected,[23] and this thwarts the purpose of God in our creation.

Responding to Personal Injury

The fifth contrast of the two rightnesses concerns retaliation for harm done. The wrongs in question are clearly personal injuries, not institutional or social evils. How do we know that? It is clear from the parts of the old law referred to. Therefore the application of this particular passage to war and other social evils, by Tolstoy and others, which has done much damage to the understanding of Jesus' teaching, is simply a misreading.

The old rightness for the cases in question was that injurers should be injured in *exactly the same way*, so far as possible, as they had injured. This was a completely general statement to cover any kind of injury done, even to cover intended evil and property damage (Lev. 24:17–21; Deut. 19:14–21). The intent of the *lex talionis*, or law of retaliation, as it came to be called, was that reciprocity would be achieved through equalization.

There was to be redress of injury by injury being done to the doer. But more was not to be done than the injurer did. That was a major point of the old law and a great advance of civilization. If someone broke your arm, you were not to break both arms in return, or even one arm and a finger. There was to be equalization of injury, and then a stop to injury and counter injury. No insignificant or easy task, of course, as contemporary life around the world or in our homes and workplaces shows. And in fact it rarely succeeds. Obviously a better approach is needed.

So what, in the situation of personal injury, is the rightness of the kingdom heart? Here we must once again recall the point about order: that we have *already* heard and received the word of the kingdom, and that anger, contempt and absorbing desire have been dealt with so that our lives are not being run by them. If they occasionally test us still, that is very natural. But they do not control us and leave us unable to reliably and happily carry through with our sober intention to do what is good and avoid what is evil.

This being so, when we are personally injured our world does not suddenly become our injury. We have a larger view of our life and our place in God's world. We see God; we see ourselves in his hands.

And we see our injurer as more than that one who has imposed on us or hurt us. We recognize his humanity, his pitiful limitations (shared with us), and we also see him under God. This vision, and the grace that comes with it, enables the prayer: 'Father forgive them, for they do not really understand what they are doing.' And in fact they don't, as Jesus well knew when he prayed this prayer over his murderers.

Some Cases of Non-resistance

What are characteristic ways in which one fully alive in and to The Kingdom Among Us may respond to personal affronts, injuries and impositions? Jesus mentions four different types of kingdom responses:

1. They will 'turn the other cheek' (Matt. 5:39). That is, they will remain vulnerable. Negatively, they will not take their defence into their own hands and do whatever they may regard as necessary to protect themselves.

   So long as it strictly concerns themselves alone – and Jesus never suggests that we turn *someone else's* cheek or make someone else vulnerable – they will allow themselves to be injured by others who mean to hurt them rather than injure the would-be injurer. This will be characteristic, predictable behaviour for them.
2. 'Let him have your shirt' (5:40). They will conscientiously try to help, as is appropriate, those who have won legal cases against them in court. Or: they will meet someone about to sue them in the spirit of love and may even give them more than they are about to sue for. They are, after, all, deeply interested in what the other person needs and are prepared to help that person as much as they can.

3. 'Go with him two' (5:41). If a policeman or other responsible official exercises a right to require assistance from them, they will do more than is strictly required of them, as an expression of their goodwill towards the official and his or her responsibility. They will have regard to the person involved and act from the kingdom in their behalf. They will consider the problem of the official to be something of importance to themselves.
4. 'Give to him who asks of you' (5:42). They will often give to people who have no prior claim of any kind to what they are asking for. The request itself is the only claim required to move them. And they will not evade, ignore, or 'turn away from' those who would borrow from them. The parallel passage in Luke's Gospel says, 'Whoever takes away what is yours, do not demand it back' (6:30).

I think it is perhaps these four statements, more than any others in the Discourse, that cause people to throw up their hands in despair or sink into the pit of grinding legalism. This is because the situations referred to are familiar, and they can only imagine that Jesus is laying down *laws* about what they *have* to do regardless of what else may be at issue.

All is changed when we realize that these are illustrations of what a certain kind of person, the kingdom person, will characteristically do in such situations. They are not laws of 'righteous behaviour' for those personally imposed upon or injured. They are not laws for the obvious reason that they do not cover the many cases. Additionally, if you read them *as* laws you will immediately see that we could 'obey' them in the wrong spirit. For example, as is often actually said, 'I'll turn the other cheek, but then I'll knock your head off.'

Will there, then, be cases in which persons of kingdom *dikaiosune* will *not* do what is said here by way of illustration? Quite certainly, but they will be very rare, so long as it is only an individual injury that is at stake and no issues of a larger good are concerned. After all, this is *characteristic* behaviour of the person with the kingdom heart and it does express who that person is at the core of his or her being. Though we are not talking about things one must do to 'be Christian' or 'go to heaven when we die', we are looking at how people live who stand in the flow of God's life now. We see the interior rightness of those who are living – as a matter of course, not just in exceptional moments – beyond the rightness of the scribe and Pharisee.

Reversing the Presumption

We have already spoken of 'the great inversion' between the human order and the kingdom order. In the light of this inversion of realities, we can now understand the corresponding reversal of presumptions governing human action. Within the human order, the presumption is that you return harm for harm ('resist evil'), that you do only what legal force requires you to, and that you give only to those who have some prior claim on you (those who are 'family' or have done you a favour, etc.).

The presumption is precisely reversed once we stand within the kingdom. There the presumption is that I will return good for evil and 'resist' only for compelling reasons, that I will do more than I strictly must in order to help others, and that I give to people merely because they have asked me for something they need.

If someone has taken something valuable from me through the courts, I will, as appropriate, give him something else (my shirt) if he needs it. I will still help him in other ways, as I reasonably can.

If a government official compels me to carry a burden for one mile to aid him in his work – as any Roman soldier could require of a Jew in Jesus' day – I will, again 'as appropriate', assist him further in his need. Perhaps he has a mile yet to go, and I am free to assist him. If so, I will. I will not say, 'This is all you can make me do,' and drop the burden on his foot. I also will not carry it another mile whether he wants me to or not, and say, 'Because Jesus said to.'

If I know people want to borrow something they need, I will not avoid them and their request, and I may, as appropriate, give to those who ask me for something even though they have no 'claim' on me at all – no claim, that is, other than their need and their simple request. That is how God does it, and he invites us to join him.

Of course in each case I must determine if the gift of my vulnerability, goods, time and strength is, precisely, *appropriate*. That is my responsibility before God. As a child of the King, I always live in his presence. By contrast, the way of law avoids individual responsibility for decision. It pushes the responsibility and possible blame on to God. That is one reason why people who *must* have a law for all their actions lead such pinched and impoverished lives and develop very little in the way of genuine depth in godly character.

If, for example, I am a heart surgeon on the way to do a transplant, I must not go a second mile with someone. I must say no and leave at the end of the first mile with best wishes and a hasty farewell. I have other things I know I must do, and I must make the decision. I cannot cite a law and thus evade my responsibility of judging.

If I owe money to a shopkeeper whose goods I have already consumed, I am not at liberty to give *that* money to 'someone who asks of me' – unless, once again, there are very special factors involved.

If turning the other cheek means I will then be dead, or that others will suffer great harm, I have to consider this larger context. Much more than my personal pain or humiliation is involved. Does that mean I will 'shoot first'? Not necessarily, but it means I can't just invoke a presumed 'law of required vulnerability'. I must *decide* before God what to do, and there may be grounds for some measure of resistance.

Of course the grounds will *never* be personal retaliation. And there will never, as I live in the kingdom, be room for 'getting even'. We do not 'render evil for evil', as the early Christians clearly understood and practised (Rom. 12:17; 1 Pet. 3:9). That is out of the question as far as our life is kingdom living. That is the point Jesus is making here.

If someone has taken my coat by lawsuit, I or someone else may well have a greater need of my shirt than he does. If not, I give it with generous love and blessing. Or perhaps the other's need is so great I should give my shirt even if I suffer greatly. But what if the other doesn't need it at all? Then I won't impose it 'because Jesus said so' and I must keep this 'law'.

In every concrete situation we have to ask ourselves, not 'Did I do the specific things in Jesus' illustrations?' but 'Am I being the kind of person Jesus' illustrations are illustrations of?'

Shifting the Scene

What actually happens when one derives one's response from the reality of the kingdom is that the dynamics of personal interaction are transformed. What does the person do who has been offered the other cheek? Or perhaps has now slapped it? Keep on slapping? For how long? And then what? We must always be alert for acceptable ways of removing ourselves from the situation. In the case of abuse of any kind, one should begin by involving others, and especially appointed authorities.

Our tormentors, no doubt, count on our resistance and anger to support their continuation of the evil that is in them. If we respond as Jesus indicates, the force of their own actions pulls them off their stance and forces them to question what kind of people they are. Of course they are acting from anger and worse. But now with our other cheek facing them, slapped already or soon to be slapped, the justification of their anger and evil that they were counting on has been removed. As anger feeds on anger, so patient goodness will normally deflate it. Whether it does or not, the larger community should be appropriately involved.

And we, for our part, following the order of Jesus' teaching and example, have already dealt with our anger, contempt and fantasized desire, so they do not come into play. Our response allows the kingdom of God, with all its resources, to begin its work. We 'venture on the kingdom', as we have already said, and suddenly our attackers or the ones imposing upon us sense that they are not playing the game they thought they were, that they are not in control. Their behaviour will, in most cases, undergo a radical change and will always be profoundly affected. That is why one who stands with Jesus in his kingdom need never worry about becoming a 'doormat'.

And if it doesn't change? If they just harden themselves the more and keep on coming at us? Well, then we must act or not act as we judge best. Here, as in the other situations Jesus uses to exhibit the kingdom heart, we know there are certain types of attitudes, with corresponding responses, that we are not to slip into. But what action we *are* to take is something we must decide. We will decide, as best we know how, on the basis of love for all involved and with a readiness to sacrifice what we simply want. And in every situation we have the larger view. We are not passive, but we act always with clear-eyed and resolute love.

We know what is really happening, seeing it from the point of view of eternity. And we know that we will be taken care of, no matter what. We can be vulnerable because we are, in the end, simply invulnerable. And once we have broken the power of anger and desire over our lives, we know that the way of Christ in response to personal injury and imposition is always the easier way. It is the only way that allows us to move serenely in the midst of harm and beyond it.

What to Do with Enemies

Few of us manage to go through life without collecting a group of individuals who would not be sorry to learn we have died. By far most of the people who have lived on earth have been confronted with certain kinds of other people – other 'tribes' – who would gladly kill them. There is a standard list of 'enemies' in the daily news, which in fact hardly scratches the surface of the reality of standing hatreds that define people as enemies ever against one another in this world.

The final illustrative contrast between the old rightness and the rightness of the kingdom heart has to do with our attitude towards our enemies: those with standing contempt and hatred for us who regularly fantasize our pain and destruction. Here the old 'rightness' was very simple. It was really just another application of the *lex talionis*. They seek our destruction, so we seek theirs in the same way. They hate us, so we hate them. It is only right to do so (Matt. 5:43).

Jesus, on the other hand, tells us to love our enemies and to carry that love through with the highest act of love, prayer. 'Love your enemies and pray for those persecuting you. In this way you take on the nature your Father, the one in the heavens, who routinely gives good things, such as sunshine and rain, to both the evil and the good, to those who are godly and those who spit in his face' (Matt. 5:44–45).

Loving those who love us and lavishing care and honour on those of our own group is something that traitorous oppressors, the Mafia and terrorists do. How, then, could *that* serve to distinguish the goodness of someone born into God's family or the presence of a different kind of reality and life? Even those with no knowledge of God at all, 'the gentiles', do it.

But, Jesus says to his disciples, because you are living from God as citizens of the kingdom, have the kind of wholeness, of full functionality, that he has. 'Be perfect [*teleioi*] in the way your Father, the one in the heavens, is perfect' (5:48).

Goodness is Love

Completing the Picture of the Kingdom Heart: *Agape* Love

With this contrast Jesus brings to completion his exposition of the kind of 'goodness beyond' that goes hand in hand with the blessedness of the eternal kind of life. When he thus comes to completion in the *agape* love that characterizes the Father, he has moved beyond specific acts and illustrations of kingdom goodness. Love does not illustrate, it simply is the goodness beyond the goodness of scribes and Pharisees. All the illustrations he has given in the various situations discussed in 5:20–48 are illustrations of it.

In it we achieve living union with, have fully entered into, the kingdom of the heavens. We have sought and found the reigning of God and the kind of *dikaiosune* he himself has (6:33). Out of that union we discover love as a life power that has the marvellous, many-sided expression spelled out by Paul in 1 Corinthians 13. But this beautiful statement by Paul is commonly misunderstood in exactly the same legalistic way as is Jesus' Discourse on the Hill.

Love, Paul there tells us, is patient, kind, free of jealousy and arrogance, is not rude or self-seeking, is not easily angered and keeps no record of wrongs, takes no joy in things that are wrong but instead in what is true. It always protects, always accepts, always hopes and endures everything. And it never quits (1 Cor. 13:4–8).

People usually read this, and are taught to read it, as telling *them* to be patient, kind, free of jealousy and so on – just as they read Jesus' Discourse as telling them to not call others fools, not look on a woman to lust, not swear, to go the second mile and so forth.

But Paul is plainly saying – look at his words – that it is love that does these things, not us, and that what we are to do is to 'pursue love' (1 Cor. 14:1). As we 'catch' love, we then find that these things are after all actually being done by us. These things, these godly actions and behaviours, are the result of dwelling in love. We have become the kind of person who is patient, kind, free of jealousy and so on. Paul's message is exactly the same as Jesus' message. And no wonder, for as Paul was always the first to say, he learned what he taught from Jesus (Gal. 1:12).

Are These Things Hard to Do?

Is it then hard to do the things with which Jesus illustrates the kingdom heart of love? Or the things that Paul says love does? It is very hard indeed if you have not been substantially transformed in the depths of your being, in the intricacies of your thoughts, feelings, assurances and dispositions, in such a way that you are permeated with love. Once that happens, then it is not hard. What would be hard is to act the way you acted before.

When Jesus hung on the cross and prayed, 'Father, forgive them because they do not understand what they are doing,' that was not hard for him. What would have been hard for him would have been to curse his enemies and spew forth vileness and evil upon everyone, God and the world, as those crucified with him did, at least for a while. He calls us to him to impart himself to us. He does not call us to do what he did, but to be as he was, permeated with love. Then the doing of what he did and said becomes the natural expression of who we are in him.

Bertrand Russell, a well-known British philosopher of this century, was raised a Christian, though he later adopted atheism. He was familiar with the teachings of Jesus, if not their actual meaning. In one place he comments, 'The Christian principle, "Love your enemies" is good … There is nothing to be said against it except that it is too difficult for most of us to practise sincerely.'[24]

He was, of course, right as he understood it, for he was thinking of himself and others remaining what they were inwardly and nevertheless trying to love their enemies as occasion arose. Of course, they would fail, at least most of the time. As for Russell personally, some of long acquaintance with him and Russell himself knew he was filled with hatred. No wonder he found love difficult.[25]

Russell's fallacy is the fallacy of the Pharisee. By now it should be recognizable. The Pharisee takes as his aim keeping the law rather than becoming the kind of person whose deeds naturally conform to the law. Jesus knew the human heart better than Bertrand Russell did. Thus he concludes his exposition of the kingdom kind of goodness by contrasting the ordinary way human beings love, loving those who love them, with God's agape love. This is a love that reaches everyone we deal with. It is not in their power to change that. It is the very core of what we are or can become in his fellowship, not something we do. Then the deeds of love, including loving our enemies, are what that agape love does in us and what we do as the new persons we have become.

The Intellectual Vacuum of Current Moral Thought

Towards the beginning of this chapter we made the statement that the centuries-long attempt to devise a morality from within merely human resources has now proven itself a failure. Now we want to return to this point in the light of Jesus' exposition of the rightness of the kingdom heart.

What is the basis of such a statement? Simply this: that, as noted in the opening of Chapter 1, there is in fact no body of moral knowledge now operative in the institutions of knowledge in our culture. This is the outcome of the now centuries-long effort to develop a moral guide to life within the framework of human thought and experience alone, unassisted by revelation.

By contrast, the Christian teaching about moral goodness that derives from the principles laid down by Jesus does have a historical, theoretical and practical claim to constitute the true body of moral knowledge. This is not said to encourage blind acceptance but precisely the opposite. It is said to encourage the toughest of testing for those teachings in all areas of thought and real life.

We saw in Chapter 1 the young lady who went to Professor Coles on her way out of Harvard and said to him, 'I've been taking all these philosophy courses, and we talk about what's true, what's important, what's *good*. Well, how do you teach people to *be* good?' Then she added, 'What's the point of *knowing* good, if you don't keep trying to *become* a good person?' But, as we pointed out, *knowing* good is not seriously proposed in college or university courses today. Any 'knowing' in such matters is thought to be totally impossible.

In fact, both knowing good and being good are for the most part treated with open scorn in the academic settings which determine so much of our lives. That is the outcome of the long effort to establish a secular ethic in the modern period. But the concern for becoming good and being good remains, as the words of both President Bok and Professor Coles show, for it is a real-life issue that will never go away.

And it is with regard to this issue of what kind of people we are to be that the teachings of Jesus about the rightness of the kingdom heart show him to be the unrivalled master of human life. Any serious inquirer can validate those teachings in his or her own experience. But they cannot invalidate them by simply refusing to consider them and hiding behind the dogmas of modern intellect.

Chapter 6

INVESTING IN THE HEAVENS: ESCAPING THE DECEPTIONS OF REPUTATION AND WEALTH

> How can you have faith when you seek glory from one another and do not seek the glory that comes from the One who alone is God?
>
> JOHN 5:44

> Now the Pharisees were lovers of money, and when they heard Jesus' teachings they scoffed at him. But he responded: 'You try to look good in the eyes of men. But God sees your hearts. And what men think highly of is a stench before God.'
>
> LUKE 16:14–15

From Jesus' Discourse on the Hill we have learned thus far his answers to the two great questions forced on all of us by human life: Who is really well off? and Who is a genuinely good person? One is blessed, we now know, if one's life is based upon acceptance and intimate interactions with what God is doing in human history. Such people are in the present kingdom of the heavens.

And genuinely good people are those who, from the deepest levels of their understanding and motivation, are committed to promoting the good of everyone they deal with – including, of course, God and themselves. In this they have, with God's assistance, gone beyond rightness understood as merely 'not doing anything wrong' – beyond the goodness of scribes and Pharisees – and are acting from their inward union of mind and heart with 'the heavens'.

It is their confidence in Jesus that has placed them into a living union with The Kingdom Among Us. Their union with Jesus allows them now to be a part of his conspiracy to undermine the structures of evil, which continue to dominate human history, with the forces of truth, freedom, and love. We can quietly and relentlessly align ourselves with these forces, wherever they are, because we know what is cosmically afoot. To 'overcome evil with good,' in the apostle Paul's words, is not just something for an individual effort here and there, is actually what will come to pass on this earth. The power of Jesus' resurrection and his continuing life in human beings assures of this.

Having shown us true well-being and the goodness of the kingdom heart, Jesus now, in Matthew 6, alerts us to the two main things that will block or hinder a life constantly interactive with God and healthy growth in the kingdom. These are the desire to have the approval of others, especially for being devout, and the desire to secure ourselves by means of material wealth.

If we allow them to, these two desires will pull us out of the sway of the kingdom – 'the range of God's effective will,' as we have described it – and back into the barren 'righteousness' of the scribe and the Pharisee. But as we keep these two things in their proper place, through a constant, disciplined and clear-eyed reliance on God, we will grow rapidly in kingdom substance. We will progressively incorporate all aspects of our life into the kingdom, including, of course, the social and the financial. By now, multitudes have proved this to be so.

The Respectability Trap

The Lure of Religious Honours

Desire for religious respect or reputation will *immediately* drag us into the rightness of scribes and Pharisees because that desire always focuses entirely upon the visible action, not on the source of action in the heart. The scribes and Pharisees, Jesus pointed out, 'do everything they do with the aim of being noticed by others. They enlarge the religious symbols on their clothing. They like to have the most prominent seats at dinners and in the synagogues. They relish loudly respectful greetings in malls and public places, and being called "Professor" or "Doctor"' (Matt. 23:5–7).

The hunger for titles and public awards in human life – indeed, in religious life – is quite astonishing. The bragging and exhibitionist content of many car window stickers, the almost routine puffing of credentials and curricula vitae, and much that passes for normal as part of our 'self-esteem' culture, are part of a life with no sense of our standing in the presence of God.

The children of the kingdom, by contrast, are to have none of all this. 'Don't seek to be called "Professor" or "Doctor",' Jesus says, 'for you have only one teacher, and all of you are students. And call no one on earth "Father", for you have only one Father, the one in the heavens. Also, do not be called "leader". The Anointed One is your leader, and it is not the leaders but the servants who are greatest among you' (vv. 8–11).

What a refreshing difference! But, unfortunately, if you have to bet on what text will be used for next Sunday's sermon, better not bet on this one. The public forms that our Christian devotion take are all too similar to the kind that Jesus here pushes aside. You have only to consider who is lionized, and for what, in our local congregations and religious associations and media. We have much reason to be concerned about the effects of religious respectability on our faithfulness to God.

Playing to the Audience of One

Of course by now we surely know that we are not to be in bondage to external forms, or to their absence. The form could be wrong and the heart be right, or the form right and the heart wrong. The fact that I call someone 'Father' as a formality does not mean I regard that person as my father, just as my taking an oath before giving testimony in court does not mean I am trying to manipulate my hearers. My wily heart could even use my very refusal to take the oath in court as a way of going beyond yes and no. What matters are the intentions of our heart before God.

Jesus gives us his guiding principle at the outset of the discussion in Matt. 6:1. 'Be sure not to do your rightness (*dikaiosune*) before human beings with the intent of being seen by them. Otherwise your Father, the one in the heavens, will have nothing to do with it.'

Two things should be noted immediately.

First, the teaching is not that we should *hide* our good deeds. That might be appropriate in some cases, but it is not Jesus' point. There is nothing inherently wrong with their being known. Just as in the case of 'adultery in the heart', the issue here is one of intents and purposes. Not did we look at someone *and* sexually desire them, as we have seen, but did we look at someone *in order to* sexually desire them. And now: not are we seen doing a good deed, but are we doing a good deed *in order to be seen*. In any case where we use, on ourselves or others, promised recognition as a motive for doing what should be done for its own sake, we are pre-empting God's role in our life.

Second, our intent is determined by what we want and expect from our action. When we do good deeds to be seen by human beings, that is because what we are looking for is something that comes from human beings. God responds to our expectations accordingly. When we want human approval and esteem, and do what we do for the sake of it, God courteously stands aside because, by our wish, it does not concern him.

This goes along with the personal nature of God and of our relationship to him. As we saw earlier, God does not like to be present where he is not wanted. And he knows when he is wanted and when he is not. Similarly, where people are really seeking a response from someone else, he does not intrude – generally speaking. So when our aim is to impress human beings with how devout we are, he lets us do that and stands aside. Of course, he will eventually have his day. There will be a 'day of the Lord', his turn to bat, as it were.

On the other hand, if we live unto God alone, he responds to our expectations – which are of him alone. Os Guinness, a well-known United States Christian thinker and leader, has said of the Puritans in American history that they lived as if they stood before an audience of One. They carried on their lives as if the only one whose opinion mattered were God. Of course they understood that this is what Jesus Christ taught them to do.

But the principle of 'the audience of One' extends to all that we do, and not just to deeds of devotion or charity. The apostle Paul charges us to do all our work, whatever our situation, 'with enthusiasm, as for the Lord and not for men, knowing that he is the one who rewards you and whom you serve.' Indeed, we are to do all that we do 'on behalf of the Lord Jesus, in that way giving thanks through him to God the Father' (Col. 3:17–24). Even more so for our 'rightnesses'.

Don't Let the Left Hand Know

Now Jesus gives us three *illustrations* – illustrations, remember, not laws – of a correctly Godward motivation in commendable actions.

First, he speaks of philanthropic deeds or acts that bring relief to the needy, often called 'alms' or 'almsdeeds.' The Greek term usually translated 'alms' (6:2) here is actually the same as our English term *eleemosynary*, which has come to refer to non-profit charitable operations and institutions.

When you do such deeds, Jesus says, 'do not act like the hypocrites, who have trumpets blown before them, in the synagogues and streets, as they go to do their good deeds in order to be glorified by human beings' (6:2). 'In fact,' he continues to say, 'they have received their reward in full.' What they wanted, they got. They wanted people to recognize their good deed and people did. The ego is bloated and the soul shrivels.

A special word about 'the hypocrites' is required here. It is a term used by Jesus alone in the New Testament, and he uses it seventeen times. The term *hypocrite* in classical Greek primarily refers to an actor, such as one sees on the stage, but it came to refer also to anyone who practises deceit. It is clear from the literary records that it was Jesus alone who brought this term and the corresponding character into the moral vocabulary of the Western world.[1] He did so because of his unique emphasis upon the moral significance of the inmost heart before God. As we are creative beings, our heart is who we really are. Jesus therefore made repeated and unmistakable distinctions between our face to the world and our person before God.

We now know that the Palestine of Jesus' day had numerous fine theatres, and he certainly was familiar with them. One was located in the city of Sepphoris, within a few miles of his home in Nazareth. This one was built while Jesus was a young man, and he and his father Joseph may have been workmen there. Herod the Great had previously built fine theatres in Jericho and Samaria, as well as in Jerusalem.[2] When Jesus spoke of 'the hypocrites', he was using a very vivid image that effectively seized the minds of his hearers because of their familiarity with stage characters. They were thus able to see much of the most obvious religious behaviour of their day as the sham it in fact was.

It may be hard to believe that anyone could ever do such a thing as Jesus calls attention to. But they certainly did. Literally blowing a trumpet to call attention to one's good deeds is not our style today; however, this particular behaviour illustrates enduring human traits. Fund-raisers know that it is much easier nowadays to get someone to build a building for some social institution than it is to get them to endow the maintenance on a building. You can name the building after the contributors or their family, or at least put up a plaque with their name upon it. But you can't do that for the maintenance of the building; no one seems to want their name on a mop or a broom. There are many ways of seeking glory with gifts other than by sounding a trumpet. We all too often find a way.

Jesus' contrasting teaching is that when we do an 'almsdeed' we should 'not let our left hand know what our right hand is doing.' Now how do you do that? If you *set out* to do it, you will certainly not succeed. What would you say to your left hand? 'Now ignore what the right hand is doing'? Then, of course, it will be impossible for it to do so. Ignoring the right hand is precisely a way of watching it, of being conscious of it.

The comedian Bill Cosby used to perform a routine about his childhood in which, when 'the gang' wanted to exclude a child from some activity, they would tell him he had to stand in a corner and not think about a pink polar bear for fifteen minutes before he could play. Of course it is impossible to do that deliberately because you have to think of not thinking of a pink polar bear and hence think of a pink polar bear!

But we must never forget that Jesus points *beyond* action to the source of action in character. This is a general principle that governs all he says. The kind of people who have been so transformed by their daily walk with God that good deeds naturally flow from their character are precisely the kind of people whose left hand would not notice what their right hand is doing – as, for example, when driving one's own car or speaking one's native language. What they do they do naturally, often automatically, simply because of what they *are* pervasively and internally. These are people who do not have to invest a lot of reflection in doing good for others. Their deeds are 'in secret' no matter who is watching, for they are absorbed in love of God and of those around them. They hardly notice their own deed, and rarely remember it.

And because they really are looking towards God and living towards God, God responds to them: 'Your Father, the one who sees in secret, will reward you' (6:4). The one who gives without regard to who is looking and does not even notice it as anything special themselves, no 'big deal', is the very one who has God's attention and becomes God's creative partner in well-doing. He or she will know the fellowship of God and see the effects of these deeds multiplied for good in the power of God. Characteristically, people like this are well known for how much they can accomplish. But we should know, as Jesus knew, that it is because of 'the hand of God' engaged along with them.

And When You Pray

Similarly 'the hypocrites' pray in order to be seen by others. But, as hypocrites, in the very meaning of the term, they are not what they seem to be. They seem to the onlooker to be devout before God. But they are interested only in making an impression on people. 'They stand and pray in the synagogues and on the street corners, in order to be seen of men' (Matt. 6:5). They may or may not think that God too is impressed. But that is not essential. What is essential is that they be seen.

And guess what. They *are* seen by other people. That is the reward they wanted. They got it. The entire operation lay within the range of human competence. Because they had not involved God in what they were doing, he does not intrude on their project. They are at the level of pharisaical righteousness, which never 'enters the kingdom'. Again, the ego swells, and the soul shrivels.

Often something close to this happens with very well-meaning people who simply have not accustomed themselves to disregarding the human context as they pray. When they pray, therefore, they only think of how they are sounding to others, or perhaps their main concern is with how they will look to others if God does not answer. Some even are obsessed with impressing God as they pray. All such ego concerns must be simply dropped as we pray in the kingdom.

So when the children of the kingdom pray, they may even disappear from sight, for they have learned to be indifferent to whether others know of their prayer or not. They enter a private room and close the door. There they pray to their Father, who not only *sees* in secret, but, Jesus here says, *is* in secret (v. 6). This is very significant. The secret place is where God is. There we stand 'under the shadow of the Almighty' (Ps. 91).

Prayer, it is rightly said, is the method of genuine theological research, the method of understanding what and who God is. God is spirit and exists at the level of reality where the human heart, or spirit, *also* exists, serving as the foundation and source of our visible life. It is there that the individual meets with God 'in spirit and in truth'.

The effect is, once again, a remarkable difference in the life of the believer. 'Your Father who sees in secret will repay you' (v. 6). The visible side of your life will involve highly significant events that cannot be explained in terms of the visible world. The 'spiritual' person is understood by no one, as Paul says (1 Cor. 2:15). That is because they are operating from the reality that is 'in secret'.

Jesus also warns in this passage about mistaking prayer for a mechanical process. That too would turn it into an event in the physical or visible world, not a matter of the heart. Those who do not understand God, 'the gentiles' or *ethnikoi*, falsely imagine that mere sounds, repeated over and over, will gain the desired effect. The word *battalogasate*, translated 'vain repetition' in the familiar King James Version (6:7), refers to senseless repetition, like that of one who stammers or is babbling. It has nothing to do with thoughtfully used litergy.

The 'gentiles' do not understand that prayer to the God of Israel and of Jesus, the living and personal God of the universe, is *intelligent conversation about matters of mutual concern*. This takes place in a society of shared ends and efforts, where *agape* love and the spirit of forgiveness are basic to every relationship (6:14–15). Hence they grind away at their senseless routines, hoping to use 'god' to get what they want.

This misunderstanding is illustrated by a story from the book of Acts, Chapter 8. Under the apostles, the invisible kingdom of the heavens was in powerful manifestation in Samaria, a place where Jesus himself had, some time earlier, been well received. Simon 'the great' was a local magician who observed the visible effects of the words and deeds of the apostles. He thought this was in his own line of work as a magician, and that he could buy 'the secret' from the apostles and use it in his business.

He did not understand that what he saw in the visible world in response to the apostles was a matter of who they were at the heart level before God and was a result of spiritual connectedness. A similar mistake is made by a group of Jewish exorcists in Acts 19:11–17.

Kingdom praying and its efficacy is entirely a matter of the innermost heart's being totally open and honest before God. It is a matter of what we are saying with our whole being, moving with resolute intent and clarity of mind into the flow of God's action. In apprenticeship to Jesus, this is one of the most important things we learn how to do. He teaches us how to be in prayer what we are in life and how to be in life what we are in prayer.

It is at this point in his Discourse that Jesus, very fittingly, gives the model prayer commonly known as the Lord's Prayer. Indeed, it is the disciple's prayer, and it has an absolutely vital role in kingdom living. We are going to look at it intensively in our next chapter, where we consider the community of prayerful love that God is now building.

Readers who have understood what has been said thus far will not be lulled into thinking that, in his teaching on prayer, Jesus is giving a law that forbids prayer in public, or that requires one to pray only with the words he gives in the model payer, and so forth. Given the prevailing misunderstandings, however, we cannot say too often that in the Sermon on the Mount we are not looking at laws, but at a life: a life in which the genuine laws of God eventually become naturally fulfilled.

Similarly, nothing he is teaching rules out the use of written prayers or liturgy. You can be just as 'man pleasing' and 'fleshly' in extemporaneous and informal religious exercises as in pre-established and formal ones – perhaps even more so – especially if you are proud of being informal.

Fasting Before God Alone

Fasting, too, had frequently been turned into an exercise in exhibitionism and respectability. Those who fast deprive themselves for some time and to some degree of normal food and drink. It is a thoroughly biblical practice that forms one dimension of the believer's interactive life with God. But 'the hypocrites' of Jesus' day tried to look as gloomy as possible when they fasted. They had even developed special ways of disfiguring their faces with special markings in order to make sure people knew they were fasting.

Here again Jesus points out that they get what they want. They want to be noticed in being 'devout', and they certainly are noticed. 'I tell you the truth,' he says again, 'they have their reward' (Matt. 6:16); that is, the one they were looking for.

And then he points us in the right direction for fasting as a practice in kingdom living. 'Take a shower,' he says, 'and fix yourself up. Brush your teeth. Put on lotion and cologne and nice clothing, so that others won't know you are fasting. Your Father who is in secret will see your hidden heart and enrich your life' (6:17–18). Once again, one is impressed with what refreshing good sense characterizes Jesus' words.

Of course, if we are not well experienced with fasting in the spirit of Christ, we may think that we will be miserable when we fast. If we are miserable, shouldn't we look that way? Could Jesus be asking us to 'fake it'? And indeed those who do not fast with God alone in view, or who have not yet learned *how* to do it well, will be miserable – as, no doubt, 'the hypocrites' were.

But Jesus himself knew that when we have learned how to fast 'in secret', our bodies and our souls will be directly sustained by the invisible kingdom. We will not be miserable. But we certainly will be *different*. And our abundant strength and our joy will come in ways a purely physical human existence in 'the flesh' does not know. It will come from those sources that 'are in secret'.

When Jesus was in his long fast between his baptism and entering public life, he was tempted by Satan to turn stones into loaves of bread that he might eat. His reply is profoundly important for understanding the kingdom and kingdom living. He cites a passage from Deuteronomy: 'The human being is not nourished by bread only, but by every word that comes out of God's mouth' (Matt. 4:4; Deut. 8:3). What we must take care to understand is the phrase 'every word that comes out of God's mouth.'

'Manna' as One Kind of Word of God

The passage from Deuteronomy 8 gives us the key. The primary reference of 'word that comes out of God's mouth' was the 'manna' that the Israelites lived on during their years of wandering in the desert between Canaan and Egypt. Now *manna* is an interesting term. It basically means 'whatever it is', or 'what is it?' Manna was a form of physical substance that was unknown. It was, in fact, a digestible form of *matter* suited to the physical needs of human beings and produced directly by God's action, or 'word', not by a process already in place in nature.

It is significant that not only were needs for food in the desert met by the direct action of God, but also needs for clothing and shoes. The Israelites wore the same shoes and clothing, continuously renewed by God, for forty years (Deut. 8:4). That was a fundamental part of the training they received in kingdom living. Centuries later, Nehemiah recalls God's provision in the desert just as another great historical deliverance is taking place by the hand of God: 'Yes, for forty years you provided for them out in the wastelands, and they lacked for nothing. Their clothing did not wear out nor did their shoes become too small' (Neh. 9:21).

All of this must, of course, be seen in the context of a God who in the first place created the entire physical order by his word/deed, who brought water out of a rock and caused an almond branch cut from the tree 'to grow and produce buds and blossoms and ripe fruit' (Num. 17:8).

This God is master of all basic equations that govern reality, physical and otherwise, such as the famous $e=mc^2$ discovered by Albert Einstein. (Here, *e* is energy, *m* is matter, and *c* is the speed of light.) Now, from the human perspective, it is mainly *matter* that is available to us. To meet our needs we are, within narrow limits, able to manipulate it to produce useable forms of energy, by processes such as digestion, combustion, atomic fission or fusion and so forth.

But to God, the 'energy' side of the equation is also available. He has inexhaustible supplies of it. And so he can feed thousands by 'multiplying' a few loaves and fishes, or he can directly supply the physical needs of the body of one fasting with faith towards him. His *rehma* 'word' (Matt. 4:4) to me is a concrete reality that becomes, in fasting, physical sustenance to my needy body.

Of course Jesus ate normal food, as all of us do and must. That is the God-appointed normal course, to be received with humility and thankfulness. But he also knew the direct sustenance of God to his body. He would have us know it too. The Gospel account of his meeting with a woman of Samaria (John 4) is one of the theologically richest passages in all of scripture. But one of the greatest teachings occurs right at the end of the story and is often overlooked.

It was late afternoon, and his apprentices had gone into the town to obtain food while he rested from the journey by the town well. They returned to find him conversing with – 'a woman'! They were startled that he would do such a disreputable thing. But, as people are coming out of town in response to the reports of 'the woman' who had rushed back to tell of him, they urged him to eat of the food they had brought.

His reply teaches us much about fasting and about what happens when we are engaged with the kingdom of the heavens. He says, 'I have some food you don't know about.' The disciples, from their limited understanding of the possibilities of human nourishment, immediately began to ask if someone else had brought him food. Then Jesus explained the heavenly food that nourished him: 'My food is to do what the One who sent me wants done and to accomplish his purposes' (John 4:34).

Here, as with so many of the biblical statements keyed to the realities of God's full world, we have to decide whether or not these are just 'pretty words'. No doubt they mean *something*, many will say, but really nothing more than, possibly, some vaguely devout human condition or state of mind. For example, in this case, Jesus is often thought to mean that when you do God's will, or possibly just 'good things', you feel better about yourself and life, and perhaps also that those around you will support and encourage you. Thus the good news from Jesus is reduced in practice to some vaguely hopeful outlook on the human condition.

But before taking this approach we should at least ask, What would it be like for his statement, 'I have some food you don't know about,' to be true in the sense it was obviously taken by those who initially heard it. In the case of John 4, the issue being addressed with his disciples was precisely the need for physical nourishment and how it might be met. Jesus indicates that physical nourishment too was available directly from spiritual sources.

In John 3, by comparison, the matter of an *additional kind of life* is being addressed. The idea of a birth 'from above' is presented by Jesus to explain how such an additional kind of life enters human beings here on earth. This 'birth' is a *reality*, an actual event or condition, not pretty words that perhaps refer to getting a new start in life.

Of course what really comes into play in all such passages are the beliefs we actually hold concerning 'reality', especially about God and his world. Lack of confidence in the kingdom will force us to take the 'pretty words' reading of the words of scripture. Many people simply put all of the scriptures and even religion as a whole in that category. Thus George Santayana once described religion as only 'a lyric cry in the business of life', a brief indulging in pleasant feelings.

The story is told of a man who lost his composure and cursed in the presence of his pastor. After an embarrassed silence, he looked sheepishly at the pastor and said, 'Oh, it's all right, pastor. I cuss a little and you pray a little, but neither one of us means anything by it.' The challenge to our faith in the kingdom is to mean something by our talk of it.

That Jesus himself 'meant something by it', and what he meant was precisely shown in his character and in his power to love and help people around him. His remarkable life and ministry came from his relationship to his Father. Of course none of us has exactly the same relationship, but something of what we see in him is sure to come to us as we nourish ourselves on him and his kingdom.

Feasting on Jesus Himself

He told us that he was to be 'eaten': 'He who eats me shall live by me, … and shall live forever' (John 6:51). He, not the manna, is 'the bread which comes down out of heaven, so that one may eat of it and not die' (vv. 48–50). The practice of fasting goes together with this teaching about nourishing ourselves on the person of Jesus. It emphasizes the direct availability of God to nourish, sustain, and renew the soul. It is a testimony to the reality of another world from which Jesus and his Father perpetually intermingle their lives with ours (John 14:23). And the effects of our turning strongly to this true 'food' will be obvious.

Here are some words from a pastor who had recently learned about kingdom fasting and began to put it into practice:

> The discipline of fasting has taken on new importance and regularity for me … There is an admonition in 'The Rule of St Benedict' that exhorts the monk 'to love fasting'. It is now my regular practice to fast every time I preach. I have a deeper sense of dependency and of the immense power of the spoken word. This has been demonstrated by the dear individual in my congregation who runs our tape

> ministry. She said that since January of this year, her order for sermon tapes has doubled. 'I can't explain it,' she said, 'but whatever it is, keep it up!'

He had learned to fast before the Father who is in secret, and the Father 'repaid' him by acting with his efforts in ministry. The effects in the visible world were far more than could be attributed to his own capabilities. Just as Jesus said.

Secrecy as a Fundamental Discipline

What Jesus is teaching us to do in this important passage from his Discourse is to be free of control by the opinions of others. Paul's wonderful term for this type of control is *eyeservice*, or being enslaved to eyes (*ophthalmodoulian*; Col. 3:22; Eph. 6:6). Of course it concerns just as much our not doing things that are bad for fear of being seen as it does our doing what is good in order to be seen. The decisive motivation for acting as well as not acting must be our regard of the kingdom of God in which we live as Jesus' people.

The effect of both action and non-action for human approval is to push the presence of God aside as irrelevant and to subject ourselves to the human kingdom. In both avoiding evil and doing good, our respect should be for God alone. We may think it is OK to avoid evil for fear of being seen, for in any case we do avoid the evil. But that only shows we have no respect for God and would disobey him but for the opinions of others. The basic principle is the same in both cases.

The *discipline* of secrecy will help us break the grip of human opinion over our souls and our actions. A discipline is an activity in our power that we do to enable us to do what we cannot do by direct effort. Jesus is here leading us into the discipline of secrecy. We from time to time practise doing things approved of in our religious circles – giving, praying, fasting, attending services of the church and so on – but in such a way that no one knows. Thus our motivation and reward for doing these things cannot come from human beings. We are liberated from slavery to eyes, and then it does not matter whether people know or not. We learn to live constantly in this way.

This is a rather important point for understanding what Jesus is teaching us to do in this part of the Sermon on the Mount. In particular, because of the always threatening legalism – which thinks of rightness only in terms of particular actions – we must see why he does not make it a law that we only do good deeds, pray and fast in secrecy. Biblical practice and the practice of Jesus himself obviously show that it is not a law.

Recall that Jesus often teaches against a background practice that is wrong. We have commented on this in earlier chapters. The background practices presupposed in Matt. 6:1–18 are, obviously, doing good deeds, praying and fasting to be seen. He teaches us not to engage in these practices, and he does so by saying, 'Let your alms [prayer, fasting] be in secret.' But he does *not* mean, 'Never, on pain of sin guilt, let anyone see you or know you to do a good deed [pray, fast].'

That is why there is here no inconsistency with his earlier directive in the Discourse: 'Let your light shine before men in such a way *that they may see your good works* and glorify your Father, the one in the heavens' (6:16). His teaching leads to a discipline, not a law, and a discipline that prepares us, precisely, to act in a way that fulfils the law of whole-person love of God.

'Religious Evasion'

A thoughtful examination of local gatherings of Christian believers may reveal that in this teaching Jesus lays his finger upon a primary cause of their ineffectiveness as schools of eternal living. Truthfully, it seems to be a general law of social/historical development that institutions tend to distort and destroy the central function that brought them into existence. A few years ago Clyde Reid wrote a painfully incisive discussion of how our church activities seem to be structured around *evading* God. His 'law of religious evasion' states, 'We structure our churches and maintain them so as to shield us from God and to protect us from genuine religious experience.'[3]

Along with many other telling observations of church life, he notes,

> The adult members of churches today rarely raise serious religious questions for fear of revealing their

> doubts or being thought of as strange. There is an implicit *conspiracy of silence* on religious matters in the churches. This conspiracy covers up the fact that the churches do not change lives or influence conduct to any appreciable degree.[4]

There is very little time and occasion for openness in most of our gatherings because we fear it. We think it may lead to confrontation, anger and divisiveness. We are not open because we fear what others will think of us and do to us. If we honestly compared the amount of time in church spent thinking about what others think or might think with the amount of time spent thinking about what God is thinking, we would probably be shocked. Those of us in congregational leadership need to think deeply about this.

Often the 'eyeservice' that occurs in present-day church services comes in the form of trying to 'move' people. 'Wasn't that a great service,' we often say. But what do we mean? Are we really thinking of how God felt about the service? What is the correlation between God's view of a great service and the human view? We need to be very careful about this, or the rule, 'Truly, they have their reward,' may apply to us.

Suppose I am a pastor. If, truly, God did nothing in my church service, or in response to my efforts in ministry, how much would it really matter if the people in attendance still thought and spoke well of things and returned for the next service and brought their friends? I may be tempted to think I have to attract people to hear me but could get by without God.

How can one in a leadership position not be haunted by what the Lord said to his prophet Ezekiel:

> Everyone is talking about you all the time. They say, 'Come and let's hear what the word is from the Lord.' And they sit before you as my people, and they hear your words, but they do not do them. For their mouths talk devotion but their hearts seek wicked gains. Why, you are just like one who sings about love with a beautiful voice and a well-played

> instrument. They hear what you are saying, but do not do it. (Ezek. 33:31–32)

Whatever our position in life, if our lives and works are to be of the kingdom of God, we must not have human approval as a primary or even major aim. We must lovingly allow people to think whatever they will. We may, if it seems right, occasionally try to help them understand us and appreciate what we are doing. That could be an act of love. But in any case we can only serve them by serving the Lord only.

The Bondage of Wealth

Where Your Treasure Is

Jesus continues his warning about seeking security outside of the kingdom by teaching us about our treasures. Treasures are things we try to keep because of a value we place upon them. They may be of no value whatsoever in themselves; nevertheless, we take great pains to protect such things. Thus we are said to treasure them. For example, we may have a 'safe' at home or at a bank. Isn't that an interesting term for a box, *a safe*? A dictionary describes a 'safe' as 'a place or receptacle to keep articles (as provisions or valuables) safe.'

Of course we may also treasure things other than material goods: for example, our reputation, or our relationship to another person, another person, or the security or reputation of our school or our business or our country. The most important commandment of the Judeo-Christian tradition is to treasure God and his realm more than anything else. That is what it means to love God with all your heart, soul, mind and strength. It means to *treasure* him, to hold him and his dear, and to protect and aid him in his purposes. Our only wisdom, safety and fulfilment lies in so treasuring God. Then we will also treasure our neighbours rightly, as *he* treasures them.

Everyone has treasures. This is an essential part of what it is to be human. To have nothing that one treasures is to be in a non-human condition, and nothing degrades people more than to scorn or destroy or deprive them of their treasures. Indeed, merely to pry into what one's treasures are is a severe intrusion. Apart from very special considerations, no one has a right even to know what our treasures are. A main part of intimacy between two persons is precisely mutual knowledge of their treasures. Treasures are directly connected to our spirit, or will, and thus to our dignity as persons. It is, for example, very important for parents to respect the 'treasure space' of children. It lies right at the centre of the child's soul, and great harm can be done if it is not respected and even fostered.

When our son John Samuel was a little boy, he had a stuffed animal that he called Sleepy Dog. You can easily imagine what it looked like, I think. He kept it near him at play and slept with it right beside him. Over time it became emaciated and threadbare. His mother cleaned and repaired it as best she could, of course. But I, in my infinite wisdom – of which I had so much more when I was younger – eventually decided that Sleepy Dog must be replaced. So we obtained another little stuffed animal, and Sleepy Dog disappeared. John never really accepted the replacement, and in his gentle spirit he grieved for his little stuffed friend for a long time. Of course there was no really good reason why he could not have kept him.

People in concentration camps and those homeless folk who come to live on the streets go to great lengths and even risk their lives to hold on to things that may be simply ridiculous to others. None of them is without some treasure. It will be perhaps a photo or old letter or some ornament or trinket. We reveal what our treasures are by what we try to protect, secure, keep. Often our treasures are totally worthless to other people. Sometimes, of course, they are not. And that is the case with money, wealth, material goods.

So, to discuss our treasures is really to discuss our *treasurings*. We are not to pass it off as dealing merely with 'external goods', which are 'non-spiritual' or just physical stuff. It is to deal with the fundamental structure of our soul. It has to do precisely with whether the life we live now in the physical realm is to be an eternal one or not, and the extent to which it will be so.

Beyond Moths, Corrosion and Thieves

The first thing that Jesus tells us with respect to treasures is that to treasure things that are 'upon the earth' is not a smart strategy for treasuring. Treasures of the earth, by their very nature, simply cannot be held intact. Here is where 'moth and rust destroys things, and thieves dig through walls and steal' (Matt. 6:19). Even cyberspace is not safe from 'viruses', power failure and the disappearance of backups.

This can be very depressing to think about if you know of no alternative. We spoke about Leo Tolstoy and his journey to faith some chapters back. As is well known, he fell into a lengthy, suffocating depression because of the vision that everything he valued would die or otherwise pass away.[5] This was after he had become one of the most successful authors the world has ever known. But the 'world-view of the educated' that imposed itself on him was one of utter hopelessness, much as it is today. Through the teachings of Jesus he found an alternative, and such an alternative as soon delivered him from hopelessness about life and from the meaninglessness of human work.

So the wisdom of Jesus is that we should 'lay up for ourselves treasures in heaven' (6:20), where forces of nature and human evil cannot harm what we treasure. That is to say, direct your actions towards making a difference in the realm of spiritual substance sustained and governed by God. Invest your life in what God is doing, which cannot be lost.

Of course this means that we will invest in our relationship to Jesus himself, and through him to God. But beyond that, and in close union with it, we will devote ourselves to the good of other people – those around us within the range of our power to affect. These are among God's treasures. 'The Lord's portion,' we are told, 'is his people' (Deut. 32:9). And that certainly includes ourselves, in a unique and fundamental way. We have the care of our own souls and lives in a way no one else does, and in a way we have the care of no one else.

And we also care for this astonishingly rich and beautiful physical realm, the earth itself, of which both we and our neighbours are parts. 'You have established the earth and it continues. All things stand this day according to your directions. For all things are your servants' (Ps. 119:91). God himself loves the earth dearly and never takes his hands off it. And because he loves it and it is good, our care of it is also eternal work and a part of our eternal life.

There is a natural order of things that is good to respect. Human beings naturally understand this if they have not been robbed of good sense by their experiences and their education. We see many expressions of this in the ancient law given by God to the Israelites. For example, one homely provision of this law was that a baby goat should not be cooked in its mother's milk. It is an important aspect of the kosher Jewish home. A thoughtless person might say, 'How silly!' And of course one should say that if there is some vital need or reason why, in a given case, it is necessary to do what this law forbids, by all means do it.

But anyone who has lived closely with baby goats and their mothers, and has seen deeply into how they belong to one another, will understand the wrongness of using what the mother is given to sustain the little goat's life to cook it in. Indeed, life is naturally structured throughout by such appropriateness and inappropriateness.[6] Thus, to 'lay up treasures in heaven' is to treasure all of these intimate and touching aspects of heaven's life, all of what God is doing on earth. It is to do so in the order and manner heaven has indicated, and especially as we see it illumined in Jesus himself. And when we live in this way, our treasures are *absolutely secure*. All that we do counts and counts forever. It is preserved in our life within God's eternal life.

This is a large part of what the apostle Paul calls 'sowing to the spirit'. And, when we do such sowing, 'of the spirit we reap what is everlasting.' So 'let us not lose heart in doing good,' he continues, 'for when the time is right we shall reap, if we don't quit. Therefore as we have opportunities let us do good to all men, and most of all to the family of faith' (Gal. 6:8–10). This is, precisely, *how* we deposit treasures in heaven on a daily, hourly basis.

Life Organizes Itself Around Our Heart

Not only can we have complete protection and security of our treasures in this way, but our life as a whole, our living, also now comes into proper alignment with reality. Our souls are now suited to deal with things because we see clearly. Our treasure focuses our heart. 'Your heart will be where what you treasure is,' Jesus tells us (Matt. 6:21). Remember that our heart is our will, or our spirit: the centre of our being from which our life flows. It is what gives orientation to everything we do. A heart rightly directed therefore brings health and wholeness to the entire personality.

To bring this truth home to us, Jesus compares our 'heartsight' to our eyesight. We know how our eyesight affects our body in its environment. 'The eye is the lamp of the body.' If the eye works well, then the body easily moves about in its environment. As Jesus puts it, 'Our whole body is well directed,' is 'full of light' (6:23).

The person who treasures what lies within the kingdom sees everything in its true worth and relationship. The person who treasures what is 'on earth', by contrast, sees everything from a perspective that distorts it and systematically misleads in practice. The relative importance of things is, in particular, misperceived. The person who is addicted to a drug or to some activity is but an extreme case. All else is seen only in its relation to the object of the addiction and enjoyment of it – even one's own body and soul.

Thus, 'if your eyes are bad, your body as a whole is in the dark.' But if the eye of your soul, 'the light within you', is not functioning, then you are in the dark about *everything* (6:23). You are, simply, lost. You don't know where you are or where you are going. This is what it means to be a 'lost soul', a dead soul.

Impossibility of Serving Both God and Earthly Goods

We cannot but serve our treasures. We labour all day for them and think about them all night. They fill our dreams. But it is not uncommon for people to think that they can treasure this world *and* the invisible kingdom as well, that they can serve both. Perhaps we can make this work for a while. But there will come a time when one must be subordinate to the other. We simply cannot have two *ultimate* goals or points of reference for our actions. That is how life is, and no one escapes.

You cannot be the servant of both God and things 'on earth', because their requirements conflict. Unless you have already put God first, for example, what you will have to do to be financially secure, impress other people, or fulfil your desires will invariably lead you against God's wishes. That is why the first of the Ten Commandments, 'You shall have no gods who take priority over me,' is the first of the Ten Commandments.

So treasuring and serving both God and mammon is an nonsensical idea, and in any case you cannot imagine God would endure it. Of course you can serve material goods – value them, use them well – for the sake of God. But that is just to do what Jesus said in the first place and locate your treasures in the heavens. We shall have a great deal more to say about this two chapters hence, in connection with being a disciple or student of Jesus.

The Treasures in the Heavens Are Now

There is, I think, a tendency to regard this treasure in heaven as something that is only for the 'by-and-by'. It is thought to be like life insurance, so called, whose benefits only come after death. And indeed it is crucial to understand that, because we are friends of Jesus Christ, we do have 'an inheritance that is imperishable, untarnished, unfading, reserved in the heavens for those of us who by faith are guarded by the power of God unto a salvation set to be revealed in due time' (1 Pet. 1:4–5). This is important. As the Egyptians discovered long ago, we are going to be 'dead' a lot longer than we are alive on this earth.

But the treasure we have in heaven is also something very much available to us now. We can and should draw upon it as needed, for it is nothing less than God himself and the wonderful society of his kingdom even now interwoven in my life. Even now we 'have come to Mount Zion and to the city of the living God, the heavenly Jerusalem, and to countless angels, and to the assembled church of those born earlier and now claimed in the heavens; and to God who discerns all, to the completed spirits of righteous people, and to Jesus, the mediator of a new agreement' (Heb. 12:22–24). This is not by-and-by, but now.

What is most valuable for any human being, without regard to an afterlife, is to be a part of this marvellous reality, God's kingdom now. Eternity is now ongoing. I am now leading a life that will last forever. Upon my treasure in the heavens I now draw for present needs. If, with a view to my needs in this life, I had to choose between having good credit with a bank and having good credit with God, I would not hesitate a moment. By all means, let the bank go!

What my life really is even now is 'hid with Christ in God' (Col. 3:3). What I 'treasure' in heaven is not just the little that I have caused to be there. It is what I love there and what I place my security and happiness in there. It is God who 'is our refuge and strength, a very present help in time of trouble' (Ps. 46:1). And as the apostle Paul has taught us from his own experience, 'My God shall supply every need you have in terms of his riches in glory in Christ Jesus' (Phil. 4:19). This is the constant witness of the biblical record to The Kingdom Among Us.

How Many Birds Are You Worth?

It is from this background that we now return in the flow of Jesus' Discourse to themes earlier struck in this book: 'We have no reason ever to be anxious.' 'This present world is a perfectly safe place for us to be.' That certainly is what Jesus, and the Bible as a whole, has to say to us. 'Surely goodness and mercy shall follow me all the days of my life, and I shall dwell in the house of the Lord forever' (Ps. 23).

I recognize how strange, even *strained*, it sounds. But that is only because the entire posture of our embodied self and its surroundings is habitually inclined towards physical or 'earthly' reality as the only reality there is. Hence, to treasure anything else *must* be wrong. It is to rest on illusions. We must be prepared to be treated as more or less crazy unless we value what is 'on earth' as supreme for human existence.

But of course if we do value 'mammon' as normal people seem to think we should, our fate is fixed. Our fate is *anxiety*. It is worry. It is frustration. The words *anxious* and *worry* both have reference to strangling or being choked. Certainly that is how we feel when we are anxious. Things and events have us by the throat and seem to be cutting off our life. We are being harmed, or we fear what will come upon us, and all our efforts are insufficient to do anything about it.

Perhaps more energy has gone into dealing with this human situation than into anything else – from songs about 'Don't Worry! Be Happy!' to expensive sessions with a therapist.

Because we have the option, in reliance upon Jesus, of having abundant treasures in the realm of the heavens, Jesus gives us another of his 'therefores'. 'Therefore don't be anxious for your physical existence, concerning what you will have to eat or drink, or how you will clothe your body' (Matt. 6:25). Life is not about food, he continues to say, nor the body about clothes. It is about a place in God's immortal kingdom now. Eternity is, in part, what we are now living.

Jesus reminds us to look at living things around us in nature. In particular he refers us to birds and wildflowers. What is most relevant about the birds is that they do not 'lay up treasures upon earth'. They receive from their world, under God, daily food for daily needs. When we watch them we are reminded of the phrase in the Lord's Prayer, 'Give us today the food we need for today.'

The reality of kingdom immediacy – which also produced the manna in the wilderness, which had to be gathered each day and would not keep without spoiling except over the Sabbath – comes into play again with birds. Also we see it in the place of children in the Gospels. They are called 'greatest in the kingdom'. The little child has no capacity to command a store of goods on its own that would allow it to live independently of others. It simply must assume that provisions are made for it by others.

And as for the birds, it is not so much that birds do not work. They are among the busiest citizens of our world. Some, such as domestic chickens, are observed to work very hard. We too should work, and sometimes work hard. But our feathered friends do not seem to worry about the physical supports of their life, such as food and water and shelter. They simply seek it as they need it and take what they find. And that is how we should be. Having our treasures in heaven frees us to live simply in the present so far as our vital needs are concerned. We work hard, of course, and we care for our loved ones. But we do not worry – not even about them. Having food and clothing and God, we can be content (1 Tim. 6:8).

The regular provision of God for birds was the basis for some humour in Jesus' teaching, repeated a number of times in the Gospels. In the Sermon on the Mount he emphasizes his Father's provision for us by asking rhetorically, 'Aren't you better than birds?' But in Matthew 10 he is teaching about freedom from fear of physical death: 'Do not fear those who kill the body,' he says, 'but are unable to kill the soul.' Of course physical death only concerns the treasures that are 'upon the earth'. For most people, perhaps, the thing they most treasure is staying alive on earth. As a result they live their entire lives in bondage to fear of physical death (Heb. 2:15).

But the only one to fear, Jesus points out, is him who is able to destroy both soul and body in 'gehenna', the eternal cosmic landfill (Matt. 10:28). Now this just happens to be the same one who gently cares for sparrows. Two sparrows are sold for a 'penny' – really, the smallest copper coin then in circulation. On a bargain day, apparently, you can get five for two pennies (Luke 12:6). Yet God is watching over every one of them. And he watches you so closely that he knows how many hairs are on your head at any given moment. 'Don't be afraid,' then, 'you are of greater value than several sparrows' (Matt. 10:31).

Elsewhere he puts the joke in terms of ravens, birds far less attractive to me than sparrows. Yet God feeds them. 'And how much more valuable you are than birds' (Luke 12:24). Have you ever tried to price someone in terms of birds? Perhaps five sparrows, a hawk, two cockatoos and a bald eagle?

And the Lilies

All of this about food and treasuring food, but of course some people would rather starve than look bad. Thus one of the three things that make up 'the world', the human order, according to the apostle John, is 'the lust of the eyes' (1 John 2:16). Jesus understood how much people treasure their physical appearance. And a major part of appearance is size. We see its importance today in several dimensions: thick and thin, short and tall and so forth. But height has been specially valued by men and, within limits, by both men and women. A girl who is 'too tall', taller than most boys, may suffer for it. And 'Short People', as the popular song of some years back indicated, have no reason to exist.

But, of course, treasuring height and worrying about it – perhaps returning to it over and over to bemoan its absence or feel inferior – doesn't make one any taller. 'Which of you by worry can add a single inch to your height?' (Matt.6:27). And in any case one's height has no bearing on one's attractiveness and beauty as a human being: 'an unceasing spiritual being with an eternal destiny in God's great universe,' as we have said.

Nature provides its own beauty to all of God's creations. To try to be beautiful in terms of physical things never succeeds. And without the inner beauty of soul, beauty is simply garish. 'Like a golden ring in a pig's nose,' the proverb says, 'is a gorgeous woman who lacks sense' (Prov. 11:22). Some of the most beautiful people I have ever seen are elderly people whose souls shine so brightly their bodies are hardly visible: Dorothy Day, Malcolm Muggeridge, Agnes Sanford, Golda Meir, Ethel Waters and on and on. And this beauty is not just for old people. The natural beauty of the human being is given from the kingdom to every person who will receive it.

The little flowers that grow wild on the hillsides, Jesus points out, effortlessly exhibit a radiance of beauty that the most powerful human beings 'fixed up' to the greatest possible extent – 'Solomon in all his glory' (6:29) – cannot begin to match. If you look at one of these little flowers and then at the strained ladies and floppy gentlemen who come out to opening nights and award dinners in our centres of power and culture, you can only feel sorry for the people. They can't even begin to compete.

But as we live from God and God's world, a beauty is ours that overwhelms the flowers. If God adorns the grasses that pass in a day, to be burned as fuel or as trash, 'will he not do much more for you? You little-faiths!' (6:30). Here Jesus uses a term that may have been his own invention: *oligopistoi*, 'little-faiths'. It occurs ten times in five verses in the Gospels. It seems to have been a nickname that he invented as a way of gently chiding his apprentices for their lack of confidence in God and in himself. The faith that sees human beings in place in The Kingdom Among Us sees them as radiant beings of eternal value. And then of course, eventually, 'When Christ, who is our life, shall be revealed, you will also be revealed with him, a glorious being' (Col. 3:4).

People who are ignorant of God – the *ethne*, or 'nations,' who also pray, we have seen, with mechanical meaninglessness – live to eat and drink and dress. 'For such things the "gentiles" seek' – and their lives are filled with corresponding anxiety and anger and depression about how they will look and how they will fare.

By contrast, those who understand Jesus and his Father know that provision has been made for them. Their confidence has been confirmed by their experience. Though they work, they do not worry about things 'on earth'. Instead, they are always 'seeking first the kingdom'. That is, they 'place top priority on identifying and involving themselves in what God is doing and in the kind of rightness [*dikaiosune*] he has. All else needed is provided' (6:33). They soon enough have a track record to prove it.

The reference to seeking to have the *rightness* of the Father ties the discussion of reputation and treasures back to the culminating verses of Chapter 5 and to 'being the children of your Father in the heavens,' 'being whole as your Father in the heavens is whole' (5:45, 48). In both cases the reference is to the character of divine love, which only those in the family of God actually possess. This is the golden thread that winds its way through the entire discussion of kingdom living by Jesus, continually correcting our vision and giving us hope.

Jesus now concludes this section of his discourse (Matt. 6:19–34) with another touch of humour. 'You have no need to be anxious about what will happen tomorrow,' he says. 'You can do your worrying about tomorrow tomorrow. Each day contains just enough problems to last to the end of that day' (6:34).

Soberly, when our trust is in things that are absolutely beyond any risk or threat, and we have learned from good sources, including our own experience, that those things are *there*, anxiety is just groundless and pointless. It occurs only as a hangover of bad habits established when we were trusting things – like human approval and wealth – that were certain to let us down. Now our strategy should be one of resolute rejection of worry, while we concentrate on the future in hope and with prayer and on the past with thanksgiving.

Paul, once again, *got* it: 'Don't be anxious about anything,' he says, 'but in every situation, with prayer and supplications, with thanksgiving, let God know what you want. And the peace which God himself has will, beyond anything we can intellectually grasp, stand guard over your hearts and minds, which are within the reality of Jesus the Anointed' (Phil. 4:6–7).

We will find all this so much easier, of course, once we have been freed from our old dependency upon the opinions of others and upon our 'treasure' of material goods.

'In the World You Are Distressed'

We noted earlier that if we do not treasure earthly goods we must be prepared to be treated as more or less crazy. This is also true if we escape the delusions of respectability and so are not governable by the opinions of those around us, even though we respect them in love. After all, the world's 'Beatitudes' include 'Blessed are the rich' and 'Blessed are you when all men speak well of you' (Luke 6:24–26).

So Jesus told his students that 'the world' would hate them (John 15:19). I'm sure they must have been quite shocked by this, as they were by 'the establishment's' rejection and murder of their teacher. The 'world' (*kosmos*), as used in such New Testament statements, does not refer to the planet Earth and physical reality but to the historically developing organization of natural human abilities into the social and cultural structures within which we all must live. It does not refer to individuals as such. Of course Jesus was greatly loved by multitudes of individuals, as were his immediate and his later followers. But they were murdered nonetheless. And that is not uncommon today.

In sixteenth-century Holland, the Mennonites were outlawed and, when caught, often executed. One of them, Dirk Willens, was being chased across an icefield when his pursuer broke through and fell in. In response to his cries for help, Willens returned and saved him from the waters. The pursuer was grateful and astonished that he would do such a thing but nevertheless arrested him, as he thought it his duty to do. A few days later Willens was executed by being burned at the stake in the town of Asperen. It was precisely his Christlikeness that brought on his execution.[7]

So we want to be clear, as we come to the end of this chapter, that the one who takes on the character of the Prince of Life will not be exempted from the usual problems of life, and in addition will have the problems that come from 'not fitting in' and being incapable of conforming to the world order, new or old. This will not infrequently mean death or imprisonment or exclusion from the economy or education, and so on. All of these things have happened repeatedly in our history.

Indeed, it is said that more Christians have died as martyrs in the twentieth century than in all the period from the beginning to 1900.[8] The 'Western' segment of the church today lives in a bubble of historical illusion about the meaning of discipleship and the gospel. We are dominated by the essentially Enlightenment values that rule American culture: pursuit of happiness, unrestricted freedom of choice, disdain of authority. The prosperity gospels, the gospels of liberation, and the comfortable sense of 'what life is all about' that fills the minds of most devout Christians in our circles are the result. How different is the gritty realization of James: 'Friends of the world (*kosmou*) are enemies of God' (James 4:4). And John: 'If anyone loves the world, the love of the Father is not in him' (2 John 2:15).

Accordingly, when we speak of freedom from dependency on reputation and material wealth, we are *not* suggesting an easy triumphalism. Indeed, there will be times when we have no friends or wealth to be free from dependence upon. And that, of course, is precisely the point. In such a case we will be undisturbed. Life is hard in this world, and also for disciples of Jesus. In his 'Commencement Address', as we should perhaps call John 14–16, Jesus tells his distressed friends plainly, 'In the world (*kosmou*) you will have trouble.' This is not denied but transcended when he adds, 'Cheer up! I have overcome the world' (16:33). 'Many are the afflictions of the righteous,' the psalmist discovered long ago, 'but the Lord delivers from them all' (Ps. 34:19).

Chapter 7

THE COMMUNITY OF PRAYERFUL LOVE

God did not send his Son into the world to condemn it, but to save it.

JOHN 3:17

Within the spiritual community there is never, nor in any way, any immediate relationship of one to another, whereas human community expresses a profound, elemental, human desire for community, for immediate contact with other human souls, just as in the flesh there is the urge for physical merger with other flesh.

DIETRICH BONHOEFFER, LIFE TOGETHER

Ask, and it shall be given.

MATT. 7:7

No Condemnation

Jesus looks outward to the cosmos and to the sweep of human history before and after. He tells us we have no need to be anxious, for there is a divine life, the true home of the soul, that we can enter simply by placing our confidence in him: becoming his friend, and conspiring with him to subvert evil with good. He also shows us how we can be renewed in the depths of our soul, stepping 'beyond the goodness of scribes and Pharisees' to become the kinds of persons who are genuinely at home in God's world.

In the concluding parts of his Discourse on the Hill, now, he continues to alert us to specific practices and underlying attitudes that are so 'human, all too human' but sure to isolate us from the goodness and power flowing within The Kingdom Among Us.

In the first twelve verses of Matthew 7, he deals with the deadly way in which we try to 'manage' or control those closest to us by blaming and condemning them and by forcing upon them our 'wonderful solutions' for their problems. This too is a sure way of stepping outside *Torah*, *Logos*, The Kingdom Among Us, and undertaking to manage our world on our own. Disaster awaits – greater or smaller, sooner or later.

This almost universal human practice is the subject of verses 1–6, and after his brief but incisive treatment of it, he then shows us a truly effective and gracious way of caring for and helping the people we love in verses 7–12. It is the way of *the request*, of *asking*, which naturally progresses into kingdom praying. It is a way that actually works, because it draws people into the kingdom rather than into the web of our devices and plans for them. It creates the community of prayerful love.

Once Again, the Centrality of the Order

We recall, as we approach these passages, that we have already laid aside anger and contempt, cultivation of lusting, verbal manipulation, payback and getting even, along with the burdens and anxieties of 'looking good' and securing ourselves through wealth.

If we are still dominated by anger, contempt, and lusting – still 'ruling our house with an iron lung', and so forth – the tender areas into which Jesus now moves will simply be incomprehensible. We must start at the point Jesus himself chose – the nature of true well-being or 'blessedness' – and follow his order through the setting aside of anger, contempt, absorbing lust, manipulation and payback, and on to the forsaking of dependence upon human reputation and material wealth. Then we will be ready for what comes next. For as the Master of knowledge, he here deals with personal and moral reality as it really is, and it really does have an order. We omit that order at our peril.

For the teachings in Matt. 7:1–12, this point about order and progression may be even more important than for other parts of the discourse. Verses 1–5, 6, and 7–11, taken in isolation – as they usually are – appear to be just a few striking but unrelated points about this and that that the speaker dropped along the way to the end of his talk. But they are not. They are absolutely vital points in the overall teaching and its progression. They illustrate the inner texture of kingdom life with family, friends, co-workers and 'next door' neighbours. They illustrate the kingdom attitude towards those closest to us. Without them, the rest of the Sermon would never do as a plan for building the 'house' of one's life upon the rock.

Of course, we already know that the positive characterization of the kingdom attitude is *agape* love, and we have already discussed it at some length. But this love is an inexhaustible subject, and now Jesus gives a further look at it. His treatment of it here still takes in the area of action, of 'doing'. But it also involves a new look at the inward attitude, and it characterizes that attitude in a helpful way for specific contexts.

Thus verse 12: 'Therefore, treat others as you want them to treat you.' This is, of course, his world-famous Golden Rule, which every subsequent moral thinker has had to come to terms with. It, Jesus says, 'is the law and the prophets.' In other words, this is love, and everything that is intended for us by God is included within it.

The 'therefore' in verse 12 refers back to verses 1–11, and we must, as always, notice carefully what the 'therefore' is there for. It is there to indicate that verse 12 makes the general point that the earlier verses illustrate. In kingdom life we extend the respect to others that we would naturally hope others would extend to us. That is how love behaves, and it still behaves that way when we come to our intimate relationships.

In the previous verses (1–11) *agape* love has been concretely illustrated in three ways:

1. Not condemning or blaming those around us (vv. 1–5).
2. Not forcing 'wonderful things' upon them (v. 6).

3. Just asking for what we want from them – and from God (vv. 7–11).

Judge Not

If we would really help those close to us and dear, and if we would learn to live together with our family and 'neighbours' in the power of the kingdom, we must abandon the deeply rooted human practice of condemning and blaming. This is what Jesus means when he says, 'Judge not.' He is telling us that we should, and that we can, become the kind of person who does not condemn or blame others. As we do so, the power of God's kingdom will be more freely available to bless and guide those around us into his ways.

But when we first hear this we may feel as we did when we heard about laying aside anger, contempt and cultivated lusting – disbelieving. Can we *really* live that way? Could we successfully negotiate personal relations without letting people know that we disapprove of them and find them to be in the wrong? Condemnation – giving it and receiving it – is such a large part of 'normal' human existence that we may not even be able to imagine or think what life would be like without it.

At least we need the choice of giving others a good dose of blame and condemnation when it seems appropriate, don't we? We have great confidence in the power of condemnation to 'straighten others out'. And if that fails, should we not at least make clear that we are on the side of the right – no small matter itself?

But what is it, exactly, that we do when we condemn someone? When we condemn another we really communicate that he or she is, in some deep and just possibly irredeemable way, bad – bad as a whole, and to be rejected. In our eyes the condemned is among the discards of human life. He or she is not acceptable. We sentence that person to exclusion. Surely we can learn to live well and happily without doing that.

Who Can 'Correct' Others

To be fair, we rarely intend such total rejection, but that is usually what comes across. To correct another without making this happen requires great spiritual and personal maturity. That is why Paul wrote to the Galatians, 'Brothers, if someone really is caught in a sin, the spiritual ones among you are the ones to restore him. Do it in a lowly and non-presumptuous spirit, considering yourselves, lest you too be put to the test. Feel the weight others are feeling, and thus you will fulfil Christ's teaching' (6:1).

The wisdom that comes from Jesus to us through these words of Paul is astonishingly rich. First, we don't undertake to correct unless we are absolutely sure of the sin. Here the language of 1 Corinthians 13 comes into play: love 'believes all things, hopes all things.' If there is any lack of clarity about whether the sin occurred, assume it did not. At least, don't start correcting.

Second, not just anyone is to correct others. Correction is reserved for those who live and work in a divine power not their own. For that power is also wise, and it is loving beyond anything we will ever be. These are 'the spiritual ones' referred to. Only a certain kind of life puts us in position to 'correct'.

Third, the 'correcting' to be done is not a matter of 'straightening them out'. It is not a matter of hammering on their wrongness and on what is going to happen to them if they don't change their ways. It is a matter of *restoration*. The aim in dealing with the one 'caught' is to bring them back on the path of Jesus and to establish them there so their progress in kingdom character and living can continue. Nothing is to be done that is not useful to this specific end.

Fourth, the ones who are restoring others must go about their work with the sure knowledge that they could very well do the same thing that the person 'caught' has done, or even worse. This totally removes any sense of self-righteousness or superiority, which, if it is present, will certainly make restoration impossible. To aid in this direction, the restorers are to endeavour to feel the weight, the 'burden', that the one being restored feels as he or she stands trapped in the sin.

Of course, these teachings were never intended to apply only to church fellowships and community. They are most important for human life as they apply to our closest relationships, to our mates and children, our close relatives and associates of all types. This is the place where, in our twisted and upside down condition, familiarity is most likely to breed contempt. Most families would be healthier and happier if their members treated one another with the respect they would give to a perfect stranger.

C. S. Lewis's discussion of *storge*, familial love, is endlessly instructive on this point and is required reading for all who intend to have a decent family life.[1] He notes that he has 'been far more impressed by the bad manners of parents to children than by those of children to parent.'

Parents are seen to treat their children with 'an incivility which, offered to any other young people, would simply have terminated the acquaintance.' They are dogmatic on matters the children understand and the elders don't, they impose ruthless interruptions, flat contradictions, ridicule of things the young take seriously and make insulting references to their friends. This provides an easy explanation to the questions, 'Why are they always out? Why do they like every house better than their home?' 'Who,' Lewis inquires, 'does not prefer civility to barbarism?'

Saint Dominic, who lived in the thirteenth century and founded the great Dominican Order of Preachers within the Catholic Church, beautifully illustrates the tender way of Jesus. His brother Paul of Venice, among others, bore testimony to it by relating, 'He [Dominic] wanted the Rule [of the Dominican Order] to be observed strictly by himself and by the others. He reprimanded offenders justly and so affectionately that no one was ever upset by his correction and punishment.'

Brother Frugerio also said of Dominic, 'He himself observed the Rule strictly and wanted it to be observed by the others. He convicted and corrected offenders with gentleness and kindness in such a way that no one was upset, even though the penances were sometimes very severe.'[2] This is the natural effect of a non-condemning spirit.

It is obvious how different this is from the usual human treatment. Sometimes it is said even now of someone that they are 'beyond the pale'. This ancient way of speaking refers to the old tribal practice of cutting people off from the group. They are then forced by communal solidarity to live in the darkness, beyond the point where the communal fire and light allowed things to be barely visible – that is, *beyond* the pale.

For millennia it was the leper who was the most potent symbol of condemnation and exclusion. The 'immoral' person has had an equally long run in history, the divorced woman also. One of the major lessons of the Gospels is how Jesus was with such people, accepting them, touching them and eating with them. He did this in a very natural way. It was for them, not for show or to make a point.

Today homeless people and people with AIDS are, sadly, apt to find themselves looked upon as a combination of the leper and the immoral. Jesus certainly would make a point of being with them, too, in any natural connection of life. Although he certainly let his condemnation fall upon self-righteous and deeply corrupted leaders (Matt. 23; Luke 11:29–54), we never see it in other contexts. And we can trust him to express it appropriately towards such people, though we ourselves could rarely if ever do so. Anger and condemnation, like vengeance, are safely left to God. We must beware of believing that it is OK for us to condemn as long as we are condemning the right things. It is not so simple as all that. I can trust Jesus to go into the temple and drive out those who were profiting from religion, beating them with a rope. I cannot trust myself to do so.

Condemnation's Involvement with Anger and Contempt

Now a moment's reflection is all that is required to make one realize how terribly powerful condemnation is. It knifes into vulnerable areas at the core of our being. That is why it hurts so badly and at the same time why we rely upon it so heavily. The decision to step aside from it, neither giving it nor receiving it, is a major turning point in one's life. If, as Christians often say, we really are 'different' as followers of Christ, this is a point where it should be most obvious. We would not condemn, nor would we 'receive' condemnation directed upon us.

Of course, more than half the battle with condemnation is won once we have given up anger and contempt. Condemnation always involves some degree of self-righteousness and of distancing ourselves from the one we are condemning. And self-righteousness always involves an element of comparison and of condemnation. Jesus spoke to 'some who were relying upon themselves for their rightness *and* were despising others' (Luke 18:9). The combination is not accidental. Contempt is a major part of condemnation in the usual case, and when we drop contempt from our soul and our bearing, condemnation rarely occurs, and never with its most devastating effects.

Anger is not as closely intertwined with condemnation as is contempt, but in fact there is a close association. Watching anger in action, we see that it almost always leads to condemnation – partly, no doubt, because condemnation is such a handy way of hurting people deeply. And anger desires to hurt. On the other hand, condemnation makes the road to anger a quick and easy trip. The one condemned is seen as deserving of suffering and, in any case, as not worthy of protection and respect. The condemned, in turn, responds with anger to the pain of being condemned. And around and around.

Clearly, then, if we are to come to terms with condemnation we must deal with anger and contempt, and if we have dealt with anger and contempt there will be little condemnation left to deal with. Little, but still some. For there seems to be something righteous about condemnation.

There actually is a 'ministry of condemnation', and it has a certain 'glory' (2 Cor. 3:9). I have observed many good people who seem to feel a positive obligation to condemn others, and in some cases they do it without anger or contempt, even with some degree of sorrow and compassion. Yet the effects of condemnation remain the same. It remains a stinging attack, a shocking assault upon the one condemned. Whatever good it may do in human affairs comes at a very high price.

And often it grows into shame. Shame seems most widespread and deepest among the very people who take rightness and goodness most seriously. It is a dimension of condemnation that reaches into the deepest levels of our souls. In shame we are *self*-condemned for being the person we are. It touches our identity and causes self-rejection. We feel ourselves to be a failure just for being the person we are. We wish to be someone else. But of course we cannot. We are trapped, and our life is made hopeless.

This explains why discrimination against people because of the *kind* of person they are, their identity, is so hateful and destructive. It also explains why the gospel of the kingdom has such transforming power in human life. For that gospel opens the kingdom to everyone, no matter their classification, and it enables us really to become a *different kind* of person, beyond all condemnation, blame, and shame, and to know it. Those who mourn, when they step into the kingdom of the heavens, are 'given beauty in place of ashes, the oil of gladness instead of grief, and garments of praise in place of a spirit of despair' (Isa. 61:3).

That You Be Not Judged

The result of condemning and blaming is sure to be a counter-attack in the very same terms. The parents who have reproached a child for using drugs, for example, soon find themselves condemned for coffee, tobacco or alcohol use. This is a well-known case of exactly what Jesus said: 'Don't condemn or you will be condemned. As you have meted out condemnation to others, so they will mete out condemnation to you' (Matt. 7:1–2).

And if it isn't in terms of the usual 'respected' dependencies, it will be in terms of food or overwork or some other excess, real or imagined. But a counter-attack there will be, even if it requires a trip through the unconscious mind or the body of the one condemned.

If our counter-attack is unacceptable to ourselves, as it is very likely to be in a family setting, it may be shoved beneath the surface and will then come out in the many forms of behaviour that look like something else, for example, perfectionism, procrastination, rejection of authority, or passive/aggressive tendencies such as chronic tardiness or the constant aborting of success – or even in physical symptoms. For condemnation brings anger in return, and anger will attack. And that will very likely move on to contempt, to 'You fool!' to shame, or even to physical injury and abuse. And this attack can be and often is turned against oneself by the amazing chemistry of the mind.

This reciprocity explains why condemnation as a strategy for correcting or 'helping' those near and dear to us will almost always fail. It is extremely rare that anyone who is condemned will respond by changing in the desired way. And those who can so respond are most likely to be spiritual giants already. 'Rebuke a wise man,' the proverb says, 'and he will love you for it' (Prov. 9:8). Yes, but in most cases where we condemn we are not dealing with wise people. We are dealing with people, even very young people, who will simply be deeply injured, become angry and repay us in kind.

A few decades ago there emerged in American society something called the generation gap. It did not exist in the world of my youth, in the forties and fifties. It was caused by exactly what Jesus here calls our attention to: 'the law of reciprocity of condemnation', we could call it. Popular arts, sexual morality or immorality, disenchantment with 'the establishment', the Vietnam War, and the draft, racial segregation, the role of education in society, and other factors, were all a part of the mix.

But it really doesn't matter much now what 'caused' it and who 'started' it. The fact is, we are now saddled, as a people, with a conceptualization of youth against age and age against youth, of generation against generation. There is a mixture of blame, misunderstanding, mistrust, condemnation, and even shame between age groups. We now have names that more or less strongly incorporate this mixture, such as 'boomers', 'busters', 'Xers' and so forth. And we have many other ways of clustering people into mutual condemnation groups. Heartfelt acceptance of the gospel of the Beatitudes alone can offer relief from this dreadful battle of condemnation and counter-condemnation.

Eliminate Condemnation and Then Help

Jesus shows us how to proceed in another way, a better way, to help the ones we care about. He says, 'Why do you concentrate on the little speck in your brother's eye, but do not take into consideration the board in your own eye? How can you say to your brother, 'Let me get that little speck out of your eye,' when you are standing there with a board covering your own eye?' (Matt. 7:3–4). How, we might ask, does Jesus know there is a board in your eye, that you have a serious character problem that needs to be removed? In the next verse he even goes on to say, 'You hypocrite! First take the board from over your eye and then you will have clear vision to extract the little speck from your brother's eye.'

How does he know that those who 'judge' in the sense of condemning others, are hypocrites? Is it merely that there must be *something* wrong with us, because there is something wrong with everyone, and that we should not condemn others until we are perfect? Is it just the let-him-who-is-without-sin-cast-the-first-stone routine? No, that's not it. Rather, it is because he understands what condemnation is and involves.

Condemnation is the board in our eye. He knows that the mere fact that we are condemning someone shows our heart does not have the kingdom rightness he has been talking about. Condemnation, especially with its usual accompaniments of anger and contempt and self-righteousness, blinds us to the reality of the other person. We cannot 'see clearly' how to assist our brother, because we cannot see our brother. And we will never know how to truly help him until we have grown into the kind of person who does not condemn. Full stop. 'Getting the board out' is not a matter of correcting something that is wrong in our life so that we will be able to condemn our dear ones better – more effectively, so to speak.

'Judging' and Discerning

But some are troubled with giving up 'judging' because of another sense of the word that marks an absolutely central aspect of life, one that Jesus is in no way suggesting we omit. The term *krino*, a form of which Jesus uses here in Matthew 7, has as its primary meanings 'to separate, make a distinction between, exercise judgement upon', 'to estimate or appraise'.

For example, a dentist may examine a patient's teeth and say, 'I see you have not been brushing regularly. Your gums are receding, and there is a cavity over on this right lower side.' When he does this, he is indeed judging the condition of the patient's teeth and gums and practise of dental hygiene. He is discerning, seeing and saying what it is.

But he would not usually be thought of as condemning us or our teeth and gums. He is appraising their condition in distinction from other, more desirable conditions. That is his business. Of course I suppose he could be condemning us. He might be someone who just hates or has contempt for anyone who does not take care of his or her teeth. He then would naturally place that person 'beyond the pale'. But that certainly would not be the usual case and would be thought unprofessional.

We do not have to – we *cannot* – surrender the valid practice of distinguishing and discerning how things are in order to avoid condemning others. We *can*, however, train ourselves to hold people responsible and discuss their failures with them – and even assign them penalties, if we are, for example, in some position over them – without attacking their worth as human beings or marking them as rejects. A practised spirit of intelligent *agape* will make this possible. Recall the words of Paul and the example of Saint Dominic referred to earlier.

But that is a complicated task at best: not only because we may not know how to do it, which is often the case, but also because those we appraise may not know how to take our appraisal in any other way than as an attack on their person. This is especially true today, when people are so desperately seeking approval. Having no adequate sense of themselves as spiritual beings, or of their place in a good world of God, they regard any negative appraisal of what they do as condemnation of themselves as persons. They have nowhere to stand to do otherwise.

It is interesting and important to observe that today the old phrase 'hate the sin and love the sinner' no longer is accepted. If you disapprove of what I do or how I do it, it is now generally thought, you can only be condemning me and rejecting me. This is another evidence of the devastating effect of the loss to our culture of any idea of the self as a spiritual being that not only has but is an inner substance. 'I *am* my actions,' it is thought, 'and how then can you say you disapprove of my actions but love me?'

But, of course, this attitude may also be a manipulative device I use to try to drive you into approving of everything I do. Then perhaps I can enjoy without reproach my sovereign liberty – so dear to the American heart – to do exactly what I want. Or at least I can hotly reproach you in turn for trying to 'impose your ideas on me'. Few people today can stand up to this device in public or private discourse while retaining with equanimity their own sense of truth and reality. Better just to not think, or at least to be quiet.

Such easy misunderstandings as are now current make it all the more important that we be very clear in our own minds what condemnation is and how it relates to the more basic sense of judgement that only involves 'separating' one thing from another to the best of our ability. We simply cannot forsake discernment, and Jesus himself devotes the last half of Matthew 7 to urging us precisely to discern and, in that sense, to 'judge'. But we must forsake the practice of condemning people, and that will not be difficult at all once we see clearly what it is to condemn and have previously rid ourselves of anger and contempt.

A Family Without Condemning

It is a great help, of course, if the absence of condemning has been modelled for us as a way of life. When I was quite a young child, in 'grade school' as it then was called, I came to know a wonderful family in the region of southern Missouri where I was brought up. It was the VonAllman family, the family of my sister-in-law Bertha VonAllman Willard.

Now, I think my own family was a remarkable group of people, very caring and responsible, but the VonAllman family, presided over by the grandparents, Elmer and Nora, had in them a spirit that I, at least, had never before encountered, and perhaps never since. They did not condemn. They worked hard, were upright almost to a fault, and carefully disciplined their children. But I never saw or felt with them the slightest element of condemnation or condemnatory blaming.

Among them, I quickly noticed, children were to be heard as well as seen. (How brutal that saying is, 'Children are to be seen and not heard.') And as I watched their children through the years, and grew up along with their grandchildren, the same non-condemnatory spirit seemed on the whole to prevail throughout their lives.

I came to live with my older bother, J. I. Willard, and his wife, Bertha, when I was in the second grade, and intermittently thereafter. It was the VonAllman family – and most of all Bertha – that demonstrated to me how one could live a strong and good life without using condemnation to punish and control others.

Never once in all those years, or since, did she condemn or blame me, though I frequently deserved it. I thought in those years long ago that it was 'just her way'. Now I understand it was her heart, which she learned from her father and mother and, through them, from Christ.

It is not easy to imagine the real-life possibility of living without condemning when we grow up in a world such as ours. The steadying influence of a very clear and very real example can do much to help us understand the gentleness of the way of Jesus. Unfortunately I did not immediately learn to live in the spirit of my sister-in-law and her family and continued for many years to use condemnation on those close to me. I still could think of Jesus' teachings as 'impossible laws'.

When we enter the life of friendship with the Jesus who is now at work in our universe, we stand in a new reality where condemnation is simply irrelevant. There is before God, Paul says, 'no condemnation for those who are in Christ Jesus' (Rom. 8:1). And as for the condemnation we may receive from others, I endeavour not to receive it, to just ignore or drop it. I have learned to look at it only while simultaneously holding in full view the fact that Jesus, far from condemning me, died for me and is right now intervening on my behalf in the heavens. This helps me stay out of counter-condemnation, with its pain and anger.

'Who is this one condemning me,' I ask, 'when set beside that One who does not condemn me?' I think I shall not be depressed about this condemnation of me, then, especially since I know that 'nothing can separate me from the eternal love of Christ' (Rom. 8:33–35). And in this context it seems only intelligent just to have done with the whole condemning game.

When Good Things Become Deadly

Of Pearls and Pigs

Our practice of 'condemnation engineering', as it might be called, usually goes hand in hand with another device mistakenly used to manage the lives of those we truly care about. That is the practice of pushing the things of God upon them whether they want or are ready for them or not. Or it may just be good things generally we are pushing, for example, education or proper diet.

The very idea of 'compulsory education', of forcing young people to be in school – except where, very wisely and gently, quite small children are concerned – illustrates this misguided practice of pushing valuable things on people; and its disastrous outcome in contemporary society exactly confirms the truth of what Jesus had to say. His comment has actually become a proverb but unfortunately with a meaning far removed from what he had in mind.

'Do not,' he said, 'give dogs sacred things to eat, nor try to get pigs to dine on pearls. For they will simply walk all over them and turn and take a bite out of you' (Matt. 7:6).

The long-standard use of this verse is directly opposed to the spirit of Jesus and his teachings. That use suggests that we may have certain wonderful treasures, of truth and of service perhaps, that we could give to others. Perhaps the 'treasure' is the very gospel itself. But there are some who are not *worthy* of those treasures. We have to watch for such people. Normally they are thought of as people who will not accept our 'treasure' or would not use it rightly. They are the 'pigs' or the 'dogs' in question. And we are not to waste our good things on these worthless or evil people. So goes the standard reading of verse 6.

But it is hard to imagine anything more opposed to the spirit of Jesus than this. Indeed, the very coming of Christ, the pearl of God, into the world, would be a case of pearls before pigs thus understood.

So let us be clear once and for all that Jesus is not suggesting that certain classes of people are to be viewed as pigs or dogs. Nor is he saying that we should not give good things and do good deeds to people who might reject or misuse them. In fact, his teaching is precisely the opposite. We are to be like the Father in the heavens, 'who is kind to the unthankful and the evil' (Luke 6:35).

The problem with pearls for pigs is not that the pigs are not worthy. Worthiness is not in question here at all, but helpfulness. Pigs cannot digest pearls, nor nourish themselves upon them. Likewise for a dog with a Bible or a crucifix. The dog cannot eat it. The reason these animals will finally 'turn and rend you', when you one day step up to them with another load of Bibles or pearls, is that *you* at least are edible. Anyone who has ever had serious responsibilities for caring for animals will understand immediately what Jesus is saying.

And what a picture this is of our efforts to correct and control others by pouring our good things, often truly precious things, upon them – things that they nevertheless simply cannot ingest and use to nourish themselves. Often we do not even listen to them. We 'know' without listening. Jesus saw it going on around him all the time, as we do today. And the outcome is usually exactly the same as with the pig and the dog. Our good intentions make little difference. The needy person will finally become angry and attack us. The point is not the waste of the 'pearl' but that the person given the pearl is not helped.

How often this happens between child and parent! Along with condemnation – they usually go hand in hand – the counter-attack is the number one cause of alienation between the generations. Our children or others do not know what else to do with us pearl pushers. And even though they love us – as parent or friend, for example – they simply cannot take any more of our 'pushy irrelevance', as they see it, or possibly our stubborn blindness.

Forcing religion upon the young even though it makes no sense to them is a major reason why they 'graduate' from church about the same time they graduate from secondary school and do not return for twenty years, if ever. The gap is only widened when the elders are in turn condemned for not responding to the new-found wisdom of the young.

Frankly, our 'pearls' often are offered with a certain superiority of bearing that keeps us from paying attention to those we are trying to help. *We* have solutions. That should be enough, shouldn't it? And very quickly some contempt, impatience, anger and even condemnation slips into our offer.

And the very goodness of our 'pearl' may make us think that we couldn't possibly have the wrong attitude towards the intended recipient. Would we be offering them such pearls if our heart were not right? Unfortunately, we just might. It has been done. And how we honestly feel when our 'pearl' is left there on the ground to be walked on by the unenthusiastic recipient will be a pretty good sign of where our heart was in the first place.

What we are actually doing with our proper condemnations and our wonderful solutions, more often than not, is taking others out of their own responsibility and out of God's hands and trying to bring them under our control. This was never meant to be, and usually we ourselves do not consciously intend it. We are perhaps filled with anxiety about the ones we care for. But, just as we saw earlier with 'swearing' or making oaths, we are always to respect other people as spiritual beings who are responsible before God alone for the course they choose to take of their own free will.

God has paid an awful price to arrange for human self-determination. He obviously places great value on it. It is, after all, the *only* way he can get the kind of personal beings he desires for his eternal purposes. And just as we are not to try to manipulate others with impressive language of any kind (Matt. 5:37), so we are not to harass them into rightness and goodness with our condemnings and our 'pearls' or holy things.

The Serpent and the Dove

But what are we to do in our desire to help others? Nothing? That would be unacceptable. It is not consistent with really loving those around us. Thus Saint Augustine understood love of our neighbour as requiring that 'we must endeavour to get our neighbour to love God.' He understood this to apply to our family, our household and 'all within our reach.'[3] And he is right. To a great extent, what matters in our approach to people is not just what we do, but how we do it, and when. And we can count on it that a superior attitude or condemnation will never help us help them.

The instructions that Jesus gave to his apprentices when, on one occasion, he sent them out to minister the kingdom of the heavens to the needs of human beings was this: 'Have the practical good sense of the snake, and be as undevious or innocent as doves' (Matt. 10:16). These homely images begin to open up the positive side of an association with others that will help them without condemning them or forcing upon them good things that they simply cannot benefit from.

What is the wisdom of the snake? It is to be watchful and observant until the time is right to act. It is timeliness. One rarely sees a snake chasing its prey or thrashing about in an effort to impress it. But when it acts, it acts quickly and decisively. And as for the dove, it does not contrive. It is incapable of intrigue. Guile is totally beyond it. There is nothing indirect about this gentle creature. It is in this sense 'harmless.' The importance scriptural teaching places on guilelessness is very great. One of the traits of the small child, greatest in the kingdom, is its inability to mislead. We are to be like that as adults.

These are qualities we must have to walk in the kingdom *with* others, instead of trying to drive them to change their ways and attitudes and even who they are. These qualities are in turn founded in still deeper qualities, such as patience, confidence, hopefulness, truthfulness and genuine respect for the freedom and individuality of others.

The Request As the Heart of Community

The Dynamic of *the Request*

And with such qualities, once again, as we saw in 'turning the other cheek', the dynamics of the personal relations involved are radically transformed. The most important element in the transformation is this: As long as I am condemning my friends or relatives, or pushing my 'pearls' on them, I am their problem. They have to respond to me, and that usually leads to their 'judging' me right back, or 'biting' me, as Jesus said.

But if I back away, maintaining a sensitive and non-manipulative presence, I am no longer their problem. As I listen, they do not have to protect themselves from me, and they begin to open up. I may quickly begin to appear to them as a possible ally and resource. Now they begin to sense their problem to be the situation they have created, or possibly themselves. Because I am no longer trying to *drive* them, genuine communication, real sharing of hearts, becomes an attractive possibility. The healing dynamic of *the request* comes naturally into play. And this is the final illustration, the positive one, of how to really be of help to those near us (7:7–11).

When we stand thus in the kingdom, our approach to influencing others, for their good as well as ours, will be simply *to ask*: to ask them to change, and to help them in any way they ask of us. It is a natural extension of this dynamic when we turn to ask God to work in their lives and hearts to bring about changes. These changes will certainly involve more than any conscious choice they could make or we could desire.

And as long as we respect them before God, and are thoughtful and gracious, we can keep asking, in appropriate ways, keep seeking and keep knocking on the door of their lives. We should note that the ask-seek-knock teaching first applies to our approach to others, not to prayer to God. We respect and never forget that the latch of the heart is within. We are glad for that fact and would not override it. We can gently but persistently keep our hopeful expectation before them and at the same time before God. *Asking* is indeed the great law of the spiritual world through which things are accomplished in co-operation with God and yet in harmony with the freedom and worth of every individual.

The Unity of Spiritual Orientation

To understand Jesus' teachings, we must realize that deep in our orientations of our spirit we cannot have one posture towards God and a different one towards other people. We are a whole being, and our true character pervades everything we do. We cannot, for example, love God and hate human beings. As the apostle John wrote, 'Those who do not love their brother who is visible cannot love God who is invisible' (1 John 4:20). And: 'The one who does not love does not know God, who is love' (4:8).

Similarly James rules out the blessing of God and the cursing of human beings, 'made in the likeness of God,' coming from the same mouth (3:9). He also indicates that humility before God and humility before others go together. Those humble before God do not 'judge' their brothers and sisters (4:6–12).

The same basic point of the necessary unity of spiritual orientation is seen in Jesus' teachings about forgiveness and about forgiveness and prayer. 'If you forgive men the wrongs they do you, your Father in the heavens will also forgive you. But if you don't, neither will he' (Matt. 6:14–15). And again with confession of Jesus, or being ashamed: 'Whoever is ashamed of me and my teachings in the midst of these adulterous and sinful people, the Quintessential Man will be ashamed of them too, when he comes in the midst of the glory of his Father and the holy angels' (Mark 8:38).

And with explicit regard to prayer: 'When you stand praying, forgive anything you may have against anyone, so that your Father also, the one in the heavens, may forgive you your wrongdoings' (Mark 11:25). Forgiving is but one case of giving, and one who does not forgive does not live in the spiritual atmosphere and reality of giving, where prayers are answered.

Life in the kingdom of God is not something we *do*, like investing in the stock market or learning Spanish, that allows us to reserve dominion over our own life and use the kingdom for our purposes. We have to surrender the innermost reality of the self to God as expressed in Jesus and his kingdom. We cannot 'use' it while holding our innermost self back from it. There are few one-way streets in the kingdom: for example, God forgives me but I do not forgive, Jesus confesses his friendship to me before the heavenly company but I do not own him before those less than glorious ones around me, and so forth. All of this must be kept firmly in mind as we contemplate Jesus' teaching about the power of *the request*, as it functions between human beings and between us and God.

When I *ask* someone to do or to be or to give something, I stand *with* that person in the domain of a constraint without force or necessitation. We are together. A request by its very nature unites. A demand, by contrast, immediately separates. It is this peculiar 'atmosphere' of togetherness that characterizes the kingdom and is, indeed, what human beings were created to thrive in.

We teach our children to say 'please' and 'thank you'. This is understood to be a matter of respect, and rightly so. But it is also a way of getting what we want or need. It is a way of getting that requires us to go through the freedom of the person asked, however. In the very act of asking, in the very nature of the request, we acknowledge that the other person can say no, and, 'innocent as doves', we accept that response. We are not set to punish him or her for saying no. Yet we ask, and we are supposed to ask, and in by far the most cases he or she does not say no. 'Ask,' Jesus said, 'and you shall receive. Seek, and you shall find. Knock, and it shall be opened to you.' That is how we are to relate to others. And that is the primary intention of this much-quoted passage.

As Emily Dickinson has written,

> The soul selects her own society,
> Then shuts the door;
> On her divine majority,
> Obtrude no more.[4]

The Continuum of Prayer

How beautiful it is to see relationships in which asking and receiving are a joyful and loving way of life. Often we see those who cherish one another each seriously or playfully trying to outgive the other. That is how relationships should be. Of course, we must never eliminate the asking side of the relationship. A balance must be kept, for giving is not the same as imposition. That is why God does not just give us what we need without being asked. Prayer is nothing but a proper way for persons to interact. Thus Jesus very naturally moves in Matt. 7:7–11 from asking for what you want of others to asking for what you want from your Father, the one in the heavens. These two relationships, he clearly taught, are on a continuous line.

'Who of you,' he asks, 'would give a stone to their child that had asked for a biscuit?' (7:9). He is simply reading the ways of the actual human heart. And truly there might be some monster who would do such a cruel thing, or would place a snake in the hand of a child that has asked for a fish (v. 10). But that would not make it any less true that the very act of asking brings to bear a power that usually secures the desired result. Any exception would only prove the rule.

The power of asking is so great that it makes many people uncomfortable. Don't you know of people who will go considerably out of their way to avoid someone who is apt to ask them for something? It may even be someone whom they do not know and will never meet again. But they do not wish to feel the power of *the request*. Who really enjoys eating a sandwich in front of the family dog?

No matter that it is your favourite sandwich, which you have lovingly prepared as part of a tiny vacation with your book in a quiet and pleasant place, here is the face, the eyes, perhaps a paw on your knee. You know the rest. You are up against a fundamental force of the universe.

In our intimate relationships and associations, the request is by itself usually enough to bring the desired result, unless those relationships and associations have been damaged by previous experience or the persons involved are too deeply scarred. And sometimes there are good reasons why the request should not be granted. But that is by far the less common situation.

These realities of asking are facts that we all can observe. Jesus uses them to help us understand the power of prayer, as he moves on to consider requests of God. 'So if you, twisted as you are, know to give good gifts to your children, how much more will your Father, the one in the heavens, give good things to those who ask him!' (7:11).

And here, finally, is the basic answer to the urgent need we all feel to influence others for good. That answer is prayer, asking God. This is the sure way in which the good that we can accomplish in others can be accomplished. *Our confidence in God is the only thing that makes it possible to treat others as they should be treated.* Hence we must look yet again at the 'therefore'. Having made clear the power of prayer to achieve the good ends we desire, Jesus says, 'Therefore, whatever you would like others to do to you, do that to them.' That is, *because* the power of asking and prayer is what it is, treat others as you would like to be treated. 'For that is what the law and the prophets, God's revealed will, requires of us' (7:12).

Where Quarrelling and Fighting Come From

Still another perspective on the communal harmony that comes through the power of prayer is seen in James 4. There prayer is seen as the alternative to fighting others over what we want. 'What is the cause of all the quarrelling and fighting among you?' James asks. These are Christians he is talking to. He replies, 'The pleasures marching around in your body are the cause. You obsessively desire things, but do not get them. You kill and burn with envy, and are not able to obtain what you want. You struggle and fight' (vv. 1–2).

But what should we do? We should ask. That is the solution to competition. We should turn to God in request and request what is good rather than only what we want. We should pray that others succeed. 'You do not have because you do not ask, and you do not get when you ask, because you only want to feed those pleasures of yours' (v. 3). This whole approach to life is misguided.

We need to love our neighbours as ourselves, do to them as we would be done to. Receiving the good news of the kingdom will enable us to do that, for it obliterates scarcity and win-lose relationships. Then, in deed as well as in prayer we will seek their good as well as our own. A life of prayer shows us the way to what we need and harmonizes the desires of everyone in the group. Because we are living in the kingdom of the heavens, we are released from absorbing desires that would deflect us from what is really good. In many ways it is the life of prayer that discovers a space in which all can live.[5]

The Mediator in the Community of Love

Thus Jesus' teaching about asking, about *the request*, takes us into the deepest nature of our life together in the kingdom of God as it is now present on earth. This life is shown in both its horizontal (human) and its vertical (divine) dimensions. To understand it totally revolutionizes how we deal with our families, our fellow Christians and our fellow citizens on earth, both in the kingdom and out.

In a lengthy section of his indispensable book *Life Together*, Dietrich Bonhoeffer provides a striking characterization of the community of prayerful love. I have taken from it an epigraph for the opening of this chapter. There he stresses that in the spiritual community there is never any *immediate* relationship between human beings.

Another way of saying this is that among those who live as Jesus' apprentices there are no relationships that omit the presence and action of Jesus. We never go 'one on one'; all relationships are mediated through him. I never think simply of what I am going to do with you, to you or for you. I think of what we, Jesus and I, are going to do with you, to you and for you. Likewise, I never think of what you are going to do with me, to me and for me, but of what will be done by you and Jesus with me, to me and for me.

Bonhoeffer's insights and language are so powerful on this point that it would be a mistake not to dwell on his own words:

> Because Christian community is founded solely on Jesus Christ, it is a spiritual and not a psychic [merely human] reality. In this it differs absolutely from all other communities … Christian brotherhood is not an ideal that we must realize; it is rather a reality created by God in Christ in which we may participate. The more clearly we learn to recognize that the ground and strength and promise of all our fellowship is in Jesus Christ alone, the more serenely shall we think of our fellowship and pray and hope for it.[6]

The quality of love in the prayerful community is radically different from the highest form of human loves, according to Bonhoeffer.

> Human love is directed to the other person for his own sake, spiritual love loves him for Christ's sake. Therefore, human love seeks direct contact with the other person; it loves him not as a free person but as one whom it binds to itself ... It desires to be irresistible, to rule. Human love has little regard for truth. It makes the truth relative, since nothing, not even the truth, must come between it and the be-loved person.'

Truth must yield to desire, which drives the psychic community.

By contrast, in kingdom love

> Jesus Christ stands between the lover and the others he loves ... Because Christ stands between me and others, I dare not desire direct fellowship with them. As only Christ can speak to me in such a way that I may be saved, so others, too, can be saved only by Christ himself. This means that I must release the other person from every attempt of mine to regulate, coerce and dominate him with my love ... Thus this spiritual love will speak to Christ about a brother more than to a brother about Christ. It knows that the most direct way to others is always through prayer to Christ and that love of others is wholly dependent upon the truth in Christ.

Laughter and Redemption

These words perfectly capture the meaning and purpose of Jesus' teachings in Matt. 7:1–12. Instead of harassing those near us with our judgements and treasures, we stand before them with our helpless requests, while simultaneously standing before the wise and mighty King with our requests for them. We only need to add a comment about how our humanity enters into the spiritual community of 'indirect' love. This, too, Bonhoeffer understood very well. All the natural relationships of life – to family, classmates, co-workers, neighbours and even to those in the political and artistic and intellectual realms – are very good in themselves, when taken rightly. They too are essential to life together in the kingdom. There is no human spirituality apart from those relationships. We must seek our spirituality in them.

Purely 'spiritual' relationships with others would, therefore, be dangerous at best, for they are inherently false to the human condition. That condition is one of labour, glory, dust and death. It is one of constant incongruity between human dreams and dignity, on the one hand, and human realities, on the other. We are incarnate and finite beings, trailing clouds of over-aspiration and ragged incompleteness. When our 'spirituality' disconnects from the natural contexts and relationships that are always *there* nevertheless, one of the chief signs of what is happening is that we lose our ability to laugh.

Laughter is the automatic human response to incongruity, and incongruity is never lacking on the human scene, no matter how far advanced we may be into the kingdom. It is indelibly imprinted in our finiteness. There will be lots of laughter in heaven, you can be sure, as well as joy, for our finiteness will always remain. Just imagine an eternity in which no one laughs!

And we should note that one of the things that disappear when we are grinding away at others with our condemnations, blamings and 'pearls' is, precisely, laughter. We become insufferably grim. But genuine shared laughter is one of the surest ways for human beings to come together and break the stalemates of life. It is essential to genuine community.

No wonder, then, that laughter is so good for our health. It is even a symbol of redemption, for there is no greater incongruity in all creation than redemption. When deliverance comes, 'we are like those who dream: our mouth filled with laughter, our tongue with shouts of joy' (Ps. 126:1–2).

Thus Abraham fell on the ground laughing when told by God that he, a one-hundred-year-old man, would have a child by ninety-year-old Sarah (Gen. 17:17). Later Sarah herself laughed at the same 'joke' (18:12–15). God specified to Abraham that the child of promise would be named 'Laughter'. *Isaac* means 'Laughter'. 'Your wife shall bear you a son, and you shall call his name Laughter, and I will establish my covenant with him' (Gen. 17:19). Was this a *penalty* imposed upon them because they laughed? Hardly. Rather, it was a perpetual reminder that God breaks through. What joy they had when little Laughter came into their home and as he grew to become a young man!

We have commented several times on how the currently accepted image of Jesus all but makes it impossible to find him interesting and attractive, lovable. The responses of common people to him throughout the pages of the Gospel show how false that image is. He was such an attractive person and such a powerful speaker that, from the human point of view, the leaders of the day killed him out of envy of his popularity (Matt. 27:18). He was a master of humour and often used it to drive home the truths he imparted, as any good speaker does.[7] But few today would put him on their guest list for a party – if it were really going to be a *party*. Just as we don't think of Jesus as intelligent, so we don't think of him as pleasant company, someone to enjoy being around. Is it any wonder that someone would rather not be his student?

Prayer in the Cosmic Setting

On Not Getting What We Ask For

But the request, while powerful, does not always get us what we have in mind as we make it. This is true when it is addressed to other human beings and true when it is addressed to God as prayer. And that is entirely appropriate. It is a great advantage of requesting and prayer that it not be a fail-safe mechanism. For human finiteness means that we are all limited in knowledge, in power, in love and in powers of communication. Yet we must act. We must go on. Even disregarding ill will, it is small wonder that we do not, and often cannot, grant or be given what is requested of us or by us.

We do not know enough, and our desires are not perfect enough for us safely to be given everything we want and ask for. It is as simple as that. C. S. Lewis gives a lovely picture of how sane this is as we pray to God:

> Prayers are not always ... 'granted'. This is not because prayer is a weaker kind of causality, but because it is a stronger kind. When it 'works' at all it works unlimited by space and time. That is why God has retained a discretionary power of granting or refusing it. Except on that condition prayer would destroy us. It is not unreasonable for a headmaster to say, 'Such and such things you may do according to the fixed rules of this school. But such and such other things are too dangerous to be left to general rules. If you want to do them you must come and make a request and talk over the whole matter with me in my study. And then – we'll see.'[8]

We human beings have two different kinds of causation, as Lewis also points out. One is entirely under our control. The other, which works through the request, is not. If you have weeds in your garden or a flat tyre, it will be better not to just pray that the weeds will die or the tyre be fixed. You can, of course, ask someone else to take care of the situation. And they may or may not refuse. But you had better just pull the weeds or fix the tyre if you can. Basically, that is your domain by nature and divine appointment. If you have a friend who is addicted to heroin, however, or lost in the jungles of intellectual faddishness, then whatever else you may do to help him, you had better pray. Not just because 'fixing him' is beyond you, but because it is good it should be beyond you.

It is deeply instructive of the nature of human life and its redemption that, when Jesus knew Peter would deny him, he did not just 'fix him' so that he wouldn't do the terrible thing. Surely he could have done that. But it would not have advanced Peter towards being the person he needed to become. So Jesus said to Peter, with sadness perhaps, but with great confidence in the Father, 'I have requested, concerning you, that your faith might not die. And when you have straightened up, uphold your brothers' (Luke 22:32).

I think there is perhaps no other scene in all scripture that so forcefully illustrates the community of prayerful love as this response to Peter. How earnestly Jesus longed for Peter to come out right in his time of testing! But he left him free to succeed or fail before God and man – and, as it turned out, before all of subsequent human history. He used no condemnation, no shame, no 'pearls of wisdom' on him. And he didn't use supernatural power to rewire his soul or his brain. It was just this: 'I have requested, concerning you, that your faith might not die.' And it corresponds perfectly to Matt. 7:1–11. It is Jesus' beautiful pattern for us to practise in our relationships to those close to us.

Reaching for Further Understanding of Prayer As Such

This, then, is the community of prayerful love that Jesus brings us to in his kingdom. Its centre is, obviously, prayer, and there are several matters concerning prayer and how to pray that need to be discussed before we leave his Discourse on the Hill. We also recall that we postponed discussion of the Lord's Prayer, as given in Matthew 6, and we will soon have to go back and integrate it into our practice of kingdom living. That prayer forever stands squarely at the heart of the life and earthly community of Christ's disciples.

It is hoped that the few necessary points to be covered here will be practically helpful in opening the way into a deeper experience of the life of request. Prayer, like all of the practices into which Jesus leads by word and example, will be self-validating to all who will simply pray as he says and not give up.[9] It is much harder to learn if we succumb to the temptation to engage in 'heroic' efforts in prayer. This is important. Heroism, generally, is totally out of place in the spiritual life, until we grow to the point at which it would never be thought of as heroism anyway.

There are, of course, people who pray heroically, and they are to be respected for what God has called them to. One thinks of people like Rees Howells or John 'Praying' Hyde.[10] But that is a special calling and is for very few of us. To look to this calling as the ideal for our prayer life is only to assume a burden of uncalled-for guilt, and, quite surely, it is to choose an approach that will lead to abandoning prayer as a realistic and pervasive aspect of life in the kingdom. There will be heroic periods as they may be called for, but with no intention to be heroic. Always, we are simply children walking and talking with our Father at hand.

Prayer Is Basically Request

And now we turn to a number of specific points where progress in kingdom praying seems frequently blocked. The first concerns understanding the central matter of exactly what prayer is. The picture of prayer that emerges from the life and teaching of Jesus in the Gospels is quite clear. Basically it is one of asking, requesting things from God.

The relevant texts – for example, the Lord's Prayer itself – leave no doubt about this, as we shall see, and that is consistent with the remainder of the New Testament and with the Bible as a whole. Compare, for example, the prayer and the picture of prayer in 1 Kings 8:22–56. Nevertheless, many people are uncomfortable with this picture, especially with the idea that we would be requesting things *we* want from God.

A lovely couple once gave me a ride from a conference back to the airport a few hours away. As we rode along and chatted, the conversation turned to difficulties their son was having in his business. I then inquired as to how they were praying about it and what their experience in prayer had been. They were astonished. Should we really pray for our son's business, they asked? I think they would have quickly and easily prayed for his health or for his salvation. But business? And especially business in which they had a personal interest? That seemed to them entirely out of the question.

Now there was an important element of truth, and a certain goodness of heart, behind their discomfort. Prayer is never *just* asking, nor is it *merely* a matter of asking for what I want. God is not a cosmic butler or fix-it man, and the aim of the universe is not to fulfil my desires and needs. On the other hand, I am to pray for what concerns me, and many people have found prayer impossible because they thought they should only pray for wonderful but remote needs they actually had little or no interest in or even knowledge of.

Prayer simply *dies* from efforts to pray about 'good things' that honestly do not matter to us. The way to get to meaningful prayer for those good things is to start by praying for what we are truly interested in. The circle of our interests will inevitably grow in the largeness of God's love.

What prayer as asking presupposes is simply a personal – that is, an experientially interactive – relationship between us and God, just as with a request of child to parent or friend to friend. It assumes that our natural concerns will be naturally expressed, and that God will hear our prayers for ourselves as well as for others. Once again, this is clear from the biblical practice of prayer. It is seen at its best in that greatest of all prayer books, Psalms.[11]

Accordingly, I believe the most adequate description of prayer is simply, 'Talking to God about what we are doing together.' That immediately focuses the activity where we are but at the same time drives the egotism out of it. Requests will naturally be made in the course of this conversational walk. Prayer is a matter of explicitly sharing with God my concerns about what he too is concerned about in my life. And of course he is concerned about my concerns and, in particular, that my concerns should coincide with his. This is our walk together. Out of it I pray.

Other Valid Aspects of a Praying Life

But often in discussions of prayer we confuse it with other valid aspects of any life in which prayer is functioning as it ought. And that is not helpful. In fact, it can result in prayer's being replaced and omitted. We may confuse prayer with special states or activities that, although of some importance, are simply not prayer. Thus, well-intentioned people wind up not praying at all without even being aware of it. What they do is good. It is just not prayer and does not have the results of prayer. I have often seen this, even in whole congregations, and the harm it does to our life and to our confidence in God is very great.

So we must carefully consider, for example, that just talking to God is not prayer, though prayer is talking to God. And praise is not prayer, though praise is a wonderful exercise, and we will do very little praying unless our hearts are full of praise. Indeed, for anyone who has a genuine knowledge of God, praise is the only appropriate attitude in which to live. It is the only sane attitude.

Only a vivid assurance of God's greatness and goodness can lay a foundation for the life of prayer, and such an assurance will certainly express itself in praise. The great 'faith chapter' in the New Testament, Hebrews 11, tells us in simple words, 'Those who come to God must believe that he is and that he becomes a rewarder of those who seek him out' (v. 6). Praise is the inevitable result in the heart of the person who thus understands God and is actually living interactively with him.

Thanksgiving too is an inevitable accompaniment of vital prayer. The purpose is not to manipulate God into thinking we are grateful and that he should therefore give us more. That unfortunate idea is quite ridiculous, of course, and yet many people toy with it or even try to put it into practice. Nevertheless, prayer in the manner of Jesus will have incredible results, and thanksgiving will be a constant theme just because that is the reality of our relationship to God. Thanksgiving goes hand in hand with praise. We *are* thankful when we know we are living under the provisions of his bountiful hand.

Accordingly Paul told the Philippians, 'Be anxious for nothing, but in every situation with prayer and beseeching, with thanksgiving, make your requests known to God. Then the kind of peace God himself has will, far beyond anything you can understand, guard your hearts and minds in Christ Jesus' (4:6).

So prayer is a total activity, incorporating many elements essential to a personal relationship between two persons – persons different from and related to one another as the Father is to his children on earth. But still the *heart* of prayer is the request.

Can We Change God?

And God's 'response' to our prayers is not a charade. He does not pretend that he is answering our prayer when he is only doing what he was going to do anyway. Our requests really do make a difference in what God does or does not do. The idea that everything would happen exactly as it does regardless of whether we pray or not is a spectre that haunts the minds of many who sincerely profess belief in God. It makes prayer psychologically impossible, replacing it with dead ritual at best. And of course God does not respond to this. You wouldn't either.

Suppose your children believed that you never did anything differently because they asked you. For example, you will give them money on Friday evening regardless of whether they ask you for it or not. But they also believe that you require them to go through the ritual of asking. And so they do it. On Friday evening they approach you and ask you to give them some weekend money. They do it even though they believe that you will or will not give it to them regardless of what they do, and that you know that they believe this. This, unfortunately, is the idea some people have of prayer.

Of course, this is not the biblical idea of prayer, nor is it the idea of people for whom prayer is a vital part of life. It was two Old Testament scenes that changed my own mind about these matters and permitted me to enter into the teachings of Jesus about prayer. For I too was raised in a theology that presents God as a great unblinking cosmic stare, who must know everything whether he wants to or not, and who never in the smallest respect changes his mind about what he is going to do.

The first scene is set in the aftermath of the rebellion of the Israelites that occurred while Moses was on the mountain receiving the tablets with the Ten Commandments for the first time. They had made an idol and worshipped it and, with hearts turned back to Egypt, had indulged in a massive orgy. Now God tells Moses he intends to destroy them all and raise up a new nation from Moses alone (Exod. 32:10).

Moses' response to God in this situation is one of the most instructive passages on prayer in all of the Bible (vv. 12–14). First, notice that Moses reasoned with God, asking him why God should be defeated in his project with the people he had brought out of Egypt. Wasn't God able to complete it? And the Egyptians, Moses also pointed out, would be sure to say that God brought them out of Egypt intending to destroy them in the wilderness. Is that a good God, a great God, they would ask? And then there is the matter of promises made to Abraham, Isaac and Jacob. These rebellious people about to be destroyed were their descendants. Certain commitments had been made to them about their descendants. Would destroying these descendants be consistent with those commitments?

Moses boldly asked 'Jehovah', the special name for the covenant-making God of Israel, to 'change your mind' about harming 'Thy' people (v. 12). And the response was, 'So Jehovah changed his mind about the harm which he said he would do to his people' (v. 14).

The second Old Testament scene involves one of the really good kings in Judea, Hezekiah. He was a man who had already seen astonishing answers to prayer, especially in his confrontation with Sennacherib, king of Assyria (2 Kings 19:8–37). That is one of those magnificent biblical stories that even capture the artistic imagination. Lord Byron wrote 'The Destruction of Sennacherib' to memorialize it in verse.

But now Hezekiah has fallen mortally ill, and his friend Isaiah the prophet comes with the word from God: 'You shall die and not live' (20:1). In the face of this declared intent at least to allow death to come, Hezekiah does exactly what Moses did. He 'prayed to Jehovah'. He 'turned his face to the wall', and 'weeping bitterly' he reasoned with God on the basis of how he had walked before him in truth and with an undivided heart and had done what is good in his sight (vv. 2–3).

Before Isaiah could get halfway out of the palace, God told him to go back and tell Hezekiah, 'I have heard your prayer, I have seen your tears; behold, I will heal you ... And I will add fifteen years to your life' (vv. 4–6). And so, in fact, he did.

Now what we see here is a God who can be *prevailed upon* by those who faithfully stand before him. We should recall here our earlier discussion of how parents respond to the requests of their children. There is nothing automatic about requests. There is no 'silver bullet' in prayer. Requests may be granted. Or they may not. Either way, it will be for a good reason. That is how relationships between persons are, or should be.

God is great enough that he can conduct his affairs in this way. His nature, identity, and over-arching purposes are, no doubt, unchanging. But his intentions with regard to many particular matters that concern individual human beings are not. This does not diminish him. Far from it. He would be a lesser God if he could not change his intentions when he thinks it is appropriate. And if he chooses to deal with humanity in such a way that he will occasionally think it appropriate, that is just fine.

A Universe Responsive to Personality

This opens up a deep truth about our universe as a whole. It is a world that responds to desire and to will, and in many ways. That is what we should expect of a universe that is fundamentally Trinitarian, based in the ultimate reality of an interpersonal union too 'one' to be many and too 'many' to be just one.

On the physical side of this universe, many scientists now tell us, every thing and event is totally derived from and determined by certain subatomic particles called quarks.[12] These are taken to be the ultimate physical constituents of the physical universe. For the strictly scientific analysis of strictly physical reality, we should assume nothing beyond quarks, it is often said.

But not all of reality is physical. There is, as a matter of fact, no *science* that even attempts to demonstrate that all that exists is physical. Anyone is invited to point out which one does so, and where. If there were such a 'science', it would certainly fail. And in any case quarks themselves are not absolute beings. They must derive both their existence and their nature – including the laws by which they, supposedly, determine everything else – from something other than themselves.

Because that 'something other' is God, all of physical reality, quarks and all, is subject to his will. Our own body is, to a significant degree, immediately responsive to our thought, desire, and will. That is what enables us to act and to perceive. We all know this to be true in life, no matter what our philosophical theories about it may be. If we did not, we could not act, organize a life or live. But this central fact of life shows that matter is not indifferent to personality. It is influenced by it and influences it in turn. This is an actual *fact* about our world and our place in it.

Within a narrow range, then, desire and will directly influence physical reality by simply desiring and willing it to behave in certain ways. Our bodily actions are cases of this, as just noted. Whether willing and desiring – or merely thinking – influences things other than our own soul and body is far less clear. One would not, at present, want to venture greatly on the reality of psychokinesis, the alleged ability to move things by thought and will alone. But recent scientifically organized studies of prayer strongly indicate a power very like it.

Scientific Studies of Prayer

Empirical studies of the effects of praying have been around for quite some time. In the 1950s William R. Parker, of Redlands University in California, developed a programme of 'prayer therapy groups'. He tracked changes in the lives of individuals in small groups that did, or else did not, use prayer for the healing of various physical difficulties. He also studied the effects of different kinds of prayers and attitudes in praying. Prayer in what we might accurately call the spirit of Jesus Christ was found to have noteworthy effects for good in those who learned to use it. The book recording all of this, *Prayer Can Change Your Life*, is still very much worth reading and is especially useful in learning some aspects of the practice of healing prayer.[13] When it appeared, it was quite unusual.

Since the late 1980s, however, there have been more than 130 studies of the effects of prayer published in medical and other professional journals. Many of these have been set up under the most careful of scientific controls, and some have even involved prayer for non-human living things. Perhaps the most well known is the one by Randolph Byrd, at the University of California San Francisco Medical School, published in 1988. It dealt with 393 coronary care patients who had had heart attacks or severe symptoms. It was a double-blind study; neither the patients nor the medical staff caring for them knew who was being prayed for and who was not.

The results were so impressive that every major television network and newspaper in the United States reported them in some detail. Of the group prayed for, significantly fewer died, fewer required use of the most potent drugs, and not one had to be put on life support. These results, along with many other studies, are discussed in great detail by Larry Dossey, M.D., in his *Healing Words*.[14]

Dossey also reports on prayer experiments with non-human forms of life, such as germinating seeds, plants and bacteria (pp. 190, 218–21). Also, distance was found to have no bearing on the effects of prayer. Prayer was as effective for things on the other side of the earth as for things nearby. It continued to be effective when the object was enclosed in a lead-lined box that shuts out all known forms of physical energy – waves, particles and so on.

Finally, in Dossey's interpretation of the research material, it does not matter, within broad limits, how you pray or to whom you pray. There is no how-to in the sense of methodical procedure (pp. 9–10). We are on 'the pathless path' (p. 18). And this is no doubt mainly because, in his view, there is no 'external God' we have to go through to achieve the effects of prayer (p. 8). God is in any case unknowable (p. 23). What we pray 'to' is within ourselves.

Indeed, as Dossey approvingly quotes from the biologist R. Davenport, 'Physical reality ... emerges from our consciousness during our changing experience within nature' (p. 68). This is currently a well-known philosophical understanding of things that we need not accept in order to take seriously the scientific studies of prayer.

Now this interpretation of prayer – or, for Dossey, better: prayerfulness – as a strictly human enterprise only involving interaction with non-personal forces is obviously different from Jesus' interpretation of prayer. But my purpose here is to understand, not to criticize it. Prayer is, under any interpretation, a particular exertion and expression of thought, will and desire.

These carefully researched examinations of the effects of prayer on life show, I believe, that personality in its human form has effects – through appropriate exertions of thought, will and desire – that work beyond the familiar channels of physical causation. That is the heart of Dossey's position and, less clearly, of Parker's. Both are professionals concerned about human health, and they believe that known resources for good should be implemented. Further, it is clear that both want to get on with the business at hand, healing, and not get bogged down in theological hairsplitting. Any honest person must be sympathetic.

Still, the question remains as to whether this picture of prayer in terms of impersonal powers captures prayer as an activity in the kingdom of God, or is only a further extension of the purely human realm. Perhaps the human kingdom is significantly larger, and of a remarkably different nature, than the reigning materialistic interpretation of reality would have it. I believe that it is. But that in no way sets aside the primacy and priority of the kingdom of the heavens over human life. When we have said all that is to be said of the power of a 'prayer' that does not 'go through an external God', we still have to come to terms with that God and to deal with the dimensions of human existence, especially the moral dimensions, with which Dossey's kind of prayer has no clear involvement.

This 'external' kind of prayer is a matter of coming to a person other than oneself and asking that *they* do something that one cannot do oneself. It is coming to One who has repeatedly invaded human history and continues to do so. It is intelligently working with him to accomplish ends that fulfil his purposes in creation and in fostering human life upon the earth for a short while. It is therefore prayer of the *spirit*, or kingdom prayer, not mere *soul* prayer. Soul prayer is an exercise of powers inherent in the human being without reference to a 'God beyond'. Perhaps it also involves some larger realm of non-physical reality.

Here we want to keep in mind Bonhoeffer's distinction, referred to earlier, between communities that are spiritual and those that are psychical or merely human realities. The psychical aspect of the human being is certainly real, and it must not be overlooked. But to understand the scope of prayer in God's full world, we must go far beyond the psychical as understood along Dossey's lines.

For kingdom praying, personalities are ultimate and distinct. They interact through explicit, purposeful communication, listening and speaking, not through a mere 'sense of unity'. In Numbers 12:7–8, emphasizing the kind of relationship God himself obviously prefers, he says of 'my servant Moses, he is faithful in all my house; with him I speak mouth to mouth, even openly, and not in dark sayings, and he beholds the form of the Lord' (vv. 7–8).

Jesus himself indicates that something very close to this is intended by God for anyone who loves him: 'He will keep my word, and my father will love him and we will come to him and make our home with him' (John 14:23). If you know the biblical tradition, you cannot imagine that this would only be a matter of strange sensations or warm feelings. God is above all a God who speaks and listens.[15]

Prayer Trains Us to Reign

Prayer as kingdom praying is an arrangement explicitly instituted by God in order that we as individuals may count, and count for much, as we learn step by step how to govern, to reign with him in his kingdom. To enter and to learn this reign is what gives the individual life its intended significance. This high calling also explains why prayer frequently requires much effort, continuous effort, and on some matters possibly years and years of effort. Prayer is, above all, a means of forming character. It combines freedom and power with service and love. What God gets out of our lives – and, indeed, what we get out of our lives – is simply the person we become. It is God's intention that we should grow into the kind of person he could empower to do what we want to do. Then we are ready to 'reign for ever and ever' (Rev. 22:5).

Reign is no doubt wording that is a little too grand for the contemporary mind, though what it refers to is what everyone actually pursues in life. We have been trained to think of 'reigning' as exclusive of others. But in the heart of the divine conspiracy, it just means to be free and powerful in the creation and governance of what is good. In the life of prayer we are training for, we reign in harmonious union with the infinite power of God.

And a major element in this training is experience in *waiting* for God to move, not leaping ahead and taking things into our own hands. Out of this waiting experience there comes a form of character that is priceless before God, a character that can be empowered to do as one chooses. This explains why James says that patience in trials will make us 'fully functional' (*teleion*), 'perfect' (1:4).

Sometimes we must wait for God to do as we ask because the answer involves changes in other people, or even ourselves, and that kind of change always takes time. Sometimes, apparently, the changes in question involve conflicts going on in a spiritual realm lying entirely outside human affairs (Dan. 10:13). We always live in a larger context of activities we do not see. But whatever the exact cause, Jesus emphatically taught that we are to stay with our request. That is, quite simply, an aspect of all serious human relationships. We stay with an issue until it is resolved one way or another.

He uses an illustration taken from human affairs, once again emphasizing the continuity between making requests of human beings and praying to God. On one occasion he compared praying to going to a friend at midnight to borrow food for an acquaintance who is travelling and has descended on you so late at night that you have nothing for him to eat (Luke 11:5–6).

You call out your request to your neighbour, and from inside there comes the answer: 'It's too much trouble. The door is closed, and the kids are settled with me in bed. I can't do anything for you' (v. 7). But he will. If you just stand there and wait, he will. Even if he has to awaken the kids and undo the door – no small matter in those days.

Maybe he looks out a hour later and sees you just standing there wringing your hands. What else can he do? And as Jesus points out, 'It is not because he is your friend that he will do it, but because you just keep standing there waiting for the loaves' (v. 8). Of course, if you go away he won't do it, and if he does do it you won't be there to receive it. That is common sense, and Jesus integrates it right into the life of prayer.

Another graphic illustration of the importance of staying with a request is found in Luke 18. This, like the previous one, is explicitly designed to teach us not to quit praying for what we need:

> He told them a parable in order to show how they should pray relentlessly and not give up. One of the most powerful men in the city, a judge, did not fear God and had no regard for men. And one of the

> weakest people in the city, a widow, came to him repeatedly, insisting that he apply the law to right a wrong done to her. This judge did nothing for a while, but then he thought, 'Even though neither God nor man scares me, this widow is driving me nuts. I'll give her justice to keep her from wearing me out by constantly petitioning me.' (18:1–6)

Now, Jesus says, 'Listen to what this crooked judge says. And will not God do what is right by his chosen ones, who cry out to him day and night? And will he be slow in responding? Not at all. He will be quick to their aid' (vv. 7–8). But the assumption is that the request does not go away. It is there to stay. That is our part.

The main teaching here is that we should expect prayer to proceed in the manner of a relationship between persons. Of course it will be in the manner of such relationships at their best, but the general character of requesting will remain. In fact, the contrary assumption possibly causes more people to 'drop out' of praying than anything else. Praying is mistakenly thought to be like putting your money into a vending machine or like dropping a bomb. You perform a simple act once, and then the mechanism takes over to produce the inevitable result. I have even heard people seriously teach that if you ask God for the same thing a second time, that only proves to him you didn't believe the first time – as if he didn't know already.

This view also leads to misguided efforts to word everything just right: for example, being sure to say, 'In Jesus' name', or, 'If it be thy will'. The idea that if we get it 'just right' it will work treats prayer like the vending machine. Prayer is never a mechanism. It is always a personal negotiation, as the earlier quotation from C. S. Lewis so wisely suggests. Jesus' constant effort in his teaching about prayer is to drive this point home.

Does This Offend God's Dignity?

But just as religious faith has its traditional dogmas, so does unbelief. I am acquainted with highly placed intellectuals who hold that we know nothing of the nature of God. And yet they do not hesitate to affirm that it would be beneath God's dignity to receive anything from human beings or to 'answer' a request. God is too 'great' to be bothered, like 'great' human beings, no doubt. But if we know nothing of the genuine nature of God, one might reply, we certainly do not know *that*.

This is a very old prejudice, at least as old as Plato, who regarded the belief that the gods are 'turned aside from their purpose by sacrifices and prayer' as one form of insolence towards God.[16] That prejudice is passed on through people such as Cicero and Hume.[17] We have seen in a previous chapter that it comes to expression in many contemporary theologians on the left.

We should admit, I think, that some views of prayer are degrading of God, and perhaps of human beings as well. We think, for example, of those that make his response inevitable if we can just get our words right. Or of those that have us buying him off with sacrifices of various kinds. But that is not so of the view of prayer that Jesus gives. To suppose that God and the individual communicate within the framework of God's purposes for us, as explained earlier, and that because of the interchange God does what he had not previously intended, or refrains from something he previously had intended to do, is nothing against God's dignity *if it is an arrangement he himself has chosen*.

It is not inherently 'greater' to be inflexible. That is an unfortunate human idea of greatness, derived from behaviour patterns all too common in a fallen world. It turns God into a cosmic stuffed shirt. This unfortunate idea is reinforced from 'the highest intellectual sources' by classical ideas of 'perfection', which stressed the necessity of absolute inalterability in God. But in a domain of persons, such as The Kingdom Among Us, it is far greater to be flexible and yet able to achieve the good goals one has set. And that is an essential part of the Divine Personality shown in the Bible and incarnated in the person of Jesus and presented in his message. So far from fitting the classical pattern of God as 'the Unmoved Mover', the God shown in the historical record is 'the Most Moved Mover'. This is the One who lives with us and whom we approach from within the community of prayerful love.

The Grandest Prayer of All

The Lord's Prayer

All this becomes very clear if we only pay attention to Jesus' explicit teaching and practise of prayer, as his apprentices naturally would. Although he spent much time alone in prayer, he also spent much time praying in the presence of his students. They were tremendously impressed. On one occasion he took Peter, James and John along with him to a mountain top. There, 'while he was praying his face was transformed and his clothing flashed like lightning' (Luke 9:29).

This may seem quite unrealistic. His three friends certainly hardly knew what they were looking at, and they came to understand it only much later (2 Pet. 1:16–19). But recall, as we have said, that we live in a Trinitarian universe, one where infinite energy of a personal nature is the ultimate reality. When we pray we enter the real world, the substance of the kingdom, and our bodies and souls begin to function for the first time as they were created to function. Indeed, the 'transfiguration' of Jesus must be regarded as the highest revelation of the nature of matter recorded in human history.

Matter, ordinary physical 'stuff', is the place for the development and manifestation of finite personalities who, in their bodies, have significant resources either to oppose God or to serve him. Jesus the Quintessential Man, that is, the Son of man, is the only one who has brought the role of matter to its fullness in his own personality. That is what we are looking at in the Gospels. As for each of us, this is something that lies in our future, in the worlds to come (Phil. 3:20–21; 1 John 3:2). Yet even now when we put our body and soul into prayer, the effects are remarkable.

William Penn said of George Fox, around whom the early Friends (Quaker) movement arose,

> But above all, he excelled in prayer. The inwardness and weight of his spirit, the reverence and solemnity of his dress and behaviour, and the fewness and fullness of his words, have often struck even strangers, with admiration, and they used to reach others with

> consolation. The most awful, living, reverent frame I ever felt or beheld, I must say, was his in prayer.[18]

Clearly the presence of Jesus in prayer was more impressive than even that of George Fox. Some while after the event of Jesus' transfiguration before his friends, the Gospel of Luke records, 'He was praying in a certain place' with his students. 'After he had finished one of his students said to him, "Lord, teach us to pray, just like John [the Baptizer] also taught his disciples"' (11:1). This is, of course, an exact expression of the master-student relationship. The apprentices have watched the master do some important thing, and they have heard him explain it. Now they say, show us how, induct us into the practice.

Jesus' response here must be taken very seriously. Many people make little progress in learning to pray simply because they have not seriously entered into Jesus' answer to the explicit request, 'Teach us to pray.' Praying is a form of speaking, and it is best learned by entering into the words that Jesus gave us to say to God when we pray. He is the Master of this subject too.

Of course, we have already seen in Chapter 6 that mere *repetition* is not kingdom praying. And this is still true of repetition of the words that Jesus gave. Instead, we learn to use the words given by him to speak intelligently and lovingly to our heavenly Father, with whom we are engaged in a common life. But we *do* use those words. And with them as foundation, and only so, we move out – partly on our own initiative, which God elicits and expects – into prayer over the details of our life and times 'under the sun'.

God Must Be Addressed

The variations in phrasing between the words given as the Lord's Prayer in Matthew 6 and in Luke 11 are of little significance, and we will treat the two passages as one and the same prayer or prayer outline. First, there is simply the address. 'Father', the Luke version simply says, and Matthew characteristically further identifies the one addressed as 'Our Father, the one in the heavens.' The 'address' part of prayer is of vital significance. We dare not slight or overlook it. It is one of the things that distinguishes prayer from worrying out loud or silently, which many, unfortunately, have confused with prayer.

When we speak to someone, we use a name to call to that person in distinction from everyone else. We thereby indicate that we wish to speak to *that particular person*. The name also calls attention to our standing in relation to the one addressed. This is nearly always true in intimate associations. I call my son 'My dear boy', my daughter 'Little Princess', and my wife 'Sweetheart'. No one else does that. No one else can do that. Similarly when they speak to me: when they say 'Dad' or 'Sweetheart', there is a configuration drawn around us within which we then relate. It is stronger than steel. Whatever else happens or is said will be conditioned upon this configuration.

A remarkable change in the spirit of our society is marked by recent changes in the formalities of address. These changes are not incidental, not small things. They mirror manifold profound ambiguities and uncertainties as to who we are as we go through daily life. It now is thought to be cloyingly bad taste, for example, to refer to anyone in a note or memo as 'Dear Joe'; you just write 'Joe'. If the trend continues, it will next be 'Hey, you.'

The idea is, I think, that we don't want to be hypocritical and express fondness where it is not felt. How very noble the sentiment! No one seems to understand that it was not fondness but respect that was expressed by the 'Dear Joe' form. The change of form marked the loss of respectful approach, not the loss of hypocrisy – which, from all appearances, remains in a very healthy condition.

Our Father, the One in the Heavens

When we speak to God, Jesus tells us, we are to address him as 'Our Father, the one in the heavens.' This is the configuration of reality from within which we pray. The overwhelming difficulties many people have with prayer, both understanding it and doing it, derive from nothing more than their failure or their inability to place themselves within this configuration and receive it by grace. This may be because they actually do not live within the kingdom configuration, perhaps are even in rebellion against it. But until they learn to do this routinely yet deeply, they will experience no stability and development in their practice of prayer.

If we are already 'turned' towards the Father and are recipients of the kingdom, a common way of bringing ourselves into the 'address' position is to enter a deep, meditative reading of some choice passage of scripture. Martin Luther said that those well trained in 'warming up the heart' for prayer will 'be able to use a chapter of Scripture as a lighter' – a *Feuerzeug*, the same term modern Germans use for a pocket lighter.[19]

For this purpose we will benefit most from the great passages of scripture that clearly show us our Father in relation to his creation and his earthly family. These are passages such as Genesis 1 or 15; Exodus 19; 1 Kings 8; 2 Chronicles 16 and 19; Nehemiah 9; many of the psalms (34, 37, 91, and 103, for example); Isaiah 30, 44, and 56–66; Luke 11; Romans 8; Philippians 4.

Reading or singing the great hymns, or using written prayers the Lord has given his people through the ages, are also extremely useful. This activity must not be hurried. Quiet, deeply meditative absorption of the words, receptive of images that fill out the realities they refer to, is sure to bring us to proper orientation before God.

Certain bodily postures may also be useful in this regard. Luther, once again, recommends that we 'kneel down or stand up with folded hands and eyes towards the sky.'[20]

The followers of Saint Dominic described nine different ways in which he prayed, including bowing humbly before the altar in a church, lying flat on his face before the crucifix, standing with hands and arms spread out like a cross, stretching himself to the limit and standing as upright as possible.[21]

Such matters of posture are, of course, not laws. No one *has* to do them. And the necessary address to God in prayer is, in fact, an entirely inward reality, between us and God. Reading, posture, singing, special setting and the like are all to be used only insofar as they serve to establish a gripping presence and address. They are simply matters of what is helpful and what is not. The important thing for each individual is that he or she should find some way that is effective and not assume that it does not matter how one approaches prayer.

Jesus commonly stood and 'looked into heaven' as a part of his address to the Father. He did this because the person he was speaking to was, of course, *there*. We should remember this, and though it may occasionally be useful to bow the head and close the eyes, that is not to be regarded as the 'canonical position', the only one in which we are really praying. The particular values it serves are not the only matters to be observed in prayer, and, perhaps strangely, many people have found it very enlivening to pray with open eyes, and possibly walking to and fro.

In any case, when we pray we must take time to fix our minds upon God and orient our world around him. Whatever we need to do to that end should be done. When it is done, we will see ourselves situated in the family of God across time and space, as we pray '*our* Father', and we will see God as our *Father*, and we will see our Father directly available to us for face-to-face communication. That is what it means for him to be *Our Father, the one in the heavens.*

Unfortunately, the old standard formulation, 'Our Father who art in heaven,' has come to mean 'Our Father who is far away and much later.' As explained in an earlier chapter, the meaning of the plural *heavens*, which is erroneously omitted in most translations, sees God present as far 'out' as imaginable but also right down to the atmosphere around our heads, which is the first of 'the heavens'. The omission of the plural robs the wording in the model prayer of the sense Jesus intended. That sense is, 'Our Father always near us.'

Having taught us to address God in the manner indicated, the remainder of the model prayer as given in Luke 11 consists of requests or categories of requests.

There are five of them:

1. That the name 'God' would be regarded with the utmost possible respect and endearment.
2. That his kingdom would fully come on earth.
3. That our needs for today be met today.
4. That our sins be forgiven, not held against us.
5. That we not be permitted to come under trial or to have bad things happen to us.

These are basically the same as in Matthew 6, where a little wording is added to some of them. We shall consider the two passages together.

'Hallowed' Be Thy Name

The first and second requests directly concern God's position in the human realm. The first one asks that the *name* of God should be held in high regard. 'Hallowed be thy name,' the old version has it.

In the biblical world, names are never just names. They partake of the reality that they refer to. The Jewish reverence for the name of God was so great that especially devout Jews might even avoid pronouncing it. Thus we do not really know how *Yahweh*, as we say it, really is to be pronounced. The pronunciation is lost in history.

Today very few people any longer understand what it means to 'hallow' something and are apt to associate *hallow* only with ghosts and Hallowe'en. So we would do better to translate the language here as 'let your name be sanctified.' Let it be uniquely respected. Really, the idea is that his name should be treasured and loved more than any other, held in an absolutely unique position among humanity.

The word translated 'hallow' or 'sanctify' is *hagiastheto*. It is basically the same word used, for example, in John 17:17, where Jesus asks the Father to *sanctify* his students, especially the apostles, through his truth. And it appears again in 1 Thess. 5:23, where Paul expresses his hope that God will sanctify the Thessalonians entirely, keeping them blameless in spirit, soul and body until Jesus returns. In such passages, too, the term means to locate the persons referred to in a separate and very special kind of reality.

This request is based upon the deepest need of the human world. Human life is not about human life. Nothing will go right in it until the greatness and goodness of its source and governor is adequately grasped. His very name is then held in the highest possible regard. Until that is so, the human compass will always be pointing in the wrong direction, and individual lives as well as history as a whole will suffer from constant and fluctuating disorientation. Candidly, that is exactly the condition we find ourselves in.

But the cosmic significance of this first request must not hide the fact that it is also the natural request of a child who loves its 'Abba', its Daddy. How a child's heart is wounded to hear its parents, mother or father, dishonoured or to see them attacked. Such an attack shakes the very foundations of the child's existence, for the parents are its world. The touching confidence in the parent that famously makes a child think its parents are 'the best' in every regard is really essential to the child's well-being in the early stages of life.

So when we hear this first request, and indeed the second as well, we want to remember that it is the prayer of an adoring child, somewhat jealous for its parent. And we want to let ourselves sense its longing that 'Abba', who in this case really is 'the greatest', should be recognized as such. We want to dwell on this meditatively and perhaps weep for sadness that God is not so understood. We want to enter into the alarm of the little child who stumbles across those who do not think its father or mother is the greatest and best. And we must transfer that alarm to the lack of admiration and confidence that the human world has for our Father in the heavens.

Thy Kingdom Come

The second request follows from the first. The child's confidence in the 'Abba' who supervises everything for good naturally wants his rule, his kingdom, to come into realization in any place where it is not fully present. Recall, now, that the *kingdom* of God is the range of his effective will: that is, it is the domain where what he prefers is actually what happens. And this very often does not happen on this sad earth – on Gaia, as it is often called nowadays.

The clause 'Thy will be done, as in heaven so also on earth,' added in the Matthew 6 version of the model prayer, therefore only clarifies what it means to say, 'Thy kingdom come.' We have pointed out in earlier chapters that this does not mean 'come into existence.' The kingdom of God is from everlastingly earlier to everlastingly later. It does not come into existence, nor does it cease. But in human affairs other 'kingdoms' may for a time be in power, and often are. This second request asks for those kingdoms to be displaced, wherever they are, or brought under God's rule.

We are thinking here of the places we spend our lives: of homes, playgrounds, city streets, workplaces, schools and so forth. These are the places we have in mind, and they are where we are asking for the kingdom, God's rule, to come, to be in effect. Also, we are thinking of *our* activities more than of those of other people. We know our weaknesses, our limitations, our habits, and we know how tiny our power of conscious choice is. We are therefore asking that, by means beyond our knowledge and the scope of our will, we be assisted to act within the flow of God's actions.

But we are also praying over the dark deeds of others in the world around us. We see how they are trapped in what they themselves often disown and despise. And we are especially praying about the structural or institutionalized evils that rule so much of the earth. These prevailing circumstances daily bring multitudes to do deeply wicked things they do not even give a thought to. They do not know what they are doing and do not have the ability to distance themselves from it so they can see it for what it is. That is the power of 'culture'.

Culture is seen in what people do unthinkingly, what is 'natural' to them and therefore requires no explanation or justification. Everyone has a culture – or, really, multidimensional cultures of various levels. These cultures structure their lives. And, of course, by far the most of everyone's culture is right and good and essential. But not all. For culture is the place where wickedness takes on group form, just as the flesh, good and right in itself, is the place where individual wickedness dwells. We therefore pray for our Father to break up these higher-level patterns of evil. And, among other things, we ask him to help us see the patterns we are involved in. We ask him to help us not co-operate with them, to cast light on them and act effectively to remove them.

Give Daily Bread Daily

The third request in the model prayer deals with the immediate sustenance of our body. Food, of course, is symbolically central, but whatever else we really need to live in a functional manner is included in this request. Paul speaks of being at peace if we have 'foods and clothings' (1 Tim. 6:8). And that, you may recall, fits in exactly with what we found in Jesus' discussion of birds and flowers in Matt. 6:25–34 and with what God provided in the desert wanderings of his covenant people (Deut. 8:3–5).

Of course this request embodies that confidence in our Father that relieves us from all anxiety. The emphasis is on *provision today* of what we need *for today*. This is because God is always present today, no matter which day it is. His reign is the Eternal Now. So we do not ask him to provide today what we will need for tomorrow. To have it in hand today does not guarantee that we will have it tomorrow when we need it. Today I have God, and *he* has the provisions. Tomorrow it will be the same. So I simply ask today for what I need for today or ask now for what I need now.

This is how children do it, of course. A mother who discovers that her child is saving up oatmeal, pieces of toast or strips of bacon for fear of not having food tomorrow has cause to be alarmed. The world being what it is, we can all too easily imagine situations in which the child's action would be reasonable. But in any normal situation parents will be astonished and pained that the child does not trust them to provide for it day by day. A child should never have to even think about future provision until it grows older and has that responsibility.

Now, to make it clear about the teaching and the prayer, it is quite all right, as earlier noted, to have things now that we intend to use tomorrow and to work or even pray in a sensible way for them. What hinders or shuts down kingdom living is not the having of such provisions, but rather the trusting in them for future security. We have no real security for the future in them, but only in the God who is present with us each day.

It used to be said long ago that no man's property, life or reputation was safe while Parliament was in session. And there are hundreds of things other than government action that can turn our provisions to nothing. That is the precarious condition of all who 'lay up treasures for themselves and are not rich towards God' (Luke 12:21). When we accept and practise Jesus' teaching on prayer, however, we are entirely freed from concerns about the future. You can easily imagine what a marvellously transforming effect this has on our life and our relationships with others.

Don't Punish Us for Things We Do Wrong

The fourth request is for forgiveness of sins. It asks the Father to deal with us on the basis of mercy or pity. We forgive someone of a wrong they have done us when we decide that we will not make them suffer for it in any way. This does *not* mean we must prevent suffering that may come to them as a result of the wrong they have done. It does not mean that either when we forgive others or when they or God forgive us. Of course we *may* be of help there, too, but it is no part of forgiveness. Moreover, it is usually unwise. The natural consequences of actions have been pretty well designed by God to lead us to be the persons we ought to be. To blunt their lessons may be to harm those we would help.

But it is only pity or mercy that makes life possible. We do not like to hear it, but human beings at their best are pitiable creatures that 'walk in a vain show' (Ps. 39:6). Only God's mercies keep us from being consumed because of our sins (Lam. 3:22). But as a father pities his children, so the Lord pities us. He knows what we are made of and remembers that we are dust. He does not deal with us according to our sins, nor does he reward us in proportion to our wrongdoings (Ps. 103:10–14). That is the wonderful, healing nature of The Kingdom Among Us.

Once we step into this kingdom and trust it, pity becomes the atmosphere in which we live. Of course it is his pity for us that allows us in to start with, and then it patiently bears with us. 'The Lord is bursting with compassion and full of pity' (James 5:11). But we also are to 'be of one mind, having compassion one of another, love as brethren, be pitiful, be courteous' (1 Pet. 3:8 KJV).

It is not psychologically possible for us really to *know* God's pity for us and at the same time be hardhearted towards others. So we are 'forgiving of others in the same manner as God forgives us.' That is a part of our prayer. We are not just promising or resolving to forgive, however. We are praying for help to forgive others, for, though it is up to us to forgive – we do it – we know we cannot do it without help. But we can expect help, for the 'unity of spiritual orientation' discussed earlier in this chapter covers all these matters.

Therefore I live with my family on the basis of their pity for me. My wife is given the grace to have mercy on me, likewise my children. Earlier it was my parents, grandparents, brothers and sister. They all dealt with me mercifully. They felt sorry for me and had pity on me.

Now that I have come to know The Kingdom Among Us, I also will be merciful to those close to me. It is not just that I do not condemn them. That is important, of course, but it is not enough. I must have mercy. The kingdom and its God is great enough that 'mercy and truth can meet together' (Ps. 85:7–10). And 'Mercy brags about how it wins over judgment' (James 2:13). The provision of the Father in the life and death of his Son, and in the greatness of his own eternal heart, makes it possible.

Understanding of these matters can help us with one of the most painful failures to be found in our families. We each of us have a deep, biological need to honour our parents. This need is reflected in the commandment: 'Honour your father and your mother, that your days may be long in the land that your God Jehovah has given you' (Exod. 20:12).

To honour our parents means to be thankful for their existence and to respect their actual role as givers of life in the sequence of human existence. Of course, in order to honour them in this way we need to be thankful for our own existence too. But we also will usually need to have pity on them. For, even if they are good people, it is almost always true that they have been quite wrong in many respects, and possibly still are.

Commonly those who have experienced great antagonism with their parents are only able to be thankful for their existence and honour them, as they deeply need to, after the parents have grown old. Then it is possible to pity them, to have mercy on them. And that opens the door to honouring them. With a certain sadness, perhaps, but also with joy and peace at last. One of the greatest gifts of The Kingdom Among Us is the healing of the parent-child relationship, 'turning the hearts of fathers to their children and the hearts of children to their fathers' (Mal. 4:6).

Of course, as long as we are *demanding* things, we cannot *ask* for them, and there is no place for pity. Sometimes it may be necessary to demand. Perhaps the relationship has degenerated to the point that nothing else is left. But it is always better to avoid demanding when we can. Living on the basis of pity makes it easier to ask and makes it easier to give, including forgiveness. People who are merciless, unable to pity others and receive pity, simply have a hard life full of unsolvable problems.

Today we sometimes speak of people who cannot forgive themselves. Usually, however, the problem is much deeper. More often than not, these are people who refuse to live on the basis of pity. Their problem is not that they are hard on themselves, but that they are proud. And if they are hard on themselves, it is because they are proud. They do not want to accept that they can only live on the basis of pity from others, that the good that comes to them is rarely 'deserved'. If they would only do that, it would transform their lives. They would easily stop punishing themselves for what they have done.[22]

Recently a popular book was written under the title *When Bad Things Happen to Good People*. But to complete the picture we also need to contemplate certain other situations. For example, what about when bad things *don't* happen to good people? Could not one write a fine book on that? And what of when bad things don't happen to bad people? Or when good things happen to bad people?

The book in question had an important point, and the individual case it treated was a very touching one. The answer it gives to the problem of the suffering of good people is that God cannot do anything about it. That same book has been written many times through human history, and the answer it gives is one of the standard answers. But it is important to see all dimensions of our human situation in order to have an adequate picture of our place before God.

And if you've been squirming as you read this, there's a good reason. I have used the word *pity* through much of this discussion of 'forgive us our sins', rather than the word *mercy* or the even more dignified *compassion*. This is because only *pity* reaches to the heart of our condition. The word *pity* makes us wince, as *mercy* does not. Our current language has robbed *mercy* of its deep, traditional meaning, which is practically the same as *pity*. To pity someone now is to feel sorry for them, and that is regarded as demeaning, whereas to have mercy now is thought to be slightly noble – just 'give 'em a break.'

Today even many Christians read and say 'forgive us our trespasses' as 'give me a break.' In the typically late-twentieth-century manner, this saves the ego and its egotism. 'I am not a *sinner*, I just need a break!' But no, I need more than a break. I need pity because of who I am. If my pride is untouched when I pray for forgiveness, I have not prayed for forgiveness. I don't even understand it.

In the model prayer, Jesus teaches us to ask for pity with reference to our wrongdoings. Without it, life is hopeless. And with it comes the gift of pity as an atmosphere in which we then can live. To live in this atmosphere is to be able simply to drop the many personal issues that make human life miserable and, with a clarity of mind that comes only from not protecting my pride, to work for the good things all around us we always can realize in co-operation with the hand of God.

Don't Put Us to the Test

The final request asks our Father not to put us to the test. 'Don't bring us into temptation.' The 'temptation' here is not primarily temptation to sin. Trials always tempt us to sin, however. And temptation to sin is always a trial, which we might fail by falling into sin. Moreover, the bad things that come upon us are always trials. And so the version in Matthew 6 elaborates this last request by saying, 'Spare us from bad things that might happen to us.'

This request is not just for evasion of pain and of things we don't like, though it frankly is that. It expresses the understanding that we can't stand up under very much pressure, and that it is not a good thing for us to suffer. It is a vote of 'no confidence' in our own abilities. As the series of requests begins with the glorification of God, it ends with acknowledgement of the feebleness of human beings.

God expects us to pray that we will escape trials, and we should do it. The bad things that happen to us are always challenges to our faith, and we may not be able to stand up under them. They are *dangerous*. To know this, one has only to watch how quickly people begin to attack God when bad things start to happen to them. The popularity of the book just referred to, on why bad things happen to good people, is explicit testimony to how 'bad things' tend to undermine faith.

The excessive confidence people have in the strength of their own faith – usually it is when they are *not* suffering, of course – simply makes the danger worse. The attitude of James and John, seeking in advance their own promotion in the government they expected Jesus to set up, is characteristic. He asked them if they could go through what he was going to go through. They replied, 'Yes Sir, we can do it!' (Matt. 20:22). This is precisely the attitude of self-confidence we must avoid, and the final request in the model prayer is designed to help us avoid it. Once again, we are asking for pity, this time in the form of protection from circumstances. We are asking a Father who is both able and willing to extend such pity to not let bad things happen to us.

As we attentively make this prayer a part of our constant bearing in life, we will *see* how God indeed does keep us from trials and deliver us from evil. Constantly. We will see how often good things happen even to 'bad' people – as well as to the good. And, of course, we will find that we do have trials, and that some bad things come to everyone. No one is totally exempt. We can count on that for sure.

But we will also become assured that any trial or evil that comes upon us has a special function in God's plans. As with daily provision of food, there is continuous provision for every need, no matter how dire. We may not always have it ahead of time, but often right when we need it from the God who is right there with us. Our bedrock certainty of this will stand firmly upon our many experiences of the presence and goodness of our Father. We will have first-hand experience of how his strength is brought to perfection in our lives precisely by our weaknesses, combined with hopeful faith.

Here lies the secret of Paul's astonishing testimony: 'So, living for Christ, I am delighted when I experience weaknesses, insults, desperate needs, persecutions and difficulties. For when I am weak, then I am powerful' (2 Cor. 12:9–10).

It is precisely this experience-based assurance that is expressed in the great psalms, such as 23, 34, 37 and 91. These and similar passages in the scriptures trouble many people because they seem to promise too much – to be, frankly, unrealistic. But they do not promise that we will have no trials, as human beings understand trials. They promise, instead, totally unbroken care, along with God-given adequacy to whatever happens.

Psalm 91, for example, is a great affirmation of the total protection Jehovah gives to those who 'dwell' under his presence. But isn't that just too much? 'No evil will befall you!' (v. 10). Really? And: 'Because he has loved Me, therefore I will deliver him; I will set him securely on high, because he has known My name. He will call upon Me, and I will answer him; I will be with him in trouble; I will rescue him and honour him. With a long life I will satisfy him, and let him behold My salvation' (vv. 14–16 NASV). Similar claims are made in the other psalms mentioned. We should understand that God will usually spare us from trials, especially if we are living in the Lord's Prayer. And we should also understand that, when trials are permitted, it only means that he has something better in mind for us than freedom from trials.

What we learn about God from Jesus should prove to us that suffering and 'bad things' happening to us are not the Father's preferred way of dealing with us – sometimes necessary, perhaps, but never what he would, on the whole, prefer. What the psalmist says is true of many of us: 'Before I was afflicted I went astray, but now I keep Thy word ... It is good for me that I was afflicted' (Ps. 119:67, 71 NASV). Discipline is essential to our actual place in God's earthly family, and discipline is 'not joyful, but sorrowful; though ..., afterwards it yields the peaceful fruit of righteousness' (Heb. 12:11).

This truth is twisted by our imagination to give a false view of God. That 'twist' is largely responsible for a morbid streak that runs through much of historical and even current Christianity. We project upon God the sadistic tendencies that really are present in human beings. Given the anger, hatred, and contempt that pervades human society, it is not uncommon that individual human beings actually *enjoy* the suffering of others. One of our worst thoughts about God is that he too enjoys human suffering. This gives rise to the image of *the Marquis de God*, a divine counterpart to the Marquis de Sade, after whom sadism is named:

> The Marquis de God. Ready to show you how much he cares by punishing you ... In a moment of rage, continents convulse with seismic activity. In a fit of moral indignation, he demonstrates the latest craze in viral mutations ... The Marquis de God is simply a god who hates. This is a deity who despises sin and sinners with such passion that he'll murder in order to exterminate them.
>
> He forces his noblest creation to dance like a trained poodle on the brink of annihilation. Grace, like a dog biscuit, offered or withdrawn, depending on performance.[23]

Is it any wonder that Jesus told us to forget everything we think we know about the nature of God and lose ourselves in his picture of our Father, the one in the heavens? (Matt. 11:25–27; John 3:13; 17:6–8). The last request in the Lord's Prayer is the revelation of a God who loves to spare his children and who will *always* do it upon request unless he has something better in mind, which he rarely does.

People who do not ask God to spare them from trials and evils usually do not even recognize his hand when they are spared. They then live under the illusion that their lives are governed by chance, luck, accident, the whims of others and their own cleverness. And because they do not ask, do not constantly invite God in, that may well be, to some significant extent, no illusion. If one is content with such an outlook, God will probably leave one with it. He respects us, no matter how wrong we are. But we will never know our life to be one in The Kingdom Among Us. To that kingdom Jesus' words about prayer are an ever open door.

The Enduring Framework of the Praying Life

I personally did not find the Lord's Prayer to be the doorway into a praying life until I was in my mid-twenties. In my family that prayer was, for three generations I know of, always said in unison at the breakfast table. But at some point, for reasons I cannot explain, I began to use it in a new way: taking each phrase of it and slowly and meditatively entering into the depths of its meaning, elaborating within it important details of my current life.

When I began to 'live' in the prayer in this way – for that is the only way I can describe it – there were many nights when I would awaken about two o'clock and spend an hour of delight before God just dwelling in one or more phrases from it. I had to make a point at times, as I still do, of praying thoughtfully on *through* the entire prayer. Otherwise the riches of one or two phrases in the prayer would be all I could develop, and I would not benefit from all its contents.

Sometimes now I do not begin at the first request but go immediately to the end or the middle and settle in there for a while. At other times I will use just the words of the address, 'Our Father filling the heavens', to establish and re-establish address and orientation as I go through the day. For some reason I especially profit from using those words while driving on the roads of Los Angeles. They put the vast, sprawling urban landscape, with a greater population than many nations, into its proper perspective before God. And they transform my sense of who and where I am. I have never found any situation in which they failed to be extremely powerful.

There is, of course, much more to prayer than the Lord's Prayer. It is a prayer that teaches us to pray. It is a foundation of the praying life: its introduction and its continuing basis. It is an enduring framework for all praying. You only move beyond it provided you stay within it. It is the necessary bass in the great symphony of prayer. It is a powerful lens through which one constantly sees the world as God himself sees it.

The English wording long familiar from the King James Version is a treasure now interwoven with Western consciousness. It may be of some use in practice, however, to reword the prayer to capture better the fullness of its meanings and its place in the gospel of the kingdom:

> Dear Father always near us,
> may your name be treasured and loved,
> may your rule be completed in us –
> may your will be done here on earth
> in just the way it is done in heaven.
> Give us today the things we need today,
> and forgive us our sins and impositions on you
> as we are forgiving all who in any way offend us.
> Please don't put us through trials,
> but deliver us from everything bad.
> Because you are the one in charge,
> and you have all the power,
> and the glory too is all yours – forever –
> which is just the way we want it!

'Just the way we want it' is not a bad paraphrase for 'amen'. What is needed at the end of this great prayer is a ringing affirmation of the goodness of God and God's world. If your nerves can take it, you might (occasionally?) try 'Whoopee!' I imagine God himself will not mind.

Chapter 8

ON BEING A DISCIPLE, OR STUDENT, OF JESUS

> Go therefore to every ethnic group and help them become my students.
>
> MATT. 28:19

> Jesus the very thought of Thee
> With sweetness fills my breast;
> But sweeter far Thy face to see,
> And in Thy presence rest.
>
> BERNARD OF CLAIRVAUX

Who Is Our Teacher?

Who teaches you? Whose disciple are you?

Honestly. One thing is sure: You are somebody's disciple. You learned how to live from somebody else. There are no exceptions to this rule, for human beings are just the kind of creatures that have to learn and keep learning from others how to live. Aristotle remarked that we owe more to our teachers than to our parents, for though our parents gave us life, our teachers taught us the good life.

It is hard to come to realistic terms with all this. Today, especially in Western cultures, we prefer to think that we are 'our own person'. We make up our own minds. But that is only because we have been mastered by those who have taught us that we do or should do so.

Such individualism is a part of the legacy that makes us 'modern'. But we certainly did not come by that individualistic posture through our own individual and independent insight into ultimate truth.

Probably you are the disciple of several 'somebodies', and it is very likely that they shaped you in ways that are far from what is best for you, or even coherent. You are quite certainly, as I am, the student of a few crucial people, living and dead, who have been there in crucial times and periods to form your standard responses in thought, feeling and action. Thankfully, the process is an ongoing one, and is to some extent self-correcting.

Originally we are the disciples of our parents or other family members most intimately related to us. Usually this is very good. They may be dear, strong people who know God and walk in his ways. It has mainly been so for me and for many others.

But not always. Our original family connections may be anything from mildly debilitating to disastrous. We know much more about this today than we did just a few decades ago. We have a pretty good idea, for example, of how children raised with alcoholic parents turn out. They learn from their relationship to their alcoholic parent how to be in this world – fairly tragically in many cases.

Then we are the disciples of our teachers, then of our playmates and peers – one of the most potent of 'discipling' relationships – then perhaps again of our teachers. But now, in our teens and twenties, our teachers play quite a different role. They do much to set in stone the major thrusts of our more or less consciously chosen self-image that will make or break us in the important connections of our life.

These last teachers often include some very glamorous and powerful people. They may indeed be teachers – instructors of some type, as in the armed services, or even academic professors. But they may also include public figures of various kinds: artists, musicians, writers, professionals. Nearly always they convey to us a strong impression of what life as a whole is all about. This provides the absolutely necessary orientations of conscious behaviour towards ourselves, others – and God. We must have such orientations, even if they be wrong.

It is one of the major transitions of life to recognize who has taught us, mastered us, and then to evaluate the results in us of their teaching. This is a harrowing task, and sometimes we just can't face it. But it can also open the door to choose other masters, possibly better masters, and one Master above all.

The Earthly 'Society of Jesus'

The assumption of Jesus' programme for his people on earth was that they would live their lives as his students and co-labourers. They would find him so admirable in every respect – wise, beautiful, powerful, and good – that they would constantly seek to be in his presence and be guided, instructed and helped by him in every aspect of their lives. For he is indeed the living head of the community of prayerful love across all time and space.

On that assumption, his promise to his people was that he would be with them every moment, until this particular 'age' is over and the universe enters a new phase (Matt. 28:20; Heb. 13:5–6). More generally, the *provisions he made* for his people during this period in which we now live are provisions made for those who are, precisely, apprentices to him in kingdom living. Anyone who is not a continual student of Jesus, and who nevertheless reads the great promises of the Bible as if they were for him or her, is like someone trying to cash a cheque on another person's account. At best, it succeeds only sporadically.

The effect of such continuous study under Jesus would naturally be that we learn how to do everything we do 'in the name of the Lord Jesus' (Col. 3:17); that is, on his behalf or in his place; that is, once again, as if he himself were doing it. And of course that means we would learn 'to conform to everything I have commanded you' (Matt. 28:20). In his presence our inner life will be transformed, and we will become the kind of people for whom his course of action is the natural (and supernatural) course of action.

The Narrow Way and the Good Tree

Plainly, in the eyes of Jesus there is no good reason for not doing what he said to do, for he only tells us to do what is best. In one situation he asks his students, 'Why do you call me 'Lord, Lord,' and do not do what I say?' (Luke 6:46). Just try picturing yourself standing before him and explaining why you did not do what he said was best. Now it may be that there are cases in which this would be appropriate. And certainly we can count on his understanding. But it will not do as a general posture in a life of confidence in him. He has made a way for us into easy and happy obedience – really, into personal fulfilment. And that way is apprenticeship to him. It is Christian 'discipleship'. His gospel is a gospel *for life and Christian discipleship.*

In other words, his basic message, 'Rethink your life in the light of the fact that the kingdom of the heavens is now open to all' (Matt. 4:17), presents the resources needed to live human life as we all automatically sense it should be and naturally leads one to become his student, or apprentice in kingdom living.

Therefore the practice of routine obedience from the heart is the final topic of his Discourse on the Hill. No doubt he understood ahead of time that every imaginable way would be tried to avoid simply doing the things he said and knew to be best, and now we see from history and all around us that it has been so.

So, in his conclusion to the Discourse in Matt. 7:13–27, he gives us four pictorial contrasts to help us not miss the path into the community of prayerful love, where what the law and the prophets really said is fulfilled because people actually treat others the way they would like to be treated (7:12).

You enter this kingdom community, he first points out, by a narrow gate. That is, there is a right way to enter, and not just any way – the 'wide way that leads to disaster' – will succeed (vv. 13–14).

And then he warns against those who would mislead us, those who look good, but inwardly – where we now know the real action lies – are governed merely by their own desires. Outwardly they look like sheep, but inwardly they are only thinking about eating sheep, that is, using us for their purposes (v. 15). These are the ones Jesus' other little brother, Jude, described as 'caring for themselves. … following after their own desires, speaking arrogantly and flattering people to gain advantage' (Jude 12–16).

All one has to do to identify those who would mislead us is watch what they do and pay little attention to what they say. What they do will be the unerring sign of who they are on the inside. Trees and plants manifest their nature in their fruit: figs by bearing figs and not grapes. And what people do reveals, when thoroughly and honestly considered, the kind of person they really are (Matt. 7:16–20).

Those to be trusted are the ones who actually learn to do what Jesus taught was best. Calling him 'Lord', or even doing astonishing things in his name, are no substitute. The one who enters the kingdom of the heavens is the one who does the will of Jesus' Father in the heavens (v. 21). The will of the Father is precisely what Jesus has been teaching here on the hillside, the real meaning of 'the law and the prophets' (v. 12).

The one who hears him and does what he says accordingly builds the house of his or her life to be totally indestructible. The house is built upon a rock, not upon sand, where the winds of life will knock it down. And all this is to say, in plain contemporary language, 'Just do it!' For he knows that in any case in which we do *not* 'just do it' we are, to that extent, exempting ourselves from the blessed reality of the kingdom.

The four pictorial contrasts in this passage in Matthew 7 are these:

1. The narrow gate and the wide gate (vv. 13–14).
2. The good tree with its 'insides,' and the bad tree (vv. 15–20). *Subpicture* – Wolves in sheep's clothing. False leaders contrasted with the true: They do not have the spontaneous and constant goodness of the heart of Jesus (v. 15). Internally they are 'wolves'.
3. Final judgement of those who do 'the will of my Father' and of those who try to substitute for that great deeds 'in your name' (vv. 21–23).
4. Those who hear him and do what he says (house on the rock) and those who hear him but do not do what he says (house on the sand) (vv. 24–27).

The narrow gate is not, as so often assumed, doctrinal correctness. The narrow gate is obedience – and the confidence in Jesus necessary to it. We can see that it is not doctrinal correctness because many people who cannot even understand the correct doctrines nevertheless place their full faith in him. Moreover, we find many people who seem to be very correct doctrinally but have hearts full of hatred and unforgiveness. The broad gate, by contrast, is simply doing whatever I want to do.

The fruit of the good tree is obedience, borne only from the kind of person we have come to be (the 'inside' of the tree) in his fellowship. The wolf in sheep's clothing is the one who tries to *fake* discipleship by outward deeds. But then inward realities overwhelm him or her.

'The will of my Father' is the very thing that Jesus has just gone over in his Discourse. Doing what he said, beginning from 'believe on him whom God has sent', we step into the flow of God's ways, we 'enter the kingdom of the heavens'. Naturally we will also enter into its next phase, its fullness, marked by the end of human history and the final settling of accounts.

All of this is the same as saying that, in actually doing what Jesus knows to be best for us, we build a life that is absolutely indestructible, 'on the Rock'. 'And the Rock was Christ' (1 Cor. 10:4).

The great Pauline, Petrine, and Johannine passages, such as 1 Corinthians 13; Colossians 3; 1 Peter 2; 2 Pet. 1:1–15; 1 John 3:1–5:5, all convey exactly the same message in so many words, one of an inward transformation by discipleship to Jesus. In them the central point of reference is always a divine kind of love, *agape*, that comes to characterize the core of our personality. The deeds of 'the law' naturally flow from it. The law is not the cause of personal goodness, as we have said before, but it invariably is the course of it.

How Are We to Be with Him?

But if I am to be someone's apprentice, there is one absolutely essential condition. I must be *with* that person. This is true of the student-teacher relationship in all generality. And it is precisely what it meant to *follow* Jesus when he was here in human form. To follow him meant, in the first place, to be with him.

If I am Jesus' disciple that means *I am with him to learn from him how to be like him.* To take cases from ordinary life, a child learning to multiply and divide numbers is an apprentice to its teacher. Children are with their teachers, learning from them how to be like them in a certain respect – similarly for a student of the piano or voice, of the Spanish language, of tennis and so forth. The 'being-with', by watching and by hearing, is an absolute necessity.

And provision has been made for us to be with Jesus, as one person to another, in our daily life. But it is also necessary that we have a practical – though not a metaphysical or even a theological – understanding of this arrangement in order to carry on our side of the apprenticeship relationship. Jesus accordingly took great care to instruct his immediate students – both before his death and in the interval between his resurrection and ascension – about the specific manner of his presence with them (and with us) during the long period ahead. He wanted them to understand very clearly before he left them exactly what it would be like.

In John 14, he goes carefully over the fact that he would soon be taken away from them in the visible human form they had known. Then, he explains, another 'strengthener' – 'comforter' is just not the right word to use in translating *paracleton* today – would be active and interactive in their lives. The marginal reading of John 14:16 in the New American Standard version is excellent for the meaning intended: a paraclete is 'one called alongside to help'. This other strengthener (other, that is, than the visible Jesus as they had known him) would be with them to the end.

The human order, or 'world' (*cosmos*), by contrast, cannot receive this 'spirit of truth', as Jesus describes it, because it can't see it and therefore cannot know it. The human mind in its now standard form does not, generally speaking, accept as reality what it cannot see. The spiritual nature of God, here reaffirmed by Jesus with reference to his own personality, was presented to the Jewish people early in their history (we recall Exod. 20:4; Deut. 4:12, 15, etc.). But it was something even they never quite mastered – though they did understand about idolatry. That is shown by the dominance of the highly visible 'rightness of scribes and Pharisees' as late as Jesus' day. One would never attempt to live in such a 'rightness' if one thoroughly understood that every thought and intention lay open before an always present God. But many of us still try to do it today.

God as personality is not a physical reality that everyone must see whether they want to or not. He can, of course, make himself present to the human mind in any way he chooses. But – for good reasons rooted deeply in the nature of the person and of personal relationships – his preferred way is to *speak*, to *communicate*: thus the absolute centrality of scripture to our discipleship. And this, among other things, is the reason why an extensive use of solitude and silence is so basic for growth of the human spirit, for they form an appropriate context for listening and speaking to God.[1]

Teaching the Transition

In Acts 1 we have a fascinating account of the forty days Jesus spent with his eleven apostles between his resurrection and his ascension. That account is absolutely central for our understanding of how he is with his people now. It clearly indicates that during the period in question he alternated between communicating with them *without* being visibly present and communicating with them *while* being visibly present.

We are told, 'He was taken up [the ascension] after he had given directions to the apostles *through the Holy Spirit*.'

Then the writer immediately adds, 'To them he *also* presented himself living after his execution by many unmistakable evidences, being seen by them over a forty day period and conversing with them about the kingdom of God' (Acts 1:2–3).

The Master teacher takes every step required to make sure the students get the message about how he will be with them. He tells them what is going to happen to them, it happens, and then he talks with them about what happened. And then the lessons are repeated. And so on. That is Jesus as teacher. It is absolutely essential that his friends understand in the strongest way possible how he is going to be with them and how they will continue to be his apprentices and co-workers in the kingdom when they no longer see him in the usual sense. For this is an arrangement that must stand up for the entire period of the church's existence, which means at least up to today.

'Engulfment' in the Spiritual Presence

However, the concrete reality of his non-visible interactions with them during the pre-ascension period did not immediately clear up all the questions and misunderstandings his assistants had. Pointing to the next step in their development, he reminds them of the ancient promise of engulfment in the spirit of God. This promise had been renewed in the message of John the Baptizer and was repeatedly emphasized by Jesus himself. Now he tells them that they are to stay in Jerusalem, and that in a few days they will be engulfed by the holy spirit (Acts 1:4–5). As Luke 24:49 worded it, they were to wait there until they were 'dressed in power from the heights.'

It is really unimaginable that they would have waited, as he told them to, without the *experience* of the reality of the spirit to which he had so carefully introduced them after his resurrection. And even so, they were still asking if he was about to 'restore the kingdom to Israel' (Acts 1:6), meaning the *visible* reality of a political entity. That was still the only way they could think of the promised engulfment, or 'baptism', he said was about to happen. But the promise was of a 'power' that did not depend upon a visible kingdom. It was to be a power without visible position. In the ambiance of that power, his people would exist and bear witness, starting from Jerusalem and reaching to the farthest places on the earth, from then until now (v. 8).

And thus fortified by teaching and experience, they did wait – though they did not fully understand. And they were engulfed. And they understood enough to be able to say what was happening at that moment. They understood and explained the manifestations of Pentecost in terms of God's promises to Israel and of their experience with Jesus and of what they were now and always to do (Acts 2:14–40).

The engulfment came upon them – with quite a racket, right out of that sky into which only ten days earlier they had seen Jesus disappear (Acts 2:2). Peter then stood at the heart of the Jewish world and reinterpreted the call that God had anciently placed upon the Jewish people to be a light and a blessing to all nations. 'The promise of living in a holy power other than ourselves,' he said, 'was not just for the little group of disciples at the time. It was also to all the people of Jerusalem, as well as to their children and to others no matter how far away, as the Lord draws them to himself' (2:39).

Life in the Spirit and the Kingdom of the Heavens

The personal presence of Jesus with individuals and groups that trust him was soon understood by Jesus' first students to be the *practical* reality of the kingdom of God now on earth. That is, it is what the kingdom is as a factor in their lives. This reality is the additional 'life' of which the apostle John makes so much in his writings. It is the 'in Christ' that forms the backbone of Paul's understanding of redemption.[2]

Unfortunately, the relentlessly legalistic bent of the human soul has, over time, led many to identify engulfment in the spirit with its outward manifestations, whether they be signs and wonders; other tongues; poverty, chastity and obedience; power to convert unbelievers; or certain practices and symbols that have become denominationally distinctive. But, as important as such things are, they are not the reality of the kingdom life itself. The reality of the kingdom life is an inner one, a hidden one, with 'the Father who is in secret'. And we often find it to be absent in those who convert many others or who manifest tongues, signs, wonders and the like.

Not that the genuine presence of the kingdom in a person can really be hidden. It cannot, nor, for that matter, can its absence. But it also cannot be canned, controlled, produced on demand, standardized or brought to a point at which it can be dispensed by one human being to another.

The reality of spiritual life in Jesus' kingdom, as distinct from its specific manifestations in the visible world, cannot be used to get a monopoly on God and prove that *we*, after all, are the ones who have 'got it right'. The spirit cannot be merchandised, even ever so subtly. There is, alas, an unfortunate streak of Simon 'the Magnificent'

(Acts 8:9–24), whom we met earlier, interwoven with the people of Jesus throughout the ages. We all have to struggle against this Simonizing tendency. But we can be sure that the spirit of Jesus will not co-operate with that tendency.

Thus Paul very simply says, 'All who are interactive with the spirit of God are God's children' (Rom. 8:14). The interactive movement he refers to is the inner reality, not the outward manifestations. And: 'The kingdom of God is not eating and drinking [whether you do it in one way or in another] but is inner rightness (*dikaiosune*) and peace and joy sustained by the Holy Spirit. For those serving Christ in this way are well-pleasing to God and approved by men' (Rom. 14:17–18).

And when Paul writes to the Colossians, he prays that they will walk worthy of the Lord, pleasing him in every respect, bearing fruit in every good work and constantly growing in their knowledge of God (Col. 1:10). Then he asks that they be 'strengthened with all power, in terms of God's glorious power' (v. 11). One might expect that this would be for the sake of some astounding outward manifestations! But no, it is required to enable the Colossians to have 'limitless endurance and long-suffering or patience, joyfully giving thanks to the Father who has equipped us for a role in the destiny of the saints in the light.' The most exalted outcome of submersion in the risen Christ is the transformation of the inner self to be like him.

So the kingdom of the heavens, *from the practical point of view in which we all must live*, is simply our experience of Jesus' continual interaction with us in history and throughout the days, hours and moments of our earthly existence. This is why we find Philip the Evangelist in the city of Samaria, as the new kingdom unit begins to spill out beyond Judea, 'proclaiming the kingdom of God and the name of Jesus Christ' (Acts 8:12). The kingdom was reality to them through the name of Jesus. Through the use of the name, Jesus himself still acted. And Paul, at the end of the book of Acts, situated now in Rome, was 'proclaiming the kingdom of God and teaching the things concerning King Jesus' (Acts 28:23, 31).

Thus was fulfilled Jesus' statement to the Jewish nation – not, we emphasize, to individual Jews – that 'the kingdom of God shall be taken from you and will be given to a people producing its fruits' (Matt. 21:43). And those people were the people of the name 'Jesus'.

And of course it is discipleship, real-life apprenticeship to Jesus, that is the passageway *within* The Kingdom Among Us from initial faith in Jesus to a life of fulfilment and routine obedience. That is precisely why Jesus told his people, when they saw him for the last time in his familiar visible form, to make disciples, students, apprentices to him from every ethnic group on earth. And to make disciples they would certainly have to be disciples.

Accordingly, we must take a very careful look at discipleship to Jesus. We will consider what it is to *be* a disciple of Jesus, how to *become* a disciple of Jesus, and how to *make* a disciple of Jesus.[3]

How to Be a Disciple

The Simplicity of Discipleship

First of all, we should note that *being* a disciple, or apprentice, of Jesus is a quite definite and obvious kind of thing. To make a mystery of it is to misunderstand it. There is no good reason why people should ever be in doubt as to whether they themselves are his students or not. And the evidence will always be quite clear as to whether any other individual is his student, though we may be in no position to collect that evidence and rarely would have any legitimate occasion to gather or use it.

Now this may seem very startling, even shocking, to many in our religious culture, where there is a long tradition of doubting, or possibly even of being unable to tell, whether or not one is a *Christian*. The underlying issue in that tradition has always been whether or not one was going to 'make the final cut'. And that has, in turn, often been thought a matter of whether God has 'chosen you' and you are therefore 'among the elect'. Or else it is a matter of whether or not you have sinned too much, or are good enough. Needless to say, those would be difficult questions to answer with much assurance – perhaps impossible to answer at all, because we are in no position to inspect the books of heaven.

It would take us far out of our path to enter into these hoary controversies. But fortunately there is no need. It is almost universally conceded today that you can be a Christian without being a disciple.[4] And one who actually is an apprentice and co-labourer with Jesus in his or her daily existence is sure to be a 'Christian' in every sense of the word that matters. The very term *Christian* was explicitly introduced in the New Testament – where, by the way, it is used only three times – to apply to disciples when they could no longer be called Jews, because many kinds of gentiles were now part of them.

Now, people who are asked whether they are apprentices of a leading politician, musician, lawyer or screenwriter would not need to think a second to respond. Similarly for those asked if they are studying Spanish or bricklaying with someone unknown to the public. It is hardly something that would escape one's attention. The same is all the more true if asked about discipleship to Jesus.

But, if asked whether they are *good* apprentices of whatever person or line of work concerned, they very well might hesitate. They might say no. Or yes. Asked if they could be better students, they would probably say yes. And all of this falls squarely within the category of *being* a disciple or apprentice. For to be a disciple in any area or relationship is not to be perfect. One can be a very raw and incompetent beginner and still be a disciple.

It is a part of the refreshing realism of the Gospels that we often find Jesus doing nothing less than 'bawling out' his disciples. That, however, is very far from rejecting them. It is, in fact, a way of being faithful to them, just as chastisement is God's way of showing that someone is his child (Heb. 12:7–10). A good 'master' takes his apprentices seriously and therefore takes them to task as needed.

What a Disciple Is

Following up on what has already been said, then, a disciple, or apprentice, is simply someone who has decided to be with another person, under appropriate conditions, in order to become capable of doing what that person does or to become what that person is. How does this apply to discipleship to Jesus? What is it, exactly, that he, the incarnate Lord, does? What, if you wish, is he 'good at'? The answer is found in the Gospels: he lives in the kingdom of God, and he applies that kingdom for the good of others and even makes it possible for them to enter it for themselves. The deeper theological truths about his person and his work do not detract from this simple point. It is what he calls us to by saying, 'Follow me.'

The description Peter gives in the first 'official' presentation of the Gospel to the gentiles provides a sharp picture of the Master under whom we serve as apprentices. 'You know,' he says to Cornelius, 'of Jesus, the one from Nazareth. And you know how God anointed him with the Holy Spirit and power. He went about doing good and curing all those under oppression by the devil, because God was with him' (Acts 10:38).

And as a disciple of Jesus I am with him, by choice and by grace, learning from him how to live in the kingdom of God. This is the crucial idea. That means, we recall, how to live within the range of God's effective will, his life flowing through mine. Another important way of putting this is to say that I am learning from Jesus to live my life as he would live my life if he were me. I am not necessarily learning to do everything he did, but I am learning how to do everything I do in the manner that he did all that he did.

My main role in life, for example, is that of a professor in what is called a 'research' university. As Jesus' apprentice, then, I constantly have before me the question of how he would deal with students and colleagues in the specific connections involved in such a role. How would he design a course, and why? How would he compose a test, administer it and grade it? What would his research projects be, and why? How would he teach this course or that?

The Whole of My Daily Existence Is the Focus of Discipleship

That my actual life is the focus of my apprenticeship to Jesus is crucial. Knowing this can help deliver us from the genuine craziness that the current distinction between 'full-time Christian service' and 'part-time Christian service' imposes on us. For a disciple of Jesus is not necessarily one devoted to doing specifically religious things as that is usually understood. To repeat, I am learning from

Jesus how to lead *my* life, my *whole* life, my real life. Note, please, I am not learning from him how to lead his life. His life on earth was a transcendentally wonderful one. But it has now been led. Neither I nor anyone else, even himself, will ever lead it again. And he is, in any case, interested in my life, that very existence that is me. There lies my need. I need to be able to lead my life as he would lead it if he were me.

So as his disciple I am not necessarily learning how to do special religious things, either as a part of 'full-time service' or as a part of 'part-time service'. My discipleship to Jesus is, within clearly definable limits, not a matter of what I do, but of how I do it. And it covers everything, 'religious' or not.

Brother Lawrence, who was a kitchen worker and cook, remarks,

> Our sanctification does not depend upon *changing* our works, but in doing that for God's sake which we commonly do for our own ... It is a great delusion to think that the times of prayer ought to differ from other times. We are as strictly obliged to adhere to God by action in the time of action as by prayer in the season of prayer.[5]

It is crucial for our walk in the kingdom to understand that the teachings of Jesus, which we have been examining at such length in this book, do not by themselves make a life. They were never intended to. Rather, they presuppose a life. But that causes no problem for, of course, each one of us is provided a life automatically. And we know exactly what it is. It is who we are and what we do. It is precisely this life that God wants us to give to him. We must only be careful to understand its true dignity. To every person we can say with confidence, '*You*, in the midst of your actual life there, are exactly the person God wanted.'

The teachings of Jesus in the Gospels show us *how* to live the life we have been given through the time, place, family, neighbours, talents and opportunities that are ours. His words left to us in scripture provide all we need in the way of general teachings about how to conduct our particular affairs. If we only put them into practice, along the lines previously discussed, most of the problems that trouble human life would be eliminated. That is why, as we have noted, Jesus directs his teaching in Matthew 5 to 7 towards things like murder and anger, contempt and lusting, family rejection, verbal bullying. This is real life. Though his teachings do not make a life, they intersect at every point with every life.

So life in the kingdom is not just a matter of *not* doing what is wrong. The apprentices of Jesus are primarily occupied with the positive good that can be done during their days 'under the sun' and the positive strengths and virtues that they develop in themselves as they grow towards 'the kingdom prepared for them from the foundations of the world' (Matt. 25:34). What they, and God, get out of their lifetime is chiefly the person they become. And that is why their real life is so important.

The cultivation of oneself, one's family, one's workplace and community – especially the community of believers – thus becomes the centre of focus for the apprentice's joint life with his or her teacher. It is with this entire context in view that we most richly and accurately speak of 'learning from him how to lead my life as he would lead my life if he were me.'

The Glory of My Job

But let us become as specific as possible. Consider just your job, the work you do to make a living. This is one of the clearest ways possible of focusing upon apprenticeship to Jesus. To *be* a disciple of Jesus is, crucially, to be learning from Jesus how to do your job as Jesus himself would do it. New Testament language for this is to do it 'in the name' of Jesus.

Once you stop to think about it, you can see that *not* to find your job to be a primary place of discipleship is to automatically exclude a major part, if not most, of your waking hours from life with him. It is to assume to run one of the largest areas of your interest and concern on your own or under the direction and instruction of people other than Jesus. But this is right where most professing Christians are left today, with the prevailing view that discipleship is a special calling having to do chiefly with religious activities and 'full-time Christian service'.

But how, exactly, is one to make one's job a primary place of apprenticeship to Jesus? Not, we quickly say, by becoming the Christian nag-in-residence, the rigorous upholder of all propriety, and the dead-eye critic of everyone else's behaviour. I hope that this would already be abundantly clear from our study of Jesus and of his teachings in the Sermon on the Mount and elsewhere.

A gentle but firm non-co-operation with things that everyone knows to be wrong, together with a sensitive, non-officious, non-intrusive, non-obsequious service to others, should be our usual overt manner. This should be combined with inward attitudes of constant prayer for whatever kind of activity our workplace requires and genuine love for everyone involved.

As circumstances call for them, special points in Jesus' teachings and example, such as non-retaliation, refusal to press for financial advantage, consciousness of and appropriate assistance to those under special handicaps and so on, would come into play. And we should be watchful and prepared to meet any obvious spiritual need or interest in understanding Jesus with words that are truly loving, thoughtful, and helpful.

It is not true, I think, that we fulfil our obligations to those around us by only living the gospel. There are many ways of speaking inappropriately, of course – even harmfully – but it is always true that words fitly spoken are things of beauty and power that bring life and joy. And you cannot assume that people understand what is going on when you only live in their midst as Jesus' person. They may just regard you as one more version of human oddity.

I once knew of a case in an academic setting where at noon one professor very visibly took his Bible and lunch and went to a nearby chapel to study, pray and be alone. Another professor would call his assistant into his office, where they would have sex. No one in that environment thought either activity to be anything worth inquiring about. After all, people do all sorts of things. We are used to that. In some situations it is only words that can help towards understanding.

But, once again, the specific work to be done – whether it is making axe handles or tacos, selling cars or teaching infants, investment banking or political office, evangelizing or running a Christian education programme, performing in the arts or teaching English as a second language – is of central interest to God. He wants it well done. It is work that should be done, and it should be done as Jesus himself would do it. Nothing can substitute for that. In my opinion, at least, as long as one is on the job, all peculiarly religious activities should take second place to doing 'the job' in sweat, intelligence and the power of God. That is our devotion to God. (I am assuming, of course, that the job is one that serves good human purposes.)

Our intention with our job should be the highest possible good in its every aspect, and we should pursue that with conscious expectation of a constant energizing and direction from God. Although we must never allow our job to become our life, we should, within reasonable limits, routinely sacrifice our comfort and pleasure for the quality of our work, whether it be axe handles, tacos or the proficiency of a student we are teaching.

And yes, this results in great benefit for those who use our services. But our mind is not obsessed with them, and certainly not with having appreciation from them. We do the job well because that is what Jesus would like, and we admire and love him. It is what he would do. We 'do our work with soul [*ex psyche*], to the Lord, not to men' (Col. 3:23). 'It is the Lord Christ you serve' (v. 25). As his apprentices, we are personally interacting with him as we do our job, and he is with us, as he promised, to teach us how to do it best.

Few have illustrated this better than Kirby Puckett, thirteen years the centrefielder for the Minnesota Twins baseball team. He had a career batting average of .318, made the All-Star line-up ten years in a row, and won six Golden Gloves for defensive play. He was one of the most loved men ever to play the game, and a well-known Christian.

Dennis Martinez, pitcher for the Cleveland Indians, once crushed the left side of Kirby's face with a pitch. Martinez assumed that Kirby would hate him. But when he had recovered a bit, Kirby called Martinez 'my good friend' and blamed himself for not getting out of the way of the fast ball. He was an outstanding community leader for good causes, and expressed his faith naturally in words that matched his life. Everyone knew who Kirby was trusting and why he would not hate someone who had injured him. He was living in God's world and relying upon it.

One who does not know this way of 'job discipleship' by experience cannot begin to imagine what release and help and joy there is in it. And to repeat the crucial point, if we restrict our discipleship to special religious times, the majority of our waking hours will be isolated from the manifest presence of the kingdom in our lives.[6] Those waking hours will be times when we are on our own on *our* job. Our time at work – even religious work – will turn out to be a 'holiday from God'.

On the other hand, if you dislike or even hate your job, a condition epidemic in our culture, the quickest way out of that job, or to joy *in* it, is to do it as Jesus would. This is the very heart of discipleship, and we cannot effectively be an apprentice of Jesus without integrating our job into The Kingdom Among Us.

Christian Ministers as Jesus' Apprentices

But now a special word is required concerning those of us whose 'job' – what we get paid for – is the work of opening and ministering the kingdom to others. 'Church work', we might call it, or the 'full-time Christian service' just referred to. Jesus himself began to 'make disciples' very soon after he entered his own public ministry of God's rule, or kingdom, to ethnic Israelites. That is to say, he took *apprentices* into the work that he was doing to teach them how to do what he did. His work had three main phases, clearly enumerated and illustrated in the Gospels (Matt. 4:23; 9:35; 10:7–8).

PROCLAIMING. The first was simply announcing God's new move forward in human history. In and through the person of Jesus himself, the government, or 'kingdom' of God from the heavens, was now available to every one. Heaven, we have seen, is *right now, right here*, around our bodies, hovering beside our heads – 'in Him we live and move and have our being.' Eternity is not something waiting to happen, something that will commence later. It is now here. Time runs its course within eternity.

With the coming of Jesus it was not only *here*, as it had always been, but was directly and interactively *accessible to* every one of the Israelites, no matter what their standing in life or what they had or had not done – to 'the lost sheep of the house of Israel'. They did not have to be among the glitterati, the humanly blessed. All they had to do was to trust this man Jesus as the one anointed to bring God personally into human history and therefore the Lord of that history.

This message of the present availability of God's rule to everyone was to be announced, or 'preached'. Jesus did that, and soon he sent his disciples to do the same thing. And once the foundation had been historically laid in flesh-and-blood Jews, historically prepared for that purpose, it was to be preached to all 'nations'. Those who are his disciples, his apprentices, still do announce the availability of the kingdom of heaven to all. As his apprentices in ministry, we learn from him how to do this.

MANIFESTING. The second phase of Jesus' work, in which his disciples were therefore to be apprenticed, was the *manifestation* of God's rule from the heavens. This was done by words and deeds whose powers lay beyond, or even set aside, the usual course of life and nature (as well as the effects of evil spirits). They were a revelation of God's good presence here and now. Such works were, of course, primarily acts of love done to help those in need. But they were also signs (*semeion*), or 'indications', of God's reigning. They showed God acting with the servants of the kingdom, soon to be known simply as 'saints' or 'holy ones' (Acts 9:32). Though done by human beings, they simultaneously were 'good works from the Father' (John 10:32).

So here, too, the disciples learned by watching and helping. Then they were sent away by him to do what Jesus did, preaching and working: 'As you go proclaim the message: "The kingdom of the heavens is upon you." Heal the sick, raise the dead, cleanse lepers, drive out demons. You received without cost; give without charge' (Matt. 10:7–8).

And, though far from being done with their training, they had enough confidence to *just do it*! And even from the outset they experienced a notable success (Luke 10). This seemed to confirm to

Jesus' mind, from his then incarnate point of view, that the plan for leaving his work in history with quite weak and fallible human beings would be highly successful (Luke 10:17–24). But they also had much to learn about this type of work as their experience with Jesus progressed. You see their progression clearly in the Gospels and in the book of Acts.

TEACHING. The third phase of their apprenticeship was in teaching about the nature of God and about what his rule among human beings was like. Thus Jesus' many parables that start with the words 'the kingdom of the heavens is like ...' This aspect of Jesus' work was, because of its nature, the slowest to develop in his students. It is noteworthy that, when he first sent them out to announce and to manifest, he did *not* charge them to teach. He knew that genuine understanding of the kingdom had not yet developed in them. He was counting upon their memory of what and how he had taught – along with the assistance of the *paracletos*, the helper who would be with them later in a special way – to foster their abilities to teach as he taught after he was gone (John 14:26).

But he nevertheless made it quite clear that he expected them to teach in the same general manner as he did; that is, by showing forth the nature of the rule of God in and from the things of ordinary life. They were to teach the truth revealed, but in the context of what had actually happened to them. They would compare the realities of God invading their lives with commonplace activities, such as sowing seed, fishing and so forth.

Thus, after the 'parables of the kingdom' given in Matthew 13, Jesus gives his hearers a general instruction about how to teach: 'When, therefore, a 'bible scholar' becomes a disciple (*matheteutheis*) to the kingdom of the heavens, he is like a householder who can produce from his store things old and new' (Matt. 13:52). Think of all the things one collects in one's house by living in the same place for a long period of time. The kingdom disciple teaches from his or her storehouse of personal experiences of God's rule in the commonplace events of real life.

Now obviously Jesus did not give lessons in engineering and computer networking while he was in the flesh. He didn't even give lessons in carpentry, which was his special trade and had been his job. For he was specifically training individuals to carry on his work of ministry in The Kingdom Among Us. But right now, by contrast, he is giving lessons in all subjects. He gives lessons to any of his people who are engineers, computer analysts, carpenters and so forth – and even 'full-time Christian workers', bless them. And there always is a certain priority to the work that the special ministers of the kingdom do, for they have an extraordinary role in the making and training of disciples in every area of life.

Of course, points similar to those made here about our jobs are to be made with reference to our family relationships, our recreations, our community relationships and activities, our creative and artistic experiences, and whatever else makes up a part of our lives. Always we are asking, How can these things be a part of the kingdom of God? And we expect Jesus to provide guidance and help in answering this question.

But we do not do this in a picky, self-righteous, self-obsessed manner. We know his grace and gracefulness and his desire for us to be persons in our own right. We are to count for something, not just be robots. His spirit and the spirit of our relationship rules out all paralysing and oppressive attitudes and enables every aspect of our lives to be a joyous journey through the fields of the Lord.

Joy is our portion in his fellowship. Joy goes with confidence and creativity. It is his joy, and that is not a small joy or a repressed 'joy'. It is a robust joy, with no small element of outright hilarity in it. For nothing less than joy can sustain us in the kingdom rightness that possesses us, which truly is a weighty and powerful thing to bear. It was not for nothing that Mother Teresa of Calcutta required her sisters of charity to be people who smile.

In summary, then, the disciple or apprentice of Jesus, as recognized by the New Testament, is one who has firmly decided to learn from him how to lead his or her life, whatever that may be, as Jesus himself would do it. And, as best they know how, they are making plans – taking the necessary steps, progressively arranging and rearranging their affairs – to do this. All of this will, in one way or another, happen within the special and unfailing community he has established on earth. And the apprentices then are, of course, perfectly positioned to learn how to do everything Jesus taught. That is the process envisaged in the Great Commission of Matt. 28:18–20.

How to Become a Disciple

There are many people who would like to be the constant student and co-labourer with Jesus in all the details of their life. Many of these are professing Christians; some are not. But in either case, living as an apprentice with Jesus in The Kingdom Among Us is usually not something that seems accessible to them. No wonder, then, that practical, experimental steps seem to be lacking. They do not really understand what discipleship to him is, and it therefore remains only a distant, if beautiful, ideal.

It is now generally acknowledged, as we have noted, that one can be a professing Christian and a church member in good standing without being a disciple. There is, apparently, no real connection between being a Christian and being a disciple of Jesus. And this is bound to be rather confusing to a person who would like to be a disciple. For what exactly would one do who didn't intend to go into 'full-time Christian service' but still wanted to be a disciple in something like the sense just outlined?

I believe we can identify definite steps that will prove effective. But before discussing them we need to be quite clear about our preliminary objective. Because, as we have seen, a disciple of Jesus is one who is with Jesus, learning to be like him, what, we must ask, is *the state of soul that would bring us to choose that condition?* What would be the thinking, the convictions about reality, that would lead someone to choose discipleship to him?

Obviously one would feel great admiration and love, would really believe that Jesus is the most magnificent person who has ever lived. One would be quite sure that to belong to him, to be taken into what he is doing throughout this world so that what he is doing becomes your life, is the greatest opportunity one will ever have.

The Field and the Pearl

Jesus gave us two parables to illustrate the condition of soul that leads to becoming a disciple. Actually it turns out to be a condition that we all very well understand from our own experiences. So these parables also illustrate what he meant by saying that the 'scribe' of the kingdom teaches from the ordinary things of life, 'things both old and new'.

First, he said, 'The kingdom of the heavens is like where something of extreme value is concealed in a field. Someone discovers it, and quickly covers it up again. Overflowing with joyous excitement he pulls together everything he has, sells it all, and buys the field' (Matt. 13:44).

Second, he said, 'What the kingdom of the heavens is like is illustrated by a businessman who is on the lookout for beautiful pearls. He finds an incredible value in one pearl. So he sells everything else he owns and buys it' (13:45–46).

These little stories perfectly express the condition of soul in one who chooses life in the kingdom with Jesus. The sense of the *goodness* to be achieved by that choice, of the *opportunity* that may be missed, the love for the value discovered, the *excitement* and *joy* over it all, is exactly the same as it was for those who were drawn to Jesus in those long-ago days when he first walked among us. It is also the condition of soul from which discipleship can be effectively chosen today.

Clarity About the Bargain

Only with such images before us can we correctly assess the famous 'cost of discipleship' of which so much is made. Do you think the businessman who found the pearl was sweating over its cost? An obviously ridiculous question! What about the one who found the treasure in the field – perhaps crude oil or gold? No. Of course not. The only thing these people were sweating about was whether they would 'get the deal'. Now that is the soul of the disciple.

No one goes sadly, reluctantly into discipleship with Jesus. As he said, 'No one who looks back after putting his hand to the plough is suited to the kingdom of God' (Luke 9:62). No one goes in bemoaning the cost. They understand the opportunity. And one of the things that has most obstructed the path of discipleship in our Christian culture today is this idea that it will be a terribly difficult thing that will certainly ruin your life. A typical and often-told story in Christian circles is of those who have refused to surrender their lives to God for fear he would 'send them to Africa as missionaries'.

And here is the whole point of the much misunderstood teachings of Luke 14. There Jesus famously says one must 'hate' all their family members and their own life also, must take their cross, and must forsake all they own, or they 'cannot be my disciple' (Luke 14:26–27, 33). The entire point of this passage is that as long as one thinks anything may really be more valuable than fellowship with Jesus in his kingdom, one cannot learn from him. People who have not got the basic facts about their life straight will therefore not do the things that make learning from Jesus possible and will never be able to understand the basic points in the lessons to be learned.

It is like a mathematics teacher in high school who might say to a student, 'Verily, verily I say unto thee, except thou canst do decimals and fractions, thou canst in no wise do algebra.' It is not that the teacher will not allow you to do algebra because you are a bad person; you just won't be able to do basic algebra if you are not in command of decimals and fractions.

So this counting of the cost is not a moaning and groaning session. 'Oh how terrible it is that I have to value all of my "wonderful" things (which are probably making life miserable and hopeless anyway) less than I do living in the kingdom! How terrible that I must be prepared to actually surrender them should that be called for!' The counting of the cost is to bring us to the point of clarity and decisiveness. It is to help us to *see*. Counting the cost is precisely what the man with the pearl and the hidden treasure did. Out of it came their decisiveness and joy. It is decisiveness and joy that are the outcomes of the counting.

What this passage in Luke is about is *clarity*. It is not about misery, or about some incredibly dreadful price that one must pay to be Jesus' apprentice. There is no such thing as a dreadful price for the 'pearl' in question. Suffering for him is actually something we rejoice to be counted worthy of (Acts 5:41; Phil. 1:29). The point is simply that unless we clearly see the superiority of what we receive as his students over every other thing that might be valued, we cannot succeed in our discipleship to him. We will not be able do the things required to learn his lessons and move ever deeper into a life that is his kingdom.

'Do You Love Me More Than These?'

The very same lesson, with a different background, is taught in the last chapter of John, where Jesus is working with his chosen right-hand man, Simon Peter. Peter had had a disastrous breakdown in his allegiance, as we know. But Jesus knew his man. We have already studied how he prayed for him that his faith would not disappear. And it did not disappear. But Peter needed to grow in clarity about where he actually stood.

Jesus uses a fine play on the words we translate 'love' just to help him get that clarity. After their breakfast on the beach, Jesus says to him, 'Peter, do you love me more than these?' Perhaps he was pointing to the boat and fishing equipment, which had been Peter's livelihood, or perhaps to co-workers, friends or family standing around. And he uses here the word *agapas*, for the highest kind of love. Peter replies, 'Yes, Lord, you know I love you.' But in his reply he uses the word *philo*, that is, love of friend to friend. Jesus tells him, 'Feed my lambs' (John 21:15).

The exact exchange is then repeated (v. 16), except now Jesus says, 'Shepherd my young sheep.' This is not wasted time and breath. You want to understand that Jesus is teaching, bringing his student to clarity and a decision based thereon. Repetition and rephrasing is a way of deepening impact.

Then a third time Jesus asks, 'Do you love me?' But this time he himself switched to *philo*. In other words he accepted the level where Peter was. But Peter was grieved that he kept asking, and perhaps also grieved at his own lack of *agape*. He replied, 'Lord, you know everything, and you know that I love [*philo*] you' (v. 17). He acknowledged with sadness that Jesus knew exactly what the quality and level of his love was.

But Jesus nevertheless charges him with the responsibility of feeding his young sheep. And then he also proceeds to explain to him that his calling would mean death by crucifixion in his old age. Peter was then in a position to make his choice. He made his choice, and he never again turned back. He embraced the treasure and understood what an incredible bargain he was getting, crucifixion and all. He lived his life 'believing in him, exulting with unutterable joy filled with glory' (1 Pet. 1:8). Peter thus came to understand this to be the natural condition of the disciple's soul, though he knew from experience it does not come quickly or easily.

What We Should Do

Given clarity about the condition of soul that leads to choosing discipleship, what are practical steps we can take to bring strongly before us the joyous vision of the kingdom? True, that vision can come to us at God's initiative, through experiences that may be given to us. In fact, God's initiative will always be involved, for to see Jesus in his beauty and goodness is always a gift of grace. And then, of course, there may also be a role that other people play. But these are factors over which we have no direct control. What we want to know is what I can do if I have come to suspect it would be best for me to apprentice myself to Jesus. How can we come to admire Jesus sufficiently to 'sell everything we have and buy the pearl of great value' with joy and excitement?

Ask

The first thing we should do is emphatically and repeatedly express to Jesus our desire to see him more fully as he really is. Remember, the rule of the kingdom is to *ask*. We ask to see him, and not just as he is represented in the Gospels, but also as he has lived and lives through history and now, and in his reality as the one who literally holds the universe in existence. He will certainly be aware of our request, just as you would be aware of anyone expressing their desires to you in your house.

We should make our expression of desire a solemn occasion, giving at least a number of quiet hours or a day to it. It will also be good to write down our prayer for his help in seeing him. We should do this privately, of course, but then we should share what we have done with a knowledgeable minister or friend who could pray with us and talk with us about what we are doing.

Dwell, Reside, in His Words

Second, we should use every means at our disposal to come to see him more fully. Several things might be mentioned here, but there are two in particular, and they are keyed to one of the most well known statements Jesus ever made. In John 8 he said to those around them, 'If you dwell in my word, you really are my apprentices. And you will know the truth, and the truth will liberate you' (8:31–32). As the context makes clear, he is saying that we will be liberated from all of the bondage that is in human life through sin, and especially from that of self-righteous religion. Positively, we will be liberated into life in the kingdom of God.

And what does 'dwelling', or 'continuing', in his word mean? It means to centre your life upon the very things we have been studying in this book: his good news about The Kingdom Among Us, about who is really well off and who is not, and about true goodness of heart and how it expresses itself in action. We will fill our souls with the written Gospels. We will devote our attention to these teachings, in private study and inquiry as well as public instruction. And, negatively, we will refuse to devote our mental space and energy to the fruitless, even stupefying and degrading, stuff that constantly clamours for our attention. We will attend to it only enough to avoid it.

But dwelling in his word is not just intensive and continuous study of the Gospels, though it is that. It is also putting them into practice. To dwell in his word we must know it: know what it is and what it means. But we really *dwell* in it by putting it into practice. Of course, we shall do so very imperfectly at first. At that point we have perhaps not even come to be a committed disciple. We are only thinking about how to become one. Nevertheless, we can count on Jesus to meet us in our admittedly imperfect efforts to put his word into practice. Where his word is, there he is. He does not leave his words to stand alone in the world. And his loveliness and strength will certainly be personally revealed to those who will simply make the effort to do what his words indicate.

In these efforts to see Jesus more clearly we should not dabble, but be thoughtfully serious. We should find a reliable and readable version of the four Gospels, such as the Revised New English Bible or the New Revised Standard Version. The Living Bible is also good, but it probably should be read with one of the other versions. If we can plan a week in a comfortable retreat, or at least several days, then we can read through the four Gospels repeatedly, jotting down notes and thoughts on a pad as we go.

If over a period of several days or weeks we were to read the Gospels through as many times as we can, consistent with sensible rest and relaxation, that alone would enable us to see Jesus with a clarity that can make the full transition into discipleship possible. We can count on him to meet us in that transition and not leave us to struggle with it on our own, for he is far more interested in it than we can ever be. He always sees clearly what is at issue. We rarely do.

There are a few other things we can do that will help us towards discipleship to Jesus – not least, seriously looking at the lives of others who truly have apprenticed themselves to him. Often his radiance in such people gives us very bright and strong impressions of his own greatness. To look closely at a Saint Francis, a John Wesley, a David Brainerd, an Albert Schweitzer or one of his many well-known Theresas, for example, is to see something that elevates our vision and our hope towards Jesus himself. We should, though, make sure to soak our souls in the Gospels before turning to lives of his other followers.

Perhaps because the scale is somewhat more 'human' in these great ones of the way, it is easier for us to make a few forward steps with them and then walk ever more firmly as the reality of the kingdom rises to meet us. Looking to the lives and personalities of great disciples has always been an especially potent factor in my own life. Generally, to keep company with genuine students and co-labourers of Jesus, living or 'fully living', will help us come to the place of effective intention and decision for ourselves. And, of course, we should try to find groups of his apprentices and become deeply involved with them.

Now Decide: The Power of Decision and Intention

But the final step in becoming a disciple is decision. We become a life student of Jesus by deciding. When we have achieved clarity on 'the costs' – on what is gained and what is lost by becoming or failing to become his apprentice – an effective decision is then possible. But still it must be made. It will not just happen. We do not drift into discipleship.

This may seem a simple point, but today it is commonly overlooked or disregarded, even by those who think of themselves as having a serious interest in Jesus and his kingdom. I rarely find any individual who has actually made a decision to live as a student of Jesus in the manner discussed in this book. For the greater number of professing Christians, that is simply not something that has presented itself clearly to their minds. Current confusions about what it means, and the failure of leaders and teachers to provide instruction on it and to stress the issue of discipleship, make that almost inevitable.

But in the last analysis we fail to be disciples only because we do not decide to be. We do not *intend* to be disciples. It is the power of the decision and the intention over our life that is missing. We should apprentice ourselves to Jesus in a solemn moment, and we should let those around us know that we have done so.

In the second chapter of William Law's book *A Serious Call to a Devout and Holy Life*, the author inquires into 'the reason why the generality of Christians fall so far short of the holiness and devotion of Christianity.'[7] To set the scene for his answer to this question, he raises a parallel question. Vulgarity and swearing was then an especially prominent feature of male behaviour, even among professing Christians. So he asks, 'How comes it that two in three of men are guilty of so gross and profane a sin as this is?' It is not that they do not know it is wrong, he points out, nor is it that they are helpless to avoid it.

The answer is, they do not intend to please God in this matter:

> For let a man but have so much piety as to intend to please God in all the actions of his life as the happiest and best thing in the world, and then he will never swear more. It will be as impossible for him to swear

> whilst he feels this intention within himself as it is impossible for a man that intends to please his prince to go up and abuse him to his face.[8]

And it is the simple want of that intention to please God, Law points out, that explains why

> you see such a mixture of sin and folly in the lives even of the better sort of people ... It was this general intention that made the primitive Christians such eminent instances of piety, that made the goodly fellowship of the Saints and all the glorious army of martyrs and confessors. And if you will here stop and ask yourself why you are not as pious as the primitive Christians were, your own heart will tell you that it is neither through ignorance nor inability, but purely because you never thoroughly intended it.[9]

Now perhaps we are not used to being spoken to so frankly, and it might be easy to take offence. But, on the other hand, it could well prove to be a major turning point in our life if we would, with Law's help, ask ourselves if we really do intend to be life students of Jesus. Do we really intend to do and be all of the high things we profess to believe in? Have we *decided* to do them? When did we decide it? And how did we implement that decision?

Intention and decision are absolutely fundamental in this matter of apprenticeship to Jesus, and we shall return to it shortly in connection with the last topic for this chapter: *making* disciples.

Helping Others Find Their Way into Discipleship

Clearly thought out and decisive apprenticeship to Jesus is the bridge between initial faith in him and the life of obedience and fulfilment in his kingdom. Those who have found their way in will inevitably want to share the new reality they have found with those around them. When we discover something great, we naturally want all those we really care about to be in on it. We would no more want to leave the sharing of the kingdom to 'full-time workers' than we would anything else we were really enthusiastic about.

The directions Jesus gave to his people when he last met with them in his familiar visible form was that they should 'make disciples' (Matt. 28:19). Although the language may seem somewhat intimidating, and our contemporary practice is almost unrecognizably different from what his earliest people did, there is no reason to think that he has changed his expectations and hopes for us. Our only question is a practical one: How do we do it?

The answer comes in three parts: we must, of course, be disciples, we must intend to make disciples, and we must know how to bring people to believe that Jesus really is the One.

Be Disciples

First of all, it is clear that, if we would make disciples, we should be disciples. I am sure that some have been made disciples of Jesus by those who were not. God, after all, is involved here, and you cannot limit what he will do for reasons and by means known only to him. But that kind of 'disciple making' is not something one can plan on, for it occurs only by accident, so to speak, and the grace of God. We cannot use it as the basis of a plan. And we cannot imagine that such 'accidental' disciple making is what Jesus had in mind when he told us to make people from all nations students of him.

To plan on making disciples, we need to know what one is and how people become disciples. We need to know these things by personal experience, as did the first generation of Jesus' people. They *had* been made disciples. And we need to be standing in the position of Jesus' students and co-workers, so that our efforts in making disciples will be appropriately guided and strengthened by him. They are, after all, to be *his* disciples, not ours.

Against the Tide

So we are, then, disciples in disciple making. We learn from Jesus how to make disciples as he did. We have seen that this involves proclaiming, manifesting, and teaching the kingdom of God. The teaching aspect becomes very important in making disciples. In it we help others to think accurately about 'the effective range of God's will' and to understand why it is as it is and how it works. When we have come to the point where we can do this, then in conjunction with our own experience of becoming a disciple, making a disciple is no longer something mysterious. It is only a matter of appropriately informing people about Jesus and his kingdom and helping them, through prayer and guidance, to make a decision.

But this puts us in position to see how serious a matter is the fact brought out at the end of Chapter 2. There, from the honest words of certain outstanding ministers, we saw how weak a hold the church currently has on the message of the kingdom. We saw internationally known leaders commenting on how little is said in Christian teachings about the kingdom and some admitting that they had neither heard nor preached a sermon on the topic. But, given that, what can it mean to us now to make disciples? And with the disappearance of Jesus as *teacher* – replaced by the mere sacrificial Lamb or else the prophet of social and personal 'liberation' – the prospects for the making of disciples to him become very dim indeed. You cannot have students if you have no teacher.

It also becomes clear, in the light of the disappearance of the kingdom and Jesus the teacher, why the making of *converts*, or church members, has become the mandatory goal of Christian ministers – if even that – while the making of disciples is pushed to the very margins of Christian existence. Many Christian groups simply have no idea what discipleship is and have relegated it to para-church organizations.

The Elephant in the Church

But with a picture of Jesus' people as his devoted students constantly and clearly held before us, we gain an entirely different impression of what his presence in his people is to be. Some time back, a drug rehabilitation programme ran an interesting commercial that showed an elephant walking around in an ordinary home, going by the son doing homework, the wife washing dishes and so forth. Every one studiously tries to ignore it, but it is obviously the biggest thing around the house.

Non-discipleship is the elephant in the church. It is not the much discussed moral failures, financial abuses or the amazing general similarity between Christians and non-Christians. These are only effects of the underlying problem. The fundamental negative reality among Christian believers now is their failure to be constantly learning how to live their lives in The Kingdom Among Us. And it is an accepted reality. The division of professing Christians into those for whom it is a matter of whole-life devotion to God and those who maintain a consumer, or client, relationship to the church has now been an accepted reality for over fifteen hundred years.[10]

And at present – in the distant outworkings of the Protestant Reformation, with its truly great and good message of salvation by faith alone – that long-accepted division has worked its way into the very heart of the gospel message. It is now understood to be a part of the 'good news' that one does not have to be a life student of Jesus in order to be a Christian and receive forgiveness of sins. This gives a precise meaning to the phrase 'cheap grace', though it would be better described as 'costly faithlessness'.

We have dealt with these distortions of the New Testament gospel in earlier chapters, and this is not the place to bemoan or contest this reality of our current church life. Moreover, I want it to be very clear that I am not saying only 'true disciples' of Jesus make it to heaven after death. Indeed, I believe that that is not true, though I would not encourage anyone to stop short of discipleship. Nevertheless I know that, as far as forgiveness alone is concerned, the tenderness of God is far greater than we will ever understand on earth or perhaps elsewhere.

That is surely what it means to say that he gave his unique Son to die on our behalf. I am thoroughly convinced that God will let everyone into heaven who, in his considered opinion, can stand it. But 'standing it' may prove to be a more difficult matter than those who take their view of heaven from popular movies or popular preaching may think. The fires in heaven may be hotter than those in the other place.

It might prove helpful to think occasionally of how, exactly, I would be glad to be in heaven should I 'make it'. Will it be like a nice, air-conditioned luxury hotel with unlimited room service and spectacular amenities for eternity? I often wonder how happy and useful some of the fearful, bitter, lust-ridden, hate-filled Christians I have seen involved in church or family or neighbourhood or political battles would be if they were forced to live forever in the unrestrained fullness of the reality of God, which we tried to look at in Chapter 3, and with multitudes of beings really like him.

There is a widespread notion that just passing through death transforms human character. Discipleship is not needed. Just believe enough to 'make it'. But I have never been able to find any basis in scriptural tradition or psychological reality to think this might be so. What if death only forever fixes us as the kind of person we are at death? What would one *do* in heaven with a debauched character or a hate-filled heart?

Surely something must be done now. And this brings us back to the matter of intention and decision, but now with reference to the making of disciples.

Intending to Make Disciples

The second thing for us to do if we are to make apprentices to Jesus is to intend to make disciples. This is now a familiar theme, of central importance. It must be our conscious objective, consciously implemented, to bring others to the point where they are daily learning from Jesus how to live their actual lives as he would live them if he were they. That implemented intention would soon transform everything among professing Christians as we know them.

For example, much time is spent among Christians trying to smooth over hurt feelings and even deep wounds, given and received, and to get people to stop being angry, retaliatory, and unforgiving. But suppose, instead, we devoted our time to inspiring and enabling Christians and others to be people who are not offendable and not angry and who are forgiving as a matter of course. 'Great peace,' the psalmist says, 'have they who love Thy law. Nothing trips them up' (Ps. 119:165). To intentionally make disciples is to open the doorway for people to become like that. That is why it is such a great gift to humankind.

But really to intend this is no trivial matter, of course. It means a huge change of direction. The weight of the tradition of client, or consumer, Christianity, which now without thought dominates the local congregations and denominations of Christian people – indeed, the entire Christian culture – stands against any such intention – not consciously, perhaps, but just by the inertia of 'how things are', of the daily rounds and what 'has to get done'. This established order can actually keep pastors or teachers in a church setting from thinking of making disciples as an issue that concerns them *at all*. I have been a pastor, and I understand.

Henri Nouwen well describes our common situation:

> We simply go along with the many 'musts' and 'oughts' that have been handed on to us, and we live with them as if they were authentic translations of the Gospel of our Lord. People must be motivated to come to church, youth must be entertained, money must be raised, and above all everyone must be happy. Moreover, we ought to be on good terms with the church and civil authorities; we ought to be liked or at least respected by a fair majority of our parishioners; we ought to move up in the ranks according to schedule; and we ought to have enough vacation and salary to live a comfortable life.[11]

This is why in most settings disciple making is regarded as something to be handled by para-church organizations or possibly theological schools, not the local church itself. It is assumed to be enough for church leaders to make converts or induct members and leave discipleship to take care of itself or be cared for by 'specialists'. Or perhaps we vaguely hope it will just 'happen', even though the record clearly shows that it rarely does.

On the other hand, to explicitly intend to make apprentices to Jesus could be quite upsetting to congregational life. Won't those who are mere members or converts find themselves in an embarrassing position? Second-class citizenship? It is certainly true that the implicit understanding that non-disciple Christians have with their leaders and congregations will have to be brought to light and dealt with in some appropriate way. We must deal with this in more detail in the next chapter. But we say immediately that the last thing the disciple or disciple maker will do is assume superiority over anyone, Christian or not, disciple or not. Remember, we are called to form a community of prayful love.

Discipleship Evangelism?

And what about evangelism? If we have an intentional programme to make disciples, can we simultaneously intend to make converts, or 'members', who are not disciples? Can we leave the latter to believe that they need never become disciples, and that this is actually the heart of the true message of 'grace'? What would be the effects upon evangelism for converts, or members, if we were to tell those converts explicitly that the essence of Christianity is merely a consumer, or client, relationship to Jesus and his people?

Do we now even have any idea of what discipleship evangelism, as we might call it, would look like? What message would we preach that would naturally lead to a decision to become an apprentice to Jesus in The Kingdom Among Us? I hope we can now understand what it might be, having worked our way this far. I hope that our understanding of what it is really to trust Jesus Christ, the whole person, with our whole life, would make the call to become his whole-life apprentice the natural next step. That would be *discipleship evangelism*. And it would be very different from what is now done.

So it is clear that a pervasive intention to make disciples would radically change the character of the church, the 'visible' people of God, as we know it. Just a strong minority of genuine disciples in the membership of a congregation or group would have an incredibly transforming effect. Almost every problem that we see afflicting, paralysing and even killing Christians and groups of Christians today would never even arise in a context where the primacy of apprenticeship to Jesus is accepted and developed through a corresponding course of training.

But we emphatically reiterate that the intention to make disciples is essential. It will not happen otherwise. We are, of course, *not* talking about eliminating non-disciple, consumer Christianity. It has its place. But we are talking about making it secondary, as far as our intentions are concerned. We would intend to make disciples and let converts 'happen', rather than intending to make converts and letting disciples 'happen'. And we certainly recognize what an overwhelmingly difficult task this shift would be. This is why, once again, it is absolutely necessary that those who exercise leadership must *be* close and faithful students of Jesus himself. He must be the one who shows the way.

He does not decide for us, however. Our intentions are ours, not his. We are responsible for what we intend. And to make disciples we must intend to make disciples. We are not talking about the duties of 'full-time' workers, but the duties of a friend and neighbour. Multitudes of those who constantly hear us and follow us whoever we are, as well as those who observe us from a distance, will respond with gratitude and joy that they have been given a realistic opportunity to learn how to live in the kingdom.

Changing People's Real Beliefs

So if we are to follow Jesus' directions and make students of him from all ethnic groups, or 'nations', we must be his students, and we must intend to lead others to be his students. But how do you lead someone to be his student once you intend to? Certainly not by nagging them with 'pearls'.

Some of what we have already said about becoming a disciple is relevant here, but we must apply it in a slightly different way. In short, however, you lead people to become disciples of Jesus by *ravishing them* with a vision of life in the kingdom of the heavens in the fellowship of Jesus. And you do this by proclaiming, manifesting and teaching the kingdom to them in the manner learned from Jesus himself. You thereby change the belief system that governs their lives.

But we cannot leave it at that – especially not today. We must say more specifically what that means.

Currently the minds and souls of Christians and non-Christians are constantly hammered by the innumerable fists of an 'information society' and an inescapably media-saturated social consciousness set squarely against the reality of the kingdom of God. Without necessarily intending it, these forces almost irresistibly direct our feelings, imagery, thinking and belief against the world of Jesus and his Father and against the profound needs and hungers of the human soul.

It is not a matter of conspiracy. It is actually something much more powerful. It is an anonymous and many-faceted structure of 'authority' that stipulates what is to count as knowledge and reality. It is silently but ponderously conveyed by our entire system of education, Christian and otherwise. The essential teachings of Jesus emphatically do *not* receive its stamp of approval.

A 'Glorious Accident'?

In Chapter 3 we briefly mentioned an outstanding series entitled *A Glorious Accident* that appeared on public television in the United States. It was produced in Europe, and in some countries the response to it was one of the most enthusiastic of any programme ever aired. It deserves such a response, for of its kind it is truly a magnificent piece of work. Nevertheless it should be recognized that, in it, and thus at the very heart of a civilization and intellectual culture that owes its existence to Jesus, Jesus and his teaching about life and about God are simply not a matter for discussion – not even a mention. And almost everyone would be astonished, and possibly embarrassed, by any suggestion that it should be any other way.

The programme consisted of a series of in-depth interviews with a number of internationally known scientists and philosophers. 'A glorious accident' turns out to be the human mind. Or possibly it is the physical universe as a whole. There was not the least serious consideration – hardly a mention – of the possibility that there is a God, and that the universe is something carefully planned in the light of purposes that transcend the career of physical energy and matter.

This view of reality is precisely the situation the Christian disciple maker must address. For it is quite obvious that nothing remains of discipleship to Jesus or of Christian faith if there is no God such as he obviously lived from and had faith in, if there is only 'particles and progress'. You have to be *extremely* well educated and very adept at deconstructive and reconstitutive thinking to believe any such discipleship remains, and perhaps not one in a million can qualify.

To make disciples to Jesus today, one has to make him and his God real to them, right in the face of all that stands at the centre of our world as 'official' knowledge and reality. Of course what is represented by the automatic assumptions of *A Glorious Accident* is only one belief or group of beliefs obstructive to discipleship today. In every age it is one belief system or another, but a total and exclusive confidence in the natural sciences as the key to reality is the major opposing belief now.

Not, we emphasize, the sciences themselves, but the widespread faith in them as sole source of truth. And in any case the point here is not so much about which beliefs must be challenged and changed as it is that *to enable people to become disciples we must change whatever it is in their actual belief system that bars confidence in Jesus as Master of the Universe*. That is fundamental and must be taken as an unshakeable conscious objective by any maker of disciples.

Changed Beliefs Change Action and Character

That change is fundamental. But it is also decisive. And that is the hopeful point. When we bring people to believe differently, they really do become different. One of the greatest weaknesses in our teaching and leadership today is that we spend so much time trying to get people to do things good people are supposed to do, without changing what they really believe.

It doesn't succeed very well, and that is the open secret of church life. We frankly need to do much less of this managing of action, and especially with young people. We need to concentrate on changing the minds of those we would reach and serve. What they *do* will certainly follow, as Jesus well understood and taught.

But in our culture there is a severe illusion about faith, or belief. It is one that has been produced by many centuries of people professing, as a cultural identification, to believe things they do not really believe at all. That goes hand in hand with the predominance of what was called client, or consumer, Christianity earlier. Thus there arises the misunderstanding that human life is not really governed by belief. This is a disastrous error.

We often speak of people not living up to their faith. But the cases in which we say this are not really cases of people behaving otherwise than they believe. They are cases in which genuine beliefs are made obvious by what people do. We always live up to our beliefs – or down to them, as the case may be. Nothing else is possible. It is the nature of belief. And the reason why clergy and others have to invest so much effort into getting people to *do* things is that they are working against the actual beliefs of the people they are trying to lead.

I once heard a pastor explaining to his congregation how it caused his stomach to hurt when people did not come to the evening services on which he had worked so hard. I have been a pastor, and I can understand how he felt. But he would have been more effective had he simply dealt with the beliefs of his people that kept them home on Sunday evening.

Study What the People We Speak to Actually Believe

What has to be done, instead of trying to drive people to do what we think they are supposed to, is to be honest about what we and others really believe. Then, by inquiry, teaching, example, prayer and reliance upon the spirit of God, we can work to change the beliefs that are contrary to the way of Jesus. We can open the way for others, Christians or not, to heartily choose apprenticeship in the kingdom of God.

A major part of this important work is coming to understand what the people we are dealing with really do believe, and not pretending – often with them – that they believe what they don't believe at all. In a setting where a social premium has been placed upon believing certain things for the sake of group solidarity, we must face the fact that human beings can honestly profess to believe what they do not believe. They may do this for so long that even they no longer know that they do not believe what they profess. But their actions will, of course, be in terms of what they actually believe. This will be so even though they do not recognize it, and they will lose themselves in bewilderment about the weakness of their 'faith'. That bewilderment is a common condition among professing Christians today.

Of course, this type of confusion is not restricted to religious profession. The incidence of marital unfaithfulness and abuse, of child abuse and neglect and the failure of education all stand in the midst of professions of values and beliefs that, if genuine, would simply rule them out. The truth is that these sad realities are produced by actual beliefs, which, of course, govern our actual lives. We have already once quoted the principle of management that says, 'Your system is perfectly designed to produce the result you are getting.' We need to let our minds dwell on it.

In the context of our particular family or group or congregation, to present the kingdom of the heavens will mean that we must teach about the nature of belief (which is the same as faith) and how it relates to the rest of our personality. And then we must study our friends and associates to see what they really do believe and help them to be honest about it. We understand that our beliefs are the rails upon which our life runs, and so we have to address their actual beliefs and their doubts, not spend our time discussing many fine things that have little or no relevance to their genuine state of mind.[12]

Then we must be very fair and thorough in examining those beliefs and considering to what extent they are or are not justified. There must not be the least effort to be unfair in this examination or to pooh-pooh genuine problems, for that will weaken and infect everything we try to develop thereafter. One cannot build discipleship to Jesus by dodging serious issues or not doing justice to honest doubts about him and his teachings.

Of course we do not change peoples' beliefs just by our own cleverness. We must nevertheless always be as intelligent, clever and thorough as we can. We have an indispensable role to play, and we must carefully study how to do it well.

That means that we will directly confront the opposing beliefs, such as those assumed in *A Glorious Accident*. We will name them, and we will state clearly and thoroughly how and why they are mistaken or misguided. This is standard pastoral duty, of course, but because of its importance it is the duty of a family member, a citizen, and a neighbour as well. Though it must always be joined with prayer, service and reliance on the spirit, they do not substitute for it. And we are now, and have been for some time, sorely deficient in this absolutely necessary labour. This is one more thing that contributes to the weakness of discipleship in our times. It makes it almost impossible to generate joyous confidence in Jesus and his word.

The Only Way Forward

Practically speaking, the thoughts we have covered in this chapter are among the most important for the prospects of Jesus' people on earth – and for the earth itself. If we cannot break through to a new vision of faith and discipleship, the real significance and power of the gospel of the kingdom of God can never come into its own. It will be constantly defeated by the idea that it is somehow not a real part of faith in Jesus Christ, and the church will remain in the dead embrace of consumer Christianity.

The purposes of God in human history will eventually be realized, of course. The divine conspiracy will not be defeated. But multiple millions of individual human beings will live a futile and failing existence that God never intended.

The main burden of this work of disciple making no doubt falls to those of us who teach and lead, in whatever capacity, in our churches and our society. We, especially, must ask ourselves whether, in all honesty, the information we offer and the life we live is the same as that which entered the world with Jesus and that was able, through his students, to produce the historical church and the Christian form of civilization that grew up around it. If we cannot honestly say it is, then we need to return to our sources in the gospel of Jesus and the kingdom and to discipleship and disciple making as we see it at its best in our past.

Chapter 9

A CURRICULUM FOR CHRISTLIKENESS

> So those who hear me and do what I say are like those intelligent people who build their homes on solid rock, where rain and floods and winds cannot shake them.
>
> MATT. 7:24–25

> Train them to do everything I have told you.
>
> MATT. 28:20

The Course of Studies in the Master Class

These words from Jesus show that it must be possible to hear and do what he said. It also must be possible to train his apprentices in such a way that they routinely do everything he said was best.

That may seem a dream to us today, or it may even be perceived as a threat to our current vision of the Christian hope – indeed, of our personal hope. But that is only because we now live in a time when consumer Christianity has become the accepted norm, and all-out engagement with and in Jesus' kingdom among us is regarded as just one option people may take if it suits them – but probably as somewhat 'overdoing it'. By contrast, the biblical pattern is, from beginning to end, 'Be ye doers of the word, and not hearers only.'

Because that is so, and we have insisted upon it, we now must deal with the question of ways and means. What could we teach apprentices to Jesus, and how could we train them in such a way that they would routinely do the things he said were right? Indeed, what can we do to put *ourselves* in position actually to do what he has said?

In the previous chapters we have already learned most of what we need to know to answer this question, but now we must respond to it systematically and with some fullness of detail. And this we shall do after a few preliminary clarifications.

Obedience and Abundance: Inseparable Aspects of the Same Life

Certainly life on 'the rock' must be a good way to live. Wouldn't you like to be one of those intelligent people who know how to live a rich and unshakeable life? One free from loneliness, fear and anxiety and filled with constant peace and joy? Would you like to love your neighbours as you do yourself and be free of anger, envy, lust and covetousness? Would you like to have no need for others to praise you, and would you like to not be paralysed and humiliated by their dislike and condemnation? Would you like to have the inspiration and strength to lead a constant life of creative goodness? It sounds pretty good thus far, doesn't it?

Wouldn't you also like to have a strength and understanding that enables you genuinely and naturally to bless those who are cursing you – or cheating you, beating you out on the job, spitting on you in a confrontation, laughing at your religion or culture, even *killing* you? Or the strength and understanding merely to give further needed assistance to someone who has forced you to drop what you are doing and help out? To offer the other cheek to someone who has slapped you? Clearly, our entire inner reality of thought and feeling would have to be transformed to bring us to such a place.

And if you are the usual person reading this list, you are by now beginning to experience some hesitation and some doubt. Yes, a part of this sounds very like *abundance* of life: a very desirable condition to be in that immediately recommends itself to everyone. But other parts seem like *obedience*: something that well might spoil our plans or ruin our life. And so I may be asking myself about now whether I really want to give up all the 'behavioural options' that would disappear from my repertoire if I became the person described – that intelligent person who builds his or her house upon the rock.

But the truth about obedience in the kingdom of Jesus, as should be clear by now, is that it really is abundance. Kingdom obedience is kingdom abundance. They are not two separate things. The inner condition of the soul from which strength and love and peace flow is the very same condition that generously blesses the oppressor and lovingly turns the other cheek. These Christlike behaviours are expressions of a pervasive personal strength and its joy, not of weakness, morbidity, sorrow – or raw exertion of will – as is so often assumed. And those old 'options' that we might think should be kept in reserve, just in case they turn out to be 'necessary', will not even be missed.

However, this truth about obedience seems a secret very well kept today. And the correlation between *faith in Christ* and the obedience/abundance of *life in Christ* has now become, apparently, something of a mystery. Yes, it is a relationship that has functioned well in many periods of Christian history. The cultural and literary record is there for all to see. And there still are those today for whom faith in Christ progressively modulates into both obedience and abundance. I meet such people. But, not very many. The usual Christian experience does not progress in that way. And it is mainly because individuals are rarely offered any effective guidance into the inner substance of the path laid down by Jesus in his teachings and example.

Where Are the Training Programmes?

We have to come to terms with the fact that we cannot become those who 'hear and do' without specific training for it. The training may be to some extent self-administered, but more than that will always be needed. It is something that must be made available to us by those already farther along the path.

That clearly was the understanding of Jesus for his people. Training in Christlikeness is a responsibility they have for those who enter their number. But at the present time intentional, effective training in Christlikeness – within the framework of a clear-eyed apprenticeship commitment and a spiritual 'engulfment' in the Trinitarian reality – *is just not there for us*. In the last chapter we said that non-discipleship is 'the elephant in the church'. What feeds that elephant and keeps it strong is the absence of effectual programmes of training that enable his people to do what Jesus said in a regular and efficient manner.

Imagine, if you can, discovering in your church newsletter or bulletin an announcement of a six-week seminar on how genuinely to bless someone who is spitting on you. This primitive form of desecration is still practised, much more commonly than is thought. We all recall the ceaselessly repeated television images of a professional baseball player recently spitting in the face of an umpire. You can just feel what incredible grace and maturity would be required for that umpire to respond with heartfelt blessing. And, of course, no one even thought he should give such a response, though it would have been the way of Jesus.

Or suppose the announced seminar was on how to live without purposely indulged lust or covetousness. Or on how to quit condemning the people around you. Or on how to be free of anger and all its complications. We recall the whole range of real-life enactments Jesus talked about in explaining kingdom goodness from the heart. (See Chapter 5.)

Imagine, also, a guarantee that at the end of the seminar those who have done the prescribed studies and exercises will actually be able to bless those who are spitting on them, and so on. In practical matters, to teach people *to do* something is to bring them to the point where they actually do it on the appropriate occasions.

When you teach children or adults to ride a bicycle or swim, they actually do ride bikes or swim on appropriate occasions. You don't just teach them that they *ought* to ride bicycles, or that it is *good* to ride bicycles, or that they should be ashamed if they don't. Similarly, when you teach people to bless those who curse them, they actually do bless those who curse them – even family members! They recognize the occasion as it arises for what it is and respond from the heart of Jesus, which has become their own. They do it and they do it well.

Imagine further, if your imagination is not already exhausted, driving by a church with a large sign in front that says, We Teach All

Who Seriously Commit Themselves to Jesus How to Do Everything He Said to Do. If you had just been reading the Gospels – especially Matt. 28:20, quoted on the title page of this chapter – you might think, 'Of course, that is exactly what the founder of the church, Jesus, told us to do.'

But your second thought might be that this is a highly unusual church. And then, 'Can this be *right?*' And: 'Can it be *real?*' When do you suppose was the last time any group of believers or church of any kind or level had a meeting of its officials in which the topic for discussion and action was how they were going to teach their people actually to do the specific things Jesus said?

The Necessity of a *Curriculum* for Christlikeness

My hope in this chapter is to enable us to begin a gentle exploration of these issues within our own minds and possibly in our own group context. Of course, the very last thing we intend is to blame anyone for the situation we now find ourselves in or to condemn institutions and persons now in place. No one really is to blame, in any case. We now live in the outcome of a largely unconscious historical drift over many years. Moreover, it is human nature to resist deep inward change, for such change threatens our sense of personal identity. The need now is to understand our situation. Where exactly are we now, as the people of Jesus, and why are we at this spot? And then we can begin to ask what might be done about it?

The *fact* is that there now is lacking a serious and expectant intention to bring Jesus' people into obedience and abundance through training. That would be discipleship as he gave it to us. What we have just said about seminars and signs demonstrates beyond a doubt the lack of intention. This is true even though leading writers, such as Alister McGrath, now acknowledge that 'God wishes his people to possess … the fullness of life' that Christian spirituality recognizes in Jesus.[1] What a stunning thought, once you allow it to sink in. Somehow the seriously thought out intention – not just a vague idea or wish – to actually bring about the fullness of life in Christ must be re-established.

One must recognize that numerous programmes in local congregations and wider levels of organization are frequently spoken of as discipleship programmes. We do not wish to detract from the good they do, and they do much good. Here we have in mind everything from Sunday school and special courses and seminars to Twelve-Step programmes and various types of national movements.

However, the emphasis all too often is on some point of behaviour modification. This is helpful, but it is not adequate to human life. It does not reach the root of the human problem. That root is the character of the inner life, where Jesus and his call to apprenticeship in the kingdom place the emphasis.

Behind our many praiseworthy activities there still lie many-sided theological and institutional disconnections between faith and obedience. We have discussed a number of them in previous chapters, but a much more thorough examination of these is needed than we can supply here. These disconnections reflect the profound brokenness of the human condition, and they stand squarely at the centre of contemporary Christian life, yet they also are not a matter of intention. There is no human conspiracy involved. No one has intended them, and in the midst of oceans of good intentions, few are even aware of them. But there they are, radiating their deadly effects on daily faith and life.

These deeper theological and institutional disconnections are just a matter of how, through gradual historical development, we have come *automatically* to think about Jesus Christ and the eternal kind of life that he brings to us. Jesus as the actual teacher of his people has disappeared from the mental horizon of our faith. In that capacity he is not a part of how we 'do' our Christianity today.

It is a main purpose of this book on Jesus and his kingdom to help us face this fact of the absence of Jesus the teacher and to change it. And now we have come to the point where we must propose a 'curriculum for Christlikeness': A Course of Study and Practice for Apprentices to Jesus in The Kingdom Among Us. We must begin to think about what, exactly, we would do to help people already committed to learning to do the things Jesus taught, so that they would actually come to do them routinely. Or possibly it is we ourselves who have been 'ravished by the kingdom of God'. What would we then study, how would we train *ourselves* to 'learn from Jesus how to live our life as he would live it if he were us'? This, you will recall, is what discipleship to Jesus is.

Not Just More Information

As we approach this task, it is very important to understand that the 'teaching' to be done at this point – whether directed towards ourselves or towards others – is not a matter of collecting or conveying information. The task is not to inform the disciple, or student, about things that Jesus believed, taught and practised. Usually that will already have been done, and more of that alone will be of very little use. The student will already possess almost all of the correct *information*. If tested for accuracy on it, he or she would probably pass.

And that information is essential. It is even a large part of the reason why the students have confidence in Jesus at all. Very likely they deeply want it all to be true. They want heartily to believe it. But they do not really understand it, and their confidence in its reality is shaky. They are like Peter in his truly earth-shaking confession that Jesus was the One anointed to save humanity. He had it right, of course, but had no real idea of what it meant (Matt. 16:16–19, 23).

Often those who are disciples initially only believe that *Jesus* believed the message of the kingdom. They are perhaps somewhat strengthened by that. But what the information they have actually represents does not form a part of their real life. In their bodily and social being they continue to be ready to act as though it were *not* true, even though in their conscious affirmations they accept it. Here is the point where the training 'to hear and do' must begin.

Getting the Answers Right – And *Believing* Them

And here also is one of those points where the educational practices that have developed in our society deeply injure our souls and impede the coming of the kingdom into our lives. In our culture one is considered educated if one 'knows the right answers'. That is, if one knows which answers are the correct ones. I sometimes joke with my students at the university where I teach by asking them if they believe what they wrote on their tests. They always laugh. They know belief is not required. Belief only controls your life.

It is, I suppose, actually funny. You could never lower a student's grade for simply giving the right answer but not believing it. Someone who doesn't believe it still 'knows' it. Indeed, on some types of exams if the student marks the 'right' answer by accident – a slip of the pen – he or she still gets 'credit.' A student who by pure chance got all of them 'right' would get an A.

So, as Jesus' current assistants in his on-going programme, one important way of characterizing our work of 'training disciples to do everything I told you' is 'bringing them to actually believe all the things they have already heard'. Our task in ourselves and others is to transform right answers into automatic responses to real-life situations.

The ordinary members of a church have an immense amount of information about God, Jesus, what they ought to do and their own destiny. It has come to them through the Christian tradition. Some parts of it are false or misguided, to be sure. No one completely avoids that – even *me*. But generally we have the 'right answers', and those answers are very precious indeed. But as things stand we are, by and large, unable to believe them in the way we genuinely do believe multitudes of things in our 'real' life.

For example, nearly every professing Christian has some information about the Trinity, the incarnation, the atonement and other standard doctrines. But to have the 'right' answers about the Trinity, for example, and to actually *believe* in the reality of the Trinity, is all the difference in the world.

The advantage of believing in the reality of the Trinity is not that we get an A from God for giving 'the right answer'. Remember, to believe something is to act as if it is so. To believe that two plus two equals four is to behave accordingly when trying to find out how many coins or apples are in the house. The advantage of believing it is not that we can pass tests in arithmetic; it is that we can deal much more successfully with reality. Just try dealing with it as if two plus two equalled six.

Hence, the advantage of *believing* in the Trinity is that we then live as if the Trinity is real: as if the cosmos surrounding us actually is, beyond all else, a self-sufficing community of unspeakably magnificent personal beings of boundless love, knowledge and power. And, thus believing, our lives naturally integrate themselves, through our actions, into the reality of such a universe, just as with two plus two equals four. In faith we rest ourselves upon the reality of the Trinity in action – and it graciously meets us. For it is there. And our lives are then enmeshed in the true world of God.

So, to drive home the crucial point, a great deal of what goes into 'training them [us] to do everything I said' consists simply in *bringing people to believe with their whole being the information they already have* as a result of their initial confidence in Jesus – even if that initial confidence was only the confidence of desperation.[2]

The Disciple Is Not Perfect – Yet

Understanding this also helps dispel the common misconception that those who are studying with Jesus have already realized in themselves the vision and practice of the kingdom. You often hear being a disciple spoken of as if it were an advanced spiritual condition. Not necessarily. The disciple has made a major step forward, to be sure, but may in fact still have a solid hold on very little of kingdom reality.

Jesus' disciples are those who have chosen to be with him to learn to be like him. All they have necessarily realized at the outset of their apprenticeship to him is, *Jesus is right*. He is the greatest and best. Of this, they are sure. That initial faith is God's gift of grace to them. So they have *him*. They do not yet have it. Living as his apprentices, they are increasingly getting 'it'. And as they move along they do indeed attain, by increasing grace, to an 'advanced spiritual condition'. They increase in the amount and quality of grace (interaction with God) they have in their real life. That is the same as increasing in their experiential knowledge of the real person, Jesus Christ, which in our current condition just is the eternal kind of life (2 Pet. 3:18; compare John 17:3).

Towards the beginning of their course they do not, for example, really believe that the meek and the persecuted are blessed, and certainly not the poor. That is, they do not automatically act as if it were so. But they know that Jesus does believe this, and they believe that he is right about what they themselves do not yet, really, believe.

Further, they want to believe it because, seeing his strength and beauty, they admire him so much and have such confidence in him. That is why they have become his students and have trusted him – or *intend* to trust him – for everything. Their cry is that of the desperate but honest man in the Gospels: 'Lord, I believe! Help thou my unbelief!' (Mark 9:24). This man believed in Jesus and cast himself upon him for help with his afflicted son. But as for the rest, well, he was very much less sure about the kingdom and the larger scene. Hence, 'Help my unbelief!'

The apostle Peter puts the belief structure involved here in a correct and helpful manner by saying, 'For Jesus was in the plan before the world started, but for your sake he has come at the end of the times, for you who *through him believe in God* who raised him from the dead and gave him glory, so that your faith and hope are *in God*' (1 Pet. 1:21). We are captivated by Jesus and trust ourselves to him as his apprentices. He then leads us to genuine understanding and reliance upon God in every aspect of our life. But that progression takes some time, and it is supposed to come in part through the efforts of others among his people, who are prepared to train us so that we are able to do, and routinely do, all of the things he said we should.

In order to become a disciple of Jesus, then, one must believe in him. In order to develop as his disciple one must progressively come to believe what he knew to be so. To enter his kingdom, we believe in him. To be at home in his kingdom, learning to reign with him there, we must share his beliefs.

As his apprentices, we pass through a course of training, from having faith *in* Christ to having the faith *of* Christ (Gal. 2:16–20). As a proclaimer and teacher of the gospel of his kingdom, I do not cease to announce a gospel *about* Jesus. That remains forever foundational. But I also recognize the need and opportunity to announce the gospel *of* Jesus (Mark 1:1) – the gospel of the present availability to every human being of a life in The Kingdom Among Us. Without that, the gospel about Jesus remains destructively incomplete.

Getting Clear on Objectives

Four Things We Must Not Take As Primary Objectives

To correctly form a curriculum for Christlikeness, we must have a very clear and simple perception of the primary goals it must achieve, as well as what is to be avoided.

Two objectives in particular that are often taken as *primary* goals must not be left in that position. They can be reintroduced later in proper subordination to the true ones. These are *external conformity* to the wording of Jesus' teachings about actions in specific contexts and *profession of perfectly correct doctrine*. Historically these are the very things that have obsessed the church visible – currently, the latter far more than the former.

We need wait no longer. The results are in. They do not provide a course of personal growth and development that routinely produces people who 'hear and do'. They either crush the human mind and soul and separate people from Jesus, or they produce hide-bound legalists and theological experts with 'lips close to God and hearts far away from him' (Isa. 29:13). The world hardly needs more of these.

Much the same can be said of the strategies – rarely taken as primary objectives, to be sure, but much used – of encouraging faithfulness to the activities of a church or other outwardly religious routines and various 'spiritualities', or the seeking out of special states of mind or ecstatic experiences. These are good things. But let it be said once and for all that, like outward conformity and doctrinally perfect profession, they are not to be taken as major objectives in an adequate curriculum for Christlikeness.

Special experiences, faithfulness to the church, correct doctrine, and external conformity to the teachings of Jesus all come along as appropriate, more or less automatically, when the inner self is transformed. But they do not produce such a transformation.

The human heart must be ploughed much more deeply. Thus these four emphases are good in their place, and even necessary when rightly understood. But when taken as *primary* objectives, they only burden souls and make significant Christlikeness extremely difficult, if not impossible. With respect to these four emphases, we need to say loudly and repeatedly, to everyone concerned, 'You cannot build your house on the rock in this way.'

The Two Primary Objectives of the Course of Training

By contrast, the *primary* objectives of any successful course of training for 'life on the rock', the life that hears and does, are twofold.

The first objective is to bring apprentices to the point where they dearly love and constantly delight in that 'heavenly Father' made real to earth in Jesus and are quite certain that there is no 'catch', no limit, to the goodness of his intentions or to his power to carry them out.

When the elderly apostle John, who had been the 'kid' among the apostles, came near to the end of his long life he said, 'This is the message we heard from Jesus ...' (1 John 1:5). It will be very useful in helping us see where we actually stand today if we ask ourselves, before looking at the rest of his statement, how we would automatically finish his sentence for him. What is *the* message Jesus brought, according to us? And then we might also ask our friends and acquaintances. If you do this, and write down the answers you elicit, I think you will be both astonished and enlightened by what you get.

But the aged apostle, on the basis of a lifetime of first-hand experience of Jesus, said that *this* was his message: 'God is light, and darkness in him there is not, none' (v. 5). That is *the* message he brought, according to John. It is also, according to him, the message 'we proclaim to you' (v. 5). It is the message we today are to proclaim. It is, as we shall further develop later, the message that impels the willing hearer to dearly love and constantly delight in that 'heavenly Father' made real to earth in Jesus. And it is the message that, finally, gives us assurance that his universe is 'a perfectly safe place for us to be'. Love perfected eliminates all fear.

When the mind is filled with this great and beautiful God, the 'natural' response, once all 'inward' hindrances are removed, will be to do 'everything I have told you to do'.

The second primary objective of a curriculum for Christlikeness is to remove our automatic responses against the kingdom of God, to free the apprentices of domination, of 'enslavement' (John 8:34; Rom. 6:6), to their old habitual patterns of thought, feeling and action. These are the 'automatic' patterns of response that were ground into the embodied social self during its long life outside The Kingdom Among Us. They make up 'the sin that is in my members' which, as Paul so brilliantly understood, brings it about that 'wishing to do the good is mine, but the doing of it is not' (Rom. 7:18).

It is not enough, if we would enable Jesus' students to do what he said, just to announce and teach the truth about God, about Jesus, and about God's purposes with humankind. To think so is the fallacy underlying most of the training that goes on in our churches and theological schools. Even relentlessly pursued, it is not enough.

Very little of our being lies under the direction of our conscious minds, and very little of our actions runs from our thoughts and consciously chosen intentions. Our mind on its own is an extremely feeble instrument, whose power over life we constantly tend to exaggerate. We are incarnate beings in our very nature, and we live from our bodies. If we are to be transformed, the body must be transformed, and that is not accomplished by talking at it.

The training that leads to *doing* what we hear from Jesus must therefore involve, first, the purposeful disruption of our 'automatic' thoughts, feelings and actions by doing different things with our body. And then, through various intentional practices, we place the body before God and his instrumentalities in such a way that our whole self is retrained away from the old kingdoms around and within us and into 'the kingdom of the Son of His love' (Col. 1:13 NAS).

This part of the curriculum for Christlikeness consists of 'disciplines for the spiritual life.' We shall discuss them later in this chapter.

But for now let us only add the comment that these two 'primary objectives' of the curriculum are not to be pursued separately but interactively. We do not first bring apprentices to love God appropriately and then free them from pattern enslavement. Nor do we do it the other way around.

Pursuit of the two primary objectives goes hand in hand. They are to be simultaneously sought. This would be expected in the case of persons such as we are, who live at the mercy of their thoughts, to be sure, but also are bodily beings with a social context that all too easily takes over our life.

Now let us consider in some detail what we would have to do in order to achieve the two primary objectives. And here we enter the substance of the curriculum for Christlikeness.

Enthralling the Mind with God

Turning the Mind Towards God

With regard to our first primary objective, the most important question we face is, How do we help people love what is lovely? Very simply, we cause them, ask them, help them to place their minds on the lovely thing concerned. We assist them to do this in every way possible. Saint Thomas Aquinas remarks that 'love is born of an earnest consideration of the object loved.' And: 'Love follows knowledge.'[3] Love is an emotional response aroused in the will by visions of the good. Contrary to what is often said, love is never blind, though it may not see rightly. It cannot exist without some vision of the beloved.

As teachers we therefore bring the lovely thing – in this case, God – before the disciple as fully and as forcibly as possible, putting our best efforts into it. But we never forget that in the last analysis, as we have already learned from Emily Dickinson, 'the soul selects her own society, then shuts the door.'[4] Though we act, and as intelligently and responsibly as possible, we are always in the position of *asking*: asking them, asking God, and responding to their responses.

God has placed the only key to the innermost parts of the human soul in its own hands and will never take it back to himself or give it to another. You may even be able to destroy the soul of another, but you will never unlock it against his or her will. The soul, to continue the words of the poet just quoted, can 'close the valves of her attention, like stone.' She can even lose the key, and have to have help finding it. She can even refuse the help she desperately needs. But she will never cease to need to love, which is deeper than the need to be loved.

A popular saying is 'Take time to smell the roses.' What does this mean? To enjoy the rose it is necessary to focus on it and bring the rose as fully before our senses and mind as possible. To smell a rose you must get close, and you must linger. When we do so, we delight in it. We love it.

Taking time to smell the roses leaves enduring impressions of a dear glory that, if sufficiently re-engaged, can change the quality of our entire life. The rose in a very special way – and more generally the flower, even in its most humble forms – is a fragile but irrepressible witness on earth to a 'larger' world where good is somehow safe.

This simple illustration contains profound truths. If anyone is to love God and have his or her life filled with that love, God in his glorious reality must be brought before the mind and kept there in such a way that the mind takes root and stays fixed there. Of course the individual must be willing for this to happen, but any genuine apprentice to Jesus will be willing. This is the very lesson apprentices have enrolled in his school to learn.

So the question for the first part of our curriculum is simply *how* to bring God adequately before the mind and spirit of the disciple. This is to be done in such a way that love for and delight in God will be elicited and established as the pervasive orientation of the whole self. It will fill the mind of the willing soul and progress towards an easy and delightful governance of the entire personality. Our first primary objective will then have been achieved.

Our Mind and Our Choices

Now we need to understand that what simply occupies our mind very largely governs what we do. It sets the emotional tone out of which our actions flow, and it projects the possible courses of action available to us. Also the mind, though of little power on its own, is the place of our widest and most basic freedom. This is true in both a direct and an indirect sense. Of all the things we do, we have more freedom with respect to *what we will think of*, where we will place our mind, than anything else. And the freedom of thinking is a direct freedom wherever it is present. We need not do something else in order to exercise it. We simply turn our mind to whatever it is we choose to think of. The deepest revelation of our character is what we choose to dwell on in thought, what constantly occupies our mind – as well as what we can or cannot even think of.

But the mind is also at the root of our indirect freedoms – of things we can do if we do something else. For example, the highly successful Alcoholics Anonymous programme is designed to free people from drinking alcohol. They have learned they cannot be free by just trying. Steps 1 to 4 in the well-known Twelve-Step programme are exercises of the direct freedom of the individual, the freedom to place their minds where they need to: on themselves as they really are and on God, who can help them.[5]

But these first steps make it possible to do other things (the remaining eight steps) that they could not do if their minds were not directed as the first four steps require. Eventually, they want to be free of drink day by day. That is the goal. But this 'freedom' will never be realized unless the individual involved takes constant care over the direct placement of his or her mind.

What we see in this wondrously life-saving programme is a general arrangement of the human personality that, really, is totally obvious to any thoughtful person. But we are rarely thoughtful. As the line from A. E. Housman says, 'We think by fits and starts.' Thus a part of the call of God to us has always been to think. Indeed the call of Jesus to 'repent' is nothing but a call to think about how we have been thinking. And when we come to the task of developing disciples into the fullness of Christ, we must be very clear that one main part, and by far the most fundamental, is *to form the insights and habits of the student's mind so that it stays directed towards God*. When this is adequately done, a full heart of love will go out towards God, and joy and obedience will flood the life.

What we have just explained is the constant testimony of biblical writers. As only one illustration, in Psalm 16 we read,

> The Lord is what I have in life and what sustains me ... My mind teaches me through the night times about this. I hold the Lord continually before me; because he is involved in all I do, I will not be

> troubled. Therefore my heart is glad, and all that is best in me rejoices; my flesh also will be secure. You will not desert me in the grave, nor allow your godly friend to experience decomposition. You will show me the path through life. Around you one has joy to the full. Your right hand offers everlasting pleasures. (Ps. 16:5–11)

The distortion, or 'wrungness', of the will, on the other hand – theologians of another day called it 'corruption' – is primarily a matter of our *refusal* to dwell in our minds on right things in the right way.[6] We 'refuse to retain God in our knowledge,' as Paul says (Rom. 1:28).

To illustrate from lesser things, if I do not want to keep a promise or contract, I will choose to dwell on how to avoid keeping it, not on how to keep it. This is an observable fact. And if I dwell on how to keep it, I pretty certainly will keep it, as far as matters truly are in my control.[7] That is how human personality is organized, and how it is organized must always be kept in mind as we train disciples.

The Three Areas of Necessary Intellectual Clarity

There are three main ways in which God comes before the mind, where we can lose ourselves in love of him. These are, of course, also ways in which we may present God to others, as well as ways by which we individually may seek to fill our minds with him. Through them, the lovely God wins the love of the disciple. He comes to us (1) through his creation, (2) through his public acts on the scene of human history, and (3) through individual experiences of him by ourselves and others.[8]

1. 'God the Father Almighty, Maker of Heaven and Earth'

In training ourselves or others for fullness of life in The Kingdom Among Us, the first task is to present our Father, the one in the heavens, as maker and sustainer of everything else, of 'heaven and earth'. From the very beginning of the Judeo-Christian experience, he is understood to be 'God most high' (*El Elyon*), creator and therefore possessor of 'heaven and earth' (Gen. 14:18–19).

The basis for this assurance about God lies in the common understanding or impression that all of 'natural' reality, including you and me, owes its existence and therefore its astonishing order and magnificence to something other than itself. We have no experience of any natural object or event that is self-productive or self-sustaining. Yet we are very familiar with the role of human thought and planning in the production of food, furniture, computers, aeroplanes and so forth. So it is an easy inference for human beings, which they have always drawn, to find a great 'God most high' through all that exists around us.

The famous Greek philosopher Epictetus, a contemporary to Peter and Paul, commented that 'any one thing in the creation is sufficient to demonstrate a providence to a modest and grateful mind.'[9] Paul himself explains that all human beings remain responsible, no matter how far they fall, because of the clear way in which God stands forth in natural reality. 'Since the creation of the world,' he says, 'God's invisible nature is clearly presented to their understanding through what has been made' (Rom. 1:19–20).

In a later passage in Romans (10:18), he comes close to identifying the very 'word of Christ', the gospel, with the word of God that goes out from nature to 'the ends of the earth', according to Psalm 19. Through the ages and up to today, outstanding thinkers have continued to be convinced of the soundness of such thinking.

But though the rational processes involved in seeing the Creator through nature are important – and, I believe, conclusive – they are not all that is involved. It may be that for most people God is more *sensed* through nature than inferred – somewhat as I 'sense' or 'read' your thoughts, feelings and presence when I am around you, but do not *infer* them.

The words of the poet Wordsworth express the situation best for many people:

> And I have felt
> A presence that disturbs me with the joy

Of elevated thoughts; a sense sublime
Of something far more deeply interfused,
Whose dwelling is the light of setting suns,
And the round ocean and the living air,
And the blue sky, and in the mind of man;
A motion and a spirit, that impels
All thinking things, all objects of all thought,
And rolls through all things.[10]

However that may be, the point is that in the training that brings apprentices of Jesus to live on that rock of 'hearing and doing', 'God the Father almighty, maker of heaven and earth' must be made present to their minds in such a way that they can see his magnificent beauty and their love can be strongly and constantly drawn to him. This will make a huge and indispensable contribution to their ability to love him with all their heart, soul, mind and strength.

Our Seeking and Teaching Must Be Thorough and Completely Honest

In the seeking and teaching to be done, we will, of course, open up every term – *God, Father, Maker* – and so on, as carefully and as fully as we can to the disciples. We will use the goldmine of conceptualization in the scriptures for this purpose and the best of human thinking and writing available to us. Of utmost importance, we will take care to do this work in constant interplay with the rest of the education that we have received or are receiving at the time.

We then listen prayerfully to those we teach. We encourage every question, and we make it clear that dealing honestly with the questions that come up is the only path to a robust and healthy faith. We will *never* 'pooh-pooh' difficulties, or take any problem with anything less than utter seriousness, or direct the slightest reproach or shame on anyone for having questions and doubts. When we don't honestly know what to say at the time, we will just say so. We will go away and find an answer through study, conversation and prayer.

After times of study and teaching, we will pay most attention precisely to the puzzles and ambiguities in our own minds and in the minds of our hearers. What makes no sense? What is not understood? These unclarities are more important than questions about evidence or proof, though the latter are not to be slighted. Most but not all uncertainties in the minds of *disciples* – and this is only somewhat less so for people in general – are the result of unclarities and failures to understand. These shut down confidence and love, and we must never rest until they are cleanly dispersed from the mind.

In doing this, we of course are not just counting on our own cleverness and ability but stand in expectation of help from the Spirit of truth who is constantly at work in the disciples of Jesus. We do all we do in the knowledge that we are working alongside him. Moreover, we do this kind of work hand in hand with the cultivation of the mind and spirit through art and imagination, poetry and song, praise, prayer and worship. These all help our minds to lay hold of this God, this most lovable being in all of reality.

Theology Tested by the Love of God

The bane of the more liberal branches of Christian theology today is that they are unable to present a God who could be actually loved. They say a great deal about love – especially in connection with things such as community and respect and liberation – but what comes out in the end is something very like the words of the song, 'Falling in Love with Love.'

What is to be loved is love itself, very often identified with nothing more than a certain sense of community. And then perhaps some words about God being love are tacked on. But what is actually conveyed is that love is *ultimate*. That says something quite different, however, from the New Testament revelation of God in Jesus, which made it clear that the love of God is like no love known among humanity.

Basically, modern attempts to think about God independently of historical revelation have been thoroughly victimized by currents of nineteenth- and twentieth-century philosophy that simply make knowledge of God – and maybe everything else – an impossibility. Indeed, something laughable. This forces one to handle the texts and traditions of Jesus in such a way that he can never bring us to a personal God whom we can love with all our being.

But things often turn out little better for theology on the right. It tends to be satisfied with having the right doctrines or traditions and to stop there without ever moving on to consuming admiration of, delight in, and devotion to the God of the universe. On the one hand, these are treated as not necessary, because we have the right answers; and on the other hand, we are given little, if any, example and teaching concerning how to move on to honest and full-hearted love of God.

The acid test for *any* theology is this: Is the God presented one that can be loved, heart, soul, mind and strength? If the thoughtful, honest answer is 'Not really', then we need to look elsewhere or deeper. It does not really matter how sophisticated intellectually or doctrinally our approach is. If it fails to set a *lovable* God – a radiant, happy, friendly, accessible and totally competent being – before ordinary people, we have gone wrong. We should not keep going in the same direction, but turn around and take another road.

Theologians on both the left and the right, and those on no known scale of comparison, are all loved by God, who has great things in mind for every one of them. They are our neighbours, and we are to share God's vision and love for them. *They* need to love God. The theologian who does not love God is in great danger, and in danger of doing great harm, for he or she needs to know him and believe with assurance concerning him.

Whether or not they stand within the professing community, they are human beings and, like human beings generally, they think about God more than about any other thing. But if they do not understand him rightly, they can have no confidence in him. More often than not, it is not evidence or proof they need. They need someone to make sense of God in relation to what they are sure, rightly or wrongly, they know about themselves and their world. Surely there is reason by now to conclude that this cannot be done except through God's self-disclosures and, I think, through Jesus above all.

Two Harmful Myths

Unfortunately, a number of myths associated with this part of disciple training on behalf of Jesus are now dominant. One is the idea that questions about God as creator have recently been conclusively settled in the negative by the progress of 'scientific knowledge', and that nothing of significance can be known of God from examining the order of nature – or anything else there may be.

One hundred years ago, by contrast, the general assumption was that those questions had been settled in the positive: God was regarded as manifestly present in nature. These positive answers were routinely taught *as knowledge* in schools at all levels, and the few dissenters were heard. No doubt the dissenters often were not treated with dignity.

Now the pattern is almost exactly reversed. But just as the positive answers in earlier times were sometimes based more on readiness to believe than on accurate thinking – though there was really no need for that – so the negative 'answers' that now dominate our culture are mainly based on a socially enforced readiness to disbelieve. And *those* negative answers, which find no God in nature, really do need help from social conditioning.

As I said earlier in a similar connection (Chapter 3), absolutely nothing of substance has changed in the last century or more with regard to the basic issues about God, the world, and the human self.[11] In this type of book we can only state that the reasons for believing God is the Creator, which were good reasons in other years still are good reasons, and in training the apprentices of Jesus we should present them thoroughly and carefully, updating them in any way appropriate.

To understand why the negative prejudice is so strong now, just reflect on how the entire system of human expertise, as represented by our many-tiered structure of certification and accreditation, has a tremendous vested interest in ruling God out of consideration. For, if it cannot do that, it is simply wrong about what it presents as knowledge and reality – of which God is no part. As we noted earlier, God currently forms no part of recognized human competence in any field of knowledge or practice.

But if this actually is God's universe, the current lords of knowledge have made what is surely the greatest mistake in human history. Believing the world is flat or the moon is cheese would be nothing in comparison to their mistake. To believe that the current lords of 'knowledge' are right, on the other hand, is to omit the spiritual God and the spiritual life from the literally real. It is to take them to be illusions; and two or more centuries of 'advanced thinking' have now been devoted to showing that they are illusions. So the battle to identify our universe as God's and our existence as part of his creation simply has to go on. We cannot stand aside. And in training people to 'hear and do', we must take an open, loving, and intelligent stand on these fundamental matters.

The other harmful myth that I should mention here is the idea that one has to be some kind of profoundly technical scholar to deal effectively with questions about God as creator. Certainly we do need technical scholars, and we should treasure them and pray for them. Today they are in short supply among Jesus' people. Perhaps you should become one. But the work of presenting the lovely God through his creation is basic pastoral work, and it is the work of a friend or neighbour. The technical scholars can assist, but the work required can be done by any teacher who will simply decide to do it, follow the material where it leads (that is, devote the necessary time to study), and rely upon the co-operation of the Trinitarian God who is being presented.

But what we must never forget, in moving towards the faith 'on the rock', is that our 'doing' comes – or fails to come – from what our beliefs actually are. Hence, if we would train people to do 'all things', we must change their beliefs. Only so can we change their loves. You cannot change character or behaviour and leave beliefs intact. It is one of the major illusions of Western culture, deriving from a form of Christianity that is merely cultural, that you can do this. We cannot work around that illusion, but must dispel it.

Just as we must change the beliefs of individuals for them to become disciples in the first place, so we must further change their beliefs if they are to develop as disciples into that fullness and abundance of kingdom life that has obedience as a by-product. And to help disciples towards intelligent assurance that this universe really is God's world is to advance them greatly towards 'loving the Lord their God with all their heart, soul, mind and strength' (Mark 12:30).

Jesus, in stating that as the primary, or 'first', commandment, understood that if such love were in place all else of importance would follow, including 'hearing and doing'. And that is why hearty and clear-headed love of God must be the first objective in any curriculum for Christlikeness. That objective is substantially gained when God is clearly and constantly present to the mind as our 'faithful Creator' (1 Pet. 4:19).

2. The God of Jesus and His People

Although knowledge of God through his creation is fundamental to our love for him, it is not enough and was never meant to be. It does not begin to make clear the extent to which God loves, and loves human beings in particular. It cannot make clear, to humans as they are, the 'Father heart' of God towards us. But the 'faithful Creator' does not leave himself to be a topic of speculation. His love reaches out. From the very beginning of the biblical revelation, human beings are blessed by God personally and engaged by God in a face-to-face relationship renewed by periodic visits (Gen. 1:27–31; 2:7–3:8).

This is such a striking arrangement that it poses a puzzle to the biblical writers about their own nature. 'Compared to the cosmos, what are human beings,' the psalmist cries, 'that you pay attention to them? Or human offspring that you care about them? You created them a little less than supernatural beings. But you let glory and majesty rest on them! You cause them to rule over the works of your hands and put everything on earth under their feet!' (Ps. 8:4–8).

Even when they turn their back on the Father and put themselves on the cosmic throne, he continues to visit human beings and makes every possible provision for their salvation. Apparently even the angels don't understand this (1 Pet. 1:12). It seems that through the ages they will be constantly admonished and instructed concerning the nature of God by the eternal presence of the redeemed community of human beings among them (Eph. 2:7; 3:10). And God not only interacts with every individual human being (John 1:9; Acts 10:30–31; 14:17; Rom. 1:14–15), but also establishes a *public* presence in human history through a covenant people in which he is tangibly manifest to everyone on earth who wants to find him.

The magnificent prayer in Neh. 9:5–38 expresses how creation and covenant come together in the historical tradition of a redeemed and redemptive people. The occasion is one of corporate confession of a disastrous failure to keep the covenant, and of renewal before the gracious God who does not give up on us. The first part of the prayer is the 'address', which we studied in Chapter 7. The two crucial elements stated in the address are, precisely, creation and covenant:

CREATION. 'You alone are the Lord. You made the heavens and the highest heaven, with all their angelic hosts. You made the earth and all on it, the seas and all in them. You give life to all, and the hosts of the heavens adore you' (vv. 5–6).

COVENANT. 'You are the covenanting God, who selected Abram and led him out of Ur of the Chaldees, and gave him the covenant name "Abraham", meaning "father of multitudes"' (v. 7).

This name change was made because in Abram now 'all the peoples of the earth shall be blessed' (Gen. 12:3). Abraham and the tradition of faith that comes down from him through the ages was to be *the publicly appointed place in history* where the nature of God's Father heart was to be accessible to all.

Of course, the people that later came to follow Jesus, a child of Abraham – claimed by Paul to be the seed of Abraham – understood themselves to be the continuation and fulfilment of the covenant with Abraham. Thus they understood themselves to be parties to a 'New Covenant', a 'New Testament'. The first chapters of the New Testament book of Acts portray how they understood the transition and continuation of the covenant through Jesus, and their prayers reflect the same creation-covenant combination as we saw in Nehemiah 9.

Thus in Acts 4 the apostles and others with them, under severe threat from the authorities, respond by 'lifting up their voices to God and saying: "O Lord, it is you who made the heaven and the earth and the sea and all in them"' (v. 24). Then they quote the great Old Covenant king David, and an association is established between him and 'your holy servant Jesus' (vv. 25–30). God then responds to the new covenant people by shaking the place where they are gathered and filling them with the holy spirit to 'speak the word of God with boldness' (v. 31).

'Knowledge of the Glory of God in the Face of Christ'

Accordingly, we bring the heart-wrenching goodness of God, his incomprehensible graciousness and generosity, before the mind of disciples by helping them to see and understand the person of Jesus. On a wearying, dreadful night, Jesus was saying a lot of things that were confusing and upsetting those in his little circle of friends. Philip blurted out, 'You talk about the Father all the time. Just show us the Father and that will satisfy us' (John 14:8). Jesus patiently replied, 'Haven't you yet understood who I am, Philip? Whoever has seen me has seen the Father' (v. 9). No doubt Philip and the others experienced this as just too good to be true. Could the character of God really be that of Jesus? The stunning answer is, 'Yes indeed.'

The key, then, to loving God is to *see Jesus*, to hold him before the mind with as much fullness and clarity as possible. It is to adore him. For purposes of training disciples, we should divide this into four main aspects.

First, we teach his beauty, truth, and power while he lived among us as one human being among others. The content of the Gospels should be explained and brought to life in such a way that the Gospels become a permanent presence and possession of the mind of the disciple.

Second, we teach the way he went to execution as a common criminal among other criminals on our behalf. We don't have to understand exactly how it works. Anyone who thinks he or she does fully understand what theology calls the atonement undoubtedly has some surprises coming. Nowhere, I think, is theological arrogance more commonly displayed than on this subject. But the *fact* is something we must always have before our minds. That is the good reason to wear or display a cross. For all the false and misleading associations that may surround it, it still says – even without the knowledge of the one displaying it – 'I am bought by the sufferings and death of Jesus and I belong to God. The divine conspiracy of which I am a part stands over human history in the form of a cross.'

The individual disciples must have indelibly imprinted upon their souls the reality of this wonderful person who walked among us and suffered a cruel death to enable each of us to have life in God. It should become something that is never beyond the margins of their consciousness. 'God,' Paul said, 'makes clear the greatness of his love for us through the fact that Christ died for us while we were still rebelling against him' (Rom. 5:8).

The exclusiveness of the Christian revelation of God lies here. No one can have an adequate view of the heart and purposes of the God of the universe who does not understand that he permitted his son to die on the cross to reach out to all people, even people who hated him. That is who God is. But that is not just a 'right answer' to a theological question. It is God looking at me from the cross with compassion and providing for me, with never-failing readiness to take my hand to walk on through life from wherever I may find myself at the time.

Paul's sense of the meaning of the death of the Son for the individual is spelled out in ecstatic detail in Rom. 8:31–39:

> God is for us! Who is against us? Since he did not spare his own Son in reaching us, he obviously is ready to give us every good thing. Who will charge us with anything? God has cleared us of all his charges. Who condemns us? Jesus died for us. Yes, and he passed through death intact, and now stands in the place from which God acts, looking after our interests. Of all the terrible and frightening things the human mind discovers, not one can take us out of his loving hands. We don't just 'manage' or cope. We *thrive* on it all! Nothing shall be able to separate us from the love of God which is in Jesus the Anointed, our Lord.

With this radiant passage before us, the last two aspects of Jesus' person to be imprinted on the disciple's soul in training are already in view.

Third, we teach the reality of Jesus risen, his actual existence now as a person who is present among his people. We present him in his *ecclesia*, his motley but glorious crew of called-out ones. We trace him from those uncomprehending encounters on the first Easter morning and on through the amazingly different historical periods of the church. But we also show him now active among his disciples. Who he is, is revealed in an essential way in his people.

So the *continuing* incarnation of the divine Son in his gathered people must fill our minds if we are to love him and his Father adequately and thus live on the rock of hearing and doing. And to see how he has been and is lived with and loved and served and presented and celebrated by all kinds of people across time and space adds to the force of our love for him.

But fourth, we teach the Jesus who is the master of the created universe and of human history. He is the one in control of all the atoms, particles, quarks, 'strings' and so forth upon which the physical cosmos depends.

Human beings have long aspired to control the ultimate foundations of ordinary reality. We have made a little progress, and there remains an unwavering sense that this is the direction of our destiny. That is the theological meaning of the scientific and technological enterprise. It has always presented itself as the instrument for solving human problems, though without its theological context it becomes idolatrous and goes mad.

But this Jesus is master of it all through his word. Satan in tempting him claimed to be in possession of all the kingdoms of the earth. But he was lying, as is his nature. Lies are his only hope. It is Jesus himself who is king of the kings of the earth, and who for good purposes allows Satan and evil to have some influence on humanity for a little while. And it is he, as the *Logos*, who maintains and manipulates the ultimate laws of the physical universe.

Thoroughly presented in all these ways, the love of Jesus for us, and the magnificence of his person, brings the disciple to adore Jesus. His love and loveliness fills our lives. An older Franciscan brother said to Brennan Manning on the day he joined the order, 'Once you come to know the love of Jesus Christ, nothing else in the world will seem as beautiful or desirable.'[12]

Jesus himself knew that this was the key. The keeping of his commandments was the true sign of love for him, because that love is what made it possible and actual. In this love of Jesus everything comes together: 'If anyone loves me, my word he will keep, and my Father will love him, and we will move in with him and live there' (John 14:23).

3. God's Hand Seen Through the Events of the Disciple's Life

The third area of teaching required to bring disciples to the place where they love the Lord with all their heart, soul, mind, and strength concerns the goodness of their own existence and of the life made theirs through their natural birth and the following course of life.

God, as our 'faithful Creator' and as presented 'in the face of Jesus Christ', is lovely and magnificent. But he will remain something to be admired and even worshiped at a distance if that is all we know of him. In order for disciples to be brought into a full and joyous love of God, they must see their very own life within the framework of unqualified goodness. Perhaps 'see' is too strong a word, though it is certainly what we should hope for. But they must at least be sure in their heart of hearts that their life *must* be a good thing. And those who teach disciples to 'do all things' must aim to help them to this assurance.

Saint Clare, won in her youth to a life of complete devotion to Jesus by Saint Francis of Assisi, had these for her last words: 'Lord God, blessed be thou for having created me!' This should be the daily breath of a disciple of Jesus.

Just previously, as she lay near death, Brother Rainaldo had exhorted her to bear her infirmities with patience. She replied, 'Dearest brother, ever since I have known the grace of my Lord Jesus Christ through his servant Francis, no suffering has troubled me, no penance has been hard, no sickness too arduous.'

Then, before her last words, she was heard to murmur to her soul, 'Depart in peace, for thou wilt have a good escort on the journey. Go forth confidently to Him who has protected thee and loved thee as a mother loves her child.'[13]

We will never have the easy, unhesitating love of God that makes obedience to Jesus our natural response unless we are absolutely sure that *it is good for us to be, and to be who we are*. This means we must have no doubt that the path appointed for us by when and where and to whom we were born is good, and that nothing irredeemable has happened to us or can happen to us on our way to our destiny in God's full world.

Any doubt on this point gives force to the soul-numbing idea that God's commandments are, after all, only for his benefit and enjoyment, and that in the final analysis we must look out for ourselves. When the 'moral failures' of well-known Christians (and unknown Christians, for that matter) are examined, they always turn out to be based on the idea that God has required them to serve in such a way that they themselves must 'take care of their own needs' rather than being richly provided for by God. Resentment towards God, not love, is the outcome, and from such a condition it is impossible to consistently do the deeds of love.

A beautiful illustration of the faith and love to be developed in the disciple is provided by the Old Testament figure Joseph. His story is found in Genesis 37–50. Out of a sense of blessedness that was with him from childhood, he remained completely faithful to God. Attacked and sold into slavery by his envious brothers (37:18–36), then buried and forgotten for years in prison on false charges deriving precisely from his moral rectitude (39:7–23), he remained sure of the goodness of his own life before God. Later on, after becoming the governor of all of Egypt, he could say to his brothers concerning their betrayal of him, 'You intended to do evil to me, but God meant for it to achieve good' (Gen. 50:20).

It is confidence in the invariably overriding intention of God for our good, with respect to all the evil and suffering that may befall us on life's journey, that secures us in peace and joy. We must be sure of that intention if we are to be free and able, like Joseph, to simply do what we know to be right.

Honouring Father and Mother: A Vital Need

Most of our doubts about the goodness of our life concern very specific matters: our parents and family, our body, our marriage and children (or lack thereof), our opportunities in life, our work and calling (which are not the same thing) and our job.

At the heart of our own identity lies our family, and our parents in particular. We cannot be thankful for who we are unless we can be thankful for them. Not, certainly, for all the things they have done, for they may have been quite horrible. And in many cases we must come to have pity on them before we can be thankful for them. Nevertheless, the fifth of the Ten Commandments says, 'Honour your father and your mother,' and then adds, 'that you may enjoy a long life in the land the Lord your God gives to you' (Exod. 20:12). And Paul notes that this is 'the first commandment with a promise attached to it' (Eph. 6:2).

The promise is rooted in the realities of the human soul. A long and healthy existence requires that we be grateful to God for who we are, and we cannot be thankful for who we are without being thankful for our parents, through whom our life came. They are a part of our identity, and to reject and be angry with them is to reject and be angry with ourselves. To reject ourselves leads to sickness, dissolution and death, spiritual and physical. We cannot reject ourselves and love God.

When the breach in the human soul that is self-rejection remains unhealed, the individual, and thereby society, is open to all kinds of terrible evils. This is where the Hitlers come from. And for every Hitler who rises to power, there are millions who consume themselves and die in quiet corners of the earth. The final words of the Old Testament address this profound problem. Speaking of an 'Elijah' to come, they state that 'he will turn the heart of the fathers to the children and the heart of the children to their fathers, lest I come and smite the land with a curse' (Mal. 4:6). This 'turning of hearts' is the deep human need that the Promise Keepers movement and other individuals and groups are trying to address in our time.

Thus, in training disciples to 'hear and do' the words of their master, a major point will often be to help them honour their parents. This is not something that can be bypassed. In some cases it may be easy, and in a few cases it will be unnecessary because it will already have been done. But these cases will be very few indeed, especially in contemporary society.

The training in question has clearly discernible stages. First, the individual disciples must be honest about who and what their parents really are and how they truly feel about them. Then they must confess the wrongs of attitude and act they have done their parents and ask for forgiveness. Then they must accept their parents for who and what they are, have mercy on them and forgive them.

All of this will require careful advice and much prayer and perhaps intense personal presence by the teacher on occasion. The assistance of specially trained counsellors may be required. It will take a lengthy period of time in some cases, and the child must take care not to get caught in old damaging patterns of interaction with the parent: for example, trying to make the parent understand, or trying to have the 'last word', or proving he or she was right. Such matters must be simply surrendered to God for him to work out as he will.

Similar teaching, training and guidance must be given with reference to the other aspects of the disciples' lives: body, love and sexuality, marriage and children, success with work and jobs. The object in each case is to enable the disciple to be thankful for who they are and what they have. And much the same progression will be required: from honesty to acceptance to compassion and forgiveness and then on to thankfulness to God and the honouring of our lives in all of the aspects indicated. And when this training has been completed, Paul's words will make perfect sense: 'Always giving thanks for all things on behalf of our Lord Jesus Christ to God, even the Father' (Eph. 5:20). And again: 'I have learned how to be content whatever the circumstances ... I can do all things in him who gives me strength' (Phil. 4:11, 13).

It is being included in the eternal life of God that heals all wounds and allows us to stop demanding satisfaction. What really matters, of a personal nature, once it is clear that *you are included*? You have been *chosen*. *God* chooses you. This is the message of the kingdom.

Paul says to the Corinthians, fighting among themselves over who is right or best in this and that regard, 'All things belong to you, whether Paul or Apollos or Cephas or the world or life or death or things present or things to come; all things belong to you, and you belong to Christ; and Christ belongs to God' (1 Cor. 3:21–23 NAS).

Jesus, of course, taught the same thing about the personal plenitude of every one of his people (Mark 10:30). And a very touching passage occurs in the writings of Isaiah the prophet on this point. In his day, non-Israelites were always 'on the outside looking in', as we say. And likewise eunuchs, who could never have a family of their own. But God says to them, 'I will give them a place forever in my house, and a name better than sons and daughters; a name that will stand forever' (Isa. 56:2–5).

It is noteworthy that when Job finally stood before God he was completely satisfied and at rest, though not a single one of his questions about his sufferings had been answered. His questions were good questions. He did not sin in asking them. But in the light of God himself they were simply pointless. They just drop away and lose their interest.

Let us now be perfectly clear. Your life is not something from which you can stand aside and consider what it would have been like had you had a different one. There is no 'you' apart from your actual life. You are not separate from your life, and in that life you must find the goodness of God. Otherwise, you will not believe that he has done well by you, and you will not truly be at peace with him.

You must find the goodness of God and the fellowship of Jesus in who you are, or your love for the Father and his unique Son cannot become the foundation for a life of abundance/obedience. They desire to dwell with you in your life and make glorious every aspect of it in the light of the whole that God has planned (John 14).

Today many will say that this simply does not do justice to the bitter facts of life. What of victims of sexual abuse or of dreadful diseases, birth defects, war and other terrible things? But if we have suffered terribly, we must choose not to let that be our life focus. We must, if we can, focus on God, God's world, and ourselves as included in it with a glorious destiny of our own. And when we cannot, we should seek out those who bring or can help us find the power of the kingdom to do so. Gratitude then focuses forward on redemption, and on the future that is given to us in God's future, come what may. In the light of that, we return to receive, to even welcome, our life as it actually has been and is.

Acquiring the Habits of Goodness

Breaking Bondage to the 'Sin in Our Body'

We have spoken of bringing the disciple to behold the loveliness of God in himself, in the face of his incarnate Son, and in his personal appointment and care of our individual existence. This is a process that must go hand in hand with the *second main objective* in a curriculum for Christlikeness. That, as we have said, is the breaking of the power of patterns of wrongdoing and evil that govern our lives because of our long habituation to a world alienated from God. We must learn to recognize these habitual patterns for what they are and escape from their grasp.[14]

Frankly, there are many people who believe that this simply cannot be done. In Rom. 7:14–25, Paul gives a description of persons who are torn between their conscience and their inability to do what they know to be right. He identifies 'indwelling sin' (v. 17) as a power in my body and its members to act for what is wrong without regard to my conscious intentions and desires (vv. 20–24). Evil takes on a life of its own when it inhabits my body in its social setting. It is not unlike how the AIDS virus lives and grows through the cells of the body. What Paul is describing is a reality. But this passage is mistakenly regarded by many as Paul's personal statement of what his own life was like all the time.

However, Paul's life after meeting and growing in Christ was totally different from this, as his writings and the remainder of the New Testament record makes clear. The entire assumption of the very passage (Rom. 6–8) on which this misinterpretation is based also shows that.

It is assumed by Paul that 'sin will not govern in our physical bodies to make us do what it wants, and that we will not go on giving our bodily parts to sin as tools of unrighteousness, but give ourselves to God as those whose physical bodies have already died, and our bodily parts to God as tools of righteousness' (6:12–13).

The problem currently is that we have little idea – and less still of contemporary models – of what this looks like. Consumer Christianity is now the norm. The consumer Christian is one who uses the grace of God for forgiveness and the services of the church for special occasions, but does not give his or her life and innermost thoughts, feelings and intentions over to the kingdom of the heavens. Such Christians are not inwardly transformed and not committed to it.

Because this is so, they remain not just 'imperfect', for all of us remain imperfect, but routinely and seriously unable and unwilling to do the good they know to do, as Paul so accurately describes.

They remain *governed* by, or 'slaves' of (John 8:34; Rom. 6:16), sin. For example, their lives are dominated by fear, greed, impatience, egotism, bodily desires and the like, and they continue to make provision for them. It is this condition that the curriculum for Christlikeness must aim to abolish, in a very intelligent and businesslike manner.

What the 'Sin in Our Members' Is

To make a good beginning we must have it very clearly fixed in our minds that what dominates the individual in the course of 'normal human existence' is not some invincible, overpowering cosmic force. It is not, as older theologians used to say, a metaphysical necessity we are under, but a personal or 'moral' form of constraint.[15] And if we think we are facing an irresistible cosmic force of evil, it will invariably lead to giving in and giving up – usually with very little resistance. If you can convince yourself that you are helpless, you can then stop struggling and just 'let it happen.' That will seem a great relief – for a while. You can once more be a normal human being. But then you will have to deal with the consequences. And for normal human beings those are very severe.

Now, in fact, the patterns of wrongdoing that govern human life outside the kingdom are usually quite weak, even ridiculous. They are simply *our habits*, our largely automatic responses of thought, feeling, and action. Typically, we have acted wrongly before reflecting. And it is this that gives bad habits their power. For the most part they are, as Paul knew, actual characteristics of our bodies and our social context, essential parts of any human self. They do not, by and large, bother to run through our conscious mind or deliberative will, and often run exactly contrary to them. It is rare that what we do wrong is the result of careful deliberation.

Instead, our routine behaviour manages to keep the deliberative will and the conscious mind off balance and on the defensive. That leaves us constantly in the position of having to deal with what we have *already* done. And the general 'pattern of wrongdoing' that takes over in that case is to defend what we have already done by doing further wrong: by denying, misleading and rationalizing – or even killing someone, as King David did.

Therefore it is primarily in the body and its social context that the work must be done to replace wrong habits with automatic responses that flow with the kingdom of Jesus and sustain themselves from its power. Certainly there must first come the profound inward turnings of repentance and faith. But the replacement of habits remains absolutely essential to anyone who is to 'hear and do' and thus build his or her house on the rock. Without it, direct efforts in the moment of action to do what is right will seldom succeed.

A Matter of What Is 'in' Us

This point that bodily habits are the primary form in which human evil exists in practical life is absolutely essential for an understanding of the curriculum required, so we must emphasize it.[16] We will never be able to deal with that evil as long as we take it, in the popular manner, to be external to the self (Satan, the 'world') or something other than precisely the humdrum routines we accept as our habits.

James writes of those who, rather than standing firm under testing, blame their temptations on God. Of course, they were paving the way to 'letting it happen'. But James points out that being tempted to do what is wrong is not a matter of God, it is a matter of one's inner condition, of one's obsessive desires (*epithumias*). Without these, even God cannot tempt anyone. But when one receives and harbours them, one is 'pregnant with evil, gives birth to sin and the consequence is death or separation from God' (1:12–15).

The responses we make to our context without thinking are simply an expression of what our body 'knows' to do. Of course, in most situations this is good. It is what our body is for. There is almost nothing we do as adult human beings that does not depend on our body's 'knowledge' taking over. Speaking, work in the kitchen and driving about in our community are things we have to think very little about as we do them. Unfortunately this remains true when what our body 'knows to do' is wrong.

One of the most instructive sayings of Jesus occurs when he is leaving his last meeting with his closest students before his crucifixion. He explains to them that he is now going to be engaged in a spiritual battle that will leave him no time to talk with them. Now the 'ruler of the world' is going to be permitted to try him as strongly as possible, tempting him in every way to show faithlessness towards his Father.

The struggle in the Garden of Gethsemane was a matter of Jesus' mind and feelings being hammered in every possible way to make him mistrust the Father. He almost died of it on the spot. But, Jesus added to this friends, '*in me* this "ruler" has not the least thing on his side' (John 14:30). It was, finally, what was *not* in Jesus that made him invincible, that kept him safe.

This is the true situation: nothing has power to tempt me or move me to wrong action that I have not *given* power by what I permit to be in me. And the most spiritually dangerous things in me are the little habits of thought, feeling and action that I regard as 'normal' because 'everyone is like that' and it is 'only human'.

Our training and experience must bring us to peace with the fact that if we do not follow our habitual desires, do not do what 'normal' people would do, it is no major thing. We won't die, even though at the beginning our outraged habits will 'tell us' we are sure to. The sun will come up and life will go on: better than we ever dreamed.

Rightly understood, the 'death to self' of which scripture and tradition speak is simply the acceptance of this fact. It is the 'cross' applied to daily existence. And it is a major part of what disciples must learn in order to break the grip of the 'motions of sin in their members' that drive them.

Patterns of anger, scorn and 'looking to lust' vividly illustrate the basic triviality of the drive to wrongdoing. 'The look' is only a habit. There is nothing deep or vital about it. One looks to lust or to covet upon certain cues. Anyone who bothers to reflect on his or her experience will be able to identify what those cues are.

This is also true of anger, scorn, and – you name it. It's not like the law of gravity. Falling when you step off a platform is not a habit. Cultivated lusting, anger and so on are. And, generally speaking, those who say they 'cannot help it' are either not well informed about life or have not decided to do without 'it'. Most likely the latter.

But the really good news here is that the power of habit can be broken. Habits can be changed. And God will help us to change them – though he will not do it for us – because he has a vital interest in who we become. If, for example, you have decided not to let anger or lusting govern you, you can train yourself (and certainly you can do so given the help of experienced disciple trainers) to use the very 'cues' that until now have served to activate habits of anger and lusting to activate thoughts, feelings and actions that will rule them out. Multitudes have found this to be so.

This is exactly the general arrangement that is used in the Twelve-Step programme already discussed, and, of course, Alcoholics Anonymous did not discover or invent it. It is a 'law', if you wish, of human personality. But even the A.A. programme will be powerless to help anyone who has not decided to avoid drinking and stay alive. As always, the intention points the way, and then habituated thought and desire must be redirected to support the intention in the moments of action.

The Training Will Not Be Done for Us

There has emerged here a truth that is fundamental for our curriculum for Christlikeness. The training required to transform our most basic habits of thought, feeling and action will not be done for us. And yet it is something that we cannot do by ourselves. Life in all its forms must reach out to what is beyond it to achieve fulfilment, and so also the spiritual life.

The familiar words of Jesus are 'Without me you can do nothing' (John 15:5). But these must be balanced by the insight that, in general, if we do nothing it will certainly be without him.

Obviously, the effects of training in any area cannot be transferred into us from another person, and rarely, if ever, will it be *injected* by divine grace. Another person cannot learn Spanish for me, nor can someone else lift weights to improve my muscles. And our deepest moral character also is not something that can be developed by anything that is done for us or to us. Others can help us in certain ways, but we must act. We must act wisely and consistently over a long period of time.

Still, we cannot 'put off the old person and put on the new' on our own. The transition and transformation are the result of several factors at work along with our inward or outward efforts. This is made clear in the magnificent passage in Philippians 2, where Paul is explaining the 'mind' or inmost character of Jesus and calling us to have the same 'mind'.

The mind or attitude in question is that of the loving servant to the good of others. This is the kingdom life. Jesus abandoned himself to the status of a voluntary slave, to the point of even dying for others. In so doing he achieved the highest possible unification of the life of God and the life of man. He is the Maestro, the Lord and that will be acknowledged throughout the cosmos, by everyone, at the appropriate time (Phil. 2:11).

Now, Paul continues, we have received the life of the kingdom through the word of the gospel and the person of Jesus. That life we have as a gift. But once we have it, there is something for us to do, for, as noted earlier, the person we become cannot be the effect of what someone else does.

Therefore we are to 'work out' the salvation we have (2:12). The word here, *katergazesthe*, has the sense of developing or elaborating something, bringing it to the fullness of what in its nature it is meant to be.

But we do not do this as if the new life were simply *our* project. It isn't. God also is at work in us, 'choosing and acting on behalf of his intentions' (v. 13). Hence we do what we do – and what will not be done *for* us – 'with fear and trembling' because we know who else is involved.

The Threefold Dynamic

The 'Golden Triangle' of Spiritual Growth

A picture of the factors involved in the transformation of our concretely embodied selves from inside (the 'mind') out (behaviour) can be conveyed by what I call 'the golden triangle of spiritual growth'. This image is designed to suggest the correlation in practical life of the factors that can certainly lead to the transformation of the inner self into Christlikeness. The intervention of the Holy Spirit is placed at the apex of the triangle to indicate its primacy in the entire process. The trials of daily life and our activities specially planned for transformation are placed at the bottom to indicate that where the transformation is actually carried out is in our real life, where we dwell with God and our neighbours. And at the level of real life, the role of what is imposed upon us ('trials') goes hand in hand with our choices as to what we will do with ourselves.

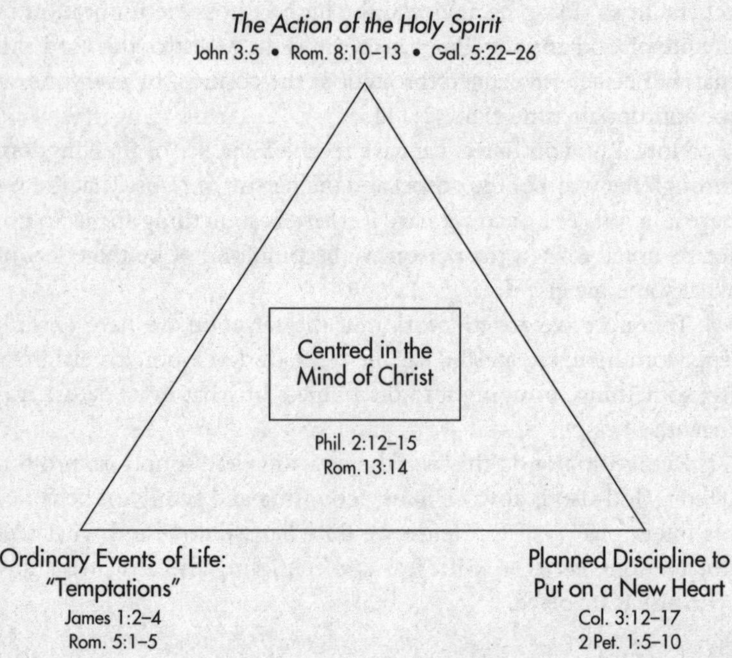

The function of the Holy Spirit is, first, to move within our souls, and especially our minds, to present the person of Jesus and the reality of his kingdom. This is through the word of the gospel, in contrast to the realities of life without God. Our confidence in Jesus as the One is always a response elicited and supported by the spiritual movements of God. Thus, as Paul says, 'No one can find Jesus to be Lord except by the Holy Spirit' (1 Cor. 12:2).

After we receive the new life, the Spirit continues to move upon and within us to enable us to do the kinds of works Jesus did (through 'gifts' of the Spirit) and to grow the kind of inward character that manifests itself in the 'fruit' or outcome of the Spirit in our outward life: love, joy, peace, long-suffering and similar traits of Christ (Gal. 2:23–25).

The importance of the work of the Holy Spirit cannot be overemphasized. But today our practice in Christian circles is, in general, to place almost total emphasis on the apex of this triangle, the work of the Spirit of God for or on the individual. This takes various forms, depending on the history and outlook of the individual or group.

Very commonly church participation is recommended on the basis of how it will change our lives, because God will be there and we will be just overwhelmed. And certainly there is an important truth to this. Public manifestations of God, 'revivals' if you wish, have made a great difference in many lives, mine included. Emphasis may also be laid upon the gifts of the Spirit, the fruit of the Spirit, the baptism or filling of the Spirit, or the anointing by the Spirit – all very important.

But reliance upon what the Spirit does *to* us or in us, as indispensable as it truly is, will not by itself transform character in its depths. The action of the Spirit must be accompanied by our response, which, as we have seen, cannot be carried out by anyone other than ourselves. This active participation on our part has two aspects, represented by the bottom angles in the triangle.

The Indispensable Role of Ordinary Events: 'Tests'

First we must accept the circumstances we constantly find ourselves in as the place of God's kingdom and blessing. God has yet to bless anyone except where they actually are, and if we faithlessly discard situation after situation, moment after moment, as not being 'right', we will simply have no place to receive his kingdom into our life. For those situations and moments *are* our life.

Our life presents itself to us as a series of tasks. Our more serious challenges are *trials*, even *tribulations*. In biblical language they are all 'temptations.' Just listen to how people carry on! For some of us the first tribulation of the day is just getting up. And then there is caring for ourselves. Then the commute. Then work and other people. But knowledge of the kingdom puts us in position to welcome all of these, because, as we have already seen, we are in a position to thrive on everything life can throw at us – including getting up in the morning! Whatever comes will only confirm the goodness and greatness of the God who has welcomed us into his world.

Thus James, the brother of Jesus, opens his letter to believers with words that truly announce the gospel of the kingdom:

> Regard it as a most joyous occasion when the various kinds of trials hit you. For you know that when your confidence in God is put to practical tests it results in the ability to stay with things – patience. And when your capacity to stay with things is fully developed you will be complete and whole, lacking in nothing. (1:2–4)

What an astonishing statement! We immediately recognize that in order to carry through with the challenges of daily life in this way we must be deeply engaged in the other two points of the triangle: we must have the constant movement of the Spirit of God accompanying us, and we must incorporate substantial 'spiritual disciplines' in our overall life plan. In fact, all three points of the triangle are absolutely essential – to one another as well as to the overall goal of spiritual growth. None will work on its own.

Paul says something similar to James in the opening of Chapter 5 of Romans. He begins with the hopefulness that is ours because of the grace, faith and peace that come to us in God's gift. Then he makes exactly James's point: 'We rejoice [*kauxometha*: 'exult,' even 'boast'] in afflictions. For we know that afflictions bring the capacity to stay with things, or patience, to its fullest form. And patience proves that the hope was right. And the hope does not let us down, for the very best happens to us, love floods our hearts through the presence of the Spirit given to us' (Rom. 5:1–5).

So it is absolutely essential to our growth into the 'mind' of Jesus that we accept the 'trials' of ordinary existence as the place where we are to experience and find the reign of God-with-us as actual reality. We are not to try to get in a position to avoid trials. And we are not to 'catastrophize' and declare the 'end of the world' when things happen. We are to see every event as an occasion in which the competence and faithfulness of God will be confirmed to us. Thus do we know the concrete reality of the kingdom of the heavens.

But few disciples will be able directly to respond to their ordinary 'trials' in this way, any more than they will be able directly to do 'all things whatsoever'. They will have to adopt certain practices that put them in position to respond appropriately. The practices in question are the disciplines that fall at the lower-right angle of the golden triangle of spiritual growth.

We Are Not Told Precisely How to Develop Kingdom Habits

Not only is the outcome of our progression in the kingdom not under our control, but we are not told in any systematic way how to do our part in the process. Well, at least we are not told in precise terms – certainly not in formulas. This is because the process is to be a walk with a person. But it is also because what is needed is very much an individual matter, a response to the particular needs of individual disciples. Perfectly general instructions simply cannot be given. That is why we do not find them in the Bible. Its 'wisdom' books, especially Psalms and Proverbs, come as close as possible.

The assumption of the way of Jesus is that we will, once we have decided to 'hear and do,' do *whatever* is required to carry out the decision. The precise details of this process will be modelled and picked up by the devoted individual from the group, from redemptive history, and from the good sense of humankind. And that is exactly what we see when we look at the history of Jesus' people.

Paul's letter to the Colossians is perhaps the best overall statement on the spiritual formation of the disciple in the New Testament. I suspect this is because it was written to people whom Paul had never met and had never had the opportunity to teach. So he gives them a well-rounded presentation of exactly what we have been talking about in this chapter.

Chapters 1 and 2 correspond quite closely to the first primary objective of a curriculum for Christlikeness as presented earlier. Chapters 3 and 4 correspond precisely to the second primary objective.

After summarizing the practical implications of the first two chapters in Col. 3:1–4, Paul moves immediately to the second primary objective in verse 5: 'Kill off the aspects of your life that run on what is earthly.' Given how his readers, and we as well, have been formed in the 'earthly', these aspects are precisely 'fornication, dirt, rage, evil desire – and covetousness, which amounts to idolatry'. You don't have to look deeply to see that this list covers the same ground as Matthew 5.

'Get rid of rage, anger, hateful intentions, God-dishonouring and bullying language. Don't mislead people in any way,' Paul continues (Col. 3:8–9). Then he shifts from acts and attitudes to the deeper level of *character*. 'You have,' he says, 'put off the old person with her habits, and put on the new person being progressively renovated to the point of fully sharing the mind of her creator' (vv. 9–10).

As those involved in this process, we are to 'put on the inner substance heart of fellow-feeling, kindness, humility, gentleness and patience, putting up with one another and forgiving each other. If you have a gripe against anyone, just forgive them, like the Lord forgave you' (vv. 12–13). Note that all this is emphatically expressed as *what we are to do*.

And Yet Everyone Knows

Nevertheless, Paul doesn't tell the Colossians *how* to do this. In other letters by him, however, we read things like 'Imitate me in exactly the way that I imitate Christ' (1 Cor. 11:1). Or: 'Put into practice what you learned and received and heard and saw in me, and the God of peace will be with you' (Phil. 4:9). What we must understand is that these words indicate not a marginal, personal oddity, but a pervasive core practice. Everyone understood it.

And, of course, it is Jesus above all who *shows* us how to live in the kingdom. Genuine apostolic succession is a matter of being with him, learning to be like him, along with all those faithful ones who have gone before us. Jesus is the ultimate object of imitation, as Paul's words to the Corinthians just quoted indicate. But then come those directly after Jesus who imitate him. And so it goes on down through the ages. The history of the people of God is an exhaustible treasure that draws its substance from the person of Jesus alive then, alive now, alive always, in himself and in others.

We do not just hear what Jesus *said* to do and try to do that. Rather, we also notice what he *did*, and we do that too. We notice, for example, that he spent extended times in solitude and silence, and we enter solitude and silence with him. We note what a thorough student of the scriptures he was, and we follow him, the Living Word, into the depths of the written word. We notice how he used worship and prayer, how he served those around him, and so forth. We have Bibles with red letters to indicate what he said. Might we not make a good use of a Bible that has green letters for what he *did*? Green for 'go', or 'do it'?

Being a man of the scriptures, Jesus understood that it is the care of the soul or, better, the care of the whole person, that must be our objective if we are to function as God designed us to function. This is the wisdom of the entire scriptural tradition. 'Put everything you have into the care of your heart,' the book of Proverbs says, 'for it determines what your life amounts to' (4:23). 'You will keep those in the peace of peace,' Isaiah says, 'whose minds are fixed on you, because they trust in you' (26:3). The blessed person is one who 'meditates in the law day and night' (Ps. 1:2; Josh. 1:8).

Paul tells his young protégé in the ministry, Timothy, to 'become a pattern for the believers, in speech, behaviour, love, faith and purity,' and to cultivate the gift deposited in him at his ordination. He calls him to 'pay attention to yourself and to the teachings, continuing in them.' For in that way Timothy will 'save both himself and the ones hearing him' (1 Tim. 4:12–16).

If we are to succeed in 'putting off the old person and putting on the new', then, or in having the mind or inner character of our Lord, we must follow an order of life as a whole that is appropriately modelled after his. This should be, and has been, something that is practised by his people and taught by them to those who enter their ranks. It would be a plan that incorporates *whatever* is necessary to enable us to have the character and then do the deeds indicated in the teachings of Jesus and his immediate followers. For simplicity's sake we could just say 'the character and deeds indicated in Colossians 3.' Our plan for a life of growth in the life of the kingdom of God must be structured around disciplines for the spiritual life.

Planned Disciplines to Put on New Heart

What Spiritual Disciplines Are

But exactly what are these 'spiritual disciplines'? What is it about a practice that makes it a spiritual discipline? Well, they are, first of all, *disciplines*. A discipline is any activity within our power that we engage in to enable us to do what we cannot do by direct effort.[17]

'Practising' can be a discipline, as in singing, playing a musical instrument, hitting golf balls or enunciating French words and phrases in the French way. Practice is discipline, but not all discipline is practice, for in many disciplines we do not engage in the very activity that we hope to be good at.

In our culture, for example, which proceeds at such a frenetic pace, simple sleep and rest may be disciplines in the sense just described. They will, as we have said, enable us to do what we cannot do by direct effort, including staying in good emotional and physical health, and possibly being loving and sensitive to our family and fellow workers. But usually when we rest we would not be practising resting – though, in the current world, that too may sometimes be needed, for some people actually cannot even rest by simply doing it.

But spiritual disciplines are also *spiritual* disciplines. That is, they are disciplines designed to help us be active and effective in the spiritual realm of our own heart, now spiritually alive by grace, in relation to God and his kingdom. They are designed to help us withdraw from total dependence on the merely human or natural (and in that precise sense to mortify the 'flesh', kill it off, let it die) and to depend also on the ultimate reality, which is God and his kingdom.

Thus, for example, I fast from food to know that there is another food that sustains me. I memorize and meditate on scripture that the order of God's kingdom would become the order and power of my mind and my life.

Centrality of Our Bodies

Somewhat ironically, perhaps, *all* of the 'spiritual' disciplines are, or essentially involve, bodily behaviours. But really, that makes perfect sense. For the body is the first field of energy beyond our thoughts that we have direction over, and all else we influence is due to our power over it. Moreover, it is the chief repository of the wrong habits that we must set aside, as well as the place where new habits are to be instituted. We are, within limits, able to command it to do things that will transform our habits – especially the inner habits of thought and feeling – and so enable us to do things not now in our power.

The deeds of the kingdom arise naturally out of a certain quality of life. We cultivate that life in its wholeness by directing our bodies into activities that empower the inner and outer person for God and through God.

In this second part of the curriculum for Christlikeness, then, the main task is, by engaging in ways of using the body differently, to disrupt and conquer habits of thought, feeling and action that govern our lives as if we or someone other than God were God and as if his kingdom were irrelevant or inaccessible to us. Once this is done – or, more accurately, hand in hand with doing it – we shift to the positive. Appropriate disciplines for developing *new* habits, kingdom habits, are practised. The ultimate effect of this part of the curriculum is to make our body a reliable ally and resource for the spiritual life.

From the stage of early discipleship, where 'the spirit is willing but the flesh is weak', we increasingly pass to the stages where the flesh – think of that as what we more or less automatically feel, think and do – is with the spirit and supportive of its deepest intentions. This is absolutely essential in training that will bring us to do from the heart the things that Jesus knew to be best.

Modelled upon Jesus Himself

A further help in understanding what spiritual disciplines are for the disciples of Jesus is to recognize them as simply a matter of following him into his own practices, appropriately modified to suit our own condition. We find our way into a life where the power of inward hindrances to obedience/abundance are broken by observing what Jesus and others who have followed him do and learning to structure our lives around those same activities. Thus, although we are indeed not told in formulaic terms what to do in order to build our life upon the rock, everyone who knows anything about Jesus' life really does know what to do to that end, or can easily find out. It is not a secret.

So, basically, to put off the old person and put on the new we only follow Jesus into the activities that he engaged in to nurture his own life in relation to the Father. Of course, his calling and mission was out of all proportion to ours, and he never had our weaknesses, which result from our long training in sin. But his use of solitude, silence, study of scripture, prayer and service to others all had a disciplinary aspect in his life. And we can be very sure that what he found useful for conduct of his life in the Father will also be useful for us. It was an important day in my life when at last I understood that if *he* needed forty days in the wilderness at one point, I very likely could use three or four.

This crucial point carries on down through the ages during which his people have been on earth. The ones who have made great spiritual progress all seriously engaged with a fairly standard list of disciplines for the spiritual life. There has been abuse and misunderstanding, no doubt, but the power of solitude, silence, meditative study, prayer, sacrificial giving, service and so forth *as disciplines* are simply beyond question. This is a field of knowledge, and we remain ignorant of it to our great disadvantage.

However, the disciplines do not confirm their value to those who only talk about them or study them 'academically' or hear others talk about them. One has to enter them with Jesus as teacher to find the incredible power they have to change one's world and character. They are self-confirming when entered in faith and humility. And you don't really need much of faith and humility if you will just stay with them. They will do the rest because they open us to the kingdom.

This is an extension of Jesus' emphasis on doing as a way of knowing the kingdom. We will be able to do what he says to do as we are inwardly transformed by following him into his life practices of solitude, service, study and so forth. This is an essential part of what Paul calls 'offering our bodies as living sacrifices' (Rom. 12:2). It will result in the mark of the disciplined person, who is able to do what needs to be done when and as it needs to be done.

Doing the Same Thing Differently

Sometimes entering spiritual disciplines is not so much a matter of doing something we have not done before as of doing it in a different way.

I began to work my way into the practice of disciplines for the spiritual life without knowing that that was what I was doing. I still remember vividly the first time I spent the better part of a day just reading and rereading the Gospel of John. It was in my second year of college. I do not recall why I did it, exactly, but I do know it was not a course assignment. I believe that it was a holiday weekend, and the campus was largely deserted. That, it turns out, is a key point.

I began by reading the Gospel while machines washed my clothes. But that was done in a hour or two, and by that time I found myself engrossed and drawn into the radiant world of John's account. I had never experienced anything like it before.

I did nothing for the rest of the day but live there in that world: reading, meditating, cross-referencing and rereading. Truthfully, my world never looked quite the same after that day. I discovered a reality in Jesus and the people and events surrounding him that I had never known before. I was not exactly 'transformed,' I think. Perhaps we use that word far too easily and often. Certain 'besetting sins' were still not eliminated. But there was a new thing at work in me. And I had learned something about how we do change – and how we do not.

In particular, I had learned that *intensity* is crucial for any progress in spiritual perception and understanding. To dribble a few verses or chapters of scripture on oneself through the week, in church or out, will not reorder one's mind and spirit – just as one drop of water every five minutes will not get you a shower, no matter how long you keep it up. You need a lot of water at once and for a sufficiently long time. Similarly for the written Word.

A year or so later I learned a related lesson with regard to prayer. In the tradition in which I was brought up, scripture reading and prayer were the two main religious things one might do, in addition to attending services of the church. But I was not given to understand that these had to be practised in a certain way if they were to make a real difference in one's life.

In particular I did not understand the intensity with which they must be done, nor that the appropriate intensity required that they be engaged in for lengthy periods of undistracted time on a single occasion. Moreover, one's life as a whole had to be arranged in such a way that this would be possible. One must not be agitated, hurried, or exhausted when the time of prayer and study came. Hence one cannot tack an effective, life-transforming practice of prayer and study on to 'life as usual'. Life as usual must go. It will be replaced by something far better.

Without my planning it or intending it, my life as a student made it possible for me to have lengthy periods to myself in an appropriate condition of soul and body. There were rooms on the third floor of a nearby building where small children met for classes in Sunday school. These rooms were filled with little chairs and tables for children, which for obvious reasons no one else could use. But I could go into those rooms Monday through Saturday and be totally alone for hour after hour. I needed no chairs. The floor alone was quite adequate for my business. And there I learned what extensive and intensive praying does for one's soul, as well as for the subjects of such prayer.

Some Specific Disciplines in the Curriculum

With these clarifications of the general nature of spiritual disciplines in mind, what are some of the specific practices that are of most use in the development of disciples? Here we need not be concerned about a complete list of such practices, and indeed there really is no such thing anyway.[18] That makes it all the more important that we understand the general concept just explained. What is clear and, for our purposes, essential is that a small number of them are absolutely central to spiritual growth. They must form a part of the foundation of our whole-life plan for growth as apprentices of Jesus.

These are, on the side of abstinence, solitude and silence and, on the side of positive engagement, study and worship.

TWO DISCIPLINES OF ABSTINENCE: SOLITUDE AND SILENCE. By solitude we mean being out of human contact, being alone, and being so for lengthy periods of time. To get out of human contact is not something that can be done in a short while, for that contact lingers long after it is, in one sense, over..

Silence is a natural part of solitude and is its essential completion. Most noise is human contact. Silence means to escape from sounds, noises, other than the gentle ones of nature. But it also means not talking, and the effects of not talking on our soul are different from those of simple quietness. Both dimensions of silence are crucial for the breaking of old habits and the formation of Christ's character in us.

Now why, precisely, are these disciplines of abstinence so central to the curriculum for Christlikeness? Remember that the second primary objective of the curriculum is to break the power of our ready responses to do the opposite of what Jesus teaches: for example, scorn, anger, verbal manipulation, payback, silent collusion in the wrongdoing of others around us and so forth.

These responses mainly exist at what we might call the 'epidermal' level of the self, the first point of contact with the world around us. They are almost totally 'automatic', given the usual stimuli. The very language we use is laden with them, and, of course, they are the 'buttons' by which the human surroundings more or less control us. They are not 'deep'; they are just there, and just constant.

They are the area where most of our life is lived. And in action they have the power to draw our whole being into the deepest of injuries and wrongs.

Now it is solitude and silence that allow us to escape the patterns of epidermal responses, with their consequences. They provide space to come to terms with these responses and to replace them, with God's help, by different immediate responses that are suitable to the kingdom environment – and, indeed, to the kind of life everyone in saner moments recognizes to be good. They break the pell-mell rush through life and create a kind of inner space that permits people to become aware of what they are doing and what they are *about* to do.

We hear the cries from our strife-torn streets: 'Give peace a chance!' and 'Can't we all just get along?' But you cannot give peace a chance if that is *all* you give a chance. You have to do the things that make peace possible and actual. When you listen to people talk about peace, you soon realize in most cases that they are unwilling to deal with the conditions of society and soul that make strife inevitable. They want to keep them and still have peace, but it is peace on their terms, which is impossible.

And we can't all *just* get along. Rather, we have to become the kinds of persons who can get along. As a major part of this, our epidermal responses have to be changed in such a way that the fire and the fight doesn't start almost immediately when we are 'rubbed up the wrong way'. Solitude and silence give us a place to begin the necessary changes, though they are not a place to stop.

They also give us some space to reform our inmost attitudes towards people and events. They take the world off our shoulders for a time and interrupt our habit of constantly managing things, of being in control, or thinking we are. One of the greatest of spiritual attainments is the capacity to do nothing. Thus the Christian philosopher Pascal insightfully remarks, 'I have discovered that all the unhappiness of men arises from one single fact, that they are unable to stay quietly in their own room.'[19]

This idea of doing nothing proves to be absolutely terrifying to most people I speak with. But at least the person who is capable of doing nothing might be capable of refraining from doing the wrong thing. And then perhaps he or she would be better able to do the right thing.

And doing nothing has many other advantages. It may be a great blessing to others around us, who often hardly have a chance while we are in action. And possibly the gentle Father in the heavens would draw nigh if we would just be quiet and rest a bit. Generally speaking, he will not compete for our attention, and as long as we are 'in charge' he is liable to keep a certain distance.

Every person should have regular periods in life when he or she has nothing to do. Periods of solitude and silence are excellent practices for helping us learn how to do that. The law that God has given for our benefit as well as his tells us that one-seventh of our time should be devoted to doing nothing – no work, not by ourselves or any of our family, employees or animals. That includes, of course, religious work. It is to be Sabbath.

What do you do in solitude or silence? Well, as far as things to 'get done', nothing at all. As long as you are doing 'things to get done', you have not broken human contact. So don't go into solitude and silence with a list. Can we enjoy things in solitude and silence? Yes, but don't try to. Just be there.

Even lay down your ideas as to what solitude and silence are supposed to accomplish in your spiritual growth. You will discover incredibly good things. One is that you have a soul. Another, that God is near and the universe brimming with goodness. Another, that others aren't as bad as you often think. But don't try to discover these, or you won't. You'll just be busy and find more of your own business.

The cure for too-much-to-do is solitude and silence, for there you find you are safely more than what you do. And the cure for loneliness is solitude and silence, for there you discover in how many ways you are never alone.

When you go into solitude and silence, you need to be relatively comfortable. Don't be a hero in this or in any spiritual discipline. You will need rest. Sleep until you wake up truly refreshed. And you will need to stay there long enough for the inner being to become different. Muddy water becomes clear if you only let it be still for a while.

You will know this finding of soul and God is happening by an increased sense of who you are and a lessening of the feeling that you *have* to do this, that and the other thing that befalls your lot in life. That harassing, hovering feeling of 'have to' largely comes from the vacuum in your soul, where you ought to be at home with your Father in his kingdom. As the vacuum is rightly filled, you will increasingly know that you do not have to do those things – not even those you want to do.

Liberation from your own desires is one of the greatest gifts of solitude and silence. When this all begins to happen, you will know you are arriving where you ought to be. Old bondages to wrong-doing will begin to drop off as you see them for what they are. And the possibility of really loving people will dawn upon you.

Soon you may even come to know what it is like to live by grace rather than just talk about it.

These are some of the fruits of solitude and silence. The apprentice will have to learn *how* to do this, of course. For most of us, wise and loving practical arrangements must be made with those around us. And we should encourage and help family members and fellow workers to enter spiritual disciplines themselves.

Obviously the effects of these disciplines will greatly benefit our first primary objective, to love God with a full heart. For the usual distractions of life greatly hinder our attention to God, and the habit of thinking about everything else is almost impossible to break in the bustle of life. Time away can help. People often complain that they cannot pray because their thoughts wander. Those thoughts are simply doing what they usually do. The grip of the usual is what must be broken. Appropriate solitude and silence are sure to do it.

TWO DISCIPLINES OF POSITIVE ENGAGEMENT: STUDY AND WORSHIP. We have already spoken of how our first area of freedom concerns where we will place our mind. Until solitude and silence have had their effects, our minds will very likely continue to be focused on the wrong things or on good things in an anxious attitude of trying to dominate them. But as we, though relocating our bodies into solitude, escape and change the inputs that have constantly controlled our thoughts and feelings, we will have additional freedom to place our minds fully upon the kingdom and its peace and strength.

This, in turn, will transform our emotional state, and thereby the very condition of our body. Most of those around us will sense that and begin to act differently themselves. The social context will change for the better, and what we have to respond to will be much more in the spirit of the kingdom. I have observed this on many occasions.

Once solitude has done its work, the key to this progression is study. It is in study that we place our minds fully upon God and his kingdom. And study is brought to its natural completion in the worship of God.

When I study anything I take its order and nature into my thoughts, and even into my feelings and actions. At one time I did not know the alphabet, for example. But then I studied it. I brought it before my mind, with the help of my teacher, and related my body to it in ways well known to all. Before very long the order that is in the alphabet was in my mind and body. From there, that order enabled me to reproduce, recognize and use the alphabet and its parts. The order that I took into myself by study gave me power to do many good things that I could not do until, by study, it had become mine.

What we learn about study from this simple example is true in all areas, from the most theoretical to the most practical. It is also true when we study what is evil. Then we take on an order and powers of evil – or they take us. But, thankfully, most of what we naturally come to study is good. A student of plumbing or singing, for example, takes into his or her mind certain orders by purposely dwelling upon the relevant subject matter and activities in appropriate ways. That is how study works. And, of course, it always enables individuals 'to do what they cannot do by direct effort.'

Now disciples of Jesus are people who want to take into their being the order of The Kingdom Among Us. They wish to live their life in it as Jesus himself would, and that requires internalization of that order. Study is the chief way in which they do it. They devote their attention, their thoughtful inquiry, and their practical experimentation to the order of the kingdom as seen in Jesus, in the written word of scripture, in others who walk in the way, and, indeed, in every good thing in nature, history, and culture.

Thus Paul's practical advice to his friends at Philippi: 'Whatever things are true, serious, right, pure, lovable, well regarded, any virtue and anything admirable, *let your mind dwell on them*. What you have learned, received, heard and seen in me, do that. And the God of peace will be with you' (Phil. 4:8–9). For all such is of God and his reign.

Of course, in all our study as and with disciples, the person of Jesus is the centre of attention. But he is not really separable, for us, from the written revelatory word, including the law, the prophets, the history and the wisdom of the Old Testament. One who would train disciples 'to hear and do' will direct them to all these, still centred on the person of Jesus.

The Twenty-third Psalm, for example, is an exquisite summary of life in the kingdom. The mind of the disciple should have it prominently displayed within, to always foster the joy and peace of the kingdom as well as to orient all of his or her actions within it. The Ten Commandments, the Lord's Prayer, the Sermon on the Mount, Romans 8, Colossians 3, Philippians 2–4, and a few other passages of scripture should be frequently meditated on in depth, and much of them memorized. This is an essential part of any curriculum for Christlikeness. Positive engagement with these scriptures will bring kingdom order into our entire personality.

I know many people who profess serious allegiance to Jesus and claim him as their Saviour but who, unfortunately, simply will not take these scriptures into their soul and body and utilize them as indicated. The result, I have to say with sadness, is that they continue to recycle their failures and make little or no real progress towards the abundance/obedience we have been discussing in this chapter. Some of them even try to use other spiritual disciplines, but with little result. An essential ingredient is missing, and the order of their mind and life remains other than that of the kingdom.

Study is by no means simply a matter of gathering information to have on hand. Intensive internalization of the kingdom order through study of the written word and learning from the Living Word establishes good epidermal responses of thought, feeling and action. And these in turn integrate us into the flow of God's eternal reign. We really come to think and believe differently, and that changes everything else.

Now we must not worship without study, for ignorant worship is of limited value and can be very dangerous. We may develop 'a zeal for God, but not according to knowledge' (Rom. 10:2–21) and do great harm to ourselves and others. But worship must be added to study to complete the renewal of our mind through a willing absorption in the radiant person who is worthy of all praise. Study without worship is also dangerous, and the people of Jesus constantly suffer from its effects, especially in academic settings. To handle the things of God without worship is always to falsify them.

In worship we are ascribing greatness, goodness and glory to God. It is typical of worship that we put every possible aspect of our being into it, all of our sensuous, conceptual, active and creative capacities.

We embellish, elaborate and magnify. Poetry and song, colour and texture, food and incense, dance and procession are all used to exalt God. And sometimes it is in the quiet absorption of thought, the electric passion of encounter, or total surrender of the will. In worship we strive for adequate expression of God's greatness. But only for a moment, if ever, do we achieve what seems like adequacy. We cannot do justice to God or his Son or his kingdom or his goodness to us.

Worship nevertheless imprints on our whole being the reality that we study. The effect is a radical disruption of the powers of evil in us and around us. Often an enduring and substantial change is brought about. And the renewal of worship keeps the glow and power of our true homeland an active agent in all parts of our being. To 'hear and do' in the atmosphere of worship is the clearest, most obvious and natural thing imaginable.

Now we have briefly touched upon four specific spiritual disciplines – solitude and silence, worship and study – around which a curriculum for Christlikeness should be framed. It must be clear how strongly they will nourish and be nourished by the first principle objective of such a curriculum, that of bringing the disciple of Jesus to love God with heart, soul, mind and strength. Other disciplines, such as fasting, service to others, fellowship and so on, might be discussed as well, and, indeed, in a full treatment of a curriculum for Christlikeness they must be discussed. But if these four are pursued with intelligence and prayer, whatever else is needed will certainly come along.

The important insight to guide us at this point is that to build our house upon the rock, putting off the old person and putting on the new, we must have a definite plan for doing so. That plan must incorporate all of the factors designated in the 'golden triangle' and be pursued on the assumption that our life as a whole will be very different, in content and organization, from lives of those not living in the kingdom. It will include major components – not just a dash and a dribble here and there – of the four disciplines discussed and of others as suitable. They are not to be undertaken as deeds of righteousness, for they are not. But they are wise counsels on how to live with Jesus in his kingdom. Each of us must face the question What is *my* plan for doing that?'

Practical Steps for Attaining the Two Curricular Objectives

An Illustration of Training-to-Do

In addition to implementing whatever is necessary to achieve the two primary objectives of the curriculum – enthralling the mind with God and breaking the power of the evil in our bodies – individual disciples will, at least in some cases, require individualized direction and help to deal with particular teachings of Jesus. For example, suppose you are someone who is struggling with the command to lay aside anger or to stop being contemptuous of others.

The key in such cases is to aim at the heart and its transformation. We want to 'make the tree good'. We do not aim just to control behaviour, but to change the inner castle of the soul, that God may be worshiped 'in spirit and in truth' and right behaviour cease to be a *performance*.

We want to become the kind of person who is not dominated by anger and who truly loves and respects others. And we want to assist others in that transition. This means, of course, that the teaching cannot be captured by rules: for example, 'Never say someone is a fool', 'Always give in', 'Never go to court' and so forth. You could follow such rules and still be filled with anger, or not follow them on appropriate occasions and be completely filled with love.

It is crucial to understand that this point applies to all of Jesus' teachings.

If we miss this point, we cannot help but fall into the worst kind of dead legalism. We can be sure that trying to follow' Jesus teachings will then ruin our lives. We have all experienced so much well-intentioned meanness in our lives, by those who felt 'responsible' and wanted us to be responsible, that Jesus, as the best-intended, will be experienced as the meanest in his 'laws'. The root of true Christlikeness will then be destroyed.

Anger and contempt towards others is only removed by the vision and experience of God being over all, ensuring that all is well with me and that others are his treasures. I no longer need to engage in the violence of name-calling, for I do not need to 'put others down' in order for me to be 'up'. I no longer need to secure myself in life, for I am secure.

Moreover, the *shock* of being dealt with in love and fairness and mercy will certainly change the behaviour of others. 'When your ways please the Lord, he causes your enemies to be at peace with you' (Prov. 16:7).

To teach the 'commandment' here, we explain (repeatedly) all of this in the context of the gospel of the kingdom, deal with any problems of understanding, and walk individual disciples through cases, helping them to experience and believe in the goodness of the rightness in Jesus' command. We give assignments relative to their tendencies to be angry or scornful. We ask them to keep a journal and report back on how things went – for a day or a week, for example – and we give further teaching and practical suggestions as needed. No doubt some of this direction will concern appropriate use of selected spiritual disciplines.

Another 'commandment' is to not 'bully' others into acceptance of our wishes and views by 'swearing': verbally invoking various things of value (from heaven to our head) in support of our beliefs and projects. This command is about the 'song and dance' or 'emphasis' we see daily in use.

The underlying teaching here is that we should respect others before God and allow them to make their judgements on the basis of our simple statements that things are this way or are not this way. We are not to attempt to drive, to control them, to manipulate them. (Matt. 7:1–7 is a companion teaching, involving not *emphasis* but our brilliant judgements as to who and what is right or wrong and why.)

To teach the 'commandment' here, we help people understand what is really going on when we are 'swearing', show them its lovelessness and how it hurts others, and teach them how to leave others in the hands of God through prayer and our own example.

Also, we will take them through the individualized practical measures previously indicated. We will walk them through their own real-life cases where verbal manipulation tempts, helping them to experience and believe in the goodness of the rightness of Jesus' command and to discover the practical measures they can take to become the kind of person who naturally obeys it.

The Pattern, or General Form, of the Teaching

Doing all this establishes a pattern of teaching, which can then be filled in in individualized ways by every 'scribe discipled unto the kingdom of the heavens' (Matt 13:52). It is in this precise way that we will successfully teach others 'to observe to do all things whatsoever I have commanded you.' The *pattern* can be applied to all cases, for example, the spirit of non-retaliation ('other cheek'), blessing for cursing (Jesus' 'method' in 1 Pet. 3:23), going the second mile, or living without intentional lusting and so on.

The pattern has two main elements:

1. Clearly positioning the context before the heavenly Father's present rule through Jesus
2. Walking the individual through actual cases in their own lives to give them experienced-based understanding and assurance

This pattern can also be applied to middle-level commandments, such as 'Let not your heart be troubled' (John 14:1), 'If you love me, keep my commandments' (14:15), and 'abide in me' (15:4). But in these cases, because they are less specific and cannot be obeyed by direct effort, the 'how-to' instructions will have to do with more general arrangements of our lives. And these more general arrangements are almost totally a matter of engagement in appropriate disciplines for the spiritual life.

The disciplines are practices that change the inner self and its relationship to the 'helper' (paraclete), so that we actually can do what we would and avoid what we would not. They of course have no point apart from the serious intent to obey Christ's teaching and follow his example.

Overview of Progress from Here to Forever

Five Dimensions or Stages of the Eternal Kind of Life

The situation of the disciple, or student, of Jesus is, we should expect, one of change and growth, in which we progress from one stage or dimension of our life in God to another. Within a few years, apparently, it is possible to move from the level of mere blindly obedient servant or 'slave' of Jesus to that of friend.

In his 'commencement address' (John 14–16) to his first apprentices, he once again gives them the all-inclusive commandment 'that you love one another just as I have loved you' (John 15:12). After clarifying that this includes 'laying down our life for our friends', and not least for Jesus himself, he makes the following observation: 'You are my friends if you keep this commandment.'

This is a very distinct and important change of status, a promotion, if you wish, based upon the progress of the apprentices. 'I no longer call you slaves [*doulous*],' he continues, 'for the slave does not know what their Lord is about. But you have become my friends because under my teaching you now have learned all that I heard from the Father' (15:15).

Of course, that does not mean we no longer serve Jesus. He remains our Master, and a favourite term of New Testament writers for themselves is 'slave of Jesus Christ'. But it is now on a different basis, a basis of loving co-operation, of *shared* endeavour, in which his aims are our aims and our understanding and harmony with his kingdom are essential to what he does with and through us.

We should be aware of, roughly, five dimensions of our eternal kind of life in The Kingdom Among Us, and these dimensions more or less arrange themselves in the following progression:

1. *Confidence in and reliance upon Jesus* as 'the Son of man,' the one appointed to save us. Relevant scriptural passages here are John 3:15; Rom. 10:9–10; and 1 Cor. 12:3. This confidence is a reality, and it is itself a true manifestation of the 'life from above', not of normal human capacities. It is, as Heb. 11:1 says, 'the proof of things not seen'. Anyone who truly has this confidence can be completely assured that they are 'included'.
2. But this confidence in the person of Jesus naturally leads to a *desire to be his apprentice* in living in and from the kingdom of God. Only a sustained historical process involving many confusions and false motivations could lead to our current situation, in which faith in Jesus is thought to have no natural connection with discipleship to him. Our apprenticeship to him means that we live within his word, that is, put his teachings into practice (John 8:31). And this progressively integrates our entire existence into the glorious world of eternal living. We become 'free indeed' (John 8:36).
3. The abundance of life realized through apprenticeship to Jesus, 'continuing in his word', naturally leads to obedience.

The teaching we have received and our experience of living with it brings us to love Jesus and the Father with our whole being: heart, soul, mind and (bodily) strength. And so we love to obey him, even where we do not yet understand or, really, 'like' what that requires. 'If you love me,' Jesus said, 'you will keep my commandments' (John 14:15). And: 'He who has my commandments and keeps them, he it is who loves me; and he who loves me shall be loved by my father, and I will love him, and will disclose myself to him' (v. 21). Love of Jesus sustains us through the course of discipline and training that makes obedience possible. Without that love, we will not stay to learn.

4. Obedience, with the life of discipline it requires, both leads to and, then, issues from the *pervasive inner transformation of the heart and soul*. The abiding condition of the disciple becomes one of 'love, joy, peace, long-suffering [patience], kindness, goodness, faith to the brim, meekness and self-control' (Gal. 5:22; compare 2 Pet. 1:2–11). And the love is genuine to our deepest core. These are called the 'fruit of the spirit' because they are not direct effects of our efforts but are brought about in us as we admire and emulate Jesus and do whatever is necessary to learn how to obey him.
5. Finally, there is *power to work the works of the kingdom*. One of the most shocking statements Jesus ever made, and once again it was in his 'commencement address', was that 'those who rely on me shall do the works I do, and even greater ones' (John 14:12). Perhaps we feel baffled and incompetent before this statement. But let us keep in mind that the world we live in desperately needs such works to be done. They would not be just for show or to impress ourselves or others. But, frankly, even a moderate-size 'work' is more than most people's life could sustain. One good public answer to our prayer might be enough to lock some of us into weeks of spiritual superiority. Great power requires great character if it is to be a blessing and not a curse, and that character is something we only grow towards.

> Yet it is God's intent that in his kingdom we should have as much power as we can bear for good. Indeed, his ultimate objective in the development of human character is to empower us to do what we want. And when we are fully developed in the likeness of Jesus, fully have 'the mind of Christ', that is what will happen – to his great joy and relief, no doubt.

Looking back over this progression, one of the most important things for us to see and accept is that, once confidence in Jesus lives in us, we must be intelligently active in stages or dimensions 2 to 5. We do this by unrelenting study under Jesus, and in particular by following him into his practices and adapting them to form an effective framework of spiritual disciplines around which our whole life can be structured. This is precisely how *we* 'through the spirit do mortify the life of the flesh' (Rom. 8:13) and 'put off the old person and put on the new' (Col. 3:9–10, etc.). Though we cannot do it by ourselves, it is nevertheless something that we do. Each of us must ask ourselves *how* are we doing it. What, precisely, is our plan? And as teachers of disciples, we must lead everyone we teach into developing his or her own plan.

The Curriculum and the Life of the Church

Such a Curriculum for Christlikeness Is Nothing New

From the perspective of contemporary Christian practice, many people will see this proposal for a curriculum for Christlikeness as radical and new. Radical it is, especially viewed against a background of all-pervasive consumer Christianity. But it is anything but new.

We have already commented on Paul's letter to the Colossians as a model of the very curriculum we are here explaining. Much the same is to be said of his other writings, especially the letter to the Ephesians and, to a lesser degree, the ones to the Philippians and the Galatians – though these are less systematic, because of his personal relationship to their situation and to specific concerns he had in mind with them.

But in order to appreciate this, you cannot read them with the 'consumer Christian' mentality, for then the ultimate objective will be seen as presenting the 'right answers' and combating the 'wrong answers' so that people will be sure to be ready to pass the test and be doctrinally correct. Of course the 'answers' are tremendously important, right and wrong. Let this be clearly understood. But they are only important in relation to life in the kingdom with Jesus now. And *that* is what Paul writes about, as do the other biblical writers.

If you keep this clearly in mind, you will then find the two primary objectives for a curriculum for Christlikeness everywhere you look in the biblical sources. And, indeed, the writings of scripture will take on an entirely new character and significance for you. None of them has in mind to sponsor or assist the position of the consumer, or 'bar-code', Christian that so pervasively occupies the contemporary Western world.

But to be fair, consumer Christianity actually emerges quite early in the history of the church. One sees the seeds of it in the New Testament writings, and it becomes prominent through the development of the monastic tradition, which distinguished those who gave their whole lives to God – 'the religious', they are sometimes called – from the supposedly lower-grade Christians who ran farms and businesses, raised families and participated in government and general cultural affairs.

Thus some of the most profound treatments of discipleship to Jesus, such as *The Rule of Saint Benedict, The Imitation of Christ*, and *The Spiritual Exercises of Saint Ignatius*, presuppose a special class of Christians for whom they are not written. But if you simply lay that assumption aside and make necessary adjustments to the content of such works, you will see that they offer, in substance, precisely what we have been discussing in this chapter: a curriculum, a course of training, for life on the rock. And that is why, century after century, they have exercised incredible power over all who open themselves to them as disciples of Jesus.

And if you look at the founding persons, events and literature of the great segments of Protestantism, you will discover much the same thing. We refer, of course, to traditions such as the Lutheran, Reformed (Calvin), Puritan, Mennonite, Friends (Quaker), Methodist and so forth. If you examine landmark works such as Calvin's *Institutes* or John Wesley's standard two-volume set of *Sermons*, you will discover nothing new in what I have said here about a curriculum for Christ-likeness, except possibly some points of organization. And certainly what I have said remains much more shallow, both theologically and practically, than these masterworks of the spiritual life. (One of the greatest hopes I have for the readers of this book is that they turn back to these true treasures of the people of Jesus.)

But if you look at what is generally accepted and done in contemporary versions of these great Protestant traditions, what I have said here will, once again, seem both radical and new – possibly outright crazy. (Who would think of putting it into actual practice in the normal congregational setting?) If so, I at least have the consolation of some wonderful company.

Book III of John Calvin's *Institutes of the Christian Religion*, for example, is a treatment of the Christian Life. In Chapter VII of Book III, he sums up the Christian Life in one phrase, 'self-denial'. Not self-esteem, certainly, nor personal fulfilment. The presentation of obedience and discipline made here by me is quite tepid compared with what Calvin has to say in that and his following chapters. But his interpretation of faith in Christ is the same as what I have said here about faith. Read it and see. A similar point is to be made with reference to the other traditions mentioned, without exception, though in other respects they retain their defining peculiarities.

It is one of the defects of an age with no true sense of its past to suppose that what is now is what has always been, and that anything else is either novel or wrong or both. But the only way forward for the people of Jesus today is to reclaim for today the time-tested practices by which disciples through the ages have learned to 'hear and do', to build their life upon the rock. Those practices are not mysteries. They are just unknown.

Some Practical Points About Implementation – Especially for Pastors

In order to implement something like a curriculum for Christlikeness in the context of a local assembly of believers, it will usually be vital to just *do* certain things and not talk a lot about them – at least until some time later.

If we are leading such a group, we must, first, be sure that the curriculum outlined is in fact the substance of our own life. Do we, or are we obviously learning to, love the Lord with all our heart, soul, mind and strength?

Second, we should prayerfully observe those we serve and live with to see who among them has already been 'ravished with the kingdom of God' and is ready to become Jesus' apprentice. These we help to consciously do so, and we then can devote serious time to leading them into and through the curriculum, adapting it as needed.

It may at first not be possible to carry this on as a congregational project, though one should not be furtive about it. We can pour ourselves into a few people without fanfare, and soon they can begin sharing the work of forming other disciples. You can count on it to spread, for, in truth, there is nothing on earth to compare it to.

Finally, we should speak, teach, and – if that is our place – preach the gospel of the kingdom of the heavens in its fullness. Practically, that means that in our various communications we focus on the Gospels and on teaching what Jesus himself taught in the manner he taught it. This, with intelligent prayer and loving deed, is our method for 'ravishing people with the kingdom of God', and thus preparing them for the step into out-and-out apprenticeship.

Once again, we do not need to talk a lot about what we are doing. In time it will be obvious. And we certainly are never to be judgemental of Christians who are, honestly, not yet disciples. In most cases they never will have had a serious opportunity to become apprentices of Jesus. But for the most part they will quite certainly respond well to the word of the kingdom and the call to discipleship when it is clearly presented to them.

We must, of course, settle it in our minds that there will always be difficulties in the local setting when one becomes serious about discipleship to Jesus and an associated curriculum. But God is always there for those who serve him, no matter what; and we can 'count it all joy' – really – and expect the manifest grace of God to be active in our midst.

Although I have not been a pastor for many years, I have always continued to teach quite regularly in churches and churchlike settings. The appeal and power of Jesus' call to the kingdom and discipleship is great, and people generally, of every type and background, will respond favourably if that call is only presented with directness, generosity of spirit, intelligence and love, trusting God alone for the outcome.

We may not soon have bigger crowds around us – and in fact they may for a while even get smaller – but we will soon have bigger Christians for sure. This is what I call 'church growth for those who hate it'. And bigger crowds are sure to follow, for the simple reason that human beings desperately need what we bring to them, the word and reality of The Kingdom Among Us.

Chapter 10

THE RESTORATION OF ALL THINGS

'Then the prophecies of the old songs have turned out to be true, after a fashion!' said Bilbo.

'Of course!' said Gandalf. 'And why should not they prove true? Surely you don't disbelieve the prophecies, because you had a hand in bringing them about yourself?

'You don't really suppose, do you, that all your adventures and escapes were managed by mere luck, just for your sole benefit? You are a very fine person, Mr Baggins, and I am very fond of you; but you are only quite a little fellow in a wide world after all!'

J. R. R. TOLKIEN, THE HOBBIT

And they shall live with His face in view, and that they belong to Him will show on their faces. Darkness will no longer be. They will have no need of lamps or sunlight because God the Lord will be radiant in their midst. And they will reign through the ages of ages.

REV. 22:4–5

Why We Must See a Future

Those who have apprenticed themselves to Jesus learn an undying life with a future as good and as large as God himself. The experiences we have of this life as his co-conspirators now fill us with anticipation of a future so full of beauty and goodness we can hardly imagine.

'When Christ, who is our life, shall appear,' Paul says, 'then you too will be revealed with him as glorious' (Col. 3:4). And, 'How great a love the Father has lavished upon us,' John exclaims, 'that we should be described as children of God! But it has not yet been shown what we shall be. We only know that when he appears we shall be as he is' (1 John 3:1–2). Reverting to Paul, 'He will transform our lowly body to be like his glory body, using the power he has over everything' (Phil. 3:20).

To live strongly and creatively in the kingdom of the heavens, we need to have firmly fixed in our minds what our future is to be like. We want to live fully in the kingdom now, and for that purpose our future must make sense to us. It must be something we can now plan or make decisions in terms of, with clarity and joyful anticipation. In this way our future can be incorporated into our life now and our life now can be incorporated into our future.

I meet many faithful Christians who, in spite of their faith, are deeply disappointed in how their lives have turned out. Sometimes it is simply a matter of how they experience ageing, which they take to mean they no longer have a future. But often, because of circumstances or wrongful decisions and actions by others, what they had hoped to accomplish in life they did not. They painfully puzzle over what they may have done wrong, or over whether God has really been with them.

Much of the distress of these good people comes from a failure to realize that their life lies before them. That they are coming to the end of their present life, life 'in the flesh', is of little significance. What is of significance is the kind of person they have become. Circumstances and other people are not in control of an individual's character or of the life that lies endlessly before us in the kingdom of God.

Indeed, all of this touches upon a general human need, built into our nature as intelligent, active beings. What will become of our universe? What will become of the human race, and of each of us individually? We ask these questions as naturally as we breathe.

Human life and consciousness requires, by its very nature, a projected future.[1] And everyone is deeply concerned to know what that future is.

We listen with a thrill and a shudder as our scientists and philosophers speculate on these subjects. Nearly always they speak of the future of the physical cosmos, and possibly of the human race as well. But they have no hope or thought of a future for the individual – not so much, even, as to discuss it.

Still, they hold tenaciously to a future for the cosmos. Even those who say it 'popped' into existence out of nothing do not think it will 'pop' into nothing out of existence. And they dream of humanity's securing its future by moving on to other planets in other systems. Endlessly. Thus, even the individual achieves a shadowy, vicarious future, for the future of humanity is implicitly treated as 'our' future. 'We' will go on.

This particular treatment of the future is now elevated almost to the point previously reserved for sacred dogma in our culture. That is because the human mind *must* have some picture of the future. Government money is freely and lavishly invested in its development and presentation at many levels, from the primary grades of schooling, to university courses and research grants, to series on public television. It rests on the picture of the natural world, the physical cosmos, as a *closed* system, with a future determined entirely from its own *internal* resources.

The Cosmos Open to God

The biblical tradition, centred in the teachings of Jesus, stands in sharp contrast. For it, personality is primary in every respect. It presents the universe as a created system that responds to and is pervaded by what is not a part of it but of which it is a part or product. Therefore the cosmos is not a system closed off to itself. And it is determined in its present and future course by personal factors – sources of energy and direction – that cannot be discerned by means of the physical senses or dealt with by the physical sciences.

These factors are God and his kingdom among us. They have announced themselves definitively in human history in the person and word of Jesus, but especially in his transfiguration and his resurrection. On these occasions, high points in the history of redemption, ordinary human beings *saw* the kingdom of God (Luke 9:27–28). Accordingly they lie right at the heart of the *knowledge* tradition that provides the basis for the historical and institutional reality of Christianity (2 Pet. 1:16–18; 1 Cor. 15).

The gospel of the kingdom sees the world of nature, from the tiniest particle to the farthest system of galaxies, as a great and good thing. There is, at a minimum, no reason to think that the world of nature will cease to exist or be destroyed. In a Trinitarian universe – a universe grounded in a society of divine persons – that is entirely a matter of the purpose that world serves. As long as it serves a purpose in such a universe – as it most certainly does – it will continue to exist, through whatever transformations may come. The material universe is both an essential display of the greatness and goodness of God and the arena of the eternal life of finite spirits, including the human.

The Human Future in This Universe

This present universe is only one element in the kingdom of God. But it is a very wonderful and important one. And within it the Logos, the now risen Son of man, is currently preparing for us to join him (John 14:2–4). We will see him in the stunning surroundings that he had with the Father before the beginning of the created cosmos (17:24). And we will actively participate in the future governance of the universe.

We will not sit around looking at one another or at God for eternity but will join the eternal Logos, 'reign with him', in the endlessly ongoing creative work of God. It is for this that we were each individually intended, as both kings and priests (Exod. 19:6; Rev. 5:10).

Thus, our faithfulness over a 'few things' in the present phase of our life develops the kind of character that can be entrusted with 'many things'. We are, accordingly, permitted to 'enter into the joy of our Lord' (Matt. 25:21). That 'joy' is, of course, the creation and care of what is good, in all its dimensions. A place in God's creative order has been reserved for each one of us from before the beginnings of cosmic existence. His plan is for us to develop, as apprentices to Jesus, to the point where we can take our place in the ongoing creativity of the universe.

George MacDonald has given us some lines that help us think about such a future:

> And in the perfect time, O perfect God,
> When we are in our home, our natal home,
> When joy shall carry every sacred load,
> And from its life and peace no heart shall roam,
> What if thou make us able to make like thee –
> To light with moons, to clothe with greenery,
> To hang gold sunsets o'er a rose and purple sea.[2]

Stated in other words, the intention of God is that we should each become the kind of person whom he can set free in his universe, empowered to do what we want to do. Just as we desire and intend this, so far as possible, for our children and others we love, so God desires and intends it for his children. But character, the inner directedness of the self, must develop to the point where that is possible.

This explains the meaning of the words of the prophet Daniel, used by Jesus to conclude one of his great parables of the kingdom: 'Then shall the good shine brilliantly, like the sun, in the kingdom of their Father' (Matt. 13:43; compare Dan. 12:3). We sing from this passage, 'When we've been there ten thousand years, bright, shining as the sun …' But we should understand that brightness always represents power, energy, and that in the kingdom of our Father we will be active, unimaginably creative.

The Older Prophecies

The beautiful prophecies of the Old Testament, especially its later books, captivate the heart of all who read them. When we read them, it seems to matter very little what one believes, or what one's religion or irreligion is. They are a human treasure. They express something far deeper than any particular tradition, even those singled out by God for special covenant responsibilities.

> Behold I create the heavens and the earth all over again. Be glad and rejoice forever in what I create. I create my city, Jerusalem. It is joy, and her people *are* gladness. No longer will be heard in her the voice of weeping and the sound of crying. No longer babies dying, or mature people who do not live to the end of a full life. When they build houses they will get to live in them. When they plant vineyards they, not others, will be the ones who eat the fruit. They shall not labour in vain or bear children to be destroyed. Before they call on me I will answer. Animals, even, will stop killing one another, and in my new world every kind of evil will be eliminated. (Isa. 65:17–25)

In this new city – 'Jerusalem', or 'the peace of God', is its name – 'all cultures and languages will come together to see God in his glory' (66:18). They will transmit that vision of God throughout all of the earth, and all humanity will come regularly to the centre of divine presence on earth, to delight in God and worship him (vv. 19–23).

The power of God's personal presence will, directly and indirectly, accomplish the public order in and among nations that human government has never been able to bring about. Truth and mercy will have met and kissed each other at last, like long-lost friends (Ps. 85:10). Grace and truth are reconciled in the person of the Son of man (John 1:17).

Forcing 'Jerusalem' to Happen

The greatest temptation to evil that humanity ever suffers is the temptation to make a 'Jerusalem' happen by human means.[3] Human means are absolutely indispensable in the world as it is. That is God's intention. We are supposed to act, and our actions are to count. But there is a limit on what human arrangements can accomplish. They alone cannot change the heart and spirit of the human being.

Because of this, the instrumentalities invoked to *make* 'Jerusalem' happen always wind up eliminating truth, or mercy, or both. World history as well as small-scale decision making demonstrates this. It is seen in the ravages of dictatorial power, on the one hand, and, on the other, in the death by minutiae that a bureaucracy tends to impose. It is well known how hard it is to provide a benign order within human means. For the problem, once again, is in the human heart. Until it fully engages with the rule of God, the good that we feel must be cannot come. It will at a certain point be defeated by the very means implemented to produce it.

God's way of moving towards the future is, with gentle persistence in unfailing purpose, to bring about the transformation of the human heart by speaking with human beings and living with and in them. He finds an Abraham, a Moses, a Paul – a you. It is this millennia-long process that Jesus the Son of man brings and will bring to completion. And it is the way of the prophets, who foresaw that the day would come when God's heart is the human heart: 'the law of God would be written in the heart.' That is, when what is right to God's mind would be done as a simple matter of course, and when we would not be able to understand why anyone would even think of engaging in evil. That is the nature of God's full reign.

All of the instruments of brutality and deceit that human government and society now employ to manage a corrupted and unruly humanity will then have no use. As, even now, the presence of a good person touches, influences and may even govern people nearby through the respect inspired in their hearts, the focused presence of the Trinitarian personality upon the earth will govern through the clarity and force of its own goodness, and indirectly through its transformed people.

Thus we see repeatedly portrayed in prophecy the gentleness of this government – for the first time a completely adequate government, in which the means to the good do not limit or destroy the possibility of goodness. The beautiful prophetic images portray the divine way of operating: 'Your true king is coming to you, vindicated and triumphant, humble, mounted on a donkey. His word will bring peace to the nations, and his supervision will take in all lands, from where his presence is centred to the farthest reaches of the earth' (Zech. 9:9–10).

Divine presence replaces brute power, and especially power exercised by human beings whose hearts are alienated from God's best. 'I will focus my being in their midst forever. And the nations will know that it is I the Masterful Lord who makes my people different' (Ezek. 37:26–28).

For All of Humankind – and Beyond

This Spirit of non-violent power is on the Anointed One, the Messiah:

> And he will bring justice to the nations. He will not quarrel, nor scream at people. You will not be able to hear his voice above the chatter of the street. In bringing discernment of what is good and right to the point where it actually governs human existence, he will not use even the violence it takes to finish breaking a stick that is already cracked or smother a smoking wick. (Matt. 12:18–21, quoted from Isa. 42:1–4)

The realization that this prophetic future is not just for the benefit of one special subgroup of human beings, Jews or Christians, for example, comes to full blossom in the New Testament period and writings. In the last book of the Bible, 'The Revelation', the phrase *every nation and tribe and tongue and people* becomes a characteristic bit of language that recurs in application to the outcome of God's redemptive purposes on earth. To be sure, some groups are caught up for a unique role in those purposes, but it is never for their *benefit* alone or because they have some special claim or corner on God.

Saint Augustine noted in the early fifth century,

> This Heavenly city, while it sojourns on earth, calls citizens out of all nations, and gathers together a society of pilgrims of all languages, not scrupling about diversities in the manners, laws, and institutions whereby earthly peace is secured and maintained, but recognizing that, however various these

> are, they all tend to one and the same end of earthly peace. It therefore is so far from rescinding and abolishing these diversities, that it even preserves and adapts them, so long only as no hindrance to the worship of the one supreme and true God is thus introduced.[4]

It is humanity, simply, that is God's focus in earth history, as it must be ours. It is to *the world* – the entire world – that he gave his Son. And, indeed, in the larger scene it is not even humanity that is his focus, but the entire created cosmos in the context of God's own life. We shall have more to say on this in what follows. For now we must turn to the question of what it is that makes it possible to be prophetically hopeful.

Why the Prophetic Vision and Hope?

In the midst of life as we find it, one may well ask how any intelligent person could expect such a glorious outcome for human history. The answer is a simple one. It is found in the vision of God that underlies the prophetic vision: *that* God is and *who* he is. That same vision of God that animated the older prophets is brought to striking fullness and clarity in Jesus.

The God in question, as we have seen, is an interlocking community of magnificent persons, completely self-sufficing and with no meaningful limits on goodness and power. The reality of this God, who also is the source and governor of all creation, is what we have meant by saying we live in a Trinitarian universe. This is the universe of The Kingdom Among Us.

To share the prophetic vision, then, it is not enough to 'sorta' believe in a 'sorta' God. But with the great God of Jesus squarely in the picture, everything else takes on a different nature and appears in a different light.

Human history is then no longer a human affair. It is Someone Else's project. Similarly for the individual human life: we are not puppets, either on the group or the individual level. But what is really going on is not, after all, what we are doing. The prophetic word, once again, is that 'a man's way is not in him, nor is it in a man who walks to direct his steps' (Jer. 10:23). Similarly for nations and epochs (Isa. 40:12–26). Instead of being the main show, we are of significance only as a – very important – part of an immense struggle between immense forces of good and evil.

The physical universe also, vast and dark from the merely human point of view, of dreadful dimensions and terrifying powers, is then recognized as God's place. We rightly regard nuclear power as dangerous, and therefore many are shocked to learn that we actually *live in* a huge nuclear reactor. In its basic nature, our solar system is a nuclear reactor, as is the physical universe beyond it. But in our Trinitarian universe nuclear power turns out to be simply one more provision in 'my Father's house', as Jesus called it, in which there are many places to live.

It is easy to lose this vision in today's climate of thought. We have already commented on this a number of times. The superficial view that dominates our culture holds reality to be limited to what can be discovered by scientific observation and explanation. Scientists do indeed tell us that all familiar physical things and events are determined by what goes on at the level of sub-atomic particle physics: quarks and the like. Some onlookers too quickly assume that nothing more is to be said. But there is nothing about sub-particle 'matter' that indicates it is the final level of reality, dependent only on itself – as God has been traditionally assumed to be. And a thoughtful examination of it shows, I believe, that it is not.

There is also a widespread impression that the laws of natural science make everything intelligible – or would, if we could only get the 'right' laws. But the laws of science make nothing intelligible by themselves, and for clear reasons. There must be certain 'initial conditions' before the laws of science can explain anything. In their 'explaining', those laws have to have something from which to start. And they obviously do not explain the existence or nature of those very conditions that must be in place before they can explain *anything*.

Science, then, may explain many interesting and important things, but it does not explain existence. Nor does it explain why the laws of science are the laws of nature.[5] And it does not explain science itself.[6] But we have reason to believe we live in a Trinitarian universe: a universe where the reality from which all other realities derive is a society of divine persons. And it is only the knowledge of this God whose deepest nature is love that is the source of the ancient prophecies with their radiant hopes. God has made himself known by personally approaching human beings and involving himself in their lives. The history is there for all who *wish* to see. But no one *has* to see – now. That is how the divine conspiracy works. With this God in view, the prophetic witness relentlessly speaks, with absolute assurance, of 'the times of the restitution of all things' (Acts 3:21).

Yet, standing right in the face of God's magnificent being and works, and his persistent invasions of history, is the human order, pervaded with evil. The grand old missionary hymn sings:

> What tho' the spicy breezes
> Blow soft o'er Ceylon's isle;
> Though every prospect pleases,
> And only man is vile?
> In vain with lavish kindness
> The gifts of God are strown;
> The heathen in his blindness
> Bows down to wood and stone.[7]

To wood and stone we must currently add political programmes and social groups, economic status, education, technologies and human knowledge, drugs and perhaps other things as well. To all of these, human beings bow down. They take them as ultimate points of reference for their lives and actions. And if that is all we see, certainly there are no grounds for hope. The ancient prophetic vision must then seem only a fanciful projection, nothing real.

Indeed, the very creation itself is groaning under the strain of the process through which humanity will step into its destined role in the cosmos, into 'the coming glory to be revealed in us' (Rom. 8:18–23). But in the Prophecies the way of God simply must succeed, because God is God. 'I am the Lord, he says, 'who exercises loving kindness, justice and righteousness in the earth; for I delight in these things' (Jer. 9:24). These things must, then, prevail. It cannot be otherwise.

God Is Really Knowable Only Through the Redeemed Community

In the face of humanity at its worst, now eternally represented by the killing of Jesus himself, the gospel of the kingdom steadies us against believing anything bad about God. It calls us, rather, to believe that what is good God will bring to pass.

Most important, this concerns the future of God's own people, the children of light. Throughout history they often have been far less than what they should be. That is still true today. But 'I will put My law within them, and on their heart I will write it ... And they shall not teach again, each man his neighbour and brother, saying, "Know the Lord," for they shall all know Me, from the least of them to the greatest' (Jer. 31:33–34; cf. Ezek. 11:19–20; Heb. 10:16).

Incredibly, to fulfil his intention to be known by dwelling in his people, God chose to occupy a tent – *a tent!* – for decades of grubby desert camping. 'I will consecrate the tent of meeting and the altar,' he said to Moses, 'and I will dwell among the children of Israel and will be their God. And they shall know that I am the Lord their God who brought them out of Egypt, that I might dwell among them' (Exod. 29:44–46).

The picture of a community of people to be inhabited by God is carried over to the new covenant in many New Testament passages, none more beautiful than those in Paul's letter to the Ephesians. There he says to the non-Jewish believers, who had previously been 'nobodies': 'You are fellow citizens with the holy ones, you are God's household, having been based upon a foundation of apostles and prophets, Jesus Christ himself being the stone around which the house is built. In him the entire building fits together and grows into a sacred gathering, becoming a dwelling place of God in the Spirit' (Eph. 2:19–22).

The purpose of God with human history is nothing less than to bring out of it – small and insignificant as it seems from the biological and naturalistic point of view – an eternal community of those who were once thought to be just 'ordinary human beings'.[8] Because of God's purposes for it, this community will, in its way, pervade the entire created realm and share in the government of it. God's pre-creation intention to have that community as a special dwelling place or home will be realized. He will be its prime sustainer and most glorious inhabitant.

But why? What is the point of it? The purpose is to meet what can only be described as a *need* of God's nature as totally competent love. It is the same purpose that manifests itself in his creation of the world. Only in the light of such a creation and such a redeemed community is it possible for God to be known in his deepest nature. They make it possible for God to be known. And love unknown is love unfulfilled. Moreover, the welfare of every conscious being in existence depends upon their possession of this knowledge of God.

Therefore, after long ages of preparation, redemption came among us in the form of his Son, 'so that through all the eons to come the illimitable stores of his grace would be clear to all in his kindness towards us in Christ' (Eph. 2:7).

This plan had long remained a 'mystery' to human beings, and even to the people of the Old Covenant. They were drawn into the divine conspiracy that they themselves did not understand. 'Mystery' means, in the language of the New Testament, something that had long remained hidden but then came to be known for the first time. The 'mystery' of this kindness had been 'hidden for ages in God who created all things' (Eph. 3:9). But it is gently brought to light through the gospel, 'so that the multi-faceted wisdom of God can, through the history and destiny of the redeemed people, become obvious to those who, under him, are responsible in various capacities throughout the universe' (3:10).

The Human Significance of God's Future for Us

A human life or a human world is one that holds together in terms of the future. It essentially involves *meaning*. Meaning is not a luxury for us. It is a kind of spiritual oxygen, we might say, that enables our souls to live.[9] It is a 'going beyond', a transcendence of whatever state we are in towards that which completes it. The meaning of present events in human life is largely a matter of what comes later. Thus, anything that 'has no future' is meaningless in the human order. That is why we try to avoid it as much as possible. It stifles us.

This life structure is mirrored in language, where meaning and meaningfulness most clearly display themselves. Thus, if we hear only the word *water* or see it written down somewhere, we do not know whether it is a verb or a noun. Hence we cannot know what it refers to or what it is about. If the remainder of a sentence is given, however, it may be either one: as in 'Water my plants while I'm away,' where it is a verb, or 'Water is essential to life on this planet,' where it is a noun.

Events in a human life are like that, and so is *a* human life as a whole, as well as human life itself. They resemble the opening words in an unfinished sentence, paragraph, chapter or book. In a sense we can identify them and grasp them, but we cannot know what they mean and really are until we know what comes later. Thus we are always seeking the meaning of events we live through and of our lives themselves. We wonder about the meaning of historical events and personages, or even of human history itself. And it is always true that meaning is found, when it is found, in some larger context.

From Jesus we learn of the ultimate context, God and his kingdom. In the future phases of that kingdom lies the meaning of our lives and, indeed, of the history of the earth of which we are a part. Jesus insisted, as we have seen, upon the present reality of the 'kingdom of the heavens' and made that the basis of his gospel. But he also recognized that there was a future fullness to the kingdom, as well as an everlasting enjoyment of life in God far transcending the earth and life on it.

We are greatly strengthened for life in the kingdom now by an understanding of what our future holds, and especially of how that future relates to our present experience. For only then do we really understand what our current life is and are we able to make choices that agree with reality. But it is not only Christians who have understood the importance of our eternal future. Other thoughtful people have seen it, though not the purposes of God in human history and redemption that are unique to the gospel of Jesus. Insight into the very nature of the human self has led them to it.

For example, Plato's account of the last hours of Socrates has him saying,

> If the soul is immortal, it demands our care not only for that part of time which we call life, but for all time: and indeed it would seem now that it will be extremely dangerous to neglect it. If death were a release from everything, it would be a boon for the wicked. But since the soul is clearly immortal, it can have no escape or security from evil except by becoming as good and wise as it possibly can. For it takes nothing with it to the next world except its education and training: and these, we are told, are of supreme importance in helping or harming the newly dead at the very beginning of his journey there.[10]

But, unfortunately, one of the least sensible and useful parts of current presentations of the Christian gospel is precisely where it concerns the future of individual and corporate humanity in God's world. There are numerous reasons for this, not least the confused and unhelpful pictures of heaven and hell that have come down to us, as well as the presumably 'scientific picture of man' that brands the very idea of continued existence beyond the body as whimsical nonsense.

In bringing this book on the divine conspiracy to a close, we must try to cast some light on what our future life in the kingdom will be like and to undermine some of the major hindrances to hearty confidence that the teachings of Jesus and his followers about our future really are true.

The Reasonableness of Preserving and Restoring Humanity

And first of all, is it truly reasonable to think that we will continue beyond the demise of our bodies? In the light of God and his kingdom, once again, it very definitely is. As John Hick, one of the most widely known Christian thinkers of our day, has nicely put it,

> If we trust what Jesus said out of his own direct consciousness of God, we shall share his belief in the future life. This belief is supported by the reasoning that a God of infinite love would not create finite persons and then drop them out of existence when the potentialities of their nature, including their awareness of himself, have only just begun to be realized.[11]

In other words, given the reality of God's world, it would actually be unreasonable to think we would simply drop out of existence.

We must be sure to add, however, that our continued existence is not primarily for our benefit, but God's. It is not just because we would like to continue to be that he decides to continue to put up with us. Rather, he has made a great, often terrifying, investment in individual human beings as well as in corporate humanity. Needless to say, it is something he regards as well worth the effort. And he is not about to lose the result by permitting human beings to cease to exist. 'He shall see the travail of his soul,' the ancient prophecy says, 'and be satisfied' (Isa. 53:10–11).

We exist and will continue to exist, then, because it pleases God. He sees that it is good. This is how the Twenty-third Psalm is to be understood. 'Though I walk in the valley of the shadow of death,' death looming over me, 'I fear no evil!' How, really, can this be? It is not just a frightened person whistling in the dark. It is experience-based knowledge of the reality of God's rod (protection) and staff (correction) that comfort me. 'His goodness and mercy dog my steps through the days of my life, and I shall reside in his house forever.' How does the psalmist know this? Because he knows *God*. He knows him in regular interactions in the real world. Those interactions show who God is, and what *God*, therefore, will certainly do! That is what the Twenty-third Psalm says.

And the Possibility

Thus the existence of the God of Jesus simply dissolves any problem about whether 'survival' is to be expected. Moreover, his own being proves that personal existence is not, as such, dependent upon matter. Instead, matter depends on him. He did quite well without a physical universe before he created it. He undoubtedly has the very highest quality of consciousness – and all this without a brain!

God, many are now shocked to realize, does not have a brain. And he never misses it. This is something one must never forget. Body and brain come from him, not the other way around. And in him our own personal being will be as secure without body and brain as it now is with body and brain. In fact, much more so.

Those who do not understand this, or for various reasons reject it, often speak as if believing in a future for human beings beyond the demise of their current body were a matter of emotional 'needs' – really, of moral deficiencies. What is meant is that people who do not believe in survival are brave, while others are cowards. But if you approach this issue with an open mind, and on a case by case basis, you will discover that bravery and cowardice are about equally distributed among those who do and those who do not believe in survival. Those who do not believe in an afterlife are not noticeably braver than those who do.

But in any case this is a thoughtless and childish way of approaching things. It reminds me of a lady I know who refused to talk about life beyond death with her children because, she said, she didn't want them to be disappointed if it turned out not to be there. Well, now ... If there is no afterlife they certainly won't be disappointed. If there is, they may find themselves badly prepared. The only possible way they could be disappointed is if they do continue to exist.

If, indeed, what happens at physical death is the cessation of the person, then approaching death is, at worst, like going to the surgeon. It is unpleasant, but at least it will be over soon, and there will then be no pain, no suffering, no regrets. No you. No anything, so far as you are concerned.

The truly brave person is surely the one who can cheerfully face the prospect of an unending existence. Suppose you are never going to stop existing and there is nothing you can do about it – except possibly make your future existence as desirable an existence as possible? That would call for real courage.

Accordingly, relief at the thought of the cessation of being is a theme commonly expressed throughout the ages. One of the great world religions presents it as the condition most to be desired. The ancient Epicureans were famous for stressing it. And in the words of the poet Swinburne,

From too much love of living,
From hope and fear set free,
We thank with brief thanksgiving
Whatever gods may be,
That no life lives forever;
That dead men rise up never;
That even the weariest river
Winds somewhere safe to sea.[12]

This poet goes on, in a characteristic manner, to celebrate 'only the sleep eternal in an eternal night.' But of course there will then be no one to enjoy that sleep. It will not be sleep.

Now if the self-revealing God of the biblical tradition is omitted or made hopelessly mysterious, in the manner of most modern thought and even theology, then we well might hope for an eternal night. Then we would not only have no regrets when we are 'gone', but shortly thereafter *no one* will have *any* regrets. For there will soon be no one. The career of our little planet is but a moment in cosmic time. From the human point of view, there would be little to lament – and very soon no one to lament it.

But from the point of view of 'our Father, the one in the heavens', it is quite another story. He treasures those whom he has created, planned for, longed for, sorrowed over, redeemed and befriended. The biblical language expressing their relationship to him is so intimate as to be almost embarrassing. The psalmist cries, 'Do not deliver the soul of thy turtledove to the wild beast; Do not forget the life of thine afflicted forever' (Ps. 74:19). You are never going to cease existing, and there is nothing you can do about it.

Again, Jesus' special word for the Father, 'Abba' or 'Daddy' expresses a relationship of treasuring and being treasured that simply cannot conceivably be broken. The God of Jesus will *obviously* preserve the human personality within the eternality of his own life. Once you think it through, anything else is simply inconceivable. Not because of us, once again, but because of God.

What Will Our Future Life Be Like?

Now is it true, as many suggest, 'that we know nothing concrete about the conditions of our existence after death'?[13] Strangely, the same author from whom these words are taken goes right on to acknowledge that, in describing our life after the demise of our body, Jesus

> used symbols pointing to eternal life as limitlessly enhanced life, as a state of being more intensely alive in an existence which is both perfect fulfilment and yet also endless activity and newness. If death leads eventually to *that*, then although we shall still think of it ... with trembling awe and apprehension, yet it will not evoke terror or despair; for beyond death we ... will not be less alive but more alive than we are now.

But to know 'eternal life as limitlessly enhanced life', in which we are 'more intensely alive' in 'perfect fulfilment and yet also endless activity and newness' is surely to know a huge amount 'about the conditions of our existence after death'.

For example, we can be sure that heaven in the sense of our afterlife is just our future in this universe. There is not another universe besides this one. God created the heavens and the earth. That's it. And much of the difficulty in having a believable picture of heaven and hell today comes from the centuries-long tendency to 'locate' them in 'another reality' outside the created universe.

But time is within eternity, not outside it. The created universe is within the kingdom of God, not outside it. And if there is anything we know now about the 'physical' universe, it surely is that it would be quite adequate to eternal purposes. And given that it has been produced, which is not seriously in doubt, all that one might require of an utterly realistic future for humanity in it is surely possible.

Really Knowing – for the First Time

When we pass through what we call death, we do not lose the world. Indeed, we see it for the first time as it really is. Paul makes this crucial point in 1 Corinthians 13. His own experiences of various kinds had assured him of the utter reality of God and the spiritual realm.

His understanding was that in what we call our 'normal' states and conditions we have in fact a very distorted view of reality. We are like little children, who really have no idea of what is going on around them (1 Cor. 11). But when we move through 'death' we shall, in his words, 'know fully, as I have been fully known.'

As we have been known by whom? Certainly by God, a myriad of angels, the spirits of just men perfected, and Jesus, as indicated in Heb. 12:22–23, or by the 'great cloud of witness' mentioned earlier in Hebrews 12. They see and know things as they really are. And so shall we. That is the quality of consciousness and life we will have.

Paul, like other biblical figures, actually had stood in the visible presence of these beings, and he knew that from their point of view he was fully known. He understood that when we move out of this body and into God's full world, we will have the same kind of fullness and clarity of experience as those beings now have of him and all things.

And that only reflects what is the standard biblical teaching: 'There is no creature hidden from His sight, but all things are open and laid bare to the eyes of Him with whom we have to do' (Heb. 4:13). The spiritual realm is the realm of *truth*, not of distortion (John 4:23). Angels are understood in both Old and New Testament to be 'watchers', witnesses, of the scene on earth. No doubt they too see things as they are, unassisted and unhindered by a brain or a body.

In our present embodied position, by contrast, we always see things in distortion, 'as in a mirror'. The mirrors that could be made in Paul's day were quite unsatisfactory and *never* allowed one to see things in them as they really are. When we move beyond the body in its current form, it will be like turning from the distorted mirror image (our current 'knowledge') to the real things, or like moving from a child's perception of things to the perceptions of mature adults.

Yet many who believe in this future condition treat it as a kind of dreamlike, drifting, hazy condition, or one in which we have no awareness of our selves or sense of our self-identity. One wonders why. Perhaps it is because of the often-drawn parallel of death with sleeping and its corresponding dream state. But that parallel applies only to the body, not the person. The person does not 'sleep'. Or perhaps one thinks that passing through death we are in a shocked condition, as we are in a body that has been badly hurt. But when we pass through, we are, precisely, *not* in a body that is injured and dysfunctional.

Spiritual beings such as God and his angels can hardly be thought of as being in a shocked, disoriented and dreamlike state. And it is the teaching of Jesus that those who share his life 'shall be like angels and have the basic nature of God' (Luke 20:35–36).

No Death

This accounts for Jesus' numerous indications that, for the godly, death is nothing. Have no fear of those who can only kill the body, he says (Matt. 10:28). We will not even *experience* death (John 8:51–52) and will, in fact, not die (John 11:26). We here re-emphasize points made earlier.

One of the occasions on which he is recorded as weeping was when he grieved for the agony human beings experience when dealing with the death of their loved ones (John 11:33–35). No doubt he saw how totally misguided their grief was, and yet how devoted they were to grieving. They even employed professionals to help them mourn.

Discussing his own upcoming death with his friends, he says to them, 'If you loved me, you would be happy because I go to the Father, where I am better off than here' (John 14:28). In different wording, 'I go to the Father, and my Father is greater than I.' Nothing for *him* to grieve about in that! Of course it left his friends with much to sorrow *for themselves*, which is understandable and appropriate. But they should also rejoice for him at the same time.

And, of course, this all accords perfectly with his response to the faith of the thief dying with him: 'Today you and I will be together in a wonderful place, Paradise' (Luke 23:43). This statement could only be a falsehood if it meant anything less than that the thief would be very much himself, in fine shape, in a wonderful situation with Jesus and, no doubt, with others as well.

Such is the understanding of the New Testament as a whole. Those who live in reliance upon the word and person of Jesus, and know by experience the reality of his kingdom, are always better off 'dead', from the personal point of view. Paul's language is, 'to die is gain' (Phil. 1:21). And again: 'To depart and be with Christ is very much better' than to remain here (v. 23). We remain willing, of course, to stay at our position here to serve others at God's appointment. But we live in the knowledge that, as Paul elsewhere says, 'Jesus the Anointed has abolished death and has, through the gospel, made life and immortality obvious' (2 Tim. 1:10).

The Changes To Come

What, Then, Changes?

When we pass through the stage normally called 'death', we will not lose anything but the limitations and powers that specifically correspond to our present mastery over our body, and to our availability and vulnerability to and through it. We will no longer be able to act and be acted upon by means of it. Of course this is a heart-rending change to those left behind. But, on the other hand, loss of those abilities begins to occur, in most cases, long before death. It is a normal part of ageing and sickness. The body as intermediary between the person and the physical world is losing its function as the soul prepares for a new arrangement.

But along this passage we do not lose our personal sense of who we are, and all our knowledge of and relationships to other persons will remain intact – except, once again, insofar as they are mediated through the body and its physical environment.

Indeed, *we* will then be in possession of ourselves as never before, and the limited universe that we now see will remain – though that universe will not be as interesting as what we shall then see for the first time. We will not disappear into an eternal fog bank or dead storage, or exist in a state of isolation or suspended animation, as many seem to suppose. God has a much better use for us than that.

Stated in other words, our experience will not be fundamentally different in character from what it is now, though it will change in significant details. *The life we now have as the persons we now are will continue, and continue in the universe in which we now exist*. Our experience will be much clearer, richer and deeper, of course, because it will be unrestrained by the limitations now imposed upon us by our dependence upon our body. It will, instead, be rooted in the broader and more fundamental reality of God's kingdom and will accordingly have far greater scope and power.

His Glorious Body

The key to understanding all of this for the early followers of Jesus was not just their knowledge of God himself, which we have so heavily emphasized, or their knowledge of the multitudes of non-physical beings or angels that serve him. The absolute bedrock of their confidence concerning their future was, rather, in their experience of the post-resurrection Jesus.

He had a body: a focus of his personality in space and time that was publicly observable and interacted with physical realities. But it was radiant, and therefore it was called 'the body of his glory' (Phil. 3:21). And it was not *restrained* by space, time and physical causality in the manner of physical bodies.

Accordingly, Paul says, 'there is a physical body and there is also one that is spiritual' (1 Cor. 15:44). Now it is true that the thought world of the first century allowed for this important distinction, but acceptance of the reality of the spiritual body is mainly based upon the specific experience of the earliest Christians with the risen Jesus.

In God's universe matter is ultimately subject to mind or spirit. That is a given in the tradition of Jesus and his people. Already our natural home, our 'citizenship' (*politeuma*), our 'sociopolitical order,' is 'in the heavens, out of which we eagerly anticipate the coming of Lord Jesus Christ. He will metamorphose our humiliating body, transforming it into a glory body like his, utilizing the power he has to make all things do what he wants' (Phil. 3:20–21).

When we pass through 'death' into God's full world – or 'our earthy tent is torn down,' as Paul elsewhere says – we are not thereby deprived of a body, any more than Jesus himself was. Rather, we are then 'clothed with a dwelling place of the heavenly sort' and 'not left naked' (2 Cor. 5:1–8). The mortal part of us is 'swallowed up by life'. God has prepared us for this by depositing in us a 'down payment' in the form of the Spirit (v. 5). We know even now, and by experience, the reality of a life that is not of the physical body.

'Running Steadfastly the Race Set Before Us'

What, then, should we expect to happen as we move onward in the eternity where we live even now? Let us break it down into three stages: the time of growing steadily, the time of passage, and the time of reigning with Jesus.

THE TIME OF GROWING STEADILY. We should, first of all, find ourselves constantly growing in our readiness and ability to draw our direction, strength and overall tone of life from the everlasting kingdom, from our personal interactions with the Trinitarian personality who is God. This will mean, most importantly, the transformation of our heart and character into the family likeness, increasingly becoming like 'children of our Father, the one in the heavens' (Matt. 5:45).

The *agape* love of 1 Corinthians 13 will increasingly become simply a matter of who we are. But the effects of our prayers, words and deeds – and sometimes of our mere presence – will also increasingly be of a nature and extent that cannot be explained in human terms. Increasingly what we do and say is 'in the name of the Lord Jesus Christ', and every part of our life becomes increasingly eternal, in the sense explained in earlier chapters. We are now co-labourers with God.

Ageing, accordingly, will become a process not of losing, but of gaining. As our physical body fades out, our glory body approaches and our spiritual substance grows richer and deeper. As we age we should become obviously more glorious. The lovely words of George MacDonald, once again, help us to imagine this crucial transition:

> Our old age is the scorching of the bush
> By life's indwelling, incorruptible blaze.
> O life, burn at this feeble shell of me,
> Till I the sore singed garment off shall push,
> Flap out my Psyche wings, and to thee rush.[14]

THE TIME OF PASSAGE. Common human experience, in all ages and cultures, teaches much more about transition and passage than Western culture for the last century or so has been willing to deal with. Some of it has been reaffirmed, and perhaps overembellished, by the recent interest in 'near-death experiences'. But what common human experience thus teaches is in basic accord with indications to be derived from biblical sources.

Most notably, the person in the transition begins to 'see the invisible'. Others whom they know come to meet them, often while they are still interacting with those left behind. If death is sudden, those nearby will have no opportunity to realize that this is happening. But we can be sure that even in such cases the person is not hurled into isolation. You would not do that, if you could help it, to anyone you loved. And neither will God.

Here we see the comforting mercy of God towards those who love him or seek him. Poor Lazarus died, we are told by Jesus, 'and he was borne away by the angels to where God's people are gathered' (Luke 16:22). From the 'great cloud of witnesses' come those who have been watching for us. They greet us and enfold us. And while those first few moments or hours will surely present us with one astonishing view after another, we will be joyous and peaceful because of the company we are in.

The old spiritual song says, 'I looked over Jordan and what did I see, comin' for to carry me home? A band of angels comin' after me, comin' for to carry me home.' And this seemingly simplistic picture, derived from scriptural stories and teachings, presents exactly what we should expect. We should expect it on the basis of our knowledge of God and the human soul, common human experience, and the teachings of scripture.

Of course all of this falls among those things that God 'hides' from the supposedly informed and self-righteously smart, while making it perfectly clear to babies (Matt. 11:25). But that will hardly distract anyone who, living in the kingdom, has already experienced 'the powers of the aeon to come'.

Now this understanding of the passage into God's full world spells out precisely the sense in which death has been abolished, in the New Testament vision, and in which we who live in the Logos will not die or experience death (John 8:51). Our personal existence will continue without interruption.

Perhaps, by contrast, we must say that those who do not now enter the eternal life of God through confidence in Jesus *will* experience separation, isolation and the end of their hopes. Perhaps this will be permitted in their case because they have chosen to be God themselves, to be their own ultimate point of reference. God permits it, but that posture obviously can only be sustained at a distance from God. The fires of heaven, we might suspect, are hotter than the fires of hell. Still, there is room in the universe for them.

THE TIME OF REIGNING WITH JESUS. We need not worry about there being a place for everyone in our new cosmic setting. We now know that there are about ten thousand million galaxies in 'our' physical system, with one hundred billion billion planets. That is, 100,000,000,000,000,000,000 planets. And it may be that the physical system we know of is but one of many that we have not yet discovered. A few decades ago we thought our galaxy was the entire physical universe.

In due time – I can only imagine it will be some while after our passage into God's full world – we will begin to assume new responsibilities. 'Well done, good and faithful servant,' our magnificent Master will say, 'you have been faithful in the smallest things, take charge of ten cities,' 'five cities,' 'many things,' or whatever is appropriate (Luke 19:17; Matt. 25:21).

I suspect there will be many surprises when the new creative responsibilities are assigned. Perhaps it would be a good exercise for each of us to ask ourselves: Really, how many cities could I now govern under God? If, for example, Baltimore or Liverpool were turned over to me, with power to do what I want with it, how would things turn out? An honest answer to this question might do much to prepare us for our eternal future in this universe.

Are we, for example, prepared to have everything about us known to everyone? There is nothing hidden that will not be revealed, Jesus tells us. 'What you have whispered in the inner rooms shall be announced over loudspeakers' (Luke 12:3). Are we ready to live with that kind of total transparency? And are we totally convinced that God's way is the only smart way and that his power will always guide and enable us in everything we do? Is our character such that we *automatically* act as if all this were so?

When I think about this, I am impressed with how few who want to 'rule cities' could actually be trusted to do it. If I had to assign rulers, I suspect I would try to find a few humble believers who don't look like much from the human point of view but who have learned to have no confidence in themselves and put their every hope in God. Thankfully, I will never have to make that assignment. I am sure God will know how to do it. But we can be sure that 'many who are first [in human eyes] shall be last [in God's judgement], and the last first.'

In any case, we should expect that in due time we will be moved into our eternal destiny of *creative activity with Jesus and his friends and associates in the 'many mansions' of 'his Father's house'*.

Thus, we should not think of ourselves as destined to be celestial bureaucrats, involved eternally in celestial 'administrivia'. That would be only slightly better than being caught in an everlasting church service. No, we should think of our destiny as being absorbed in a tremendously creative team effort, with unimaginably splendid leadership, on an inconceivably vast plane of activity, with ever more comprehensive cycles of productivity and enjoyment. This is the 'eye hath not seen, neither ear heard' that lies before us in the prophetic vision (Isa. 64:4).

This Is Shalom

When Saint Augustine comes to the very end of his book *The City of God*, he attempts to address the question of 'how the saints shall be employed when they are clothed in immortal and spiritual bodies.'[15] At first he confesses that he is 'at a loss to understand the nature of that employment.' But then he settles upon the word *peace* to describe it, and develops the idea of peace by reference to the *vision* of God – using, as we too have done, the rich passage from 1 Corinthians 13.

Thus he speaks of our 'employment' then as being 'the beatific vision'. The eternal blessedness of the city of God is presented as a 'perpetual Sabbath'. In words so beautiful that everyone should know them by heart, he says, 'There we shall rest and see, see and love, love and praise. This is what shall be in the end without end. For what other end do we propose to ourselves than to attain to the kingdom of which there is no end?'

And yet, for all their beauty and goodness, these words do not seem to me to capture the blessed condition of the restoration of all things – of the kingdom come in its utter fullness. Repose, yes. But not as quiescence, passivity, eternal fixity. It is, instead, peace as wholeness, as fullness of function, as the restful but unending creativity involved in a cosmoswide, co-operative pursuit of a created order that continuously approaches but never reaches the limitless goodness and greatness of the triune personality of God, its source.

This, surely, is the word of Jesus when he says, 'Those who overcome will be welcomed to sit with me on my throne, as I too overcame and sat down with my Father on his throne. Those capable of hearing should listen to what the Spirit is saying to my people' (Rev. 3:21–22).

REFERENCES

Chapter 1

1. Derek Bok, *The President's Report 1986–87* (Cambridge: Harvard University Press, 1987), pp. 2–3. Compare with the last chapter of his *The Cost of Talent* (New York: Free Press, 1994).

2. 'Point of View,' by Robert Coles, *The Chronicle of Higher Education*, 22 September 1995, p. A68. This discussion by Coles has counterparts in many, many social commentators of our time. In his *The Revolt of the Elites and the Betrayal of Democracy*, Christopher Lasch examines at length our contemporary inability to hold people responsible. He notes with approval the call of many Communitarians for compassion on those who need help, and then adds: 'But it is our reluctance to make demands on each other, much more than our reluctance to help those in need, that is sapping the strength of democracy today.' (New York: W. W. Norton, 1995, p. 107). But at present we suffer from something much worse than 'the ethical ignorance of persons thought to be learned,' as Gordon Keith Chalmers said some decades ago. (*The Republic and the Person*, Chicago, Henry Regnery Company, 1952, p. 4). We suffer from the intellectual dogma that in matters of what ought to be done there is no knowledge one way or the other, only feelings and political pressures. It is psychologically and socially impossible to hold others or even ourselves responsible in such an intellectual context. We can only shout at them, which we do.

3. John Maynard Keynes, *The General Theory of Employment, Interest and Money* (New York: Harcourt Brace, 1964), p. 383.

4. A significant treatment of this matter, from a particular point of view, is *Seven Men Who Rule the World from the Grave*, by Dave Breese (Chicago: Moody Press, 1990).

5. See the treatment of this issue, referring to this novel, in *The Christian Faith in the Modern World*, by J. Gresham Machen (Grand Rapids: Eerdmans, 1968), pp. 95–97.

6. Paul Johnson, *A History of the Modern World from 1917 to the 1980s* (London: Weidenfeld and Nicolson), pp. 654–55.

7. Leo Tolstoy, *A Confession, The Gospel in Brief, and What I Believe*, translated by Aylmer Maude (London: Oxford University Press, 1958), p. 27.

8. Jaroslav Pelikan, *Jesus Through the Centuries* (New Haven, CT: Yale University Press, 1985), p. 1.

9. This figure is taken from the *International Bulletin of Missionary Research* (January 1994), as quoted in *World Partners* (Ft. Wayne, Indiana), a publication of the Missionary Church, p. 2. Of course such figures are variable and bound to involve some degree of error.

10. Frederick William Faber, *All For Jesus: Or, The Easy Ways Of Divine Love* (Baltimore: John Murphy, 1854), p. 13. See Mark 4:33 on Jesus' method of teaching 'as they were able to hear.'
11. Huston Smith, *Beyond the Post-Modern Mind* (New York: Crossroad, 1982), p. 191.
12. Hans Küng, *On Being a Christian*, translated by Edward Quinn (Garden City, NY: Doubleday, 1976), p. 383. Towards the end of his life Karl Barth reported that 'he began by thinking that Jesus was the prophet of the kingdom and later came to see that he *was* the kingdom' (A. M. Hunter, *P. T. Forsyth* [Philadelphia: Westminster Press, 1974], p. 37). P. T. Forsyth wrote, 'Like Messiah, the Kingdom was an Old Testament phrase which served to enclose what he [Jesus] brought in himself ... The Gospel of the Kingdom was Christ in essence; Christ was the Gospel of the Kingdom in power ... He was the truth of his own greatest Gospel. It is wherever he is. To have him is to ensure it' (*ibid.*).
13. C. S. Lewis, *Mere Christianity* (New York: Macmillan, 1956), pp. 148 f.
14. John Calvin, *Golden Booklet of the True Christian Life*, translated by Henry J. Van Andel (Grand Rapids: Baker Book House, 1977), p. 28.
15. Melvin Morse, *Closer to the Light* (New York: Villard Books, 1990), pp. 179 f.
16. Frank Laubach, *Practicing His Presence* (Goleta, CA: Christian Books, 1976), p. 30.
17. Ibid., p. 5.
18. In his *The Greatness of the Kingdom*, Alva McClain comments, 'A general survey of the Biblical material indicates that the concept of a 'kingdom' envisages a total situation containing at least three essential elements: first, a *ruler* with adequate authority and power; second, a *realm* of subjects to be ruled; and third, the actual exercise of the function of *rulership*' (Winona Lake, IN: BMH Books, 1987), p. 17.
19. Charles C. Ryrie, for example, says, 'But the rule of heaven did not arrive during Jesus' lifetime because the people refused to repent and meet the spiritual conditions for the kingdom' (*So Great Salvation: What It Means to Believe in Jesus Christ* [Wheaton, IL: Victor, 1989], p. 38). This can be regarded as the preferred interpretation among conservative and evangelical Christians in this century, up until quite recently. See the more finely nuanced view of George Eldon Ladd (*The Gospel of the Kingdom* [Grand Rapids: Eerdmans, 1959], p. 123), which has been increasingly favoured of late. He has attempted to balance the 'now' and 'not yet' aspects of God's rule in the New Testament presentation. The wide range of scholarship that exists on the topic of the kingdom of God, its nature, presence and absence, without primary reference to the evangelical perspective, is represented in *The Kingdom of God in the Twentieth Century*, edited by Wendell Willis (Peabody, MA: Hendrickson, 1978).
20. C. H. Dodd, *The Parables of the Kingdom* (New York: Charles Scribner's Sons, 1958), p. 44.
21. Ibid., p. 50. Especially relevant on this point is chapter 6 in *The Life and Teaching of Jesus Christ*, by James S. Stewart (Nashville, TN: Abingdon, 1984).

James Kallas provides an extensive study of these matters in his *The Significance of the Synoptic Miracles* (Greenwich, CN: Seabury Press, 1961).

Chapter 2

1. See *Christianity Today*, 21 June 1993, p. 30.
2. *Christianity Today*, 24 September 1990, p. 17.
3. Helmut Thielicke, *The Trouble with the Church: A Call for Renewal* (New York: Harper and Row, 1965), p. 3.
4. Mike Yaconelli, 'The Terror of Inbetweenness,' *The Door* 126 (November/December 1992), p. 36. In giving permission to use his penetrating words, Mike Yaconelli indicates that he might not say things in quite the same way today.
5. On this compare Philip Yancy's intriguing article on Tolstoy and Dostoevsky in *Christianity Today*, 17 July 1995.
6. James Montgomery Boice, Pastor, Tenth Presbyterian Church, Philadelphia, quoted in *The Gospel According to Jesus*, by John F. MacArthur, Jr. (Grand Rapids: Zondervan, 1988), p. xii.
7. Stephen Neill, *The Difference in Being a Christian* (New York: Association Press, 1955), pp. 6, 11. Bishop Kallistos Ware's *How Are We Saved? The Understanding of Salvation in the Orthodox Tradition* (Minneapolis: Light and Life Publishing, 1996), provides a clear and impressive articulation of the Greek Orthodox interpretation of salvation and being a Christian.
8. Actually, this replacement has as its background 'an absorption of Christology into Soteriology', in the language of Karl Barth. There is an entire loss of any Christological concern in the preoccupation with my own salvation or that of society. (See 'Demythologization – Crisis in Continental Theology', by Peter Berger, in *European Intellectual History Since Darwin and Marx*, edited by W. W. Wagar [New York: Harper Torchbooks, 1966], p. 255.) 'Gospels of Sin Management' presume a Christ with no serious work other than redeeming humankind. On the right, they foster 'vampire Christians', who only want a little blood for their sins but nothing more to do with Jesus until heaven, when they have to associate with him. On the left, they foster the Phariseeism of a more or less brutal social self-righteousness.
9. MacArthur, *Gospel According to Jesus*, p. 28.
10. Ryrie, *So Great Salvation*, p. 40. See also Zane C. Hodges, *Absolutely Free!* (Grand Rapids: Zondervan, 1989). For a presentation of Ryrie's view of sanctification or Christian life and the indispensable role of human action in it, see his *Balancing the Christian Life* (Chicago: Moody Press, 1969), p. 64 and elsewhere.
11. Ryrie, *So Great Salvation*, p. 40.
12. Ibid., p. 38.

13. Ibid., p. 119.
14. Ibid., p. 39.
15. James Findlay, *Church People in the Struggle: The National Council of Churches and the Black Freedom Movement, 1950–1970* (New York: Oxford University Press, 1994). See the review article by William McGuire King in *Christian Century*, 6 April 1994, pp. 353–56.
16. William McGuire King, 'Shadows of the Social Gospel: White Mainliners in the Civil Rights Struggle', *Christian Century*, 6 April 1994, p. 353.
17. James Traub, 'Can Separate Be Equal?' *Harper's Magazine*, June 1994, p. 37.
18. John A. T. Robinson, *But That I Can't Believe* (London: Collins-Fontana, 1967), p. 51. It should be noted that Robinson moved to a significantly different position in later years.
19. Ibid., p. 51.
20. 'An American Bishop's Search for a Space-age God', interview with Christopher Wren, *Look Magazine*, 22 February 1966, p. 26.
21. William James, *Varieties of Religious Experience* (New York: The Modern Library, n.d.), p. 511. James finds himself to be 'among the supernaturalists of the piecemeal or crasser type', who believe that *facts* differ in some cases from what they would otherwise be because a personal God acts in this world on behalf of those who pray.
22. In the *National Forum* (the Phi Kappa Phi journal) 74, no. 1, (Winter 1994):5.
23. Ari Goldman, *The Search for God at Harvard* (New York: Random House, 1991), p. 277.
24. Thomas C. Oden, *After Modernity ... What?* (Grand Rapids: Zondervan, 1992), p. 119.
25. This and the following two references are taken from *The Coming Kingdom of the Messiah*, by A. F. Buzzard (Wyoming, MI: Ministry School Publications, 1988), pp. 14–16.
26. Buzzard, *Coming Kingdom*, p. 16n, as quoted from *The Expository Times*, October 1977, p. 13.
27. Buzzard, *Coming Kingdom*, pp. 14–15, as quoted from Wagner's *Church Growth and the Whole Gospel* (San Francisco: Harper and Row, 1981), p. 2.

Chapter 3

1. Vladimir Nabokov, from his story 'Beneficence', as quoted in *Books and Culture*, November/December 1995, p. 26.
2. Joan Beck, in the *Daily News* (Los Angeles), 26 November 1995.
3. William Cowper. This is a less-known stanza of his famous poem that begins 'God moves in a mysterious way, His wonders to perform,' Number 68 in *The Methodist Hymnal* (Chicago: Methodist Publishing House, 1939).

4. John M'Clintock and James Strong, eds., *Cyclopaedia of Biblical, Theological, and Ecclesiastical Literature*, vol. 3 (New York: Harper & Brothers, 1894), pp. 903–904.
5. Article 'Heaven' in M'Clintock and Strong's *Cyclopaedia*, vol. 4, pp. 122–27.
6. On this matter John Calvin pointedly comments, with reference to John 3:3 and 5 and our passage into the kingdom of the heavens by an additional birth, that 'they are mistaken who think the Kingdom of God means Heaven. It is rather the spiritual life, which is begun by faith in this world and daily increases according to the continual progress of faith' (John Calvin, *The Gospel According to St John*, translated by T. H. L. Parker [Grand Rapids: Eerdmans, 1959], p. 63). The apostle Paul matter-of-factly tells the Philippians that 'we have our citizenship in the heavens' (3:20).
7. Number 2, *The Broadman Hymnal*, 1940.
8. Most of my information on Singh comes from an unpublished paper by Leonard W. Thompson, 'Sadhu Sunder Singh – Man of Holiness, Man of India.' Friedrich Heiler, a well-known German theologian, studied Singh's life first-hand and wrote a book entitled *The Gospel of Sadhu Sundar Singh* (Delhi, India: Indian Society for Promoting Christian Knowledge, 1989).
9. I have related the story of my oldest brother, J. I. Willard, in my *In Search of Guidance* (HarperSanFrancisco/Zondervan, 1993), p. 42. Many contemporary books, such as those by John Wimber and Agnes Sanford, relate similar events.
10. See the passages on the language of the heavens in the Old Testament. Especially consider Exod. 29:43–46; Deut. 33:26–27; 1 Kings 8:27–61; 2 Chron. 6; 7:14–16; 16:9; 20:6, 15–17; 36:23; Ezra 1:2–3; 7:23, 8:18–23; Neh. 1:5; 2:4, 20; 9:6, 27–28; Isa. 63:15; 66:1; Dan. 5; 6.
11. C. H. Dodd, *The Parables of the Kingdom* (New York: Charles Scribner's Sons, 1958), p. 34.
12. In *The Meaning of Faith* (New York: Association Press, 1922), Harry Emerson Fosdick does a masterful job of analyzing a number of delusive interpretations of God that make him less than a person who intelligently and purposively fills and overflows the space in which we live.
13. Emmanuel Levinas, *Totality and Infinity* (Pittsburgh, PA: Duquesne University Press, 1969).
14. *Julian of Norwich: Showings*, translated by Edmund Colledge and James Walsh (New York: Paulist Press, 1978), pp. 193–94.
15. Brother Lawrence, *The Practice of the Presence of God* (Westwood, NJ: Fleming H. Revell, 1958), p. 58.
16. C. S. Lewis, *Out of the Silent Planet* (New York: Macmillan, 1975), p. 32.
17. Quoted in *Christianity Today*, 15 August 1994, p. 40.
18. Thus Frank Laubach rightly named one of his books *Prayer: The Mightiest Force in the World* (Old Tappan, NJ: Fleming H. Revell, 1946). This is because prayer moves the power on which all other powers depend.

19. William James, *The Principles of Psychology*, vol. 2 (London: Macmillan, 1918), pp. 578–79. This passage is very similar to the opening of Immanuel Kant's *Foundations of the Metaphysics of Morals*, where the sole moral worth is said to be a good will.
20. These, of course, are Paul's words from 1 Cor. 15. Wilder Penfield, a Nobel prize–winning scientist, explains: 'It is clear that, in order to survive after death, the mind *must* establish a connection with a source of energy other than that of the brain. If during life (as some people claim) direct communication is sometimes established with the minds of other men or with the mind of God, then it is clear that energy from without can reach a man's mind. In that case, it is not unreasonable for him to hope that after death the mind may waken to another source of energy.' Indeed. (Quoted in Melvin Morse, *Closer to the Light* [New York: Ivy Books, 1990], p. 127.)
21. Aldous Huxley, *The Doors of Perception* (New York: Harper and Row, 1970), p. 62.
22. The 'Rubaiyat of Omar Khayyam of Naishapur,' quatrain 72, translated by Edward Fitzgerald, in *British Poetry and Prose*, 3rd edition, edited by Paul Lieder, Robert Lovett, and Robert Root (Boston: Houghton Mifflin, 1950), vol. 2, pp. 644–51. The 'Rubaiyat' has appeared in numerous editions.
23. Vladimir Nabokov, quoted in *Books & Culture*, November/December 1995. I am extremely grateful to Larry Woiwode for his review of *The Stories of Vladimir Nabokov*, in which this and the previous quotation from Nabokov were given. Obviously Nabokov does not equal *Lolita*!
24. Dietrich Bonhoeffer, *Life Together* (New York: Harper and Row, 1954), p. 13.
25. John Henry Newman, quoted from *A Diary of Readings*, edited by John Baillie (Nashville, TN: Abingdon Festival Books, 1978), p. 153.
26. Joseph Butler, *The Analogy of Religion to the Constitution and Course of Nature*, many editions. The quotation is from the 'Advertisement' prefixed to the first edition; see the edition edited by Joseph Angus (London: The Religious Tract Society, n.d.), p. xiv.
27. One of the most important books for our self-understanding as Christians in the Western world today is George M. Marsden's *The Soul of the American University* (New York: Oxford University Press, 1994). This work deals with much more than what happened to the major universities in America in their flight into unfaith. It deeply penetrates issues affecting the prospects of the Christian Gospel for the foreseeable future.
28. Evelyn Waugh, *Brideshead Revisited* (Boston: Little, Brown, 1946), pp. 85 f.
29. Rudolf Bultmann and Karl Jaspers, *Kerygma and Myth: A Theological Debate*, edited by H. W. Bartische (London: S.P.C.K., 1957), p. 5. For incisive criticism of Bultmann's outlook and its effects on theology, see *Historical Criticism of the Bible: Methodology or Ideology?* by his former student Eta Linnemann, translated by Robert W. Yarbrough (Grand Rapids, MI: Baker Book House, 1990).

30. Obviously there are many matters in this chapter that need to be taken up for lengthy discussion. That simply cannot be done in this book.

Chapter 4

1. If you study the lives of the great moral teachers East and West, you will discover their preoccupation with these two basic questions. Plato's *Republic* and Aristotle's *Nicomachean Ethics* are good places to start, but one should continue on to the great moralists of the modern period, such as Thomas Hobbes, John Locke, Immanuel Kant and John Stuart Mill. You will note among the modern moralists that they, with few exceptions, defer to Jesus and acknowledge his authority by trying to identify their own theory with his teachings. A historically sound description and appreciation of the historical effects of Jesus' life and teaching upon morals in theory and practice is found in W. E. H. Lecky's *History of European Morals from Augustus to Charlemagne*, 3rd edition, revised (New York: D. Appleton, 1916), especially chapters 3 and following. At the opening of the twentieth century it still was not thought odd that a professor of philosophy at Harvard University should conclude a distinguished series of lectures by saying, 'Ethics is certainly the study of how life may be full and rich, and not, as is often imagined, how it may be restrained and meagre. Those words of Jesus, ... announcing that he had come in order that men might have life and have it abundantly, are the clearest statement of the purposes of both morality and religion, of righteousness on earth and in heaven' (George Herbert Palmer, *The Field of Ethics* [Boston: Houghton Mifflin, 1929], p. 213). That such a statement would be professional suicide today speaks volumes about where we now stand.
2. Alfred Edersheim correctly sees that the subject of the Sermon on the Mount is 'neither righteousness, nor yet the New Law (if such designation be proper in regard to what in no sense is a Law), but that which was innermost and uppermost in the Mind of Christ – the Kingdom of God. Notably, the Sermon on the Mount contains not any detailed or systematic doctrinal, nor any ritual teaching, nor yet does it prescribe the form of any outward observances ... Christ came to found a Kingdom, not a School; to institute a fellowship, not to propound a system. To the first disciples all doctrinal teaching sprang out of fellowship with Him. They saw Him, and therefore believed ... The seed of truth which fell on their hearts was carried thither from the flower of His Person and Life' (*The Life and Times of Jesus the Messiah*, 3rd edition, 2 vols. [Grand Rapids: Eerdmans, 1953], vol. 1, pp. 528–29).
3. It was a comparative study of the published translations of Matt. 5:3, with some assistance from Steven Graves, that first alerted me to the fact that there must be something desperately wrong in the usual interpretation of the Beatitudes of Jesus.

4. In his invaluable study of the Sermon on the Mount, Robert Guelich has distinguished two biblical usages of the 'Blessed are the ...' phraseology. One he calls the 'wisdom-cultic' and the other the 'prophetic-apocalyptic'. In the former the blessedness declared is indeed based upon the condition cited, so that condition is naturally understood as a part of wisdom. This usage is certainly present in the New Testament (e.g., Matt. 24:46; Luke 11:27–28; and James 1:12) as elsewhere. In the latter, according to Guelich, 'the beatitude is a declarative statement of future vindication and reward. It comes as assurance and encouragement in the face of trouble' (*A Foundation for Understanding the Sermon on the Mount* [Dallas: Word Publishing, 1982], p. 65). He finds that 'Luke's Beatitudes have been taken as eschatological blessings, whereas Matthew's appear more like entrance requirements for the Kingdom.' He later indicates that, in his view, this is *only* appearance.

What the distinction thus drawn continues to miss, I fear, is that in Jesus' Beatitudes the blessing, whether concerning wisdom *or* future deliverance, comes not because of the condition cited but precisely in spite of it. Although a certain balancing out of things is not foreign to Jesus' mind (Luke 16:25), being poor, in spiritual or earthly goods, being miserable, persecuted, and so on, is never taken by him or other New Testament writers as the cause or basis of blessedness in the kingdom.

In addition the eschatological element, though certainly present in obvious cases, is never thought of as exclusive of present blessedness – in the midst of the mess, as it were. For Jesus the poor, hungry, and so on, are also blessed now, because God's hand is on them now. Compare Paul's constant personal testimony on this point (Acts 16:25; 2 Cor. 1:3–12, 4:8–18, 6:4–10; Phil. 4:6–19; 1 Tim. 6:6–8). It may take our breath away to say it, but blessedness is possible to all now, *regardless* of what the situation may be. That is the hope of Jesus' gospel – which is not the least excuse for failing to change situations that should be changed.

5. Edersheim, *Life and Times*, p. 529.

6. The widely used Scofield Study Bible has long been famous for taking the dispensationalist stand. The resulting attitude towards Jesus' words is well expressed in a footnote to Matt. 5:6 in the 1988 New American Standard edition. Here we are told, 'In the Sermon on the Mount, Christ sets forth the perfect standard of righteousness demanded by the law (see 5:48), thus demonstrating that all men are sinners, habitually falling short of the divine standard, and that, therefore, salvation by works of law is an impossibility.' Christ, we gather, is meaner than Moses. His superior being enables him to turn the screws even more tightly on human inability and, it is hoped, make it more likely that humans will give up. The standard interpretation of Paul's teaching that 'the law was our schoolmaster to bring us unto Christ, that we might be

justified by faith' (Gal. 3:24) is that it does its job solely by making us know our helpless need.

Strangely, the succeeding Scofield note to the Sermon on the Mount states, 'Although the law, as expressed in the Sermon on the Mount, cannot save sinners (Rom. 3:20), and the redeemed of the present age are not under the law (Rom. 6:14), nevertheless both the Mosaic law and the Sermon on the Mount are a part of Holy Scripture which is inspired by God and therefore "profitable for teaching, for reproof, for correction, for training in righteousness" (2 Tim. 3:16) for the redeemed of all ages.' It is not clear how this is supposed to work. No doubt the distinction seen in Chapter 1 between salvation and the Christian life is presupposed.

7. There is divided opinion among scholars concerning whether Luke 6 gives us a different sermon from Matthew 5–7. See Alfred Plummer's *A Critical and Exegetical Commentary on the Gospel According to St Luke* (Edinburgh: T. & T. Clark, 1964), pp. 176 ff., for a summary of positions on the relationship between these two passages.

8. 'Come, Ye Disconsolate', Hymn Number 327 in *The Modern Hymnal* (Dallas: Broadman, 1926).

Chapter 5

1. H. Lecky, *History of European Morals from Augustus to Charlemagne*, 3rd edition, revised (New York: D. Appleton, 1916), p. 338.

2. Michael Grant, *Jesus: An Historian's Review of the Gospels* (New York: Charles Scribner's Sons, 1977), p. 1.

3. Clarence Bauman, *The Sermon on the Mount: The Modern Quest for its Meaning* (Macon, GA: Mercer University Press, 1985), pp. ix, 3. Bauman's words poignantly characterize the current situation: 'The Sermon on the Mount is an enigma to the modern conscience. Many enlightened minds admire what it says without affirming what it means. They assume, albeit regretfully, that its message does not apply to contemporary life and that the ethic of Jesus is therefore essentially irrelevant – a beautiful, irresistible impossibility, a conspiracy to ensure our failure. My first awareness of this dilemma dates back to early childhood when I pondered – in a painting of *Die Bergpredigt* by Schnorr von Carolsfeld – that perplexed face of the Roman soldier who sat listening to Jesus at the edge of the crowd while firmly clutching his sword. To my dismay I later discovered how widespread and deep-rooted that perplexity is throughout Christendom' (p. xi).

4. Tertullian, 'The Prescriptions Against the Heretics', subsection 7, in *Early Latin Theology*, edited by S. L. Greenslade, Volume 5 in The Library of Christian Classics (Philadelphia: Westminster Press, 1956), p. 36.

5. For a more realistic picture of the world in which Jesus grew up and served, see the invaluable book by Richard A. Batey, *Jesus and the Forgotten City: New Light on Sepphoris and the Urban World of Jesus* (Grand Rapids: 1991).
6. Dietrich Bonhoeffer, from *The Cost of Discipleship*, as quoted in *Disciplines for the Inner Life*, by Bob Benson and Michael W. Benson (Nashville: Generoux/Nelson, 1989), p. 127. See also the first three lines on p. 43 of Bonhoeffer's *Ethics*, translated by Neville Horton Smith (New York: Macmillan Collier Books, 1986): 'It is evident that the only appropriate conduct of men before God is the doing of His will. The sermon on the mount is there for the purpose of being done (Matt. 7:24 ff.). Only in doing can there be submission to the will of God.'
7. Bonhoeffer again: 'The error of the Pharisees, therefore, did not lie in their extremely strict insistence on the necessity for action, but rather in their failure to act. "They say, and do not do it" ' (*Ethics*, p. 43.). More deeply, they *intended* not to obey and devised elaborate schemes to appear painstaking for righteousness, while being deeply antagonistic to God's law and God's heart. To their deep and unrelenting wickedness Jesus finally responds with scathing diagnoses of their true condition. (See Matt. 15:3–14; Luke 11:17–12:5; and Matthew 23 entire.)
8. On this see the excellent 'Introduction' to *World Bible*, edited by Robert O. Ballou (New York: Viking Press, 1970).
9. See the penetrating discussions of David Hume on hatred, anger and contempt in his *Treatise of Human Nature*, Book 2, sections vi–x. It is still illuminating after more than two hundred years.
10. See the recent excellent empirical study by Redford and Virginia Williams, *Anger Kills* (New York: HarperCollinsPublishers, 1994). This kind of work is greatly needed to reverse the decades-long trend to indulge, even cultivate, anger and treat it as something good.
11. 'ABC Morning News', 15 March 1996.
12. Cornel West, 'NBC News', 2 June 1996.
13. C. S. Lewis, *The Weight of Glory and Other Addresses* (Grand Rapids: Eerdmans, 1973), p. 58.
14. Eduard Schweizer, *The Good News According to Matthew*, translated by David E. Green (Atlanta: John Knox Press, 1975), p. 119.
15. There is a deep wisdom about 'looking' that is preserved in numerous Christian traditions. See, for example, *The Rule of Saint Augustine* (many editions) on the 'look' and how it is to be communally dealt with.
16. Aristotle, *Nicomachean Ethics*, Book 2, Chapter 6.
17. Thomas Oden incisively comments about 'modernity's failure to understand marriage as the most transparent clue to the failure of modern consciousness, but … also about the failure of friendships and the failure of politics. Wherever I look in the interpersonal sphere I see the failure of relativized,

naturalistic, narcissistic values to nurture and sustain just interpersonal relationships and responsible covenant love ... The recent history of divorce is the key sign of the failure of modernity to sustain covenant accountability in the interpersonal sphere ... [Modernity has turned marriage] into a moment-to-moment hedonic calculus that can be as flippantly rejected as it was entered into' (*After Modernity ... What?* (Grand Rapids: Zondervan, 1990), pp. 195–96.
18. See Dallas Willard, *The Spirit of the Disciplines* (San Francisco: Harper & Row, 1988), p. 141.
19. At the onset of serious ethical reflection in Greece, the problem is set of why it is better to do what is right if one can do wrong completely undetected. See the story of Gyges in Plato's *Republic*, Book 2. Socrates (and Plato) work out the answer in terms of the kind of person you become, which you are whether anyone knows it or not. Who are you as you know yourself to be, and will 'getting away with it' be enough to satisfy you?
20. See the article 'Divorce' in *Cyclopaedia of Biblical, Theological, and Ecclesiastical Literature*, edited by John M'Clintock and James Strong (New York: Harper & Brothers, 1894), pp. 839–44.
21. On this research see Robert Karen, *Becoming Attached* (New York: Warner Books, 1994) for an excellent introduction.
22. The Gospel of Mark, written more for the gentile context, where, at least in some circles, it was not unheard of for a woman to divorce her husband, makes it clear that this discussion applies to women as well as men (Mark 10:12).
23. A significant tendency of recent ethical theory tries to found moral norms entirely upon the conditions of the possibility of communication between free rational beings. Karl-Otto Apel and Jürgen Habermas are leading names in this connection. See *The Communicative Ethics Controversy*, by Seyla Benhabib and Fred Dallmayr (Cambridge: MIT Press, 1990).
24. Bertrand Russell, *A History of Western Philosophy* (Bloomfield, NJ: Simon and Schuster, 1945), p. 579.
25. Stuart Hampshire, 'The Loneliness of the Long Distance Runner', *The New York Review of Books*, 28 November 1996, pp. 39–41. See quotations on p. 41.

Chapter 6

1. See the excellent article 'Hypocrisy', by Eva F. Kittay, in *Encyclopedia of Ethics*, edited by Lawrence C. Becker, 2 vols. (New York: Garland, 1992), vol. 1, pp. 582–87.
2. *Jesus and the Forgotten City: New Light on Sepphoris and the Urban World of Jesus*, by Richard A. Batey (Grand Rapids: Baker Book House, 1991), pp. 83 ff., 213.
3. Clyde H. Reid, *The God Evaders* (New York: Harper & Row, 1966), p. 41 and

all of Chapter 4, in which the author has very telling things to say about how unconscious motivation works at a group level to lock congregations into utterly superficial associations.

4. *The God Evaders*, p. 19.

5. Tolstoy, *A Confession*.

6. As we have emphasized earlier, contemporary ethical thought struggles in vain to agree upon any conclusive reason for condemning the vilest of human atrocities.

7. See Ronald A. Wells, *History Through the Eyes of Faith* (San Francisco: HarperSanFrancisco, 1989), pp. 238–39.

8. See the two excellent issues of *Christianity Today* in July and August 1996 for the startling facts.

Chapter 7

1. C. S. Lewis, *The Four Loves* (London: Collins, 1960), pp. 42–43.

2. Simon Tugwell, ed., *Early Dominicans: Selected Writings* (New York: Paulist Press, 1982), pp. 83–85.

3. Augustine, *The City of God*, Book 19, Chapter 14.

4. Emily Dickinson, 'The Soul Selects Her Own Society,' in *A Pocket Book of Modern Verse*, edited by Oscar Williams (New York: Washington Square Press, 1970), p. 77.

5. Cf. Bertrand Russell, 'The Free Man's Worship', etc., on despair as a basis for the moral life.

6. Bonhoeffer, *Life Together* (New York: Harper & Row, 1954), pp. 30–31.

7. Trueblood, *The Humor of Jesus*, (1964; reprint, San Francisco: HarperSanFrancisco, 1990).

8. C. S. Lewis, from his talk on 'Work and Prayer', in *God in the Dock* (Grand Rapids: Eerdmans, 1970), p. 107.

9. But I think it will be useful to mention a few books on prayer that have proved tremendously helpful to many, as well as to myself. If these are carefully studied along with scripture, and especially if they are studied with a small group of like-minded disciples focused on practice, they will greatly strengthen our grasp on the realities of The Kingdom Among Us. The books listed show us how to live our actual lives in effectual prayer. The books I have in mind are *Prayer: The Mightiest Force in the World* and *Game with Minutes*, by Frank Laubach; *Prayer – Asking and Receiving*, by John R. Rice; *Prayer*, by George Buttrick; and *Prayer: Finding the Heart's True Home*, by Richard J. Foster. In reading for spiritual understanding and growth, it is better not to read many books. As Richard Foster pointedly remarks, 'It is better to find a few spiritual staples and feed on

them until they have moulded you' (p. 153). And these five are simply great, healthy, strong, wise books.

A main reason why they are so useful and right is that they are written by *practitioners*. The authors are writing of what they know first-hand. This also explains why, though they are deep, they are not really hard to read. Practical mastery enables one to speak clearly and simply of what is as profound as reality itself.

Laubach's books are republished in the Heritage Collection edition of *Frank C. Laubach: Man of Prayer* (Syracuse, NY: Laubach Literacy International, 1990). Because these works are difficult to acquire through the 'usual sources,' I include here a mailing address: 1320 Jamesville Avenue, Box 131, Syracuse, NY 13210. Both works listed have been published earlier in many editions.

10. On these remarkable men of prayer, see Norman Grubb, *Rees Howells Intercessor* (Fort Washington, PA: Christian Literature Crusade, 1980); Francis McGaw, *John Hyde* (Minneapolis: Bethany House, 1970); and Basil Miller, *Praying Hyde: A Man of Prayer* (Grand Rapids: Zondervan, 1943).

11. A vitally refreshing new look at Psalms is given by Kathleen Norris, 'Why the Psalms Scare Us', *Christianity Today*, 15 July 1996, pp. 19–24.

12. On quarks as source of all, see J. C. Polkinghorne, *The Quantum World* (Princeton, NJ: Princeton University Press, 1985) and *The Faith of a Physicist* (Princeton, NJ: Princeton University Press, 1994). With specific reference to the brain and the mind, see John Searle, 'The Mystery of Consciousness', in two parts, *New York Review of Books*, 2 November 1995, pp. 61-66 and 16 November 1995, pp. 54–61.

13. William R. Parker and Elaine St Johns, *Prayer Can Change Your Life* (Englewood Cliffs, NJ: Prentice-Hall, 1957).

14. Larry Dossey, *Healing Words* (San Francisco, HarperSanFrancisco, 1993). See especially pp. 90 and 179–86 on the Byrd study.

15. The book *The Latent Power of the Soul*, by Watchman Nee (New York: Christian Fellowship Publishers, 1972), should be thoroughly though cautiously studied in this connection. Also my *In Search of Guidance*.

16. See Plato, *Laws*, Book 10 (Stephanus pagination, p. 885).

17. See the discussion by Norman Kemp Smith, editor, in his introduction to *Hume's Dialogues Concerning Natural Religion* (New York: Social Sciences Publishers, 1948), pp. 22–23.

18. James Gilchrist Lawson, *Deeper Experiences of Famous Christians* (Anderson, IN: Warner Press, 1981), p. 100.

19. Walter Trobisch, *Martin Luther's Quiet Time* (Downers Grove, IL: Intervarsity Press, 1975), pp. 3–4.

20. Ibid.

21. Tugwell, *Early Dominicans*, pp. 96–103.
22. To continue these thoughts very fruitfully, please see John Wimber's little booklet *Kingdom Mercy: Living in the Power of Forgiveness* (Ann Arbor, MI: Servant Publications, 1987).
23. Michael Shevack and Jack Bemporad, *Stupid Ways, Smart Ways, to Think About God* (Ligouri, MO: Triumph Books, 1993), pp. 17 f.

Chapter 8

1. My book *In Search of Guidance: Developing a Conversational Relationship with God* (HarperSanFrancisco/Zondervan, 1993) is devoted to helping people understand the life of listening to God.
2. Chapter 8 in *The Mysticism of Paul the Apostle*, by Albert Schweitzer, translated by William Montgomery (New York: Henry Holt, 1931), pp. 160–76, is still invaluable. See especially pages 164–70. Also see *A Man In Christ*, by James Stewart. (New York: Harper & Brothers, 1935).
3. Here, as in most of this book, I do not want to go into the relevant scholarship. But the issue of discipleship and the textual basis for understanding it is so important that I must refer the reader to two exhaustive and authoritative books by Michael J. Wilkins. *The Concept of Disciple in Matthew's Gospel* (New York: E. J. Brill, 1988) and *Following the Master: Discipleship in the Steps of Jesus* (Grand Rapids: Zondervan, 1992). These are excellent books, and the bibliographies they contain will certainly take anyone as deeply as they may desire to go into this subject. The underlying tensions run very deep. I have actually heard it argued that because the word *disciple* does not occur after the book of Acts, we are no longer supposed to make or be disciples!
4. Efforts to move people into the category of disciple are routinely directed towards those who are already Christians. Moreover, evangelism now is never, to my knowledge, directed towards getting people to be disciples. See my study of this in *Christianity Today*, 10 October 1980, under the title 'Discipleship: For Super-Christians Only?'; it is also included as Appendix 2 in my *Spirit of the Disciplines*, pp. 258–65.
5. Brother Lawrence [Nicholas Herman], *The Practice of the Presence of God* (Old Tappan, NJ: Fleming H. Revell, 1974), pp. 23–24.
6. On these matters see John Cotton's treatment of 'Christian Calling,' *Spiritual Foundations for Leadership*, ed. Os Guinness, Burke, VA: The Trinity Forum, 1995, pp. 1–14 through 1–17. The meaning of the priesthood of believers in the original Reformation was that every believer is a priest in whatever work or life they live, not just that every believer is qualified to do especially *religious* things.
7. William Law, *A Serious Call to a Devout and Holy Life* (New York: Paulist Press, 1978), p. 57.

8. Ibid., pp. 56–57.
9. Ibid., p. 57.
10. See Eusebius's work, *Demonstration of the Gospel*, excerpted in *Spiritual Foundations for Leadership*, op. cit., pp. 1–10 to 1–11.
11. Henri J. M. Nouwen, *The Way of the Heart* (New York: Ballantine Books, 1981), p. 10.
12. For anyone who senses a special calling to make disciples today, Lectures 9, 10 and 11 of Charles G. Finney's *Revival Lectures* (Fleming H. Revell, no location, no date) will be immeasurably helpful. They are somewhat dated by opinions and movements referred to, but on the essentials they are as fresh as tomorrow. Finney had a profound theoretical and practical understanding of how belief governs action and how truth can be brought to bear to change belief. And he also understood that this work can be done for Christian purposes only in cooperation with the spirit of Jesus.

Chapter 9

1. Alister McGrath, *Beyond the Quiet Time* (Grand Rapids: Baker Books, 1995), p. 5.
2. The inescapable need is for individuals to achieve their own understanding and insight into the reality of God, God's domain and their own souls. The nineteenth-century thinker John Stuart Mill, not himself exactly an advocate of Christianity, accurately points out the effects of presenting the truths of Jesus in such a way as to bypass the individual's active understanding of them: 'The words of him whose speech was in figures and parables were iron-bound and petrified into inanimate and inflexible *formulae*. Jesus was likened to a logician, framing a rule to meet all cases and provide against all possible evasions, instead of (one) ... whose object was to purify and spiritualize the mind, so that, under the guidance of its purity, its own lights might suffice to find the law of which he only supplied the spirit and suggested the general scope ... (Hence) ... religion, instead of a spirit pervading the mind, becomes a crust encircling it, nowise penetrating the obdurate mass within, but only keeping out such rays of precious light or genial heat as might haply have come from elsewhere.' From a letter, 'On Genius' (*Autobiography and Literary Essays*, edited by John M. Robson and Jack Stillinger [Toronto: Toronto University Press, 1981], p. 337). Mill's sense of the harm done to religious faith by failing to elicit the believer's own insight and understanding is profoundly right, and must be respected in practice by anyone who hopes to transform Christian 'information' into the solid basis for a Christlike life.
3. Saint Thomas Aquinas, *Summa Theologica*, Part II, Question 27, Articles 2 and 3; p. 1300 of *Summa Theologica*, translated by the Dominican Fathers, 5 vols. (Westminster, MD: Christian Classics, 1981).

4. Emily Dickinson, 'The Soul Selects Her Own Society', in *The Pocket Book of Modern Verse*, edited by Oscar Williams (New York: Washington Square Press, 1970), p. 77.
5. Because the famous 12 steps of A.A. are more talked about outside A.A. than actually studied themselves, it will be useful here to fully state them:

1. We admitted we were powerless over alcohol – that our lives had become unmanageable.
2. Came to believe that a Power greater than ourselves could restore us to sanity.
3. Made a decision to turn our will and our lives over to the care of God *as we understood Him*.
4. Made a searching and fearless moral inventory of ourselves.
5. Admitted to God, to ourselves and to another human being the exact nature of our wrongs.
6. Were entirely ready to have God remove all these defects of character.
7. Humbly asked Him to remove our shortcomings.
8. Made a list of all persons we had harmed, and became willing to make amends to them all.
9. Made direct amends to such people wherever possible, except when to do so would injure them or others.
10. Continued to take personal inventory and when we were wrong promptly admitted it.
11. Sought through prayer and meditation to improve our conscious contact with God as we understood Him, praying only for knowledge of His will for us and the power to carry that out.
12. Having had a spiritual awakening as the result of these steps, we tried to carry this message to alcoholics, and to practise these principles in all our affairs.

From *Alcoholics Anonymous*, 3rd ed., New York: Alcoholics Anonymous World Services, Inc., 1976, pp. 59–69.

Compared to this, one sees how utterly superficial the consumer Christianity of our day is. Imagine, by contrast, being a member of a Church or local assembly of Christians where these 12 steps were applied without specific reference to alcohol.
6. See the excellent study on this matter in G. B. Wyner's *Toward a Phenomenology of Conscientious Action and a Theory of the Practicality of Reason*, unpublished dissertation, 2 vols., University of Southern California, May 1988.
7. See William James's chapters on the will in *Principles*. James's colleague at Harvard, Josiah Royce, had this to say: 'The sole possible free moral action is

concentration upon the ideas of the Ought which are already present. To sin is *consciously to choose to forget*, through a narrowing of the field of attention, an Ought that one already recognizes. For while I cannot avoid acting in accordance with the Ought so long as I clearly know it, I can through voluntary *inattention*, freely choose to forget it.' *The World and the Individual*, Vol. II, (New York: Dover Publications, 1959), p. 359.

8. See my essay on 'Language, Being, God and the Three Stages of Theistic Evidence,' in *Does God Exist*, edd. J. P. Moreland and Kai Nielsen, Nashville: Thomas Nelson, 1990, pp. 196-217. Substantially reprinted in *Contemporary Perspectives on Religious Epistemology* (New York: Oxford University Press, 1992), pp. 212–24.

9. *The Moral Discourses of Epictetus*, translated by Elizabeth Carter (London: J. M. Dent & Sons, 1911), p. 35. Epictetus left several short treatments of 'Providence', as well as on God's being the Father of humankind, most contained in this volume.

10. William Wordsworth, 'Lines Composed a Few Miles Above Tintern Abbey', in *British Poetry and Prose*, 3rd edition, 2 vols., edited by Paul Lieder, Robert Lovett and Robert Root (Boston: Houghton Mifflin, 1950), Vol. 2, p. 19. To explore this very important idea further, see Norman Kemp Smith's treatment of how nature functions in our knowledge of the creator in his British Academy lecture 'Is Divine Existence Credible?' (reprinted in *The Credibility of Divine Existence: The Collected Papers of Norman Kemp Smith* [London: Macmillan, 1967], pp. 375–97).

11. The technical discussion of 'Intelligent Design' in nature is currently at a very exciting and intellectually profitable boil. See Michael J. Behe, *Darwin's Black Box* (New York: The Free Press, 1996).

12. Brennan Manning, *Abba's Child* (Colorado Springs, CO: Navpress, 1994), pp. 186–87.

13. Omer Englebert, *Saint Francis of Assisi: A Biography* (Ann Arbor, MI: Servant Books, 1979), p. 123.

14. For those informed and interested in such debates, we do not have in mind here the 'eradication of the sinful nature' or coming to a place where it is impossible for us to sin. We are speaking of the formation of the inner self in Christlikeness so that we routinely do what he would do were he in our place. Again, perfection, having no room for improvement in our conformity to Christ, is not the issue.

15. On 'moral' and 'metaphysical' necessity see the article on 'necessity' in M'Clintock and Strong, op. cit., Vol. VI, pp. 903–4.

16. Hannah Arendt observed the trial of Eichmann and wrote of the banality of evil. Eichmann was such an *ordinary* man. Many were angry with her. They wanted him to be a monster. But she was right. The magnitude of evil *done* is a

reflection of circumstances that have capitalized upon the commonplace habits of human beings in those circumstances.

17. The treatment of disciplines for the spiritual life in Jesus' kingdom given here is of necessity quite brief. For a more extensive treatment, see, above all, *Celebration of Discipline*, by Richard Foster, 2nd ed. (San Francisco: Harper Collins, 1978), and the excellent bibliography it contains. See also my *The Spirit of the Disciplines* (San Francisco: Harper Collins, 1988) and the historical treatment *Christian Spirituality*, 3 vols. (New York: Crossroad, 1987–91). On spiritual disciplines in the context of world culture, see *Spiritual Disciplines: Papers from the Eranos Yearbooks*, edited by Joseph Campbell (Princeton, NJ: Princeton University Press, 1960).

18. My 'standard list' divides the disciplines as follows:

DISCIPLINES OF ABSTINENCE	DISCIPLINES OF ENGAGEMENT
Solitude	Study
Silence	Worship
Fasting	Celebration
Frugality	Service
Chastity	Prayer
Secrecy	Fellowship
Sacrifice	Confession
Watching	Submission

The disciplines of abstinence are designed to weaken or break the power of life involvements that press against our involvement with the kingdom of God, and the disciplines of engagement are designed to immerse us ever more deeply into that kingdom. What the particular practices amount to are fairly obvious, and we cannot go further into them or how they are practised here. I have dealt with them at some length in my book *The Spirit of the Disciplines*, and Richard Foster's *Celebration of Discipline* goes even further, especially with respect to the practicalities of entering into the various disciplines.

The important point is to understand that some framework of disciplines, and pretty certainly a number of those listed, is needed to form a life plan for spiritual growth. Anyone who understands this and seeks help from Jesus and his people will certainly find what he or she needs.

19. In his *Pensées*. See p. 214 of *Pascal Selections*, edited by Richard H. Popkin (New York: Macmillan, 1989).

Chapter 10

1. See Jean-Paul Sartre's brilliant fictional exposition of this understanding of consciousness in his play *The Wall* (in *Existentialism from Dostoevsky to Sartre*, edited

by Walter Kaufmann [New York: Meridian Books, 1982], as well as in many other collections). He there expresses in a 'user friendly' form the understanding of consciousness that has been painstakingly elaborated in the phenomenological tendencies of recent philosophy.

2. George MacDonald, *Diary of an Old Soul* (Minneapolis: Augsburg, 1996), p. 30.

3. For further development of this vital point, see Peter Beyerhaus's fine book *God's Kingdom and the Utopian Error* (Wheaton, IL: Crossway Books, 1992).

4. Saint Augustine, *The City of God*, Book 19, paragraph 17.

5. For definitive discussions on these points, see Paul Davies, *The Mind of God: The Scientific Basis for a Rational World* (New York: Simon & Schuster, 1992), and John Polkinghorne, *The Faith of a Physicist* (Princeton, NJ: Princeton University Press, 1994).

6. On this vital and much misunderstood matter, one should consult the works of Edmund Husserl, especially his *Crisis of European Sciences and Transcendental Phenomenology*, translated by David Carr (Evanston, IL: Northwestern University Press, 1970). *See also* Philip Johnson, *Reason in the Balance* (Downers Grove, IL, 1995).

7. *The Modern Hymnal* (Nashville: Broadman, 1926), Number 13, and in many other collections as well.

8. In his profound lecture on 'The Weight of Glory,' C. S. Lewis reminds us that we have never seen an 'ordinary' person. This crucial point is not easy to keep in mind. G. K. Chesterton somewhere says that the hardest thing to believe in the Christian religion is the infinite value it places upon the worth of the individual person. The magnitude of our eternal destiny, of course, both depends on this and makes it clear.

9. 'The will to meaning is really a specific need not reducible to other needs, and is in greater or smaller degree present in all human beings' (Viktor E. Frankl, *The Unheard Cry for Meaning* [New York: Washington Square Press, 1985], p. 33). This book, as well as other works by Frankl, demonstrates beyond all doubt the fundamental drive and need for meaning in human nature.

10. Plato, *Phaedo*, Stephanus pagination 107c (many editions).

11. John Hick, *The Center of Christianity* (San Francisco: Harper & Row, 1978), p. 106.

12. In *British Poetry and Prose*, 3rd ed., edited by Paul Lieder, Robert Lovett and Robert Root (Boston: Houghton Mifflin, 1950), p. 704. Remember Hamlet's quandary – 'To sleep. Perchance to dream. Aye, there's the rub.'

13. Hick, *Center of Christianity*, p. 112.

14. MacDonald, *Diary of an Old Soul*, p. 32.

15. Augustine, *City of God*, Book 22, paragraph 29.

INDEX